THE ETERNAL DECLINE AND FALL OF ROME

THE ETERNAL DECLINE AND FALL OF ROME

THE HISTORY OF A DANGEROUS IDEA

EDWARD J. WATTS

OXFORD
UNIVERSITY PRESS

UNIVERSITY PRESS

Oxford University Press is a department of the University of Oxford. It furthers the University's objective of excellence in research, scholarship, and education by publishing worldwide. Oxford is a registered trade mark of Oxford University Press in the UK and certain other countries.

Published in the United States of America by Oxford University Press
198 Madison Avenue, New York, NY 10016, United States of America.

Library of Congress Cataloging-in-Publication Data
Names: Watts, Edward Jay, 1975– author.
Title: The eternal decline and fall of Rome : the history of a dangerous idea / Edward J. Watts.
Description: New York, NY : Oxford University Press, [2021] |
Includes bibliographical references and index.
Identifiers: LCCN 2021009498 (print) | LCCN 2021009499 (ebook) |
ISBN 9780190076719 (hardback) | ISBN 9780190076733 (epub)
Subjects: LCSH: Rome—Historiography | Rome—History—Empire, 30 B.C.–476 A.D.
Classification: LCC DG205 .W38 2021 (print) |
LCC DG205 (ebook) | DDC 937.0072—dc23
LC record available at https://lccn.loc.gov/2021009498
LC ebook record available at https://lccn.loc.gov/2021009499

DOI: 10.1093/oso/9780190076719.001.0001

3 5 7 9 8 6 4

Printed by LSC Communications, United States of America

To Manasi, Nate, and Zoe

CONTENTS

ACKNOWLEDGMENTS

THIS BOOK GREW out of a conversation that Stefan Vranka and I had at the Society for Classical Studies meeting in January 2019. We were concerned about how alt-right figures and white nationalists used events from the fourth- and fifth-century Roman Empire to attack immigration in the twenty-first century. We originally planned that I would write a short essay about the use and misuse of the Roman past, but, as I started digging into this topic, I realized that the rhetoric of Roman decline, the promise of Roman renewal, and the identification of people to blame for Rome's problems appeared repeatedly in sources ranging across the past 2200 years. The essay grew into a book—and the book quickly grew nearly twice as large as we had planned. I'm extremely grateful to Stefan for both the conversation that led to this book and for bearing with me as it expanded so much.

I am also grateful to the many friends, colleagues, and institutions that supported me over the past year as I put this project together. A great deal of initial work took place at the American School of Classical Studies in Athens in the summer of 2019. I am grateful to the staff there for their support and to the many colleagues who helped me hash out ideas over lunch at Loring Hall. This project also developed through engagement with audiences at Harvard University, Amherst College, Indiana University, Pomona College, UC San Diego, and the University of California Berkeley. I particularly benefited from personal conversations over the past year with Susanna Elm, Peter Guardino, Eric Robinson, Deborah Deliyannis, Colin Elliott, Cynthia Bannon, Giovanni Cecconi, Adalberto Magnelli, Carlos Noreña, Chris van den Berg, Alexander Riehle, Dimiter Angelov, Laura Nasrallah, Susan Harvey, Diliana Angelova, Richard Lim, Jason Moralee, Ben Keim, Bronwen Wickkiser, Tim Shea, Albert Joosse, Jeroen

Wijnendaele, Peter Van Nuffelen, Cathy Gere, Denise Demetriou, Maren Niehoff, and Alfons Fürst. Scott Jones gave me the great honor of previewing some of the book's ideas on his Give and Take Podcast. Michele Salzman, Nate Aschenbrenner, and Jan Willem Drijvers each shared portions of upcoming books with me. These books will be spectacular and I'm thrilled to have gotten a sneak peak at them. Leslie Safford and Rick Delaney did excellent copy editing work on the manuscript while Aishwarya Krishnamoorthy helped coordinate production.

A range of friends and colleagues from around the world have read chapters and offered suggestions on them. These readers include Anthony Kaldellis, Cristiana Sogno, Jeremy Schott, Andrew Devereux, Jan Willem Drijvers, and Nate Aschenbrenner. I would never have had the comfort to cover such a broad range of material without their comments and important suggestions. Mira Balberg read multiple drafts of multiple chapters and helped me understand why a discussion of Isaac Asimov and rockets probably was best left to the side.

Jamie Marvin worked tirelessly in tracking down materials, sorting out footnotes, compiling the index, and sharing portions of her dissertation. These efforts would have been greatly appreciated under any circumstances, but her help was vital as COVID-19 disruptions shut down libraries just as the book's first draft neared completion.

I also want to give a special thanks to my students in the COVID-19–disrupted undergraduate seminar I taught on this material in the spring of 2020. Despite the remarkably difficult circumstances they were a wonderful, critical audience who challenged my ideas and helped me to think in new ways about the Roman material and its implications for the present.

My work has also benefited greatly from the generous support of Carol Vassiliadis and from ongoing, stimulating conversations about antiquity and our current world with Alexia and Paul Anas, Jeanette Rigopoulos, and other members of San Diego's Hellenic Cultural Society.

The final word of thanks goes to my wife, Manasi, and my children, Nate and Zoe. Writing a book like this in a little more than a year is difficult under any circumstances. Doing it while chairing a university department amid a pandemic was harder than I imagined—especially when access to research materials stopped toward the project's end. I can't say how much I appreciate the sacrifices they made so that this project could be completed. Each of them served as a sounding board for my ideas and a source of support throughout the book's writing, editing, and revising. They also kept me going in those dark spring days when it seemed as if the world were coming undone—a challenging time indeed to write about decline. I love the three of you more than you know!

Carlsbad, California
July 10, 2020

MAP OF THE ROMAN EMPIRE AT ITS GREATEST EXTENT IN THE SECOND CENTURY AD.

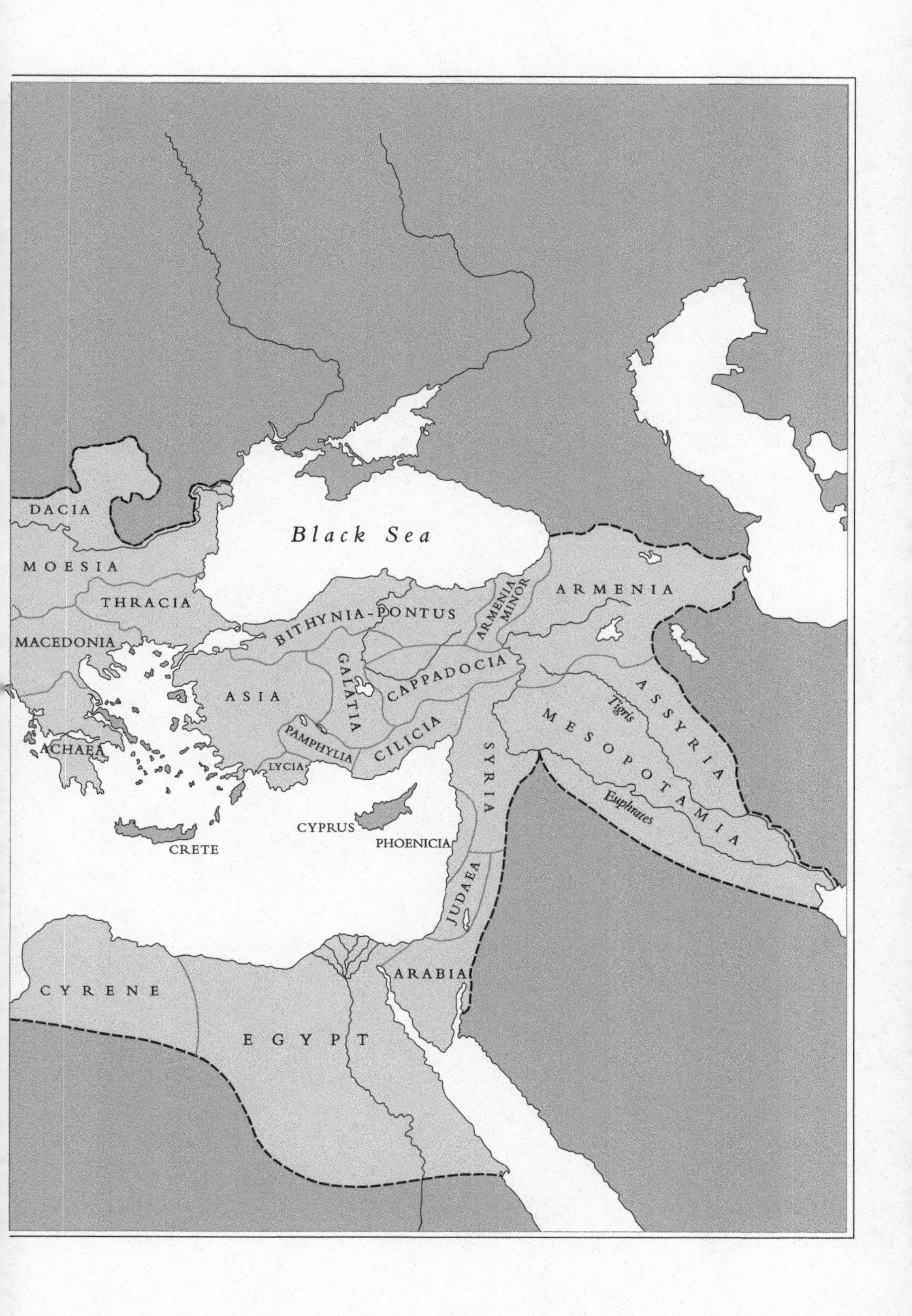

DACIA
Black Sea
MOESIA
THRACIA
ARMENIA MINOR
ARMENIA
BITHYNIA-PONTUS
MACEDONIA
GALATIA
CAPPADOCIA
ASIA
ASSYRIA
Tigris
MESOPOTAMIA
PAMPHYLIA
CILICIA
ACHAEA
LYCIA
SYRIA
Euphrates
CYPRUS
CRETE
PHOENICIA
JUDAEA
ARABIA
CYRENE
EGYPT

INTRODUCTION: A SNAPSHOT AND A STORY

ON JANUARY 20, 2017, Donald Trump's inaugural address laid out an apocalyptic scene of "American Carnage" amid "poverty in our inner cities; rusted-out factories scattered like tombstones across the landscape of our nation," and a faltering education system. Then he pivoted. "From this day forward, a new vision will govern our land." Trump bellowed, all Americans would now hear the following words:

> Together, We Will Make America Strong Again.
> We Will Make America Wealthy Again.
> We Will Make America Proud Again.
> We Will Make America Safe Again.
> And, Yes, Together, We Will Make America Great Again.

The "American Carnage" speech draws upon a deep tradition of manufacturing the perception of widespread decline in order to destabilize the present.[1] These sorts of arguments have two parts. They first make a provocative claim that society is becoming worse at a particular moment for a particular reason. They then suggest a path toward restoration that consists of rebalancing society to address the problems they identify. In Donald Trump's case, a mismatch of American priorities caused the American Carnage and the purging consists of making every decision solely so it benefits American workers.[2] The argument about social decline then exists primarily so that it might justify steps that seem necessary for renewal.

This approach is not unique to the United States. In Spain, the VOX party headed by Santiago Abascal promised to "Make Spain Great Again" through reforms designed to undo many of the legal foundations of the contemporary state that its leaders believe have eroded Spanish vitality.[3] Its "100 medidas para la España Viva" (100 steps to a vibrant Spain) offered a series of proposals to roll back laws granting regional autonomy while putting restrictions on political parties and Muslim groups blamed for terrorism.[4] In the Philippines, President Rodrigo Duterte responded to the perception of widespread crime and drug use by tolerating (or even encouraging) more than 12,000 extrajudicial killings.[5] This murderous spree has only increased Duterte's popularity. Prominent Duterte critic Walden Bello told *The Atlantic* that "I don't know if [Filipino] lives are actually better than before, but the perception is that they are. They're pro-Duterte because they feel he's cleaned up the place."[6]

Bello here points to something important. Descriptions of decline often require very few supporting facts. They are emotional things, driven by stories rather than data. Many of them require nothing more than a compelling storyteller—and people like Trump, Abascal, and Duterte tell captivating stories. In the world their rhetoric creates, facts matter less than emotions—and the emotions these men generate are indeed powerful. One can feel decline even when one cannot see it or document it. One can also feel renewal, even if it is imaginary.

Because these claims of decline often rely on emotion rather than evidence, their power depends a great deal on the way that their underlying stories are told. In fact, decline is sometimes nothing more than a snapshot and a story. The narrative usually determines what the snapshot means. To give one telling example, in 1980 young workers in Flint, Michigan earned salaries nearly 20% higher than young workers in San Francisco. In 2013, young workers in San Francisco made nearly 60% more than their peers in Flint.[7] This snapshot can support a number of different stories. It can speak to Flint's decline, San Francisco's rise, or both trends. But Flint has become emblematic of American postindustrial decline at least since Michael Moore's 1989 documentary *Roger and Me*—with the Flint water crisis of the 2010s merely the latest, most shocking evidence of the city's plight. Showing that Flint was recently a better place for young workers to begin their career than San Francisco underlines its rapid collapse. The same statistic can also tell the story of San Francisco's rise, but it does not do so with anywhere near the power. No one needs a statistic comparing San Francisco to Flint to understand how San Francisco has risen; there are many other, better ways to tell that story. This comparative statistic has then become yet another tool to tell a story of American decline rather than one of American progress or resilience.

This book is not about twenty-first-century Spain or America. It focuses on Rome, the state in history that is most strongly identified with the idea of decline—and with good reason. The decline of Rome has been a constant source of discussion for Romans and non-Romans for more than 2200 years. Everyone from American journalists in the twenty-first century AD to Roman politicians at the turn of the third century BC have used the decline of Rome as a tool to illustrate the negative consequences of changes in their world. Because Roman history is so long, it provides a buffet of ready-made stories of decline that can help develop the context around any snapshot. Rome did, in fact, decline and, eventually, fall. An empire that once controlled all or part of more than forty modern European, Asian, and African countries no longer exists. Roman prophets of decline were, ultimately, proven correct—a fact that makes their modern invocations all the more powerful.

While the claim that Rome was in decline appeared often across the centuries, the particulars of these claims evolved dramatically over time. In the early second century BC, the Roman politician Cato the Elder gave rousing Latin speeches blaming Roman moral decline on luxury goods and Greek teachers. Seventeen hundred years later, rhetoricians speaking Greek in Constantinople praised the Christian Roman emperor Manuel II Palaeologus for reversing the Roman military declines of the 1300s through his inspired policies. One cannot imagine that any Roman enchanted by Cato's anti-Greek rhetoric in the second century BC would understand the Roman decline that Manuel Palaeologus reversed. I mean this statement quite literally. Not only are the claims unrecognizably different, but also the very language in which they were made shifted from Latin to Greek. The Greek language, which Cato claimed would degrade Roman virtue, became the tongue in which claims of Roman renewal were later expressed.

Ambitious Romans often fashioned stories of decline so that they could build power for themselves by destroying present conditions. It often worked, too, but the destruction they wrought had very real consequences. Politicians who claimed they were restoring Rome sometimes trampled on the rights, property, and lives of the people whom they blamed for blocking Rome's recovery. The Roman rhetoric of decline and renewal left a trail of victims across Roman history.

I wrote this book to explain how this common, seemingly innocuous narrative of Roman decline could prove so destructive. Everyone who has a passing familiarity with Roman history or literature is aware of the pervasiveness of this story. No one has brought together the stories of the people who spun these tales of Roman decline and peddled Roman renewal. This book does.

It is not a comprehensive history of the rise of the Roman Republic, the decline and fall of the Roman Empire, or modern ideas about Rome. Each chapter will instead offer the historical context necessary to understand a moment or a series of moments in which Romans, aspiring Romans, and non-Romans used ideas of Roman decline and restoration to remake the world around them. The story begins during the Roman Republic just after 200 BC. It proceeds through the empire of Augustus and his successors, traces the Roman loss of much of western Europe in the fifth century AD, and then follows Roman history as it runs through the Eastern Roman Empire (which many people now call Byzantium) until its fall in 1453. The final chapters look at ideas of Roman decline and renewal in western Europe from the fifteenth century until today.

Rome shows that, while prophecies of decline and prescriptions for restoration may seem like inert rhetoric, they can cause deep, profound, and permanent changes to a society and its political life. This rhetoric can justify the elevation of new leaders and the overthrow of old regimes. It can upend existing customs by redefining radical innovation as the defense of tradition. Above all, it can produce victims. Romans knew the power of these ideas. They used them anyway.

But not all Romans. For long periods of Roman history, Romans told stories of their society progressing or renewing itself without undermining the conditions of the present. In the second and early third centuries, Romans spoke often about the restoration of buildings, cities, and political stability without blaming anyone for their decline. Buildings needed to be restored because they got old. Cities needed to be rebuilt because natural disasters damaged them. Civic traditions needed to be revitalized because, over time, people had lost interest in them. Outside invaders needed to be repelled and punished.

All of these real problems urgently needed to be addressed but, in these moments, Romans did not use the need for renewal to attack other Romans. A successful society repairs things that break or wear out. It defends itself against invasion and responds to military defeats. These responses, renewals, and restorations need not be destructive. In the second and early third centuries, they were often affirmative. The restorers of Rome then had collaborators, not victims. They did not upend Roman society. They confirmed its health and vitality. If Rome illustrates the profound danger of targeting other Romans who supposedly caused Roman decline, it also demonstrates the rehabilitative potential of a rhetoric that focuses on collaborative restoration when real decline sets in.

I am writing this in April of 2020, while the world reels in the face of the COVID-19 epidemic. At this moment one Roman example seems particularly poignant. In 165 AD, smallpox arrived in the Roman Empire. It horrified and terrified a population that, unlike ours, had constant experiences with death from infectious diseases. Smallpox victims endured fever, chills, upset stomach, diarrhea that turned from red to black over the course of a week, and horrible black poxes that covered their bodies both inside and out until they scabbed over and left disfiguring scars. Perhaps ten percent of the 75 million people living in the Roman Empire never recovered. "Like some beast," a contemporary wrote, the sickness "destroyed not just a few people but spread across whole cities and utterly destroyed them."[8]

The so-called Antonine Plague killed so many soldiers that military offensives were called off. It decimated the aristocracy to such a degree that town councils struggled to meet, local magistracies went unfilled, and community organizations failed for lack of members. It cut such deep swaths through the peasantry that abandoned farms and depopulated towns dotted the countryside from Egypt to Germany.[9]

The plague left even more profound psychological scars. The rhetorician Aelius Aristides survived a nearly lethal case of the disease during its first pass through the empire in the 160s.[10] He became convinced that he had lived only because the gods chose to take another instead, a young boy whom Aristides could even identify. Survivor's guilt is not a modern phenomenon—and the late-second-century Roman Empire must have been filled with it.

This catastrophe could have been a moment to focus on Roman decline, to identify culprits, and blame others for the suffering. Romans did so at other points in their history—including during another plague that hit the empire in the 250s. This was not the general response in the 160s and 170s. The emperor Marcus Aurelius reacted to the deaths of so many soldiers by recruiting slaves and gladiators to the legions. He filled the abandoned farmsteads and depopulated cities by inviting migrants from outside the empire to settle within its boundaries. Cities that lost large numbers of aristocrats replaced them by various means, even filling vacancies in their councils with the sons of freed slaves. The empire kept going despite death and terror on a scale no one alive had ever seen.[11]

The response to the Antonine Plague by the Roman historian Cassius Dio shows that one can choose not to use ideas of decline even when talking about the most serious catastrophes. Dio lived through the plague of the 160s and 170s, but he also saw the Roman recovery from it.[12] This Roman resilience prompted Dio to call the empire under Marcus Aurelius "a kingdom of Gold" that persevered admirably "amidst extraordinary difficulties."[13] Rome survived the plague. Its communities rebuilt. Just about any snapshot one could offer of the Roman smallpox epidemic would have looked horrible. But, even under those circumstances, one could use that snapshot to tell a story that affirmed the good qualities of a dynamic society.

Throughout this book, it is important to remember that the Roman prophets of decline chose to tell that story in a particular way. Some of them, like Marcus Aurelius, responded to immediate crises in ways that made Rome stronger by enhancing the bonds that held imperial subjects together. Other Romans spoke about decline with the intention of dividing their society. They had the option to do as Marcus did. They chose not to do so.

The past cannot predict the future, but it can show the dangerous consequences of certain ways of thinking and behaving. It is my hope that we can use the example of Rome to think more responsibly about how we talk about and respond to the challenges of our own changing world. Perhaps, we can then embrace a different sort of story that builds cohesion rather than division in the face of the very real, very serious social, economic, and personal challenges we now face.

1

DECLINE IN THE ROMAN REPUBLIC

DISCUSSIONS OF ROMAN decline appear in some of the earliest surviving Latin literary texts. The *Trinummus*, a play written by the early Roman playwright Plautus around 190 BC, mocks Romans concerned with moral degeneration caused by growing wealth.[1] The play opens with an allegory in which the divinity Luxury (*Luxuria*) commands her daughter Poverty (*Inopia*) to enter the house of a man whose extravagant tastes "destroyed his patrimony."[2] Megaronides, the first mortal character to appear in the play, explains that the goddess's words reflect "a sickness that has attacked our good morals here," "overcomes that which is beneficial to the common good," and "interferes with private and public matters."[3] These criticisms sound serious, but, as the play develops, Megaronides and a host of other officious characters become, in the words of a modern commentator, "moral prigs" and "self-righteous pompous ass[es]."[4] Plautus knows his audience will have heard claims like these and he wants his audience to see that these are the absurd musings of silly people.

Comedy like this works because it mocks ideas that matter. Many Romans in the 190s and 180s BC did feel that extravagance and the pursuit of luxuries were driving Rome to ruin. Some of this viewpoint grew out of the way that these extravagances had suddenly appeared in Rome after two decades of austerity and deprivation caused by Rome's war with Hannibal. Rome's long and brutal conflict with Carthage in the Second Punic War created two generations of Roman heroes. Rome survived Hannibal's invasion of Italy because of the calculated policies of established leaders like Fabius Maximus. These men enacted sumptuary laws, preached frugality, parried Hannibal's initial assaults, and gradually rolled back his Italian gains.

The old guard saved Rome from Hannibal, but the young general Scipio Africanus brought about Carthage's ultimate defeat. An incredibly charismatic and controversial figure, Scipio launched his career by winning election to a series of offices that he was technically too young to hold.[5] Empowered by strong popular support, Scipio brazenly broke with the strategy of the older generals who had saved Rome from Hannibal. He took the war to the Carthaginians, winning victories first in Spain and then in North Africa. Scipio's rapid political rise and the unconventional ways in which he secured offices aroused the initial hostility of the older generation of leaders, but they particularly resented the wealth that Scipio brought back from Africa and the public way in which he spent it.[6]

Flush with North African plunder, the dashing Scipio returned to the capital the richest Roman in history. During the war with Hannibal, the Republic had legally restricted the ownership of luxury goods and displays of wealth. Scipio's public profile excited Romans who were tired of the frugality of a wartime economy—so much so that, in 195 BC, the *lex Oppia*, the last of the legal limits on Roman spending, was repealed following a contentious public debate.[7] Scipio also had a good idea of how to use his wealth to maintain popularity. He rewarded his 35,000 soldiers with plunder equal to four months of military pay and an acre and a quarter of land in Italy.[8] He even paid for lavish games and a series of public monuments commemorating his military victories. The most evocative of these was a garish arch with seven gilded statues that Scipio erected on the Capitoline Hill in Rome.[9]

Scipio's largess helped to spark an arms race through which elite Romans used their riches to build up their public profiles. Soldiers came to expect bonuses from their commanders even if they had won only a minor victory.[10] Games became larger and more impressive. A memorable gladiatorial show in 200 BC had twenty-five pairs of fighters. By 183, a similarly memorable gladiatorial performance required sixty.[11] Returning Roman officers also sponsored more grandiose public works. By the 180s, commanders were not just decorating existing temples with war spoils but building entirely new ones as well.[12] Even dinner parties and feasts, which were often open to selected members of the public, became so opulent that, by the late 180s BC, they could stretch across multiple days and fill the Forum with reclining guests.[13]

Perhaps nothing better encapsulated this moment than the triumphal procession led in March 186 by Gnaeus Manlius Vulso following his victory over the Greek Seleucid kingdom.[14] The historian Livy describes how he "brought into Rome for the first time, bronze couches, costly coverlets, tapestry, other fabrics, and . . . pedestal tables." The slaves he captured also changed Roman banquets. Guests quickly came to expect elaborate meals prepared by skilled chefs, served by attractive waiters, and accompanied by "girls who played on the harp and sang and danced." All of these tasks used to be done in Rome by menial laborers, but now these "servile offices came to be looked upon as a fine art."[15]

These disorienting changes all happened very quickly. Within a generation, the flow of money and slaves generated by Rome's wars changed Roman political competition. Established politicians who were too old to take command in one of these lucrative campaigns had no hope of matching the glory, wealth, and popularity of successful younger men. They could, however, contrast their supposed fidelity to genuine, traditional Roman virtues with the ostentatious devotion to luxury that their younger rivals displayed. The most potent criticism they could make of this new social order highlighted its break from an idealized past.

Plautus poked fun at just this sort of moralizing. Some of the people he mocked were indeed easily dismissed old, curmudgeonly blowhards like Megaronides. But not all of them. The person who best articulated the idea that rapid moral decline now afflicted Rome was Marcus Porcius Cato.[16] Although Cato is now remembered as the very sort of old curmudgeon whom Plautus mocks, he cut a very different figure in the 190s and 180s. Cato was then at the peak of his rhetorical powers and stood out as one of the Republic's most influential politicians. Cato took it upon himself to combat the moral decline that he saw afflicting Rome.

This was a cynical move. Cato himself had benefited from a lucrative command in Spain following the conclusion of his consulship in 194.[17] Cato also understood how he could use his considerable rhetorical gifts to capitalize on the unease created by the disorienting changes affecting Roman life in the early second century. Cato had already positioned himself as the protector of traditional Roman values by arguing against the repeal of the *lex Oppia* in 195, but his attacks on the newly elegant men of Rome became fiercer as time progressed. These men possessed, Cato claimed, an avarice that "included all of the vices so that whoever was considered extravagant, ambitious, elegant, vicious, or good-for-nothing received praise."[18] Cato assailed newly fashion-conscious Romans for breaking with a past in which one dressed simply to "cover their nakedness" and "paid more for horses than for cooks." That was an age when "the poetic art was not esteemed and, if anyone was devoted to it or frequented banquets, he was called a ruffian."[19]

Cato did not just attack the Roman turn toward ostentatious consumption. Another feature of Roman life in the early second century BC also attracted his ire. Cato saw Rome's growing engagement with the Greek world as a threat to the Roman and Latin culture he idealized. His xenophobic attacks greatly exaggerated the impact of Greeks in Rome. Most Greeks would have come as slaves following a series of second-century Roman victories in the East. Relatively small numbers of free Greek philosophers, teachers of rhetoric, and doctors had come to Rome, but it was precisely these high-status, high-visibility Greeks whom Cato targeted. Cato said that Greeks "will corrupt everything" in Rome and predicted that the Romans would lose their empire when they began to be "infected with Greek literature."[20]

Cato used this malignant rhetoric to support a series of reactionary policies. When he campaigned for election as censor for 184 BC, he "proclaimed that the city needed a drastic purification" through which he could "cut away and cauterize the luxury and degeneracy of the age."[21] This message of moral decline and the promise of a radical return to a more virtuous Roman past propelled Cato into office.

Cato then used the pretext of moral renewal to attack his enemies. He expelled senators and sanctioned Roman knights who, he claimed, had fallen into degeneracy. Among them was a man named Manlius whom Cato cast from the senate because he was seen to have passionately kissed his wife while walking with her and his daughter in daylight.[22] Cato removed the brother of Scipio Africanus from the equestrian order because Cato disliked Africanus. Cato also ordered an assessment of the value of all clothing, carriages, women's jewelry, furniture, and silverware owned by wealthy Romans. Those items worth more than 1500 denarii, an arbitrary figure that

Cato had set, were then rated at ten times their actual value and taxed at this rate.[23]

Cato later turned his attention toward purging Rome of the decadent and dangerous Greek influences that he claimed threatened to corrupt Rome. To this end, he publicly rebuked Scipio Africanus for the Greek habits he had adopted while in Sicily and later backed measures expelling Greek philosophers from the city.[24] He even pushed for the deportation of the Athenian ambassador and Platonist philosopher Carneades after Carneades gave a lecture on justice that displeased Cato.[25]

Romans had mixed reactions to Cato's policies. Those who believed that avarice, excessive luxury, and foreign influence had afflicted Rome applauded the radical measures that Cato backed. They even erected a statue in Cato's honor that bore the inscription "when the Roman state was sinking into decay, he became censor and, through his wise leadership, discipline, and guidance, it returned again to the correct path."[26]

Cato's story of Roman decay seduced some Romans, but the reality of his moral renewal appalled many others. Wealthy opponents aggressively pushed back on his calls for reform and even persuaded a friendly magistrate to prosecute Cato for maladministration after his term had concluded.[27] The Republic of the early second century was robust enough to roll back the most unpalatable parts of Cato's program.

Parts of Cato's agenda that were not soon reversed aged quite poorly. His attacks against Greek teachers and doctors looked particularly misguided to later generations of Romans. By the first century BC, nearly all of the leading political thinkers in the Roman world had embraced one form of Greek philosophy or another. These Greek-trained Roman philosophers included such lions of the late Republic as Cicero and Brutus, but the most notable of all of them was Cato's own great-grandson (often now called Cato the Younger), a man defined by his devotion to Stoic philosophy.[28] Three generations later, not even his own family continued to embrace Cato's xenophobic anti-Hellenism.

While Cato's visions of Roman renewal died, his larger claim that avarice and luxury corrupted Rome endured for more than a century and a half. On the one hand, he had a point. The rapidly expanding Roman state contracted out administrative tasks like tax collection in much of its conquered territory around the Mediterranean. This decision richly rewarded the entrepreneurs who understood the new financial opportunities these contracts created.[29] Even Cato got into the act. The critic of excessive Roman wealth eventually "bought pools, hot springs, places given over to fullers, pitch-works, and land with natural pasturage and forests" while also organizing partnerships of investors who backed the commercial operations of fifty ships.[30] Other less enterprising or more poorly connected Romans were left behind.

This wealth gap fed into growing popular frustration with the Republic upon which ambitious politicians began to capitalize. None spoke more forcefully against the economic decline of the Roman poor and middle classes than Tiberius Gracchus. The grandson of Scipio Africanus, the general who defeated Hannibal, and the nephew of the Scipio who destroyed Carthage in 146 BC,[31] Tiberius stood for election as tribune of the plebs in 134 BC. This office perfectly fit an ambitious reformer. Tribunes had traditionally used their powers to protect weaker Romans from the legal and political predations of the well born. Tiberius understood how to wage a successful campaign for this office amid the anger and unease that Rome's growing wealth inequality had produced.

He told a story. His brother Gaius would later write that Tiberius was horrified by the sight of a countryside that had once been dotted with the small farms of free Roman citizens but now was full of large estates and pastures tended by barbarian slaves.[32] These estates had grown up in violation of the law, as rich men used fictitious names to rent large quantities of public land that once had been available to Roman small farmers.[33] Tiberius's supporters could point to clear consequences of these developments. "Gangs of foreign slaves, with whose help the rich cultivated their estates" had "driven away the free citizens" whose military service had won Rome its empire.[34] The unfettered corruption of the new Roman rich oppressed the poor and undermined the military preparedness of a Roman Republic that depended upon robust and enthusiastic citizen soldiers.

Tiberius's reminder of a lost agrarian ideal inflamed the anger of Roman citizens who felt that the economic revolution of the second century had left them behind. Very little of what Tiberius described was true. Archeological evidence shows that the Italian countryside was neither deserted nor filled with large estates in the 130s BC.[35] Tiberius, however, was a powerful speaker who told a resonant tale. Even if the story he told was not true, it felt true. This was enough to get him elected.

Once he had been elected, Tiberius set to work on a land reform bill. Inspired, we are told, by slogans and pleas written by his supporters on walls all over the city, Tiberius gave an impassioned speech in which he lamented the impoverishment of the people of Italy and spoke dramatically about the consequences of farms manned primarily by slaves.[36]

Despite what he claimed was at stake, Tiberius proposed a mild reform. Anyone who violated a long-standing law that limited renters to no more than 350 acres of public land would have to surrender any land above that threshold in return for fair compensation. The reclaimed public land would then be redistributed to Roman citizens.[37] The law furthermore covered only certain parts of Italy and would, at best, have allowed perhaps 15,000 families to be resettled—out of an Italian population then numbering several million.[38]

The moderation of the proposal reveals Tiberius's true objective. He did not intend to address comprehensively the conditions that led to the supposed decline of the Roman-citizen small farmers. He wanted to voice the anger that people felt about a Roman order that seemed to reward the greed of the rich while disregarding the needs of its other citizens.

When Octavius, a fellow tribune of the plebs, blocked a vote on his law, Tiberius responded with fury. Mobilizing his supporters, "he withdrew his conciliatory law and introduced one which was more gratifying to the people and harsher to the illegal owners of the land" by forcing them to "vacate the land" and offering them "no compensation."[39] Tiberius pointed out that Octavius, as a holder of large tracts of public land, had a clear motivation for opposing the reform. Then, with the flair of a demagogue, Tiberius offered to pay, out of his own funds,for the property that Octavius would lose.[40] When Octavius failed to back down, Tiberius staged a public vote to strip Octavius of his office. The newly deposed Octavius barely escaped an angry mob of Gracchan supporters.[41]

The removal of Octavius allowed Tiberius's law to pass, but at a significant cost. Not only had Octavius's deposition occurred amid threats of mob violence, but Tiberius had also "abrogated the power of a colleague who had intervened" against a law he opposed.[42] Because Octavius had objected to the law's effect on some landholders, his silencing undermined the power of tribunes to assist citizens subject to coercion by magistrates or onerous laws.[43]

Octavius's deposition set the stage for further constitutional violations by Tiberius. Land reform could not be implemented unless the senate provided funds for surveyors and supplies for the new farmers.[44] When the senate denied all funding, Tiberius again turned to his passionate supporters for a solution. Attalus III, the king of Pergamum, had recently died, leaving his kingdom and its treasury to "the Roman people." Tiberius held a vote to authorize the use of the Pergamene treasure to fund his land commission.[45] This usurpation of the senate's traditional authority over foreign policy and budgetary matters greatly unnerved senators.[46]

Tiberius's opponents in the senate blamed him for sparking two new and destructive forms of Roman political decline. Tiberius's decisions to break the norms of Roman political life presented Rome with a serious constitutional crisis.[47] But the crowds of angry supporters whom Tiberius led through the city alarmed senators even more.[48] Tiberius never ordered or even condoned violence, but he often implicitly threatened it. This attitude suggested an alarming deterioration of conditions in a Republic that had not seen this sort of political violence for centuries.

These anxieties about the trajectory of Roman life only grew as Tiberius campaigned for re-election as tribune.[49] As the day of the vote neared, Tiberius told his supporters that he feared that "his enemies would break into his house at night and kill him."[50] Many of them then camped outside of his home to protect their champion. In this charged atmosphere, it probably surprised no one that supporters and opponents of Tiberius began fighting soon after the voting commenced. Fearing that Tiberius might use this violence as a tool to seize power over the state, Tiberius's cousin, the pontifex maximus Scipio Nasica, led a group of senators and attendants out of the Senate to where Tiberius stood. They entered the crowd and began attacking the members of Tiberius's entourage who did not flee fast enough. In the mayhem, Tiberius was grabbed by the toga, pulled to the ground, and clubbed to death. He was one of perhaps 200 or 300 Romans killed.[51]

Romans understood that their Republic changed irreversibly on that day. The biographer Plutarch would write centuries later that this was the "first outbreak of civil strife in Rome that resulted in the bloodshed and murder of citizens since the expulsion of the kings" in 509 BC.[52] The only question was which sort of decline caused the damage. Tiberius's supporters "did not try to hide their hatred of Nasica" and called him "a cursed man and tyrant who had defiled with the murder of a sacred person the holiest and most awe-inspiring of the city's sanctuaries."[53] To them, Tiberius died because of the overreaction of greedy elites.

Other Romans lionized Nasica as a defender of the Republic. Writing a lifetime after the events of 133, Cicero saw Nasica as a Roman patriot who acted heroically to save a city destabilized by the constitutional violations of Tiberius Gracchus, an overly ambitious tribune who "divided one people into two factions." The heroism of Tiberius's slayers, Cicero wrote, "filled the whole world with the renown of their names."[54]

The more measured assessment of the second-century AD historian Appian blames both sides for sparking violence that, to him, was the genuine cause of Roman decline. Tiberius, Appian wrote, was both "the first to die in civil strife" and a figure whose death polarized the city between men who mourned him and those who saw in him the fulfillment of their deepest hopes.[55] Appian noted that Tiberius "was killed on the capital while still tribune, because of a most excellent design he pursued violently."[56] Rome was "no longer a Republic" but a state now governed by "the rule of the force and violence."[57]

This ominous assessment hinted at what the next century of Roman life would look like. With the benefit of hindsight, Plutarch, Cicero, and Appian all recognized that the trajectory of Roman life had changed in 133. While they each assigned blame to a different party, each man understood that, once violence has entered political life, it becomes extremely difficult to eradicate. The decline of the Republic had previously existed mainly in the rhetoric of politicians. It now looked very real.

2

THE REPUBLIC OF VIOLENCE AND THE EMPIRE OF PEACE

CALM DID RETURN following the murder of Tiberius Gracchus, for a time. But later observers correctly understood that the events of 133 BC showed Romans the disruptive power of fear, resentment, and political violence. For the next forty years, Rome would endure cycles during which people looking to address different versions of Roman decay battled over the direction of the Republic. On the one side were reformers in the mode of Tiberius Gracchus who claimed they would address the greed and corruption of the Roman elite. On the other side, Roman conservatives feared that the reformers' excessive ambitions and disrespect for constitutional norms would further destabilize the state. Everyone worried about the corrosive use of violence as a political tactic.

As these cycles reached their peaks, the contests between radical reformers and their opponents often turned bloody. Tiberius Gracchus's brother Gaius attacked Roman economic conditions that seemed to favor greedy elites until a mob alarmed at his ambition assassinated him, along with over 3000 of his followers in 121 BC.[1] Then, in the 110s BC, reformers like the future consul Marius attacked the "unlimited and unrestrained greed that invaded, violated, and devastated everything" following a series of spectacular examples of senatorial corruption.[2] This reformist push lasted longer, but it too ended with the murder of the ambitious tribune Lucius Appuleius Saturninus and "very many" of his backers after his condemnation by the senate in 100 BC.[3]

These cycles of dysfunction followed by killings forced Romans to confront a new set of questions about whether political violence could ever be acceptable. Senators argued that it could if the senate sanctioned it.

Beginning in the 120s, they used a novel legal instrument called the *senatus consultum ultimum* (the SCU) to authorize the attacks that killed both Gaius Gracchus and Saturninus.[4] The SCU was a sort of emergency declaration that ordered a magistrate to do what he could to ensure that the Republic suffered no harm. This terrifying decree permitted the use of violence—including murder—against Roman citizens while suspending a citizen's normal right of appeal.[5] Indeed, the senate's assertion of its sole right to suddenly and unilaterally deprive Roman citizens of their basic rights frightened many Romans just as much as tribunal electoral violence unnerved senators. Everyone could sense the erosion of Republican norms.

No single Roman politician active at the turn of the first century BC made more destructive use of the promise to restore Rome's political traditions than Lucius Cornelius Sulla. An ambitious and unscrupulous member of a faded consular family,[6] Sulla first rose to prominence as the person who received the surrender of the Numidian king Jugurtha in 106 BC.[7] He then starred as Rome's most successful commander in southern Italy during the Social War, a brutal struggle that began in 91 BC and pitted Rome against its Italian allies.[8]

Sulla's troops loved him. They admired his ability to undertake "successful actions . . . on the spur of the moment," his ability to make them crave combat, and the generous rewards he gave them when they won battles.[9] His army was thrilled when Sulla received a command to campaign in Asia against Mithridates, the king of Pontus, in 88 BC. Mithridates had recently followed an invasion of Roman territory with a massacre of as many as 80,000 Romans and Italians living in the cities of what is now western Turkey.[10] Sulla wanted to quench the Roman thirst for vengeance, but Sulla's soldiers also eyed the lucrative spoils they would win by capturing and looting the region's wealthy cities. This command seemed likely to satiate both Sulla's greed and his ambition.[11]

Sulla's political rivals wanted to deprive the general of this prestigious and potentially lucrative command. The old populist and former consul Marius allied with a tribune named Sulpicius to take the Mithridates command from Sulla. Sulpicius recruited a private army of as many as 3000 supporters,[12] deployed them around the city when he proposed the law stripping Sulla of the Mithridates command, and then roused them to call for the murder of Sulla and his colleague when Sulla tried to block the motion. Fearing for his life, Sulla fled the city.

Sulpicius's actions were certainly illegal. Not only had he used force to push through the votes backing his measures, but Marius was also ineligible to take the command against Mithridates because Marius was at that point a private citizen.[13] Sulpicius had, the commentator Asconius would later write, "taken possession of the Republic through force." This action, he continued, "was the beginning of the civil wars."[14]

Sulpicius used force first, but Sulla responded in devastating fashion. When he fled Rome, Sulla went to the camp of his soldiers, called an assembly, and then marched his army against the capital. Sulla described this act as a campaign "to deliver [Rome] from tyrants," words that evoked the language used against the Gracchi and other late-second-century reformers. Sulla's actions excited the enlisted men, but they so horrified his officers that all but one refused to join him "because they could not accept leading an army against their homeland."[15] Rome quickly fell to Sulla. This was the first time in over 400 years that a Roman army had taken the lives and destroyed the property of other Romans.[16]

The following morning, Sulla summoned an assembly of the people at which he "lamented the condition of the Republic, which had been so long given over to demagogues" and explained that his attack on Rome had been done "as a matter of necessity" to correct populist abuses of the political process by ambitious rabble rousers. The absolute authority of the popular vote that Tiberius Gracchus had once claimed would now disappear. From that point forward, Sulla maintained, "no law should be brought before the people unless it had been previously before the Senate" and "voting should be controlled by the well-to-do and sober-minded rather than by the pauper and reckless classes." If this was done, Roman political norms would be restored and "there would no longer be left any starting-point for civil discord."[17]

Instead of restoring the Republic, Sulla sparked a wider civil war. As soon as Sulla left Rome to attack Mithridates, Marius and his ally Cinna returned to the city with an army. Marius died soon after they took the capital, but the regime he helped establish first repealed the Sullan reforms and then ordered the execution of Sullan loyalists. The heads of the leading

Sullans were then cut off and mounted on the Rostra, the famous speaker's platform in the Forum.[18]

Sulla, however, ultimately prevailed in the fighting. He returned to Rome in 82 BC and unleashed a wave of vicious reprisals against his opponents.[19] He quickly published a list that proscribed forty senators and 1600 Roman knights. They were to be executed without trials and their property confiscated. Sulla also offered rewards to their assassins and any informer who could help find them. More people across Italy soon were added to the list, as were people suspected of helping or being kind to the proscribed. Sulla then distributed the property he had confiscated to his most loyal supporters.[20]

Sulla saved some of the most stomach-turning violence for the senate meeting in which he announced what form his restored Republic would take. He summoned the stunned senators to a temple overlooking the Circus Maximus and then timed his speech so that he delivered it while 6000 prisoners of war screamed in the circus below as they were executed.[21]

Sulla firmly believed that the excessive ambitions and violent inclinations of uppity tribunes had caused Rome to collapse into civil war. So he attacked the career path followed by reformers like the Gracchi, Saturninus, and Sulpicius. Sulla made the office of tribune unappealing to the ambitious by prohibiting any tribune from ever holding a higher office and forbidding tribunes from proposing or vetoing new laws.[22] Sulla then returned to private life in 80 BC with the belief that he had restored the Republic and put restraints in place that would prevent corrosive ambition from ever dragging Rome back into political dysfunction.

"Sulla," the historian Dionysius of Halicarnassus wrote, "was the first and only dictator who exercised his powers with such harshness and cruelty that Romans perceived for the first time . . . that the dictatorship is a tyranny."[23] The collective horror at the damage that Sulla had caused prevented the Republic from falling into another full-scale civil war for nearly thirty-five years after his retirement.[24] But the restrictive power of this terror eroded steadily. A rebellious consul prompted the senate to proclaim an SCU in 77 BC, another SCU was proclaimed to deal with a conspiracy by the failed consular candidate Sergius Catilina in 63, and the senate issued a third in 62.[25] Catilina's conspiracy also led the senate to declare a number of Roman citizens enemies of the state and strip them of their rights.[26] Within a generation of Sulla's proscriptions, the right of appeal had again come to seem like a peacetime luxury.

Sulla's restrictions on the tribunate also quickly fell away. In 70 BC, the consuls Pompey and Crassus restored the tribunate to its pre-Sullan powers. As one would predict, ambitious politicians began seeking the office again—and they quickly repeated the bad behavior of past tribunes. Less than three years after Sulla's reform was undone, the tribune Gabinius used mobs of supporters to attack opponents as Saturninus had and, borrowing from Tiberius Gracchus, he forced a colleague to rescind a veto by threatening to depose him.[27] Some of these tribunes also sought alliances with more established or more powerful figures. The most famous such incidents came when Gabinius and the tribune Manlius proposed two different grants of broad military authority to Pompey the Great so that he might campaign in the Eastern Mediterranean.[28] Both proposals rested on legally dubious grounds because Pompey then held no office, but his "lawless lust for power" prompted Pompey to accept the appointment anyway.[29]

By the end of the 60s, figures like Cato the Younger had taken to slowing down the operations of the state and engaging in electoral bribery in order to thwart both tribunes like Gabinius and more prominent Romans like Pompey and Julius Caesar.[30] His efforts only made things worse. In 59 BC, Cato's obstruction pushed Pompey, Caesar, and Crassus (Rome's richest man) into an alliance through which they would overwhelm Cato and his allies by doing "things in common on behalf of each other."[31] Caesar had won the consulship for that year and, with the backing of Pompey and Crassus, he overcame both Cato's objections and procedural blockades erected by his co-consul Bibulus to pass dramatic land distributions and other reforms.[32] Battered by increasingly unregulated political competition, the Republic no longer had the institutional strength to control Caesar and his powerful allies.

As the 50s progressed, it became clear that Roman institutions also lacked the capacity to control much less impressive figures. The most notorious such failure happened when armed supporters of the politicians Clodius and Milo, two rivals who shared a proclivity for political violence, battled on the Appian Way outside of Rome.[33] Clodius died in the fighting, his angry supporters burned the senate house, and the senate responded with an SCU that made Pompey sole consul for the year and charged him with restoring order to the city.[34]

This unrest scarred Romans deeply. Cicero argued that violence had to be used against Clodius because he was a "man whom we were unable to restrain by any laws or by any judicial proceedings."[35] He later wrote at length about how the Republic would degenerate if Romans "transformed our realm from the rule of law to violence" but it "could be eternal, if our life remained consistent with our laws and institutions."[36] This ideal mattered greatly to Cicero, who believed that there is "nothing less civil and humane that the use of violence in public affairs."[37]

Cicero's comments about Clodius are somewhat self-serving. Cicero both hated and feared Clodius, a man whose actions had forced Cicero into exile in 58 BC. Perhaps more importantly, Cicero's own political brand centered on his success in rooting out the Catilinarian conspiracy in 63 BC and his subsequent advocacy for a constitutional order that could withstand violent figures like Clodius. But this policy did not mean that Cicero manufactured the decline in Roman political norms that he described. It was very real—and it soon became very consequential.

The general Julius Caesar also came to believe that Rome had degenerated from a Republic of laws to a Republic of violence. In January of 49 BC, Julius Caesar ordered his troops to advance from the province of Cisalpine Gaul into Italy after trying and failing to negotiate terms under which he could safely return to Rome as a private citizen. At this decision's core was Caesar's inability to trust that Rome's staggering Republican institutions could protect his rights if he dismissed his army.[38] Caesar was not wrong. The senate had effectively forced his hand when it declared an SCU against tribunes allied with Caesar and forced them to seek protection beside his army.[39]

Caesar told his troops that "an innovation had been introduced into the Republic" and that "the intercession of the tribunes," which even Sulla had protected, "was now branded as a crime and suppressed by violence." Caesar then exhorted his soldiers "to defend the reputation and honor of the commander under whom they had supported the state" from the "malice of his enemies." The soldiers responded that they were "ready to defend their commander."[40] As Cicero implied, a state unable to protect the rights of its citizens and incapable of controlling political attacks was governed by the law of violence.[41] Caesar's invasion of Italy then simply obeyed the law that now prevailed in a Rome that had fallen away from its ancestral laws and norms. Another Roman civil war had begun.

Amid Rome's descent into a Ciceronian Republic of violence, Republican authors looked to explain Rome's failings. They began merging the decline caused by greed that people like the Gracchi had highlighted and that caused by the uncontrolled ambition that Sulla tried to stamp out. Writing after Julius Caesar defeated Pompey in the civil war, the historian Sallust memorably spoke of a moral decline in which greed and unseemly ambition competed to drag Romans into ill repute.[42] But he did so in a very calculated fashion. Sallust had been a notoriously corrupt official in the late 50s and early 40s and, in the introduction to one of his histories, Sallust wrote about his own career. He presented himself as a naive young politician who entered into a world in which "instead of modesty, incorruptibility, and virtue, shameless, bribery, and greed flourished" and "the craving for public office made me the victim of the same ill repute and jealousy as the rest."[43] Like foul air in the Roman summer, the toxic combination of rampant greed and uncontrollable ambition infected all who breathed it. The moral corruption of the Republic had become so complete that everyone involved in political life risked falling victim to it. Even if Rome managed to vanquish the plague of violence, Roman renewal seemed impossibly distant under such conditions.

The sometimes abstract musings about moral decline that had dotted Roman literature for the past century and a half were augmented by tales of actual, tangible horrors after Caesar's assassination in 44 BC dropped Rome back into civil war.[44] Proscriptions returned in the late 40s, but they now extended much further than even those of Sulla. Roman citizens again lost their lives without trial and without any legal appeal. Even Cicero fell victim; he was killed and his hands and head hung on the speakers' platform in the Forum as a gruesome reminder of a violent age.[45] Authors described wives betraying husbands, children betraying fathers, and slaves turning on masters as agents of Caesar's adopted son, Octavian, and his allies seized the lands of eighteen Italian communities and forced crowds of displaced Italians to flood the capital.[46] Even Brutus and Cassius, Rome's self-proclaimed liberators, extorted money from provincials, plundered their temples, and enslaved entire towns.[47]

As these civil wars wound toward Octavian's climactic victory in 30 BC, tales of Roman misfortune had already begun to be mixed with Octavian's claims that he headed a Roman renewal. Following military victories in Sicily in 36 BC and Dalmatia in 33 BC, Octavian, his general Agrippa, and other supporters paired a welcoming back of political refugees with a massive construction program in the city of Rome, a project that was designed to improve infrastructure, return stability to the food supply, and rebuild temples.[48] The returning exiles and lucky few proscribed men who had managed to avoid death credited Octavian with restoring their lives and their property.[49]

Octavian also used Marc Antony's amorous relationship with the Egyptian queen Cleopatra to rebuild a sense of common purpose among a Roman population divided by the civil war. His propaganda emphasized Antony's hesitancy to campaign when it required him to leave the luxurious Egyptian capital of Alexandria.[50] It spoke about Antony celebrating Roman victories with a triumph in Alexandria that included feasts for Cleopatra's subjects and gifts of Roman territory to the children he had fathered with the queen.[51] It encouraged rumors that Antony intended to move the Roman capital to Alexandria and rule the empire alongside Cleopatra.[52] Then in 32 BC, Octavian read to the senate what he claimed to be Antony's will, a document that named Antony's children with Cleopatra as his legal heirs and indicated that he wished to be buried in Alexandria.[53]

These rumors "show[ed] that [Antony] had degenerated from the way of life of a citizen." If Antony no longer fit the criteria of a Roman, he could be "judged an enemy" of Rome and Octavian could frame the war against him as a defense of state against the foreign queen Cleopatra and her besotted lover.[54] Capitalizing on some of the same suspicion of the Greek East that Cato the Elder once expressed, Octavian arranged for all of Italy "to swear allegiance" to him so that he could lead it to victory against Antony, their common enemy.[55] When he defeated Antony in 30 BC, Octavian then advertised both the restoration of a lawful, peaceful order in Rome and the addition of Egypt to Rome's empire. The triumphal procession he staged induced Romans to "forget all of their unpleasant experiences" and they "viewed his triumph with pleasure, quite as if the vanquished had all been foreigners."[56]

The celebration of Octavian's Egyptian conquest represented part of a larger program designed to emphasize that he had cured the disorder, violence, and lawlessness of the later Republic. In January of 27 BC, he conspicuously "transferred the Republic from my own power to the dominion of the senate and people of Rome," saying that he would now "exceed all in influence (*auctoritas*) although I possessed no more official power than others who were my colleagues in several magistracies."[57] In return, the senate granted him the title Augustus, a name that, Cassius Dio wrote, "confers no particular power" but instead "clearly shows the splendor of [his] position."[58] While the exact formula that Octavian used to define his new position as emperor evolved somewhat over the next decade and a half, he took care to always configure it so that the individual powers he enjoyed had Republican constitutional precedents. In that way, the Republic could indeed seem to be restored, after a fashion.

Romans remained somewhat uneasy about the durability of the peaceful and lawful order that Augustus claimed to have restored. In the *Georgics* (which were completed around 29 BC), the poet Vergil combined his horror at civil war with the promise of eventual peace when he wrote of future farmers plowing fields fertilized by Roman blood and turning up the old, decayed weapons of combatants.[59] The promise of renewal under Octavian (who was soon to be called Augustus) still remained uncertain as he solidified his position as Rome's first emperor. The preface to Livy's massive history, which likely appeared along with his history's first five books sometime between 27 and 25 BC, speaks about decline and renewal. Livy was not optimistic that the renewal would last. He wrote that they had now "reached the present times in which we can tolerate neither our vices nor their remedies."[60]

As the 20s turned into the 10s BC, the narrative of Republican decay and Augustan recovery began to stick better. Some of this change grew out of very real efforts that Augustus made to remind Romans that he held back a return to the degeneration and violence of the later Republic. Following a series of plagues and floods in 23 and 22 BC that contributed to a food shortage and rioting in the capital, Augustus purchased grain for the people of Rome and then, later in the year, left the city to attend to matters in the empire's eastern provinces.[61]

Rioting erupted regularly while the emperor was gone, calming only after Augustus returned to Rome in 19 BC.[62] His absences seemed like deliberate efforts to convince Romans to, as Livy said, "tolerate the remedies" to their vices. They worked. The historian Cassius Dio would later comment that "clearly it was impossible for a democratic government to be maintained" among Romans because "there was no similarity between the conduct of the people during [Augustus's] absence, when they quarreled, and when he was present."[63] Romans had come to believe that any hope of permanently reversing the troubles of the late Republic lay in Augustus.

As this idea took hold, Augustus shifted from reminding Romans of Republican instability to emphasizing the powerful renewal he delivered. At the Saecular Games that Augustus sponsored in 17 BC, a hymn composed by the poet Horace spoke of the moment as one in which "Faith and Peace, old-fashioned honor and virtue, long neglected, dare to return."[64] Horace celebrated the Augustan renewal even more openly in Book 4 of his *Odes*, a project that appeared in 13 BC and concluded with a tribute to the Augustan Age.[65]

The final poem in the book catalogs Republican decline and Augustan restoration. "Your age, Caesar," Horace wrote, has returned grain to fields left squalid by the Republic. The emperor restored peace both at home and abroad, and, perhaps most resonantly, he even "bridled runaway license, banished crime and revived the ancient arts through which the Latin name and the force of Italy grew strong."[66]

The renewal brought by Augustus fixed the devastation of the civil war and reinstated a version of the Roman constitution. It also addressed the much older, deeply entrenched narrative of Roman moral decline. This last claim was vitally important. If late-Republican politicians like Sallust could blame their misbehavior on an irresistible contagion of Roman vice, Augustus now gave them a path toward redemption. They were creatures of their time, the corrupt members of a corrupt political body victimized by the vicious conditions in which they lived. Augustus had now removed that vice. Politics were cleansed. The wretched men of the past, however many were left after the civil wars, now could return to virtuous public service in a new Roman golden age. Augustus did not just redeem Rome. He also offered a sort of personal redemption to Romans who looked to start again in his new age.

The moral decline Augustus addressed was not the avarice and ambition that troubled Sallust, however. As the massive funerary monuments erected by Augustan associates like the parvenus Cestius and Eurysaces show (see Figure 2.1), avarice and ambition remained unchecked by the emperor. This was actually a deliberate policy for an emperor who relied heavily on the support of associates born to middling families and who rewarded them with offices and wealth when they served him well. Augustus counted on their greed and ambition. He had no interest in dampening the expression of either trait, with the result that Augustus redefined moral decline as something that manifested itself in more concrete issues like adultery and family size. He then targeted those issues legislatively while letting other, more systemic moral shifts alone.

FIGURE 2.1 PYRAMID OF CESTIUS, C. 1890 (WIKIMEDIA COMMONS).

Augustus himself made similar claims about Roman renewal at the end of his life. Shortly before he died, the emperor ordered bronze pillars containing his own "account of his deeds" erected outside of his mausoleum.[67] Inscribed copies of the text soon appeared on the walls of temples around the empire. The theme that the emperor developed in this *Res Gestae* was clear. Like Livy at the beginning of his reign and Horace in its middle, Augustus used one of his final moments as emperor to frame his age as one of Roman renewal.

He began by claiming that, at the age of nineteen, he had raised an army with his own money that restored liberty to the Republic when a faction oppressed it.[68] He claimed to have "issued new laws that restored many of the traditions of our ancestors which were then being dismissed," a reference to laws on adultery and family size that he backed.[69] He described how he gave money to Italian towns whose lands had been given to soldiers,[70] how he bailed out the public treasury four different times,[71] and how he paid for public grain distributions when tax revenues could not cover them.[72] He also listed all of the public buildings he built, completed, and reconstructed.[73] Outside of Rome, he "recovered" Sicily, Sardinia, North Africa, and the territories beyond the Adriatic that had slipped from central Roman control during the civil wars.[74] He also "recovered" military standards lost by commanders in Spain, Gaul, Dalmatia, and Parthia.[75] He "replaced the ornaments in the temples of all of the cities of the province of Asia" that had been plundered by his rival Marc Antony[76] and returned to their owners all of the slaves who had taken up "arms against the Republic."[77]

Augustus's *Res Gestae* told a particular story of imperial Roman decline and renewal. The old ideas of Roman decline were everywhere in the text. But this was unlike the spiral of decline imagined by Republicans like Cicero and Sallust or the tentative, uncertain recovery described by Livy in the 20s. The decline Augustus alluded to existed in the past. It was a decline that Augustus had arrested. The violence, amoral behavior, political dysfunction, infrastructure damage, military disaster, and social dislocation belonged to the Republic and the civil wars. Augustus's imperial Rome had recovered from them and emerged stronger, more beautiful, and truer to the traditions that made Rome great.

Augustus had to make this claim. The imperial order that Augustus created did bring about peace, stability, and a return to social order—but it did so at a tremendous cost. Although the trappings of the Republican constitution remained, elections continued, and Roman magistrates again served under their old titles, Romans knew that they had traded the traditional political freedoms of the Republic for the novel security of one man's rule. This trade needed to be justified and the justification that Augustus provided was perhaps the most compelling available.

Republican authors and politicians had claimed for at least two centuries that Rome had degenerated. Much of what they said represented the self-serving rhetoric of cynical and ambitious politicians selling themselves as Rome's great redeemers, but no one could dispute that Romans suffered dreadfully in the 80s and again during the civil wars of the 40s and 30s. After nearly two centuries of Romans hearing about decline and more than a decade of them living through its worst manifestations, Augustus's claim that only he could correct Rome's course seemed plausible. When he actually succeeded in stabilizing the empire, Augustus could persuasively assert that the revolutionary political changes he put in place had created the conditions for Roman renewal. This story of Rome's restoration was now woven into Augustus's new imperial political order.

3

MANUFACTURING THE GOLDEN AGE OF TRAJAN

AUGUSTUS'S DOMINANCE OVER the Roman state rested in part on the compelling story he told of a golden age that he inaugurated. By the time that Horace penned his final *Ode* in 13 BC, Augustus's claims that he restored Rome had penetrated deeply. Their truth seemed self-evident by the end of his life when Augustus set to work on his *Res Gestae*. Augustus's success did not eliminate Romans' tendency to find social, political, and moral problems in their society, but it did alter how one could speak about change. Ambitious politicians were no longer permitted to build a following by claiming that the world around them was in decline. To do so would be to criticize the capacity and achievements of a ruling emperor—a dangerous act of sedition. The political conditions of the empire also eliminated the public occasions on which this sort of booming Catonian declinist oratory could be effectively delivered.[1] First- and second-century orators instead delivered their most impressive speeches in courtrooms or in public performances treating historical themes.[2] The only overtly political rhetoric about contemporary affairs consisted of speeches full of fawning praise of the ruling emperors.[3]

Decline now lurked in the past, appearing only when the current emperor wanted to claim credit for some sort of Roman restoration. It remained a powerful idea but, under the first emperors, Roman decline and renewal became the rarely heard cadence to which revolutions now marched. The Julio-Claudian dynasty founded by Augustus had little use for this rhetoric. The five Julio-Claudian emperors (Augustus, Tiberius, Caligula, Claudius, and Nero) reigned for nearly a century and prized stability and continuity. The transitions between their imperial regimes were usually peaceful, with the imperial successor often sharing power with his predecessor before his death.[4] The sole exception to this process of deliberately conferring power upon a successor while the ruling emperor still lived came when Claudius replaced Caligula after Caligula's murder in 41 AD. Claudius distanced himself from Caligula, but he still made extensive efforts to emphasize his connections to Augustus, his wife Livia, and other members of the Julio-Claudian family.[5] It was not until after the suicide of Nero ended Augustus's dynasty in 68 that an emperor again explicitly embraced the old language of Roman decline and renewal in a sustained way.

This language returned because Nero's death left Rome facing both a leadership vacuum and a constitutional crisis. Historians sometimes criticize Augustus for not arriving at a successful mechanism for choosing imperial successors, but, until Nero's death, there had only been one imperial assassination in the nearly one hundred years since Augustus's civil-war victory over Antony and no contested imperial successions. The Augustan model was both stable and successful, but it depended entirely upon the ruling emperor identifying a successor whom the senate would approve. Nero's suicide occurred after the senate had recognized the rebel governor Galba as the legitimate emperor and declared Nero a public enemy. No contingency existed to choose a sovereign after the senate stripped its recognition from a legitimately chosen emperor.

This vacuum meant that the new emperor Galba needed to articulate why Rome required a clean break from the Neronian regime. To do so, he put himself forward as a leader who would restore the temperance and good governance of the age of Augustus.[6] He ordered the execution of some of Nero's most notorious associates and conspicuously advertised his frugality.[7] The earliest coins issued by Galba proclaimed that liberty had been restored and Rome reborn following the end of the Neronian tyranny.[8] But Galba did not last long enough to implement his vision of what this restored Rome would look like. His frugality prompted both Vitellius, the Roman governor of Germany, and Otho, an associate of Nero based in Rome, to lead armed revolts by troops angry at Galba's failure to pay a promised military bonus.[9] A third revolt, led by Vespasian, the military commander of the powerful Roman forces in Syria, erupted soon after Galba fell.

Vespasian was the last man standing after this sprawling civil war. From the beginning of his reign, he claimed to uphold the good governmental traditions of Augustus while breaking with the supposed decadence of Nero. A fragmentary surviving document records what seems to be the text of the law conferring imperial power on Vespasian.[10] His powers are defined explicitly and then, after each is listed, the document frequently notes that Vespasian will use them lawfully "just as it was lawful for the divine Augustus, Tiberius, and Claudius."[11] Not Nero or the three short-lived emperors who followed him, because, while Vespasian valued his institutional connection to the three successful emperors of the Julio-Claudian dynasty, he wanted to distance himself from the failures of his immediate predecessors.

Many supporters of Vespasian pushed the party line that the new Flavian dynasty offered a return to the sobriety and stability of the first emperors after more than a decade of vicious leadership, military indiscipline, and personal decadence.[12] Some, like the historian Cluvius Rufus, wrote about Neronian vices so that they could distance themselves from their service to the regimes of Nero, Otho, and Vitellius.[13] Others, like the young biographer Plutarch, made their literary debuts by effectively speaking of a past to which they had little direct connection in a way that the new regime liked. Plutarch framed the year and a half between the death of Nero and Vespasian's final victory as a period in which the empire was "torn into many fragments . . . not so much through the ambition of those who were proclaimed emperors, as through the greed and lack of discipline among the soldiers."[14] The failed emperors themselves lacked either virtue or skill. Galba found himself overwhelmed by the demands of running the empire, Otho was devoted to "luxury and licentiousness," and Vitellius embodied "gluttony and drunkenness."[15] Plutarch agreed with Vespasian that the new age offered the promise of stability and renewal under an emperor who ruled with justice and wisdom.[16]

The Flavian dynasty ended with the assassination of Vespasian's younger son, Domitian, in 96. It is perhaps with some irony that the dynasty's end prompted some of the same claims of imperial dysfunction and tyranny that Vespasian leveled against Nero. The cruelest part of this was that Domitian, the longest-serving and most accomplished of the three Flavian emperors, deserved better. Domitian completed a new circus for chariot races on the site of what is now the Piazza Navona, a gladiatorial school next to the Colosseum, an Odeon for theatrical performances, and a renovation of the Circus Maximus. At the time of his death in September of 96, Domitian had also nearly finished construction on an expansion of the Roman forum.[17] Although Domitian had forgone any large wars of conquest, he had stabilized many of Rome's northern frontiers through a combination of savvy diplomacy and military force.[18] He had done all of this so economically that he increased the amount of silver in the Roman denarius, the only emperor ever to succeed in doing so for a sustained period of time.[19] While Domitian had tense and difficult relationships with many senators who came from old Italian families, he extended the highest senatorial offices to Greeks, Spaniards, and others who came from Rome's provinces.[20] He was turning his back on the old, Italian imperial past and fostering the creation of a new Roman senatorial elite that extended across the Mediterranean.

None of this prevented Domitian's assassination on September 18, 96, and his replacement by Nerva, an aged senator from an old Italian aristocratic family. The conspiracy that brought Nerva to power drew upon the grievances of a relatively small group of elites based in the capital.[21] Within the narrow social world in which these men moved, they could perhaps find others who genuinely believed Domitian to be the tyrant that later historians described. Few outside of their circle appear to have shared their view.

Although Nerva proclaimed the liberation of the state upon taking power, it is not clear how many senators saw Domitian's murder in this way.[22] The shocked crowds of people still in the city, the stunned praetorian guards who protected the emperor, and the armies outside the capital were even less inclined to do so. All of these groups, even our most hostile sources agree, had liked or perhaps even loved Domitian.[23] None of them seem to have been eager to trade the capable sovereign of the past fifteen years for an old, sickly, and disloyal senator.

Nerva proved a particularly ineffective imperial placeholder. His background as a favorite of Nero and a family member of the emperor Otho made him an odd choice as a restorer of liberty.[24] Absent any other real way to assert his authority, Nerva tried to buy support by granting cash gifts to soldiers, offering tax remissions, and creating land programs designed to benefit the Italian poor, acts that collectively washed away the budget surplus that Domitian had amassed.[25] Ultimately, the legal permissiveness and financial extravagance grew so troubling that the consul Fronto told Nerva that, while it was bad to have an emperor who permitted no one to do anything, it was worse to have one who permitted everyone to do everything.[26] The liberty that Nerva claimed to have restored quickly degenerated into exceedingly expensive chaos that bordered on anarchy.

This mismanagement nearly cost Nerva his throne. Not more than a month after taking power, Nerva suppressed a coup by a descendant of the Republican general Crassus and barely survived a rebellion by the praetorian guards in the early summer of 97.[27] In a desperate but savvy ploy to retain power, Nerva then adopted and named as his successor the respected Spanish general Trajan following what appears to have been a delicate negotiation to stave off the revolt of his troops in Germany.[28] Nerva died less than a year later.

The instability of Nerva's regime contrasted markedly with the cold efficiency of Domitian—and not in a way that reflected positively on the new emperor. After Nerva's initial attempt to claim that he had restored Roman liberty, there was little rhetoric of renewal introduced to support an emperor who was clearly inferior to the man he had replaced.

Trajan offered a far more effective and inspiring example. Under Trajan's steady hand, Romans again began to speak optimistically about the dawning of a new Golden Age. The Trajanic era was a time of bold actions when the empire's conquests of places as diverse as Dacia, Arabia, and Mesopotamia pushed Romans to forget about the more measured military objectives set by Domitian. It was a period in which Trajan remade much of the center of Rome with projects that included improvements to Rome's water infrastructure, the construction of an impressive public bath on the Oppian Hill above the Colosseum, the building of Portus (a new harbor north of the old port at Ostia), and the opening of a massive new Forum and market complex that required extensive excavations of the edges of the Quirinal and Capitoline hills (see Figure 3.1). Trajan's markets had such a dramatic visual impact that, more than 250 years later, the emperor Constantius II could only gape in amazement when he first saw "the gigantic complex around

FIGURE 3.1 MAIN BUILDING AND RUINS OF TRAJAN'S MARKET. "MERCATI DI TRAIANO" IN ROME, ITALY. BY JBCARVALHO PHOTOGRAPHY. SHUTTERSTOCK.COM.

him, [one which] prevented description and never again would be imitated by mortal men."[29] Trajan very much desired to claim that the trajectory of Rome and its empire had resumed its upward path.

Trajan also emphasized that his new age fit into the positive progression of Roman fortunes by reissuing a series of old Republican and imperial coin types. These "restitution" issues drew upon a well-established imperial convention, but Trajan's version did something quite new. Trajan put his name on coins that copied old imperial types featuring emperors who had been divinized (with one exception, a coin depicting Galba). Imperial imitations, however, make up only a fraction of this restitution issue. Trajan also put his name on reissued Republican silver coins first minted by or otherwise featuring distinguished men like Cato, Pompey, and Aemilius Paullus. He even reproduced the famous denarius featuring Libertas on the front and Lucius Junius Brutus, the traditional founder of the Roman Republic, on the back that Caesar's assassin Brutus issued in 54 BC.[30] This project tied Trajan to a systematic presentation of all of Roman history through the coins issued by the men who favorably directed it. It was, then, a refashioning of the glorious Roman past that culminated in the promise of the Trajanic present.[31]

Trajan nodded to a period of decline before his accession that he allowed others to explicitly define. Many of the best authors of the early second century rose to the challenge. But the decline they pointed to was not the chaotic reign of Nerva. They instead worked to recast the public memory of the regime of Domitian as a nightmare of dysfunction and terror. Some of the most famous historians and orators Rome ever produced cynically stepped up to manufacture this counterintuitive narrative.

The *Histories* of the senator and ex-consul Tacitus stand out as a spectacular example of this sort of production. They describe the period between the accession of Galba and the death of Domitian as one that was "rich in disasters, terrible with battles, torn by civil conflicts, and horrible even in peace." This was an age in which Rome suffered military defeats to Dacians and Germans in the north, lost cities to the eruption of Mount Vesuvius, and saw the capital burn. It also witnessed "awful cruelty" consume political life as "nobility, wealth, and the refusal or acceptance of office" made one subject to accusations of treason and "virtues caused the surest ruin." Tacitus then describes a reign of terror not unlike that which prompted the horrible social dissolution of the late Republic. Through Tacitus's skilled hand, the early 90s became a time when informers gained honors for their crimes, "slaves were corrupted against their masters, freedmen against their patrons, and those who had no enemy were crushed by their friends." If Tacitus lived long enough, he hoped to write "the history of the deified Nerva's reign and Trajan's rule, a richer and less dangerous topic, because of the rare good fortune of an age in which it is permitted to say that which one thinks and believes."[32] He never did.

The biography that Tacitus wrote of his father-in-law Agricola focuses even more intensely on the cloud of fear that supposedly loomed over all public activity under Domitian. This project represented a genuine challenge because Agricola was one of Domitian's most successful and celebrated generals. Indeed, Tacitus's sketch of Agricola's life and career had to strike a very delicate balance between celebrating the achievements of the man and attacking the emperor who empowered him. So Tacitus describes Agricola's long command in Britain during which he completed the Roman conquest of Wales and campaigned deep into Scotland.[33] Upon his return to Rome in 85, Domitian rewarded Agricola with triumphal decorations, a eulogy in the senate, and a public statue.[34]

Tacitus explains that these honors were a sham. The tyrannical emperor had marked Agricola's victories "with the smile on his face that masked a secret anxiety" amid rumors from jealous courtiers who sought to turn "an emperor hostile to excellence" against Agricola.[35] Agricola then retreated from public life and died in 93, before he had the opportunity to "see this light of a most fortunate age and Trajan as emperor."[36]

Like the beginning he would later attach to his *Histories,* Tacitus frames his sketch of Agricola's life with a powerful attack on the climate Domitian created. He recounted Domitian's execution of the authors Arulenus Rusticus and Herennius Senecio, the order that their books be burned in the Forum, and the subsequent expulsion of philosophers from the city. These outrages were, Tacitus wrote, "the extreme of slavery in which even the opportunity to speak and listen was wrested from us." Tacitus could never forget the "many years plucked from the middle of our lives" in which Romans cowered in silence, fearing punishment or death. But now, he continued, "our spirit returns." Nerva "united two things that had been formerly incompatible, the rule of one man and liberty" and Trajan "every day increases the good fortune of the age" in which all of the prayers for a hopeful future have been fulfilled.[37] The moment had finally arrived when it was safe to write the truth and honor those who deserved it.

Tacitus's biography of Agricola also notes one other aspect of the newly manufactured enlightened age of Trajan. From the emperor on down, most of the men proclaiming and defining this Roman renaissance built their careers under Domitian. If the time of Domitian had been an age of horror and tyranny, Agricola, Tacitus, and even Trajan were all complicit in it.

Tacitus acknowledges as much. He does not deny that his "political career began under Vespasian, developed under Titus, and was advanced further by Domitian," but, he claims, his commitment to truth requires him to describe the fear and servitude of those years now that the freedom of the new age permits him to speak freely.[38] Tacitus asserted that he had suffered in shameful but necessary silence under Domitian, a victim of a political moment that he lacked the power to correct or the courage to openly oppose. Lurking unspoken beneath this admission was an apology for Trajan, an emperor who had helped Domitian put down a rebellion in 89 and had received the honor of a consulship in 91 as a reward. Trajan, the man who brought about this new age of freedom and enlightened monarchy, had done more than nearly anyone else to ensure that those final years of Domitian actually took place.

Tacitus might have exaggerated his own cowardly silence during the reign of Domitian, but at least he admitted that he had benefited personally from the emperor. This honesty was more than could be attributed to some of the other men who stepped forward to proclaim Trajan's restoration of liberty and virtuous rule. Plutarch, for example, might have been selected as one of the priests of Apollo at Delphi after he gave a speech to Domitian that prompted the emperor to pay for a restoration of the god's temple in 84.[39] Under Trajan, Plutarch refused to acknowledge Domitian's interest or generosity.[40] The restoration of Delphi's "many ruined and desolate buildings" came not from Domitian but because of the "present settled condition" of the reign of Trajan.[41]

No one took this sort of hypocrisy further than the senator and orator Pliny. Pliny was the first member of his family to join the senate—and his climb to prominence took place largely across the reign of Domitian. An ambitious social climber like Pliny could not afford to turn down honors or offices when offered, but Pliny's opportunism became a problem after Domitian's fall. Pliny, however, was quick to adapt. "Once Domitian was killed," Pliny would later write, "I decided that this was a truly splendid opportunity for attacking the guilty, avenging the injured, and making oneself known."[42] Like Cato three centuries before, Pliny realized that he could use the uncertainty of a new political moment to raise his own profile by attacking enemies who were too strongly tied to Domitian's regime.

Pliny then rose before the senate and lodged a charge against Publicius Certus, the man who had prosecuted the philosopher and senator Helvidius Priscus in one of the more notorious trials of Domitian's reign.[43] Although many in the senate initially expressed horror that Pliny would revisit the actions of his colleagues under Domitian, his speech did get Certus removed from the upcoming consular list and his position at the treasury. Certus soon died in disgrace.

Writing later, Pliny expressed satisfaction with what the speech had done for his career. Pliny said that "almost the entire Senate embraced me with open arms and overwhelmed me with congratulations" because he had restarted the practice of bringing matters of public concern before the senate.[44] Pliny now posed as the voice of the senate in "the days after liberty was restored" by Trajan and Nerva. He then published a revision of his speech against Certus just to be sure that Romans knew that Pliny had announced this dawning new age.[45]

Pliny undertook other projects that reiterated his role in shaping the Trajanic Golden Age. He revised and published a panegyric of the new emperor that he originally delivered in September of 100, infusing the work with the idea of Trajanic renewal.[46] Late in his life, Pliny also collected and published the letters that he and Trajan had exchanged. These letters, which form the final book of a larger letter collection, carefully frame Pliny's relationship with the emperor as a genuine friendship in which their personal interactions and public administrative activities blend together as they regularly correspond with each other.[47] Pliny wants his readers to see that the two men collaborated to ensure that the empire functioned according to what Trajan would describe to Pliny as "the spirit of our age."[48] Pliny then had a real and significant part to play in executing the emperor's new imperial vision.

None of this should obscure the fact that the men who described the great age of Trajanic renewal had not remarked on the supposed Roman decline superintended by Domitian when it was happening. Indeed, it is likely that very few people thought about Domitian's reign in that fashion before he died. But Domitian's rule had ended with his assassination and a regime born from a political murder could never be legitimate unless the murder was justified. Just as the supporters of Vespasian had done following his victory in the civil war a generation earlier, Nerva, Trajan, and the men who looked to gain their favor set out to explain two things. First, they needed to show why the reign of Domitian was so horrible that a regime change was necessary. Then they needed to explain why the reigns of Nerva and Trajan returned Rome to a glory that Domitian's viciousness had caused it to lose.

This way of thinking about Roman decline and renewal differed from what one had seen in the Republic. In the Republic, figures like Cato and Tiberius Gracchus could claim that the present was an age of decline and use the promise of renewal to propel their political careers. Under Roman emperors, however, the present could not be a moment of decline unless one wished to undermine the authority of the sovereign. The current emperor could, however, bring about a renewal that allowed Rome to recover from the problems his predecessor had caused. Finding decline as it unfolded in the present offered no prospect of political gain, but everyone from emperors to senators to average people stood to benefit if they accepted, repeated, and amplified the imperial line that a new emperor had restored lost Roman glory. After the reign of Trajan, nearly every new imperial dynasty for more than a millennium would begin by claiming to attack and correct the degeneration of the age that preceded it. Rome's eternal restoration had begun.

4

RENEWAL WITHOUT DECLINE: THE ANTONINES AND SEVERANS

THE MEN WHO branded Trajan an ideal emperor succeeded to such a degree that, for more than two centuries, the senate greeted newly inaugurated Roman emperors with this acclamation: "May you be more fortunate than Augustus and better than Trajan!"[1] Men like Pliny and Tacitus get only part of the credit for the emperor's enduring reputation. His fame had far more to do with the simple fact that, for nearly three quarters of a century, all of the men who succeeded Trajan died of natural causes. None fell to usurpers. None were assassinated. All had been adopted by their immediate predecessor. Thus all of these emperors embraced the legacies of their predecessors. For nearly a century, Rome was said not to be in decline, because no emperor wished to blame any of the problems he confronted on a recent imperial ancestor.

Together, these emperors manufactured another Roman golden age. The period from Nerva to the death of Trajan's adopted great-grandson Marcus Aurelius in 180 is now known as the Age of the Five Good Emperors. Nearly 1600 years later, the English historian Edward Gibbon wrote of this period, "If a man were called to fix the period in the history of the world during which the condition of the human race was most happy and prosperous, he would, without hesitation, name that which elapsed from the death of Domitian to the accession of Commodus."[2]

The ancient sources written in or about this period agree with Gibbon that the period between Trajan and Marcus saw Rome ruled by the wisest and most pious emperors it would ever see. Some, like a rather ridiculous set of letters exchanged between Marcus Aurelius and his teacher Fronto, even suggest that this was an age so devoid of genuine stresses that Roman leaders now spent time worrying about things as mundane as their mother bumping into a wall or a scorpion crawling into a shoe.[3] The dramatic letters of Cicero these were not.

The apparent calm of this age supposedly grew out of the great qualities these emperors possessed. Authors speak at length about all of the aspects of Roman life these men reinvigorated, the infrastructure they rebuilt, and the military they revitalized. Trajan's successor, Hadrian, for example, took credit for rebuilding Roman military discipline without assigning explicit blame for its deterioration.[4] He expanded cities and rebuilt structures across the empire but, unlike Augustus, he never claimed or implied that any sort of inherited problem required him to do these things.[5] More typical was his decision to take no credit for rebuilding the Roman Pantheon. Hadrian adorned this architectural marvel with only a copy of the original inscription honoring Marcus Agrippa, the associate of Augustus who had paid for the old building that Hadrian's construction replaced.[6]

Hadrian took particular pride in traveling the empire, reviewing conditions in its provinces, and advertising his successes in restoring those provinces to prosperity. He issued a large series of coins that marked Hadrian as the "Restorer" of a province and showed him standing above a seated personification of that province, reaching his hand out, and pulling the province up (see Figure 4.1).[7] After Hadrian's death, the temple erected by his successor Antoninus Pius to honor him featured depictions of all of the

FIGURE 4.1 REVERSE OF A HADRIANIC DENARIUS CELEBRATING HADRIAN'S RESTORATION OF GALLIC PROVINCES (*RIC* 2.HADRIAN.325, PRIVATE COLLECTION).

empire's provinces, indicating the importance the emperor had placed on thriving provincial life.

Hadrian walked a very fine line when he made these claims. No one, least of all Hadrian, could freely claim that the age of his adoptive father, Trajan, represented a time of decline. Trajan was beloved. Both Hadrian and the senate had enthusiastically backed his divinization, and Hadrian himself energetically promoted the cult of his "father."[8] Trajan, however, had left Hadrian with a set of problems that required the new emperor to respond with radical measures. While Trajan had conquered Mesopotamia and Armenia in campaigns stretching from 113 to 115, Roman forces struggled to pacify these new territories.[9] Hadrian quickly pulled back from these new conquests, a decision that proved controversial and might have forced him to execute some of Trajan's most trusted advisors shortly after he took power.[10] A serious Jewish revolt also erupted in Libya during Trajan's last months of life. As Hadrian took power, the rebellion spread into Egypt with even the great city of Alexandria briefly coming under the control of the rebels.[11] Rumors of possible revolts by armies and coups led by Roman senators also filtered through to the new emperor as he made his way to the city of Rome.[12]

Everyone who cared to look could see evidence of decline from the empire's state in the middle of the reign of Trajan, but no one openly acknowledged it. Hadrian did what seemed most prudent. He fixed the many problems that he could identify, advertised the attention that he was paying to them as he traveled extensively around the empire, and took credit for the renewal that everyone knew was needed. Neither Hadrian nor any of the people who supported him said anything openly about the failures under Trajan that made such renewal necessary.

This pattern continued under Antoninus Pius and Marcus Aurelius, the final two of the so-called Five Good Emperors. Antoninus Pius, who was called a "savior and restorer" by some of his subjects, rebuilt cities and buildings destroyed in natural disasters and helped the city of Rome recover from food shortages.[13] Marcus Aurelius did much the same. He paid for the rebuilding of Smyrna after an earthquake and reconstructed the Temple of Demeter and shrine of Kore at Eleusis after it was sacked by barbarians in the 170s.[14] Contemporaries even celebrated Marcus Aurelius for selling furnishings from the imperial residence to pay for a war against the Marcomanni, a sort of rhetorical alchemy that transformed a dire financial emergency into proof that the empire could overcome severe challenges through the virtues of an ideal emperor.[15] In each of these cases, though, the emperors brought about a specific sort of recovery that solved a singular problem. Antoninus Pius and Marcus Aurelius restored things that were ruined by happenstance, but they did not and could not be thought to preside over a time of decline.

By the time of Marcus's death in 180, there were hardly any Romans alive who could remember life under Domitian, the most recent emperor whom Romans had been taught to consider bad. Many Romans soon came to believe that Marcus, who combined devotion to Stoic philosophy with deference to the Senate and a vigorous military response to barbarian threats, represented the best ruler in history.[16]

This was all a mirage. Despite Gibbon's confident claim, anyone who actually looked at what life was like under the Five Good Emperors would hesitate to name it the most happy and prosperous moment in human history. The Age of the Five Good Emperors was an age when it was good to be an emperor. It was a pretty bad time to be almost anyone else. Objectively speaking, life got worse for many Romans as the Age of the Five Good Emperors progressed. No rebels succeeded in toppling these emperors but, after Trajan and Hadrian had both avoided significant usurpations by their commanders, Antoninus Pius faced one rebel and Marcus confronted a serious revolt launched by the general Avidius Cassius (allegedly) with the encouragement of Marcus's wife, Faustina.[17]

The empire also endured a series of regional insurrections that began late in the reign of Trajan and continued through the middle of the reign of Marcus Aurelius. Moors revolted in Spain under Marcus.[18] Jews rebelled in North East Africa in 116–117 and in Judaea in the 130s. Egypt suffered serious violence during the Jewish revolt under Trajan, Egyptian rebels rose up again under Antoninus Pius, a group of herdsmen in the Nile Delta led an uprising against Marcus in 171–172, and Egypt also supported Avidius Cassius's failed usurpation.[19] For much of Marcus's reign, the empire's northern frontier buckled as Roman commanders suffered such severe defeats that the emperor found himself forced to campaign along it for much of the later 160s and nearly all of the 170s.

Nothing in this period compared with the horror of a plague that descended on the empire in the late 160s and kept killing its population in large numbers into the 180s. The doctor Galen described symptoms that seem to indicate that this was the first incidence of smallpox in the Mediterranean but, whatever the illness actually was, it seems that as many as ten percent of the empire's 75 million inhabitants might have perished.[20]

The plague had a host of devastating implications. Panicked citizens asked for help from the gods and posted verses from an oracle above their doorways to ward off the pestilence.[21] The army seems to have been particularly hard hit. So many soldiers died that Marcus could not campaign effectively against the Marcomanni in 169.[22] The rapid decline in the workforce also sparked both inflation and political instability.[23] The population decrease ultimately compelled the emperor to increase the recruitment of Germans into the army and sponsor the immigration of barbarians into the northern provinces of the Empire.[24] Some barbarians even settled in Italy itself. Sources tend to understate the inevitable tensions that these steps produced, but even Cassius Dio confesses that the settlement of Germans in Italy stopped following a rebellion by some of the migrants in the city of Ravenna.[25] No one would believe that this was the peak of the Roman Empire—unless they were told so.

The death of Marcus on March 17, 180, has come to be seen as the end of a Roman golden age, but, if Rome had begun to decline on that March day, no one noticed. Little changed immediately. The new emperor Commodus represented the embodiment of imperial continuity and stability. He had been born in the imperial palace, the first palace-born male child to take power in Roman history. As the child of Marcus and Antoninus Pius's daughter Faustina, Commodus was the son of one emperor and the grandson of his predecessor—another imperial first.[26] Marcus had also groomed the boy to be ready to take power. Marcus made Commodus co-emperor in 177, he had arranged for Commodus to accompany him on campaign, and he even celebrated a joint triumph with his son.[27] The official portraiture of Marcus and Commodus advertised the strong father-son bond they enjoyed by depicting them as having a nearly identical appearance.[28]

As Commodus's reign progressed, however, clear signs of change began to emerge. The young emperor was barely eighteen when his father died. He responded by entrusting much of the basics of governing to a series of advisors with ties to his father's regime. They convinced Commodus to break with Marcus's aggressive frontier policy and pull back from some of the land his father had conquered in exchange for a more enduring peace and the furnishing of German recruits to his army.[29] This justifiable shift directed Roman attention away from an expensive frontier war and back to the city itself.[30]

Commodus soon turned away from the considered policies framed by the skilled advisors he had inherited. He became increasingly unhinged as the 180s gave way to the 190s. He compelled senators to turn up at the Colosseum to watch him fight as a gladiator and engage in wild beast hunts, at one point twirling the severed head of an ostrich before a group of senators who could barely stifle their laughter.[31] He styled himself the "Roman Hercules" and issued coins and official portraits showing himself draped in the lion skin associated with that hero.[32] He had months and legions renamed in his honor and even proposed that Rome be called Colonia Commodiana to commemorate his refounding of the city.[33] All these antics occurred amid a series of crises that rattled the empire. A fresh outbreak of smallpox proved so dangerous that a witness describes 2000 people a day dying when it hit Rome in 189.[34] Then, in 192, a massive fire devastated the center of Rome, burning the Forum, the building that contained the empire's archives, and even supposedly fireproof vaults.[35]

Commodus's behavior became so unpredictable that even those closest to him feared that they might fall victim to his irrational fury. He died on New Year's Eve of 192, strangled in his bath by a wrestler after poison failed to kill the robust emperor.[36] He was replaced by Pertinax, one of the few advisors of Marcus who still retained both some measure of authority and dignity. Despite Commodus's increasingly bizarre behavior, it is notable that the coup that killed him originated from a private conflict. Had the assassins not acted, the armies, the provincial governors, and even most of the senate seem likely to have continued to indulge Commodus's eccentricities. The notion of basic imperial stability and continuity survived despite the apparent insanity of the emperor.

Pertinax played along. He clearly knew about the coup in advance and, after he viewed Commodus's body, he went to the camp of the praetorian guards, promised them a bonus, and secured their support. He then summoned the senate and feigned hesitancy to accept the office of emperor until the senate voted him the position.[37] Pertinax did nothing to stop the senate from declaring Commodus a public enemy, but he also prevented senators or angry mobs in the city from doing anything to the former emperor's body.

While he carefully distanced himself from Commodus, Pertinax also took pains to emphasize stability and continuity with the principles that had guided the reign of Marcus.[38] He ostentatiously deferred to the senate by pledging not to execute anyone without senatorial consultation. He pushed reforms that prevented the praetorian guards from seizing or destroying private property.[39] Pertinax then followed Marcus and raised money by auctioning off the extravagant furniture, statues, and other property that Commodus had accumulated, an event that very publicly contrasted the moderation of Pertinax with the gaudy excesses of his predecessor.[40] But Pertinax broke with Marcus in one very important way. He refused to announce the appointment of his own son as co-emperor or successor, a nod to the older Antonine ideal of appointing the best man as an imperial successor.[41]

These efforts to mimic Marcus and his Antonine predecessors obscured an important reality. The murder of Commodus marked the effective end of Rome's third imperial dynasty. After the previous two dynasties had fallen, a senatorial figure had stepped forward and framed himself as a champion of moderation and conservative ideals. Each of these champions claimed to correct the supposed extravagance and authoritarianism of his predecessor—a nod back to the old Republican virtues of moderation and frugality that Romans always struggled to regain. It had never turned out well. Galba's soldiers killed him because the frugality applauded by the senate made the emperor seem parsimonious and aloof. Nerva's adoption of Trajan was the only thing that prevented him from suffering a similar fate. Pertinax had no Trajan to defend him. He died less than three months after taking power, killed by praetorian guards who feared that his reforms would threaten the privileges they had built up under Commodus.[42]

The murder of Pertinax in March of 193 sparked a civil war. A wealthy, dissolute senator named Didius Julianus first won the throne by outbidding other contenders in a sordid auction conducted by the praetorian guards. He lasted barely two months, abandoned by the senate and the praetorians after the Pannonian army of Septimius Severus advanced on Rome. Severus then allied with Clodius Albinus, the rebellious commander of Roman forces in Britain, and defeated Pescinnius Niger, a third imperial claimant based in Syria, following a battle in Asia Minor in 194. Severus eventually turned on Albinus, defeating his armies in 197 and taking full control over the empire.

Severus's victories in these sprawling civil wars gave him the opportunity to define the character of the new regime he created. The combination of Commodus's apparent insanity, Pertinax's ineffective reform program, Julianus's manifest corruption, and the rivalry with Albinus and Niger gave Severus ample scope to follow Vespasian and Trajan and claim that his regime represented a restoration of Roman virtue after a period of decline.

But Severus opted to go in a different direction. His regime would not advocate radical renewal. He elected to continue the old Antonine pattern of emphasizing restoration without decline. Severus began by embracing the legacy of Pertinax. Soon after the defeat of Julianus in 193, Severus spoke before the senate, claiming that he had rebelled so that he might avenge Pertinax and pledging to rule in the same way as Marcus and Pertinax.[43] He then ordered construction of a shrine to Pertinax, arranged to have him divinized, and presided at an elaborate funeral that ended with Pertinax's consecration.[44]

As his reign progressed, Severus shifted away from the close embrace of Pertinax. He never disavowed his ties to the old senator but, in the lead-up to a war with Clodius Albinus, Severus came before the senate and advanced the strange claim that he had in fact been adopted by Marcus Aurelius.[45] Severus then pushed the senate to recognize his "brother" Commodus as a god, began to call himself the "son of the divine Marcus Antoninus," and legally renamed his son Marcus Aurelius Antoninus, the official name of the future emperor Caracalla.[46] Severus also soon ceased marking his connection to Pertinax. The name Pertinax disappeared from his coins around 199, replaced by the Antonine-evoking legend Severus Pius.[47] Severus then began doing things like erecting statues to Nerva, whom he describes as his great-great-great-grandfather.[48]

Because Severus now claimed to be an Antonine, he found himself constrained by the same Antonine rhetoric of continuity. On one level, this constraint was most unfortunate. Severus was much more successful than his immediate Antonine predecessors. He increased military morale by raising pay and permitting soldiers to marry, reforms that coincided with a rise in military effectiveness.[49] His armies fought far more capably than those commanded by Marcus. Severus captured and held territory in Mesopotamia that Trajan could not secure.[50]

In other areas of Roman life, Severus had a record of reform surpassed perhaps only by Augustus.[51] The emperor sponsored a set of laws on marriage that modified the old Augustan restrictions on adultery and reaffirmed the privileges granted to men with a specified number of children.[52] In 203, an arch was dedicated to Severus and Caracalla in the Roman Forum because of "their restoration of the state and their expansion of the boundaries of the Roman people" (seeFigure 4.2). [53]

Then, in the following year, Severus held the Saecular Games for the third time since the magnificent resurrection of the tradition under Augustus.[54] These games traditionally purified and renewed the city of Rome following a period of strife and, like Augustus, Severus could now use this event to symbolically open a new era.[55]

The new age saw a refashioning of Rome's public face. Severus constructed a number of new buildings in the city, including a bath complex, an aqueduct, and the Septizodium, a spectacular 300-foot-long, 100-foot-high fountain complex on the edge of the Palatine hill opposite the Circus Maximus.[56] He restored the Pantheon and the Theater of Pompey in the Campus Martius as well as the areas around the Forum that had burned under Commodus.[57] Severus took this last task on with great energy, rebuilding the burned Temple of Vespasian, the Temple of Peace, and the Porticus Octaviae as well as a large number of other sanctuaries across the city.[58] Then, on the western wall of the rebuilt Temple of Peace, Severus's engineers hung a massive 2000-square-foot marble map of the city of Rome

FIGURE 4.2 WESTERN EDGE OF THE ROMAN FORUM SHOWING ARCH OF SEPTIMIUS SEVERUS AND REMAINS OF THE TEMPLE OF VESPASIAN AND TITUS, RESTORED BY SEVERUS IN C. 200 AD. PHOTO C. 1890. WIKIMEDIA.

that labeled and showed the ground plans of all of the structures in the city.[59] The plan was far too large to be consulted with the naked eye. Its purpose was instead to overwhelm viewers and show them the magnificence of the city that Severus had restored.[60] Around the same time that the marble plan was erected, Severus issued a coin series marking him as the "Restorer of the City."[61]

The odd thing about Severan renewal was, of course, the emperor's unwillingness to identify any Roman decline that he had reversed. The inscriptions placed on the Pantheon, the Theater of Pompey, and a host of other structures speak about him restoring things that had been worn down by age.[62] Other inscriptions celebrate Severus for rebuilding structures in and around the Forum following fire damage.[63] Severus wanted Romans to understand that he had brought about a massive Roman renewal, but he also wanted them to know that his new age was a "rejuvenated continuation" of the Antonine era rather than a break from that glorious past.[64]

Septimius Severus died in 211. His successors maintained the fiction that they were the dynastic heirs of Marcus Aurelius and the stewards of the stable empire over which he presided. So, for example, in 212 Severus's son Caracalla extended citizenship to every freeborn person in the Roman Empire so that they might share in his salvation.[65] The edict came to be called the *Constitutio Antoniniana* in his honor and, while it profoundly and permanently altered the Roman legal landscape, even the best Roman lawyers of later centuries could not figure out which Antoninus had actually issued the law.[66] Some said it was Antoninus Pius, some said it was Marcus Aurelius, but all of them struggled to see the citizenship extension as something separate from the broader imperial stability and institutional continuity that typified the long Antonine age.[67] They had unwittingly fallen victim to the propaganda of stability and illusion of continuity around which Septimius Severus crafted the public image of his dynasty.

Reality often refused to cooperate with this picture. Four emperors rose and fell between 211 and 222, a period of political instability that bracketed one of the most significant changes to the legal status of the Roman population the state would ever see. While Alexander Severus, the final member of the Severan dynasty, did rule for thirteen years, the rise of the Persian Empire in the east, barbarian attacks in the north, and the emperor's apparent submissiveness to his mother provoked an army rebellion that overthrew the emperor.[68] The soldiers killed Alexander Severus and replaced him with Maximinus Thrax, a gigantic, burly Thracian military man who had trained many of the soldiers serving on this campaign.[69]

Maximinus Thrax simply said what everyone around him already knew. The rhetorical fiction that the Antonine dynasty begun by Nerva had continued on into the reign of Alexander Severus was now too tattered to mask the substantial problems Rome confronted in the mid-third century. Once people in the 220s and 230s had begun to see decline instead of continuity, they sought its origins.

Many of them settled on the same point. Rome's decline, they believed, began with Marcus Aurelius's catastrophic decision to allow Commodus to take over as his successor. In fact, a completely ahistorical tradition of Marcus expressing doubts about the stability of his son already appears in the works of Cassius Dio and Herodian, two men who were alive at the time of Marcus's death.[70] In Dio's case, the senator was almost certainly aware of Marcus's actual intentions. These historians knew better, but the Marcus who piously embraced his son as his heir could not work for historians who now knew what the decades after Marcus's death would bring. Decline had to begin somewhere. It made sense to place its origins at the end of the life of Rome's last unquestionably good emperor.

We can now see that this point of transition was manufactured many decades after it happened. No one at the time understood that the moment before the accession of Commodus marked Rome's imperial apogee. Dio himself admits as much.[71] His larger history grew out of a smaller book that Dio composed early in the reign of Septimius Severus that recorded the dreams and portents that made Severus believe that Fortune had ordained him to become emperor. This work clearly did not see the death of Marcus as the beginning of a period of Roman decline, because Severus read the work and sent Dio a long, complimentary letter praising his effort. The pieces of this original book that remain in Dio's history see events from the reign of Commodus through the early years of that of Severus as building in a positive direction, with developments peaking as Severus took power.[72]

This is not the trajectory one now finds in Dio's longer history. Dio narrates the progression of Roman history from the foundation of the city to Dio's own second consulship in 229. This is a history that he quite deliberately separates into distinctive periods, with the events beginning with the death of Marcus Aurelius fitting into a clearly inferior period of Roman history. Thus Dio ends book 72 by saying that, after Marcus died, "our history now descends from a kingdom of gold to one of iron and rust, as affairs did for Romans on that day."[73] The last eight books frame this period of decline before concluding with a lukewarm endorsement of the reign of Severus Alexander as a moment in which troops complain openly of being disciplined while the emperor and his advisors protect and honor the targets of their anger.[74] The Roman imperial order remained vibrant enough to resist the entitled demands of the army—but just barely.

Herodian was a few years younger than Dio and wrote perhaps a decade and a half after Dio finished his history. He too had lived under Marcus, but he also lived long enough into the third century that he believed the Roman state had lost the resiliency that Dio felt still existed in 229. Herodian saw and wrote about the coup that brought Maxininus Thrax to power, a coup he thought was caused by the army realizing it had different interests than those of the senatorial elites and the emperors they supported.[75]

Herodian also had a clearer idea of when the degeneration began. In his preface, he speaks about how the six decades between the death of Marcus and his own day had seen more civil wars, foreign invasions, enemy sacks of provincial cities, plagues, and natural disasters than those Rome had experienced in the preceding two centuries.[76] Herodian claimed that these tragedies marked a decline in which the demands of the military undercut the political stability of the empire. Of course, Herodian had also elected to forget the wars, sacks, plagues, and earthquakes of the Antonine age. The markers of Roman decline again mattered only when they reinforced a decline that an author wanted his readers to see. Like Dio, Herodian remained pessimistic about the direction of the empire.[77] After more than a century of imperial claims of renewal without decline, the 230s seemed to Herodian like a period of Roman decline without a realistic path toward renewal. His history ends in 238 AD, the so-called Year of Six Emperors. The final incidents he records trace the deaths of the distinguished senatorial emperors Balbinus and Pupienus, the exposure of their bodies along the road, and the salutation of the thirteen-year-old Gordian III as Roman emperor.[78] No words of optimism or promises of renewal greet the acclamation of the sixth emperor to hold power in 238.

Herodian's abrupt conclusion implies that his narration has stopped but the chaos and uncertainty it has described will continue. Romans had returned to the pessimism of the late Republic. Instead of a second Augustan Golden Age, the empire now descended into what modern historians call the Third-Century Crisis.

5

DECLINE AND FALSE RENEWAL

The Third-Century Crisis

THE CRISIS THAT Herodian sensed dawning in 238 lasted into the mid-280s. During that time, more than fifty men would try to claim imperial power, roughly one person per year for half a century. This half-century represented an abject failure according to the measures Romans had become accustomed to use when judging imperial regimes. Since the time of Augustus, the empire had promised stability and security in exchange for the loyalty of its subjects. The middle decades of the third century brought very little loyalty or political stability. The empire did only moderately better in terms of protecting itself, especially after its system of frontier defenses collapsed in the 250s.[1] But, just as the long-lived emperors and regular imperial successions of the Antonine age made its multiple crises seem like isolated incidents, the political instability of the third century gives the impression of a half century of unremitting catastrophe and systemic failure. The reality was far more complicated.

This impression of endless crisis grows in part from a shift in the way that Romans thought and talked about the conditions in which they lived. The rhetoric of decline, which had largely disappeared from political life by the late Antonine period, reappeared often in the middle third century. Whereas Antonine and Severan emperors framed restoration and renewal as essential maintenance on an otherwise well-running machine, the emperors of the third century returned to the rhetoric of decline and restoration that new emperors often used to discredit the final emperor of the dynasty that preceded them. The third century saw no long-lived dynasties after the death of the last Severan emperor. Many new emperors and imperial pretenders emphasized that the failings of their predecessors had brought Rome to a crisis point, and they proclaimed their accession as the dawning of an era of renewed liberty and prosperity. When they fell from power, their failings only reinforced the perception of unrelenting crisis in the empire.

No third-century emperor pushed the story of Roman decline and renewal more aggressively or recklessly then the emperor Decius, who ruled from 249 until 251. There was some logic to his decision to press this point. The period between the death of Alexander Severus and the accession of Decius saw eight emperors rise and fall as well as three abortive attempts to found new imperial dynasties.[2] Decius hoped to make the fourth post-Severan dynasty last longer. He had been born around 190 in Budelia, near the city of Sirmium in what is now northwestern Serbia.[3] He came of age in the Severan empire, had been named to a consulship under Alexander Severus, and held two major provincial governorships in 234 and 238.[4] He came to power with a reputation as a tough, serious, and conservative military man.[5]

The chaos and failures of the preceding decade offered Decius the opportunity to present himself as a restorer of traditional Roman virtues. He modeled his approach on the emperor Trajan. In fact, not long after taking power the man born as C. Messius Quintus Decius Valerinus took on a new name. From this point forward he would be C. Messius Quintus Traianus Decius—Trajan Decius.

As Trajan Decius, the new emperor inaugurated a carefully curated program of nostalgia for the great Roman past that he would bring back. Decius sponsored one of the most unusual and innovative coin issues in Roman history.[6] These featured a nearly complete selection of all of the divinized emperors of the Julio-Claudian, Flavian, Antonine, and Severan dynasties, with only Claudius, Caracalla, and Pertinax left out. Perhaps more surprising than these omissions was the inclusion of Commodus and Severus Alexander. It is also telling that Trajan Decius left out the three Gordians (who had ruled between 238 and 244), the most recent additions to the pantheon of divine emperors. Their exclusion made clear that this issue was not simply a numismatic catalog of all of the divinized emperors. It instead was a collective monument to those emperors with whom Trajan Decius wanted to be identified.[7] His was a new dynasty, but it was one that nevertheless promised to restore the virtues, traditions, and achievements of the four great and long-lasting imperial dynasties that had come before.

This message extended beyond the emperor's adoption of the name Trajan and the coins he issued. In a symbolic bow to old Roman political tradition, Decius reintroduced the old Republican office of the censor, a position that Augustus had discontinued as an independent magistracy in 22 BC.[8] Inscriptions honoring Trajan Decius as a restorer of Roman cities and the Republic began to appear around the empire soon after his accession. The Danubian town of Oescus honored him in 249 for restoring military discipline and reestablishing civic cults.[9] The Italian town of Cosa erected a statue honoring Trajan Decius as the "restorer of cults and liberty" in 251, perhaps following an effort by the emperor to reopen a local temple.[10]

These inscriptions reflect Trajan Decius's particular concerns with restoring Roman military and religious vigor. Decius's embrace of Roman tradition also manifested itself in one radical and extremely disruptive way. The senate could declare a ritual called a *supplicatio* in which temples would be opened so that the population of the city could give offerings to the gods to either thank them for their protection or ask for their forgiveness.[11] This ritual eventually became a part of the imperial cult and was celebrated each time the public marked an imperial anniversary. Decius, perfectly in character, decided to supersize this traditional ritual action.[12] Not long after taking power, he issued a law requiring every citizen in the Roman Empire to perform a sacrifice and get a receipt indicating that they had done so. He appears to have thought very little about what such a universal decree would mean to the empire's small but growing Christian community. It is a shame that he did not. Because Decius had just inadvertently launched the first empire-wide persecution of Roman Christians.[13] It is unknown how many Christians died because of his recklessness.

This was not the only unfortunate consequence of the Decian renewal. The emperor fancied himself an exceptional military commander and he provoked a war soon after taking power by canceling the regular tribute payments that his predecessor Philip I had granted to Gothic barbarians.[14] For much of 249, Decius sensibly allowed Roman commanders in the frontier area to deal with Gothic attacks but, as 250 began, Decius elected to take personal control over the campaign.

This decision was a mistake. Not long after he arrived on the scene, Goths broke through the frontier and defeated the emperor in battle. As was his tendency in most matters, the emperor continued promising dramatic results. The historian Dexippus preserves a letter supposedly sent by Decius to dissuade the city of Philippopolis (the modern Bulgarian city of Plovdiv) from organizing local resistance to a Gothic attack in 251. While undoubtedly a literary creation of the historian, the letter nonetheless reflects Decius's generally ill-informed arrogance. The emperor told the population of Philippopolis that it is reckless to fight "without a general" when they could instead by led "by a leader." Doing otherwise would be to act against their "commander."[15] Trusting its emperor, the city did not organize a defense. The Goths then sacked it. For good measure, Goths also sacked the town of Oescus, which had recently praised the emperor for restoring military discipline.

Decius's bombastic foolishness had even more serious consequences later that year. Loaded with plunder and captives taken during their raiding, the Goths had begun to move out of Roman territory when Decius and his forces confronted them outside of the city of Abritus (modern Razgrad in Bulgaria). The Goths wisely arranged their forces in three lines, with the final line placed behind a marsh. Decius gleefully charged into the Gothic forces, routed the first two lines of Goths, and then found himself and his army bogged down in the muck.[16] Trajan Decius, his son Herennius Etruscus, and much of his army perished. The emperor's body, "interred in the slime of the swamp," was never found. He was the first Roman emperor to die in battle with barbarians.

Conditions in the empire continued to deteriorate as the decade progressed. The remains of Trajan Decius's army chose his successor, Trebonianus Gallus, right after the battle. Gallus came to an agreement that paid the Goths to leave Roman territory and then turned to confront a major uprising in the east led by a Syrian nobleman.[17] Roman forces pushed the rebel to retreat, probably into Persia, and Gallus ordered his son, Volusian, to march east and lead a major campaign against Persia in 252.

Catastrophe struck before he arrived. A Persian attack wiped out the Roman army in the region. Persian sources speak about 60,000 Romans killed and then detail how the Persian troops swept through Syria, overran all of the main Roman garrisons in the province, and sacked Antioch, the third largest city in the empire.[18] Roman sources speak of Syria being burned and Antioch "no longer called a city" after the Persians left it "entirely ruined and naked, houseless, uninhabited."[19] Amid these Roman military defeats, a disease whose progression strongly resembled Ebola struck the empire. It emerged in the massive city of Alexandria in the reign of Decius, hit the capital by 251, and raged on until the early 260s.[20]

Roman decline was no longer simply a propaganda device. It was apparent to everyone that the empire was demonstrably weaker than it had been even a decade before. The Roman military owed much of its longstanding success to the effective training and relatively long service time of the professional soldiers who fought in it. The combined losses to the Goths in 251 and the Persians in 252 robbed the military of many tens of thousands of well-trained and well-drilled soldiers. Those men were neither quickly nor easily replaced. The massive destruction in Syria and the enslavement of many Roman citizens by Persian and Gothic raiders further complicated any Roman military recovery.[21] In a time of plague, the sheer numbers of people dying made large-scale recruitment exceedingly difficult. So few mourned when Gallus was assassinated in 253 by frustrated troops led by their general Aemilianus.

The situation hardly improved when Valerian, the next emperor of consequence, ended the short reign of Aemilianus. Valerian was an old and distinguished senator who had held a consulship, served as the primary senatorial negotiator during the chaos of 238, had been chosen as the president of the Senate, and had even been chosen as censor by his senatorial colleagues when Decius tried to revive the office.[22]

Valerian looked like the sort of senatorial traditionalist who could bring back Roman glory and he set about following the familiar script of promising Roman renewal amid a growing sense that the empire was rapidly declining. Like Hadrian a century and a half earlier, he traversed the empire, in one case traveling from Syria to Cologne in Germany and back to Rome in the span of a little more than a year and a half.[23] But conditions in the empire no longer resembled those of the Hadrianic era. Valerian had inherited a host of major problems, with the situation in Syria foremost among them. So he set to work rebuilding Antioch, perhaps beginning construction on the new imperial palace on an island in the center of the Orontes River that emperors marching east would use for more than a century.[24] Valerian even marked his efforts to restore the East from the damage caused by the Persians with an issue of coins depicting a personification of Oriens (the East) crowning him with a laurel wreath and calling the emperor the Restorer of the East.[25]

Valerian's claim was wildly optimistic. War with Persia continued along the Euphrates, German Alamanni threatened to cross the Rhine, barbarian raiders used ships to attack cities in Greece and Asia Minor from the sea, and plague raged on. The horrific and disgusting illness savaged Valerian's army and the empire's civilian population. Sources speak about deaths of 5000 people a day and recount how the population of Alexandria, the empire's second city, collapsed from 500,000 to 190,000 people.[26] The bishop of Alexandria described the two great harbors of the city and the Nile River all clogged with floating bodies, filling the entire city with a stench of death and decay that neither the sea breezes nor winter rains cleansed. Living through this horror, he wrote, was like watching "the human race waning and wasting away upon the earth."[27]

Valerian and many around him believed that they had identified the culprits responsible for Rome's ongoing nightmares. Christians. This was, of course, not a new notion. Christians had been blamed for disasters as far back as the great fire of Rome under Nero.[28] But the 250s were different. The empire had never before experienced this particularly noxious combination of political instability, repeated military defeat, and gruesome plague. As Cyprian, the Christian bishop of Carthage, wrote, "many people now complain and blame us because wars flare up more frequently, plague arrives, famines rage, and long droughts interrupt the showers and the rains." The world, they claimed, "is shaken and oppressed" because Christians do not worship the gods.[29]

Valerian responded violently to these concerns, whether he believed them or not. One Christian source indicates that Valerian had once been friendly with Christians and had welcomed them into his home, but he turned against them abruptly as the disasters in the empire mounted in the summer of 257.[30] In August, he issued an edict that called for bishops and other leading Christians to either sacrifice or be exiled. Many chose exile.

Then, in the summer of 258, the emperor issued a second edict that ordered recalcitrant Christians to either sacrifice or be killed. Female Christians had their property confiscated and Christians associated with the imperial bureaucracy were sent to the mines to work as slaves until they died of exhaustion.[31] Because it was specifically directed against Christians, Valerian's persecution was more systematic and deadlier than that of Decius. The total Christian deaths are again unknown, but the persecution did claim several prominent Christians, including the bishops Cyprian of Carthage and Sixtus of Rome.[32]

Christians responded to these charges that they had caused Roman decline in an intriguing way. They vigorously disputed the accusation that they were in any way responsible for the plagues, wars, and instability that simultaneously afflicted Rome. At the same time, Christian leaders like Cyprian looked within their communities and saw groups of Christians who succumbed to the pressures of the persecution. For these Christian leaders, the persecution represented both a sign of Christian decline and the beginning of a Christian renewal.

Cyprian wrote that Christians were right to be saddened at the loss of the martyrs who died for their faith, but they should not lose sight of the fact that God also chose to allow the persecution to happen. "The Lord wished to test his family," Cyprian wrote, "and because a long peace had corrupted the divine discipline among us, the divine judgement awakened the faith as if from a deep sleep." In the calm of the past few decades, individual Christians became filled with "an insatiable greed" and devoted themselves to "increasing their possessions." Even bishops were "no longer devoted to their sacred duties" but instead "hunted the markets for profits," "multiplied their profits by making loans," and "tried to amass large fortunes while they had brethren starving within the church."[33] The persecution then represented God's punishment, "correction of our sin," and "proof of our faith." These misfortunes had pushed faithful Christians to "follow Christ" without being "held back by the chain of their wealth" and to "seek heaven" without being "weighed down by earthly desires."[34] The lapsed Christians who sacrificed during the persecutions of Decius and Valerian had succumbed to the same sorts of avarice, ambition, and greed that Cato and Sallust had blamed for the decline of Rome's Republic 300 years before.

But, Cyprian concluded, the church emerged stronger now that these false believers had been discovered.

Cyprian might have believed that the persecutions made the church stronger, but they clearly did nothing to help the empire. Valerian's persecution preceded two of the most terrible years Rome ever experienced. In the West, German raiders crossed the Rhine and the Alps, penetrating deep into Italy, sacking cities, and carrying off large numbers of captives. In Asia Minor, barbarians sailing down from the Black Sea raided as far south as Cappadocia. Valerian tried to lead his army to meet them—and failed. Even worse, the Ebola-like plague hit his army hard during this campaign. Then, as 260 dawned, the weakened and depleted forces had to face a new Persian invasion of Mesopotamia. Valerian and his army were defeated and besieged near the city of Edessa. Valerian arranged to meet with the Persian shah so that they might negotiate an armistice. He was instead taken prisoner and spent the rest of his life as the Persian king's captive. According to one tradition, the emperor lived out his days serving as the footstool the shah used to mount his horse.[35]

The Persians assumed that the capture of Valerian would precipitate the collapse of Roman rule in the East, but something surprising happened as the Persian army continued its advance. Valerian's son and co-emperor Gallienus pulled back from some of his father's most aggressive and panicked policies. Most notably, he ended the Christian persecution. The people of the empire then rallied. Imperial governors, Roman allies, and even citizen militias organized to beat back the invaders who had spilled across Rome's frontiers.

Initially many of these figures responded as ambitious governors had for the past two decades. They sought to fill the power vacuum left by Valerian's capture by trying to take control over the whole empire. Although Gallienus retained power as Augustus in Italy, no fewer than five other men claimed imperial power across the empire in 260, each supported by some combination of Roman imperial and local resources. In the summer of 260, Roman forces led by a treasury official named Macrianus defeated the Persians in Cilicia. Macrianus then proclaimed his sons Macrianus and Quietus emperors.[36] Two Danubian governors also rebelled.[37] So too did Postumus, who was commanding troops in Gaul.[38] Forced to deal with a barbarian invasion of Italy, Gallienus could not immediately confront all of the usurpers. His inaction proved a blessing.

The next year saw things stabilize as Aureolus, a commander loyal to Gallienus, and Odaenathus, the leader of the city of Palmyra who was officially acting as an agent of Gallienus, defeated Marcianus, Quietus, and the Danubian rebels. These events left the regime of Postumus in control of Gaul, the Rhineland, Britain, and, after 261, much of Spain. Gallienus controlled the imperial center, North Africa, and Egypt. Odaenathus's Palmyra controlled all of the Asiatic provinces south of the Taurus mountains in Gallienus's name. None of the three pressed a claim for universal control of Roman territory. This situation would hold for much of the next decade, with each regime developing an administrative structure that drew heavily upon the local aristocracy.

The poverty of literary evidence from this decade makes it hard to know for sure why these figures behaved differently from the way other would-be emperors acted when they seized control of Roman provinces in the past. One reason for the change may be that the horrible decade of the 250s compelled Roman leaders in all parts of the empire to focus on restoring the health of the regions they controlled rather than using those regions as springboards for a campaign to take control of the entire empire. The sovereigns of the 260s privileged partnership with local leaders and local institutions. They embarked on a collaborative process of Roman rehabilitation that provided for the focused defense of cities and towns that the central government could not easily reinforce while offering resources for local reconstruction following damaging attacks.

The *Scythica* of the Athenian historian Dexippus outlines how Roman imperial power and local initiative could coexist in the 260s.[39] Dexippus often emphasizes how the combined efforts of civic and regional leaders and Roman imperial officials effectively confronted barbarian threats in Greece and the southern Balkans. In 267, for example, a band of Herulian raiders sailed down from the Black Sea and sacked Athens. The devastation was terrible, but the Roman imperial navy destroyed their ships before the Heruls could sail back. By using a force of a few thousand Athenians composed primarily of youth who had undergone the traditional ephebic military training expected of Athenian citizens, Dexippus then harried the retreating Herulian forces as they passed through Attica. Both local Athenian and Roman imperial resources then combined to help the city slowly rebuild from the destruction.

This idea of local and imperial partnership existed outside of the territory controlled by Gallienus as well. An altar from the German city of Augsburg that dates to September 11, 260, commemorates a victory won that spring against barbarians who "were killed and put to flight by soldiers of the province of Raetia but also Germaniciani and locals," an action that liberated "many thousands of Italians" whom the barbarians had captured.[40]

This is the same model that Dexippus earlier describes in which a Roman commander leads a force of locals from the region in order to mount a campaign against a barbarian invader. But there are two interesting twists to this text. The first is the emphasis the Augsburg altar places upon the success of the provincial levy in freeing thousands of Italians taken captive during the barbarian invasion of Italy. Even more interesting, though, is the fact that this altar was erected while the Gallic emperor Postumus controlled the region, thus suggesting that both Gallienus and Postumus tolerated this sort of local mobilization under Roman official supervision.

Postumus saw the marshaling of local resources to serve local needs as a path toward a novel sort of Roman renewal.[41] Indeed, this view may help to explain some of the idiosyncrasies of Postumus's regime. The regime of Gallienus spent much of the 260s minting huge numbers of low-silver-content coins and debased gold coins of poor workmanship. Postumus embarked on a distinctive numismatic program. His beautiful gold coins weighed more than those of Gallienus and his first silver coins had a greater purity and better workmanship than those of his rival. He also restarted the large-scale issuing of the traditional high-value bronze denominations of the Antonine Age, coins that had largely been discontinued by Gallienus. This initial burst of coins advertised a strong, capable emperor who tangibly returned an icon of imperial stability to his domains.

These coins also often bore images that blended the imperial and the local in much the same way that Dexippus and the Augsburg altar did. One of the earliest silver coins that Postumus issued featured a reclining representation of the Rhine and the legend Salvation of the Provinces on its reverse. Another, which bore the legend Restorer of the Gauls, evoked earlier Hadrianic coins by showing Postumus standing with his foot on an enemy and raising up a figure representing Gaul (see Figure 5.1).[42]

Postumus then offered a strong imperial regime based on partnership with his subjects and capable defense of their cities and properties. This was much the same model that Dexippus theorized, though one put in operation by a regional imperial claimant rather than by Gallienus and the central empire.

This process unfolded on an even larger stage in the Roman East where regional power brokers had already begun responding to the failures of emperors to confront the relentless Persian invasions of the 250s. In 252 or 253, a descendant of the royal house of Emesa named Uranius Antoninus mounted a successful defense of his home region. He assumed imperial titles, issued coins, and then apparently faded back into obscurity once the immediate Persian threat had receded.[43]

The response to the capture of Valerian proved even more potent. As the remains of his army scattered, some forces linked up with fighters trained

FIGURE 5.1 COINS ISSUED BETWEEN 264 AND 283 BY THE EMPERORS POSTUMUS, AURELIAN, PROBUS, AND CARUS CELEBRATING THEIR RESTORATIONS OF PROVINCES, ARMIES, OR THE ENTIRE WORLD (CLOCKWISE FROM UPPER LEFT, *RIC* 5B.POSTUMUS.225; *RIC* 5A.AURELIAN.299 AND 366; *RIC* 5B.PROBUS.731; *RIC* 5B.CARUS.106; PRIVATE COLLECTION).

by the Palmyrene Odaenathus. Odaenathus had secured an extraordinary degree of power in Palmyra and had worked closely with Roman imperial authorities since the 250s. He prevented a Persian attack on Palmyra during the devastating invasions of the 250s and, in return for his service, Valerian granted Odaenathus the status accorded to a Roman consul.[44] Odaenathus was, then, perfectly positioned to both rally Roman troops and deploy local forces.

Odaenathus did so with devastating effectiveness in the summer of 260. Attacking under the authority of Gallienus, he routed the Persian army as it retreated back into Persian territory. Gallienus then appointed Odaenathus the "commander of the East."[45] In this capacity, Odaenathus mounted an invasion of Persian Mesopotamia in 262 or 263, penetrating as far as the Persian capital of Ctesiphon and allowing Gallienus to claim the title Persicus Maximus.[46] He seems to have launched a second invasion of Persia in 267 that might again have reached the vicinity of Ctesiphon. Rome's eastern frontier was not only restored, but also its armies in the region were resurgent.

As the crises of the early 260s passed, however, Gallienus and those around him began eyeing a full restoration of central authority across all of Roman territory. The 250s had shattered the ability of the central government to marshal and organize the resources of Rome's immense empire. Those resources still existed, however, and, in the 260s, figures like Postumus and Odaenathus had efficiently deployed these local assets to save the empire and begin to restore their home regions. This was a Roman restoration, of a sort.

The seductive notion that one man should control all Roman territory undermined this particular, regionalized Roman restoration. In Gaul, Postumus was assassinated in 269 because his resistance to calls to invade Italy angered his troops.[47] Odaenathus fell to assassins enlisted by local rivals and a suspicious Gallienus in late 267 or early 268.[48] These tensions between the emperor ruling from Rome and the regional authorities ruling in Rome's name became even more pronounced after the murder of Gallienus in 268. His successor, Claudius Gothicus, had such a frosty relationship with Odaenathus's widow, Zenobia, that she attacked Egypt and pulled it away from the central empire. Once the emergencies of the early

260s had passed, Romans began rethinking the sustainability of the local and imperial partnerships that had saved their empire.

The situation became truly untenable when Claudius's general Aurelian took the throne in 270.[49] Aurelian refused to accept that Rome could thrive when multiple Roman sovereigns controlled its territory. His reign began with a series of successful campaigns against barbarians who had penetrated the Alps, attacked northern Italy, and crossed the Danube.[50] Soon after that, Aurelian resolved to reunify the empire. Palmyra was his first target. The campaign began in 272 with the negotiated handover of Egypt to Aurelian by the province's governor.[51] Aurelian then led his army toward Syria and won a major victory outside of the city of Emesa.[52]

Following the defeat of Palmyra and the capture of Zenobia in the early autumn of 272, Aurelian turned his attention to the Gallic empire. After Postumus's startling successes in the early 260s, the Gallic empire had fallen into increasing dysfunction as its soldiers assassinated a sequence of successors to Postumus.[53] Aurelian absorbed its territory following a victory at Châlons in 274. He then pardoned Tetricus I and Tetricus II, the last two Gallic emperors.[54]

By the end of 274, Aurelian felt entitled to advertise himself as the man who had restored Rome. The senate fêted him as the Restorer of the World and he issued a large number of coins bearing that legend. Nothing better expressed the pride this emperor took in that particular achievement than the massive triumphal procession in which he led Zenobia, her son Vaballathus, and Tetricus II into the city of Rome. Each was costumed, with Zenobia weighed down by so much heavy gold that she could barely walk and Tetricus dressed in a scarlet cloak, yellow tunic, and Gallic trousers. They were followed by people carrying the crowns of victory sent by all of the major cities in the empire, the residents of Rome marching in their guilds, Roman army troops, and members of the Senate.

This display celebrated Aurelian's reunification of the empire and his reintegration of the parts that had split off. But Aurelian was not finished. His imperial renewal extended even to a public reconciliation with the regional leaders who had once opposed him. Aurelian permitted Zenobia to get remarried to a Roman senator, he allowed Tetricus I to serve as a governor of an Italian province, and he decreed that Tetricus II would keep his senatorial rank.[55] The empire was truly whole again.

Aurelian had succeeded in doing the unthinkable. The surprising, almost unbelievable Roman recovery from the disasters of 260 had been completely redefined. Postumus's victories along the Rhine and Odeanathus's Persian campaigns were no longer actions that restored Roman power and prestige. They were instead continuations of the profound Roman decline that everyone knew had gripped the empire in the 240s and 250s. Perhaps even more startling was the fact that the triumphant emperor used this remaking of the past as a justification to dismantle many of the very structures that had made Rome so resilient in the 260s. After a short revolt in 273, Palmyra was again defeated, plundered, and, eventually, turned into a Roman army garrison center.[56] The Athenian ephebic initiations were discontinued not long after Athenian ephebes under Dexippus's leadership had helped the city fight back against the Heruls.[57] The local resources of the Gallic empire were reabsorbed.

Central control had been restored, but at a price. The empire that emerged out of the 270s was on a path to becoming both more centralized and more brittle. It would be much better able to absorb blows like those inflicted in the 250s and 260s, but, if enough of those blows landed at once, there were fewer local resources to fall back upon. Aurelian had brought about a Roman restoration, but it was one that radically reshaped the way that all Romans interacted with their cities and their empire.

6

DECLINE, RENEWAL, AND THE INVENTION OF CHRISTIAN PROGRESS

THE GREAT CELEBRATION of imperial unity over which Aurelian presided in 274 proved premature. He would be dead within a year. Over the next decade, six emperors would come and go until Rome again had an emperor who proved capable, ruthless, and long lived enough to re-establish strong imperial control over the entirety of the Roman world.

That emperor was Diocletian, a military man from what is now Croatia, who seized power in 284.[1] Diocletian had learned a few important lessons from recent decades. The epidemic of third-century imperial assassinations showed Diocletian that even the most powerful and capable emperors could not fend off challengers by themselves. Diocletian understood that power must be shared with a competent colleague and, because he had no sons, he chose a Balkan soldier named Maximian as his imperial partner.[2] Diocletian had also learned that emperors needed to be mobile so that they could be present in regions of greatest tension. Not long after the appointment of Maximian, the two emperors led two separate armies on campaigns in the Roman north.

Maximian faced a particularly intriguing challenge. Around the time of Diocletian's accession, a peasant revolt against increased taxation and oppression by local elites erupted in Gaul.[3] Perhaps led at first by an imperial pretender named Amandus, these so-called Bagaudae were "inexperienced farmers [who] sought military garb" so that "the plowman imitated the infantryman, the shepherd the cavalryman, the rustic ravager of his own crops the barbarian enemy" as they "ravaged the countryside far and wide" and "assailed many cities."[4] Then, as Maximian struggled to deal with this situation, Carausius, a naval commander charged with responding to Frankish and Saxon pirate attacks on Roman coastal towns, rebelled with his fleet. Carausius had evidently allowed barbarians to raid Roman settlements before he attacked them so that he and his troops could then seize the captured plunder for themselves. When Maximian ordered his execution, Carausius had the sailors in his fleet proclaim him emperor—and promptly seized Britain and northern Gaul for himself.[5] Robbed of his fleet and facing a fresh barbarian invasion across the Rhine, Maximian did not respond immediately.

Diocletian faced his own challenges in the East (including a revolt in Egypt that led to his sacking of Alexandria), but we know much more about how contemporaries responded to Maximian's successful suppression of the Bagaudae and the German invasion.[6] In a panegyric delivered at a celebration marking the day of Rome's founding, a Gallic rhetorician called Maximian and Diocletian "the founders of the Roman Empire, for you are what is almost the same thing—its restorers" and said that their rule marked "the beginning of its salvation."[7] The speaker then tells how Maximian responded to the disasters of recent years. He suppressed the Bagaudae, he pushed the Germans back and took the war into their territory, and he built a fleet with which he would soon confront Carausius.[8] All of this, the speaker concludes, rivals the deeds of great Roman Republican figures like Cato whose successes had inspired generations of Romans to strive for glory.[9]

This powerful, traditional rhetoric of Roman restoration and renewal following a period of decline appears elsewhere in the late 280s and early 290s. Soldiers in Egypt inscribed a dedication to Diocletian and Maximian that labeled them "the restorers of the entire world."[10] A birthday address given to Maximian in July of 291 spoke about how his successes in Gaul had "restored reason to our uneasy minds,"[11] how his cooperation with Diocletian had liberated the state from a "savage tyranny" whose injustices had provoked the provinces to rebel,[12] and how his efforts to secure the food supply of the empire "restored soundness to the State."[13]

These achievements reflected the regime's strong emphasis on using the army to secure the empire. In order to do this even more effectively, Diocletian and Maximian decided to share their powers with two junior colleagues in 293. This system, which would come to be called the tetrarchy (a term meaning rule by four men), gave Diocletian and Maximian two junior colleagues who could help them confront the regional uprisings of the 280s and early 290s. Instead of a pair of emperors, the empire now had four. Diocletian and Maximian, the two senior members of the imperial college, continued as Augusti. Constantius I, who came into the imperial structure as Maximian's deputy, and Galerius, who served as Diocletian's colleague, served as Caesars. Each had distinctive spheres of activity. Diocletian and Galerius operated in the East while Maximian and Constantius took responsibility for the West.

While imperial power was shared, the new tetrarchic regime took pains to emphasize the distinctiveness of the four members of the imperial college. Gone were the days of the emperor as a sort of first citizen who claimed that he exceeded his fellow citizens only in authority but not in power. The tetrarchs associated themselves directly with divinities and heroes, wore distinctive purple garments, and advertised their achievements with imperial titles that could run on for many lines when inscribed on monuments. These imperial colleagues shared power, but they did so at a distance from everyone else. The Principate of Augustus had now given way to the Dominate of Diocletian and his colleagues.

The tetrarchy gave the empire a new ruling structure, but the tetrarchs nevertheless fell back on the traditional Roman rhetoric of imperial restoration to explain the necessity of this innovation and the glory of their achievements. This reversion becomes particularly clear from a series of panegyrics delivered in Gaul to honor Constantius I. These Gallic authors praise Constantius's successes in controlling the northern Rhine frontier while rooting out Carausius from northern Gaul and Britain. A panegyric for Constantius delivered in 297 or 298 called this achievement as nothing less than a "miracle of valor" that brought about the full revival of the state after years of struggle.[14] Constantius's contributions overwhelm the orator. "So many victories have been won by your courage, so many barbarian nations wiped out everywhere, so many farmers settled in the Roman countryside, so many frontiers pushed forward, and so many provinces restored," that, the speaker proclaims, "I am nearly brought to a halt at a loss for words."[15]

The orator then tells the story of deep imperial decline that Constantius had reversed—and, tellingly he shifts from the emperor's military achievements to other Roman recoveries that Constantius sparked. He turned barbarians who had settled in northern Gaul into productive and peaceful Roman farmers.[16] He brought neglected countryside under cultivation.[17] He superintended the reconstruction of the city of Autun, with so many private homes, public buildings, and temples rebuilt under him that Constantius became the city's second founder.[18] Constantius recovered Britain, ensuring that Britons were "at last Romans" again since he had restored them to "life by the true light of the empire."[19]

Unlike the panegyrist who praised Maximian a few years earlier, this speaker has no doubt that the Roman restoration that Constantius spearheaded was real, substantial, and wide ranging. Roman decline, he claims, had begun under Gallienus when, either "through neglect of affairs or through a certain deterioration of our fortune, the state was dismembered of almost all of its limbs." "But now," he continues, "the whole world has been reclaimed through your courage." [20] The new order was working.

This panegyrist was not alone in seeing a new world emerging by the late 290s. The Roman decline that people like Herodian sensed dawning in the late 230s had most definitively ended with Diocletian's tetrarchy. The tetrarchs knew it. They did not hesitate to claim it. But with the empire now recovered, Romans wondered what came next.

By the middle 290s, the tetrarchs shifted from repairing the damage done to the empire. They began creating structures that would keep it strong in the future. The regime that promised to restore Rome in the 280s now had to keep it strong in the 290s and early 300s. To do so, Diocletian and his colleagues undertook a series of revolutionary reforms that restructured many of the basic features of the Roman Empire.[21] There were, of course, now multiple emperors—and each one of them operated far away from the city of Rome out of bases in provincial cities like Nicomedia (modern Izmit, Turkey), Thessaloniki, and Trier. They transformed the often impossibly large Roman provinces of the past into smaller, more easily governed units with military commands now separated out from civilian provincial administration.[22] These added officials made the defense of provinces more efficient and facilitated a reform in the tax system by instituting a process that regularly reassessed the tax obligations of landholders on the basis of current economic conditions.[23] They reformed the monetary system, changing the denominations of coins and adding mints across the entire empire to ensure the regular availability of the new currency.[24]

The reforms of the 290s ran up against the reality of an empire that could not change as quickly as its leaders hoped. Defeating enemy armies proved easier than convincing Romans to embrace expensive new administrative systems that improved the effectiveness of their government. The higher tax burdens and more efficient collections that the new tax system created prompted the Egyptian revolt that Diocletian fought to suppress.[25] As the 300s dawned, the tetrarchs began to show signs of impatience with their subjects' resistance. In 301, for example, the tetrarchs issued an edict that instituted a set of price controls in order to combat a crisis of confidence in the new Roman currency. The preamble of the edict betrays their frustrations: "We, who by the kind favor of the gods, have crushed the burning havoc caused in the past . . . have protected the peace established for all time with the necessary defenses of justice."[26] Yet, the emperors continued, the avarice of Romans threatened to undo all of this progress. It could be controlled only by establishing a fair maximum price that anyone could charge for a good or service—and punishing those who exceeded it.

The tetrarchs' concern for preserving the gains of the past decade and a half became increasingly malignant in the first years of the fourth century. They began to target those whom they blamed for undermining the Roman restoration they had collectively achieved. In 302, Diocletian sent a legal instruction to the proconsul of Egypt, ordering him to begin a persecution of Manichees, a religious group that had emerged in third-century Persia, because they threatened to infect "the temperate and tranquil Roman people as well as our entire empire with . . . their malevolent poisons." The proconsul was to act quickly "so that this iniquitous disease is completely cleansed from our most happy age."[27] Diocletian ordered the proconsul to arrest Manichean leaders and burn them alive along with their books. If doing so did not eliminate the cult, their followers were to suffer capital punishment. Radical measures were required if the restored empire was not to again fall into decline.

A similar logic seems to have underpinned the emperor's decision in 303 to embark on a persecution of Christians. The status of Christians had changed dramatically since Gallienus's decision to effectively legalize the church following the capture of Valerian in 260. By 303, nearly two generations of peace had helped Christianity to become a visible feature of Roman public life. Large and wealthy churches had sprung up across the empire—including a beautiful church perched on a hill above Diocletian's palace in the city of Nicomedia.[28] That Christian leaders were publicly known and that openly practicing Christians served in the army and imperial court [29] meant very little to Diocletian, the "father of a golden age," as he and his colleagues struggled to defend their own achievements.[30] Forty years of imperial protection of Christians meant nothing to emperors who saw much of that time as a period of Roman decline. Like Manichees, Christians were now regarded as a threat to the tetrarchic Roman restoration.

On February 24, 303, officials in Nicomedia posted an edict that ordered churches destroyed, holy books burned, Christians of high legal and social status stripped of all privileges, and imperial freedmen who were Christians re-enslaved.[31] To Diocletian's almost certain shock, the new persecution immediately prompted fierce resistance. Violence greeted the posting of the order in cities in the provinces of Syria and Commagene while other acts of defiance popped up around the empire.[32] Further edicts that followed across the summer and fall of 303 and into early 304 mandated the arrest of clergy and, in 304, the requirement that all Romans registered on public census rolls perform a sacrifice.[33]

After this first year, the persecution became a more haphazard affair. It flared up or flickered out on the basis of the particular concerns of individual emperors and governors.[34] One still cannot discount the horrific effect that this persecution had on Christian communities. While the persecution did not widely target ordinary Christians, and a number of imperial officials (including the Caesar Constantius I) declined to do much of anything against Christians, church leaders did suffer seriously—especially in the Eastern Mediterranean. The Christian authors Lactantius and Eusebius both describe mass imprisonment, Christians being burned alive, the seizure of Christian property, and the destruction of Christian scriptures.[35] A little more nuanced view of events comes from a few surviving administrative documents showing how these orders were executed by the powerful new bureaucracy the tetrarchs had created. A papyrus from Egypt, for example, records the confiscation of all the goods in a local church, categorized according to what was and was not found.[36]

Christian authors counterattacked powerfully. Far from preserving the tetrarchs' Roman restoration, they claimed, the persecution had instead tipped the empire right back into decline. Indeed, this message was delivered to the emperors themselves when a prominent Nicomedian Christian seized the document containing the very first public announcement of the persecution, ripped it up, and proclaimed that the persecution of Christians represented a victory for the Goths, Decius's murderers, and the Sarmatians.[37] Both Galerius and Diocletian were in the city when this event happened. This man became the persecution's first martyr.

Lactantius and Eusebius offer less dramatic but no less potent statements about the Roman decline that persecution precipitated. Lactantius describes a degeneration of the empire and gruesome personal fates for the persecuting emperors. "Good fortune soon deserted" Diocletian as Galerius orchestrated his retirement as well as that of Maximian. Galerius and Constantius became the new Augusti while two incompetent and venal friends of Galerius were elevated to the ranks of Caesar.[38] The cruelty with which Galerius had attacked Christians now turned against all Romans. The census of 306, Lactantius says, was so harsh that large numbers of people and animals starved to death—and Galerius then forced the living to pay taxes for the dead.[39]

Lactantius also explains how the persecuting emperors suffered for the violence they inflicted. Diocletian died in retirement, passing in and out of lucidity.[40] Maximian was executed following an attempted coup.[41] Galerius, the instigator of the persecution, died of a horrible disease that saw his stinking flesh putrefy when he still lived.[42] Not only did the tetrarchic imperial renewal fail because of persecution, but Christians could also gleefully recount how the tetrarchs themselves were punished horribly.[43]

While Lactantius blamed Christian persecutions for the destruction of the tetrarchic imperial restoration, Eusebius, the future bishop of Caesarea, saw the Great Persecution fitting into an even more sweeping historical narrative. Eusebius treated the tetrarchic persecution in three historical works, all of which overlapped to some degree. One of these, the *Martyrs of Palestine*, recounts the sufferings of the persecution's Palestinian victims.[44] The other two texts, Eusebius's *Chronological Canons* (now often called the *Chronicle*) and his *Ecclesiastical History*, fit the persecution into a history of

Christian events that traced the church's integration into Roman society and marked persecutions as breaches in the basic continuity of Roman and Christian history.[45] Rome thrived when Christians and the empire worked together and it suffered when venal emperors turned against Christian Romans. Like Lactantius, Eusebius emphasized that Christian persecutions made the empire weaker and endangered the Roman recovery that the tetrarchs claimed to be protecting.

Then the conversation changed dramatically.

In 312, the emperor Constantine I, the son of the tetrarch Constantius I, converted to Christianity. Constantine began his career as a pagan usurper who seized power by convincing his father's army to acclaim him as Augustus after Constantius's death in 306.[46] He spent much of the next six years strategically positioning himself to take advantage of the rivalries that were beginning to tear the tetrarchy apart.

The key turning point for Constantine came when he invaded Italy to destroy the regime of his imperial rival Maxentius.[47] The campaign's final victory defied easy explanation. Maxentius, an experienced commander who had held Italy against two other tetrarchic attacks in earlier years, had cut the bridges to Rome and filled the city with supplies so that its residents could endure a siege.[48] Despite these careful preparations, Maxentius made the strange decision to march his troops out of Rome and meet Constantine's army on a field north of the city. They were put to flight and retreated to the Tiber; in the chaos, Maxentius fell into the river and drowned.[49] Maxentius's decision to fight what is now called the Battle of the Milvian Bridge seemed so out of character that even Lactantius struggled to find an explanation.

A range of contemporary sources reflect on the seemingly miraculous victory that Constantine won. In a panegyric delivered in Trier shortly after Constantine's successful campaign, the orator asked the emperor "what God, what majesty so immediate, encouraged you when almost all of your comrades and commanders were . . . openly fearful" of undertaking the campaign?[50] The speaker then guessed that "you must share some secret with that Divine Mind . . . that deigns to reveal itself to you alone."[51] The orator might have known the identity of the God to whom Constantine attributed this victory, but, if he did, he does not say so.

Lactantius and Eusebius were less shy. Lactantius describes the size of Maxentius's forces, their superiority to Constantine's army, and their initial success before "Constantine received a warning in a dream to make the heavenly sign of God on his shields and then join battle." Constantine did so, "the Hand of God hung over the battle line," and Maxentius's army was routed.[52] Lactantius's Christian God assumed an active role in assisting an obedient Christian emperor take and exercise power.

Eusebius did not live under Constantine's direct authority in the 310s and thus he knew relatively little about the emperor when he wrote the *Ecclesiastical History*. Eusebius still felt confident enough to assert that the Christian God had taken an active role in ensuring Constantine's victory. He spoke about how Constantine, "calling upon the heavenly God and . . . Jesus Christ, as his ally, marched with his army" against Maxentius and then "God himself . . . dragged the tyrant out far from the gates" of the city of Rome so that the population would be spared the horror of a sack. This victory, Eusebius continued, was like that won by Moses at the crossing of the Red Sea, a victory that freed the Israelites from captivity. Praises echoing those sung to Moses rang out as Constantine triumphantly marched into Rome.[53]

Eusebius continued to develop the idea of Constantine as a second Moses for more than a quarter century. As he did, he became more and more explicit about the sovereignty God exercised over the course of Roman history.[54] The paths of the empire and the church remained intertwined, but God had now put a Christian emperor in place to ensure that Rome functioned as God intended.

This line of argument pointed to a radically different way of thinking about what an emperor ought to do. The glorious Roman past suddenly was irrelevant. The empire was not supposed to be, like the empire of the Antonines, one that maintained the traditional order of Rome. Nor was it to be like the one of Augustus or Diocletian that brought about Roman renewal after a period of decline. The empire of Constantine was supposed to be something new—radically new. It would be a Christian Empire and, as a second Moses, Constantine would create a new social order by leading Christians from persecution into power. This new order required a new language for describing imperial achievements.

Constantine, however, did not use the language of revolution to describe the Christian empire he sought to inaugurate. Drawing upon a conception he perhaps borrowed from Lactantius's theological work the *Divine Institutes*, Constantine proposed a different sort of renewal.[55] Instead of harkening back to Roman predecessors, Constantine grounded his Christian empire on a more distant and glorious biblical past. The Constantinian empire would return to Romans the worship of the one true God that they and their ancestors had forgotten.

Constantine laid out this vision in a few surviving texts. In an oration now called "To the Assembly of the Saints," Constantine argued that it was his mission to lead the people of the world back to "the light of truth" by overturning all of the "schemes" that "wicked injustice" had crafted to draw them away.[56] Horrible things had crept into local religious practices as different cities and peoples wandered from true religion. Egyptians and Assyrians began to perform sacrifices, other peoples developed mythologies in which gods committed terrible acts, and some even began to worship dead human beings as gods.[57] The worst thing that these divergent traditions came to do, however, was to persecute the devotees of the true God. Egypt and Babylon both persecuted the Jews before the coming of Christ and, Constantine claims, now their capitals have been destroyed because of their behavior. Moses's leadership led to the destruction of the army of Egypt and Daniel's resistance before Nebuchadnezzar prompted God's destruction of the Babylonians.[58]

Constantine was seldom modest and, as his oration continued, he placed himself in the tradition of these heroic champions of true religion. The Roman emperors who had persecuted Christianity over the preceding three quarters of a century represented another link in this chain of violence against God. They were insane and their claims that they acted against Christianity "on account of the laws of preceding generations" prove it.

"These traditions" and the actions of the persecution, he writes, "derive from the same madness."[59] Like their Egyptian and Babylonian predecessors, Decius and Valerian suffered horrible reverses as punishment for their persecution. Echoing Lactantius, Constantine describes how Diocletian went insane after he attacked Christians.[60] Constantine, by contrast, has prospered because of God. His "brave deeds, victories in war, and triumphs over conquered foes" show the truth of his claim.[61] Through God, Constantine defeated Maxentius on his way to taking sole control of the empire. He ended the persecutions that these emperors had begun against the church, astonishing spectators who saw the persecutors fail to break the church and then fall to its champion.

Constantine did not just see his Roman, Christian religious renewal as an effort to punish the persecutors and undo the effects of the persecution. It was also his mission to change religious behavior so that Romans could enjoy the benefit of the Christian God's divine favor. Most of this encouragement was rhetorical. So, in a letter written to provincials in the East soon after the defeat of his last remaining imperial rival, Licinius, in 324, Constantine emphasizes that "there is nothing new or revolutionary" in Christianity, since it brings the human race back from "errors" into which it has fallen over time.[62] This was not a Roman renewal after a period of Roman decline. Constantine instead promised that Rome will lead a human renewal that brings all men the benefits that accrue to those devoted to the true religion of the original, true God.

Constantine's Christian empire emerged gradually through a series of calibrated legislative and administrative measures.[63] Some of these explicitly favored Christianity. Constantine exempted Christian clergy from mandatory public service in their home cities,[64] he supplied Christian bishops with large amounts of money and goods that they could use to support their congregations,[65] he paid for the construction of new churches, and he gave bishops a form of judicial power that they could use to free slaves and resolve legal disputes within their communities.[66]

Constantine also made clear that he disapproved of the traditional religious institutions and practices that pulled his subjects away from God. Constantine emphasized that, unlike the persecutors of old, he would not use force or compel people to embrace Christianity.[67] The emperor proved true to his word. He made his opinions clear, but he did not compel anyone to agree with them.

Some of the measures he took show how carefully Constantine walked this line. Soon after he took control of the Eastern half of the empire in 324 Constantine issued a law "intended to restrain idolatrous abominations" so that "no one should erect images, or practice divination and other false and foolish arts, or offer sacrifice in any way."[68] His hope, we are told, was that "now the madness of polytheism was wholly removed, pretty nearly all mankind would henceforth attach themselves to the service of God."[69] No compulsion was used. Constantine's anti-pagan laws had no enforcement mechanisms and they specified no penalties for people who violated them. They were legally binding but toothless suggestions about how the emperor wanted his subjects to behave.[70]

Other laws specifying how churches were to be built, ordering the destruction of four pagan temples, and mandating the seizure of some property belonging to temples had a bit more bite—but only a bit.[71] The only truly vicious acts of religiously motivated violence he initiated involved the torture of Didyman priests who pushed for the Great Persecution to begin and the former governor Theotecnus, an official who had overzealously persecuted.[72] Other than these incidents, there is no good evidence that Constantine ever went back on his pledge to avoid violence aimed at punishing Roman pagans or prompting their conversion.

Constantine based his revolution on suggestion and persuasion rather than force, but this approach did not make the emperor any less of a revolutionary. For the first time in Roman history, Roman tradition did not underpin a new regime. In modern parlance, Constantine did not particularly care about making Rome great again. He had a bigger aim. He believed that, with the backing of the Christian God, he and Rome could return the nations of the world to the ancestral piety all humans once shared. Reaching this goal would make Rome greater than it had ever been before. The Christian revolution had begun.

7

ROMAN RENEWAL VERSUS CHRISTIAN PROGRESS

CONSTANTINE WAS AN extremely skillful revolutionary. In the eyes of Christians, his embrace of the Christian God and his efforts to promote its worship resonated clearly. Not more than two or three years after the emperor's death, Eusebius set to work on a monumentally influential biography of Constantine that crafted a template of the ideal Christian emperor around his actions. To Eusebius, Constantine was a new Moses selected by God to get Romans to embrace Christianity.[1] Romans, as the followers of the new Moses, needed to follow God's command that they "demolish completely all the places where the nations whom you are about to dispossess served their gods."[2] Eusebius imagined a Christian empire filled with churches and believing congregations that would naturally emerge when imperial support for the church combined with active and widespread Roman de-paganization. He also claimed that Constantine's religious policies suggested his sympathy with that goal.

Constantine carefully differentiated the world he worked to create from the one that he actually ran. He expressed clear support for the sort of goals Eusebius attributes to him, but Constantine also continued to perform the traditional religious duties of a Roman emperor.[3] Constantine remained pontifex maximus until his death,[4] he issued laws reiterating well-established religious practices,[5] and, in the 330s, the emperor agreed to the request of the city of Hispellum to construct a temple honoring him and his family.[6] This flexibility enabled many of his subjects to pretend that Constantine remained as devoted to the empire's traditional religions as his predecessors. These pagan Romans insisted on treating Constantine as they would any previous emperor.[7]

Constantine's sons proved less capable of maintaining the balance between Roman tradition and Christian revolution. Some of this was unavoidable. Constantine had done a great service to Christians by ending the persecutions and speaking openly about his vision for a Christian empire. He reigned for more than thirty years, the longest tenure of any Roman emperor since Augustus, and a new generation of Christians who had not experienced persecution led the church by the time of Constantine's death. A rhetorical revolution meant little to them. They wanted a real, tangible Christian empire—and they were impatient.

The political drama that unfolded in the decade and a half following Constantine's death did little to help matters. Constantine had directed that the empire should revert back to a tetrarchy upon his death, but Constantine's body was barely cold when this arrangement collapsed. A series of family murders and civil wars destroyed most of Constantine's male relatives and left his two sons Constantius II and Constans sharing power from the early 340s through January 350.[8] As the 340s progressed, however, a growing conflict over Christian doctrine caused their relationship to deteriorate. In the late 310s, an Alexandrian presbyter named Arius began teaching that God and Christ had different natures.[9] This teaching was condemned at a church council summoned to the city of Nicaea by Constantine in 325, but adaptations of Arius's theological ideas continued to exert a great deal of influence over many people in the Roman East—including Constantius II. Constantius acted against Nicene bishops and even forced Athanasius, the Nicene bishop of Alexandria, into exile in Gaul. Athanasius returned east only when Constans threatened civil war unless Constantius reinstalled the bishop.[10]

Imperial dynamics changed again when, in January 350, the usurper Magnentius overthrew Constans and thus provoked a civil war with Constantius that did not conclude until 353. The two years following the defeat of Magnentius were only slightly more settled. Constantius sent his cousin Gallus to the East to run affairs there while he fought Magnentius, but Gallus proved to be such an arrogant and unpopular administrator that Constantius recalled and executed him in 354.[11] Then, in November 355, Constantius named Julian, his last living male cousin, as Caesar and sent him to the Rhine frontier to keep an eye on both the Alamanni and the Roman commanders tasked with fighting them.

All of this political instability did little to dissuade Constantius II from pushing Rome in revolutionary new directions. Unlike his father, Constantius unapologetically advertised this fact. The change in tone became apparent early in the 340s when Constantius and Constans issued the first Roman law that mentioned a penalty for traditional Roman religious practices. In 341, the two emperors commanded that "the madness of sacrifices shall be abolished" and, if any man "should dare to perform sacrifices, he shall suffer the infliction of a suitable punishment."[12] Although the emperors explained that this law only reinforced a legal position taken by their father, they went further than Constantine ever had in mandating a penalty—though what constituted a "suitable punishment" was so unclear that no governor is known to have punished a person who sacrificed.

By the time that the political challenges of the early 350s were sorted out, Constantius felt empowered to remake the empire as he wished. This empowerment meant that he could give his anti-pagan policies more teeth. In February 356, the emperor took the legislative step of prescribing the death penalty for sacrifices.[13] More anti-pagan legislation followed that December when the emperor ordered that "all temples should be immediately closed in all cities and access to them forbidden" while reiterating the death penalty for sacrifice.[14] Disregard for these laws seems to have been so widespread that there is no record of anyone being charged under them. At the same time, it was lost on no one that this law offered a mirror image of the death penalty the tetrarchs had inflicted fifty years earlier on Christians who refused to sacrifice.[15]

Other anti-pagan efforts made more of an impact. Constantius transferred to the Christian church some temples belonging to the emperor, including the Caesareum, a large seaside temple in Alexandria that he gave to the city's bishop.[16] He sanctioned a small number of temple destructions[17] and he permitted people to take materials and statuary from temples for use in the construction or decoration of their homes.[18] Constantine had laid out the principles of a Roman, Christian revolution, but Constantius II took many of the first steps necessary to create the empire that his father imagined.

Some Christians felt that he did not move fast enough. In the mid-340s, the Christian convert Firmicus Maternus repeatedly urged Constantius and his brother Constans to ban sacrifice and overthrow pagan temples.[19] Maternus describes temples as tombs and appeals to the emperors to destroy pagan practices through "the severest laws so that the deadly error of this delusion no longer stains the Roman world."[20] Later he informs the emperors that "the benevolent Godhead of Christ has reserved the extermination of idolatry and the overthrow of the pagan temples for your hands."[21] Maternus concludes that "after the destruction of the temples, you will be advanced greatly by the power of God" so that "you might rule the entire world successfully" and the empire would be stronger than ever before.[22]

This sense of a dawning new Roman era extended beyond Constantius's religious policies. Constantius also helped formalize Constantinople's status as the empire's second capital. The city was founded by the emperor Constantine and dedicated in 330, but there was nothing particularly revolutionary about an emperor expanding and redeveloping a city. Second- and third-century emperors from Hadrian to Philip the Arab had adopted favorite cities, built impressive new infrastructure, and renamed existing cities after themselves.[23] The Constantinople that Constantine left was a superficially beautiful place with no permanence.[24] Like a modern Olympic venue, the buildings were built quickly, and many had to be torn down soon after they were opened because they were unsafe.[25] Constantine even supposedly resorted to paying people to move to the city he named after himself.[26] Constantine's Constantinople was "the object of desire for an impatient lover," a vanity project unlikely to endure for long beyond its patron. It was Constantius II who made it into a capital that would "surpass even the most ancient cities in her permanence."[27]

In 357, the philosopher Themistius came before the senate in Rome and stunned the audience by speaking at length about Constantinople's new prominence. He described how Constantius had decided to make Constantinople fully and completely into a New Rome. The emperor had expanded its infrastructure, granted it privileges that accorded with its status as an imperial capital, and elevated the Constantinopolitan senate so that it enjoyed parity with that of Rome.[28] The result, Themistius concluded, was that Constantius had become a second Romulus because, through him, Constantinople has genuinely become a New Rome.

Themistius said something even more inflammatory that day. He told the Roman senators that the empire no longer needed Rome—it could and did defend its interests solely with the resources Constantinople provided. He described how, when "barbarian revolt broke out and the Roman Empire hung in the balance," it was Constantinople "that preserved the embers" of the Roman line.[29] It was because of Constantinople's patron Constantius "that Rome's proud and mighty name has not been utterly abused nor erased." It was from Constantinople that "he set out and inflicted a deserved punishment on" Magnentius, "the man who had raged drunkenly against this people, who had hacked at the Senate, and had filled the Tiber . . . with slaughter and pollution."[30] Old Rome lay prostrate. New Rome saved the empire.

Words like these had never before been spoken to the Roman senate. This was the proclamation of a new Roman Empire, one in which both East and West now had their own Romes. Old Rome basked in the traditions that had brought it an empire. Names like Cato, Cicero, and Trajan bridged the centuries between that deep, glorious Roman past and the Roman present that emulated it. A thousand miles to the East sat a gleaming new city with a new senate, new churches, and a Christian imperial patron that offered a different, modern Rome. Constantinople looked forward in a way that Old Rome could not. It was a dynamic, shiny city rapidly rising. If Rome was Boston, Constantinople was Los Angeles—with all of the energy, optimism, and glitz that implies.

It is interesting to imagine where Constantius's revolution would have taken the empire had the emperor not died suddenly at the age of forty-four on November 3, 361.[31] He was on the verge of winning a civil war against his cousin Julian, his new wife was pregnant,[32] and he still seemed to have many years left to live. Constantius's death abruptly ended many of his most cherished projects. On his deathbed, he had ordered his army to recognize Julian as his successor (or, at least, his advisors prudently reported that he had so ordered). Since Julian had an army nearby and there was no other logical choice, his succession was natural.

This change in emperor did not mean that there would be much political or religious continuity between the regimes of Constantius and Julian. The reason was partly personal. Julian loathed his cousin. He blamed Constantius for the murder of Julian's brother Gallus in 354 and for the murder of his father in the great purging of Constantine's relatives in 337. Julian was an austere man who had little patience for the court ceremonial that Constantius embraced. Julian had also secretly converted from Christianity to paganism while a student in Athens in the early 350s. He had no interest at all in helping to build a Christian empire. He much preferred to dismantle the work on that project his uncle and cousin had begun.

Something even stronger motivated Julian. Like Constantine, Julian had prayed before deciding to march on his imperial rival and, also like his uncle, he "begged the god to give [him] a sign." Zeus, not Christ, answered him. The god told Julian "not to oppose the will of the army."[33] Julian's victories in Italy and the Balkans during the civil war against Constantius and Constantius's shocking death all proved to the new emperor that he enjoyed a particular sort of favor from the king of the old gods.[34]

Julian then determined to rule the empire in a fashion that both honored the old gods who had protected him and improved the moral, material, and spiritual conditions of his subjects. The new emperor firmly believed that these goals were linked. He was trained as a Platonic philosopher in a curriculum that emphasized the philosopher's spiritual progress toward communion with god and the ruler's obligations to his subjects.[35] Julian was convinced that many of the religious and administrative policies his uncle and cousins had put in place worked against that goal. He would pull Rome back from the revolution Constantius II had begun.

The reforms Julian initiated are breathtaking in their scope and vision. Famously unkempt, Julian had no interest in the "thousand cooks, as many barbers, and even more butlers" that his cousin employed.[36] The barbers were not replaced, but a host of mid-level imperial secretaries and other advisors were—by pagan philosophers and other intellectuals whom Julian trusted.[37] Julian had the strongest possible aversion to Constantius's executions of political opponents and convened a tribunal to investigate high officials who might have abused power in the later years of Constantius's reign.[38]

Julian is best remembered for the work he did to recalibrate imperial religious policies. As soon as he assumed power, the pagan historian Ammianus Marcellinus wrote that Julian "directed in plain, unvarnished terms, that the temples should be opened, sacrifices brought to their altars, and the worship of the old gods restored."[39] He soon ordered the return of the temples given to Christian bishops in the reign of Constantius, a seemingly straightforward policy that neglected to take into account how one could undo the Christian renovations of large buildings like the Alexandrian Caesareum, reconstruct the sacred objects that had been destroyed, or recover the materials originating from temples that had been sold or reused.[40]

Julian also hoped to revitalize traditional religion in ways that improved the spiritual condition of his subjects. He fashioned a pagan priesthood modeled on imperial provincial administration in which worthy figures were placed in charge of all of the temples in a defined region. In keeping with the emperor's philosophical ideals, these priests would "take care to exhort men not to transgress the laws of the gods."[41]

Julian broke with Roman convention nearly as much as Constantius had, but, unlike his cousin, Julian did not adopt the language of revolution or progress. His reforms instead leaned very heavily on a rhetoric of Roman decline and renewal. In the letters he sent to cities in Italy and Greece at the time of his initial revolt, Julian spoke about arriving in Gaul and finding it overrun with Franks and Alamanni who had "settled themselves with impunity" near forty-five towns that they had sacked and around other cities "deserted by their inhabitants." They controlled "on our side of the Rhine the whole country as it extends from its sources to the Ocean" and raided so regularly that the Romans "could not even pasture their cattle there."[42] Over the next two years, Julian continued, he fought until "all of the barbarians had been driven out of Gaul" and then built a fleet of 600 ships, crossed the Rhine, and took the fight to the barbarians. He concluded that "I have now, with the help of the gods, recovered all of the towns" that were lost and returned to Roman territory "twenty thousand persons who were held on the far side of the Rhine."[43]

Contemporary observers praised Julian's Gallic restoration just as effusively as their ancestors had celebrated the successes of his grandfather Constantius I nearly six decades earlier. The orator Mamertinus told Julian how "the Gauls were recovered by your valor" and "all barbary was subdued."[44] Between barbarian raiders and corrupt governors, "no one was safe from injustice or untouched by abuse" unless he paid for this security.[45] Julian confronted all of these problems simultaneously. "In one engagement, Germany in its entirety was destroyed, in one battle the war ended." The correction of "morals and the reform of the law courts" proved more difficult, but Julian confronted these energetically and ably.[46]

Julian's efforts extended beyond Gaul. Dalmatia found "the weight of its misery lightened" as Julian "re-established [the Dalmatians] on the road to a life of wealth and luxury."[47] In Greece, the city of Nicopolis had "collapsed into dismal ruins" with houses crumbling, aqueducts cut, and the roofs of public buildings caving in while Eleusis was "nothing more than a pile of rubble."[48] Julian restored them all. A "joyfulness permeated the whole region" as everywhere saw a "magnificence displayed" in "newly risen public buildings, the fields prolific with abundant crops appropriate to the terrain, the vintage surpassing the prayers of the peasants, the steep hills, the deep valleys and the broad plains resounding to the cries of domestic animals."[49]

Julian's panegyrist added a new note to these standard verses of Roman renewal. Julian had not just restored the material and military prosperity of the empire; he had also restored its virtues. Julian, Mamertinus said, "restored within the State the virtues condemned to exile and rejection." He "rekindled the extinguished study of literature"; he "freed philosophy from condemnation" and "clothed it in purple and placed it . . . on the imperial throne."[50] Perhaps even more importantly, "the ancient freedom of former ages has been given back to the Republic" following a period in which the "haughtiness of those who wore the purple" corrupted the state by ignoring the worthy and rewarding only their friends.[51]

Julian himself wrote of this moral decline in an oration he addressed to the Cynic philosopher Heraclius in the spring of 362.[52] Outraged by a speech in which Heraclius had compared himself to Zeus and Julian to Pan, Julian responded with a strong attack on the Cynic's abandonment of the gods, laws, and social norms. Julian narrated a myth that offered a barely disguised attack on Constantine and his sons. Constantine was a rich man who had many wives and many children and divided his property equally among them. He "took no thought for how to make them virtuous" so that, after his death, a "general slaughter ensued." "Everything was thrown into confusion" as the sons "demolished the ancestral temples."[53] Horrified that "the laws of mankind" had been "profaned along with those of the gods," Zeus spoke to his son Helios, pointed out Julian, and told him that it would be Julian's task to "cleanse the house of your forefathers" and restore the virtue and traditional piety of the Roman world.[54]

Although Julian concluded this myth with the qualification "I do not know whether this account is a myth or truth," he certainly believed that Zeus had chosen him to repair the empire his uncle and cousins had nearly ruined. In 361, he wrote to the philosopher Maximus that he sacrificed openly and often because he communed regularly with Zeus, Helios, and Athena.[55] In his *Against the Galileans*, Julian expressed frustration that some Romans still turned their backs on tools offered by the gods to protect the Roman state[56] and instead preferred to "overturn temples and altars" and slaughter "those of us who remained true to the teachings of their fathers."[57]

Five centuries of Roman history had shown that the claim that one is restoring Rome's idealized past does not mean that past ever existed. As Julian's short reign progressed, it became clear to both his supporters and his opponents that the traditions Julian said Zeus, Helios, and Athena wanted him to restore never existed in the form he imagined. Traditional Roman paganism had no priesthood like the one Julian organized. It had no expectation of regular animal sacrifices. It took a flexible view of when and where one participated in religious life. The convert Julian had little personal experience with these traditions. The gods had charged him with restoring the virtue, power, and proper religious behavior in the empire. He knew what they asked for—and he had little patience for pagans or Christians who did not share his view of the pagan, philosophical Roman future.

By early 363, Julian seems to have understood that his abrupt return to these imagined Roman traditions made many of his subjects uncomfortable. In a scathing self-parody that he wrote and published in Antioch that year, Julian acknowledged that Antiochenes felt "the affairs for the whole world have been turned upside by me"[58] Other critics were even more forceful. Writing soon after Julian's death, the Christian author and bishop

Gregory Nazianzen framed Julian as "a tyrant who rebelled and has taken a fall worthy of his impiety."[59] Even the friendly historian Ammianus Marcellinus, who generally approved of much of Julian's reform program, found some of Julian's actions severe.[60] Julian might have couched his new world in the language of Roman tradition and renewal, but it was no less revolutionary than the one spearheaded by his forward-looking cousin.

Julian's reign lasted far less time than that of Constantius II, but it too ended unexpectedly. Julian's fraught months in Antioch during the winter of 362–363 had been spent in preparing for a Persian campaign that he hoped would definitively prove both the certainty of his divine calling and his superiority over Constantine and Constantius II, the two Christian emperors who had been unable to defeat the Persians decisively.[61] Combining the same speed and tactical riskiness that had worked in Gaul and Germany, Julian planned for two armies to proceed into Persian territory. They would meet outside of the capital of Ctesiphon, take the city, and disable the empire. But Julian's northern army was delayed; the Persians mobilized a large counterattack and then killed the emperor in a skirmish as his forces retreated.[62] Perhaps trusting too much in the divine protection of Zeus and Helios, Julian had fought without his breast plate. His army hastily chose a successor, a military officer named Jovian. Jovian then negotiated a peace treaty with the Persians that traded Roman territory in Mesopotamia for the army's safe passage home.[63]

This defeat meant that the Roman Empire would never again be as big as the one Julian ruled. After one emperor pushed a new form of Roman progress and another pursued a rather dubious Roman renewal, the steady territorial decline of Rome had begun. Questions of progress, decline, and renewal soon took on a new urgency in an empire that was now becoming progressively smaller and weaker.

8

WHEN RENEWAL FAILS TO ARRIVE

THE ROMAN TERRITORIAL contraction that began in 363 continued, in fits and starts, for more than a century, but the high costs of Julian's failed Persian campaign became clear immediately. Jovian's peace treaty pushed the legal limits of the Roman Empire back from the flatlands of Northern Mesopotamia for the first time since the 290s.[1] Not only had the frontier moved more than a hundred miles farther from the Persian capital of Ctesiphon, but Persia could advance its forces into Syria much more easily—a development that would have profound consequences for Roman Syria in the centuries to come.

Perhaps because the Persian king wanted to garrison this territory with Persian settlers, the Roman residents of the strategically located city Nisibis were told to evacuate and move west to land that remained in Roman territory.[2] The Syriac church father Ephrem lived in Nisibis until 363 and left as one of these Roman refugees. He wrote occasionally about the traumatic loss of his home during the final ten years of his life that he spent in the Roman city of Edessa. What galled him most was that Roman Nisibis had endured three massive Persian sieges between the late 330s and 350s. Ephrem described epic confrontations against Persian war elephants, fights pushing Persian forces back from breaches in the city wall, and even a naval battle fought on plains around the city that the Persian king had flooded. Roman Nisibis survived all of this, Ephrem wrote, because it had remained faithfully Christian.[3] Nisibis wavered under Julian and its people "did not hold fast to the banner of He who redeems all." Instead, "they were turning to paganism."[4] In the summer before the Persian takeover, "an idol was set up in the city" and "empty sacrifices . . . expelled the [Christian] altar" that had long preserved the city.[5] With this protection lost, the Persians took the city peacefully.

Ephrem described the final days of Roman Nisibis in a hymn written while he was in exile. He wrote about "a fortuitous wonder" that he witnessed as he prepared to leave his home. "There met me near the city the corpse of [Julian], that accursed one, as it passed by the wall" while, at the same time, "the banner that was sent from the East . . . was fastened on the tower so that a flag might point out to the spectators that the city was the slave" of the Persian king.[6] Ephrem was "amazed as to how it was that the body and the standard were there at the same moment," but he knew "it was a wonderful preparation of justice" that "while the corpse of the fallen one was passing" the Persian flag would be raised and would proclaim "that the injustice" of Julian "had delivered the city" to them. As the chanter sang these words, the congregation was instructed to respond, "Praise be to Him who clothed his corpse in such shame!"[7]

This was the flip side of the Christian empire Constantine and his sons had worked to build. Their new way of thinking about the link between Rome and the Christian God powerfully reinforced a Christian's identification with the empire and its leadership when the church and the empire both thrived together. It also opened up a choice for Christians when imperial leadership and church priorities diverged. Ephrem was a loyal Roman. This is why he followed the Roman frontier's retreat from Nisibis. But he also felt that a non-Christian emperor like Julian deserved a divine rebuke and the pagans who followed him deserved punishment. If God elected for that punishment to consist of the loss of Ephrem's home city, Ephrem accepted the justice of His sentence.

Other Romans took a different view. None except for Jovian's most unprincipled propagandists tried to frame his peace treaty as a victory.[8] Even they did not have to pretend for long. Jovian never made it all the way back to Constantinople before he died of asphyxiation after staying in a freshly painted room that the overzealous townspeople of Dadastana had made airtight.[9] His reign had lasted barely seven months. The Persian peace treaty would remain his most important legacy.

The twin nightmares of Julian's defeat and Jovian's treaty opened up the door for Jovian's successor Valentinian I to define himself as an emperor devoted to the restoration of traditional Roman strengths and virtues. Valentinian largely delivered on this promise. His success probably surprised many people. Valentinian's reign began unexpectedly following a chaotic conference of Jovian's officers outside of Dadastana. The new emperor was chosen without any evident enthusiasm, a capable candidate who also had the advantage of being nearby.[10] After learning of his selection as emperor in the winter of 364, Valentinian quickly appointed his brother Valens as his co-emperor.[11] The two emperors spent the spring and summer of 364 deciding how they would share the empire's military and administrative responsibilities. Valentinian took control of the West and Valens the East, with the dividing line passing just to the west of Thessaloniki.

The brothers staked their claim to imperial authority on a set of individual qualities that, collectively, they hoped would spearhead a Roman recovery. Valentinian presented himself as a strong, industrious, and militarily effective monarch.[12] Valens, for his part, advertised the management skills that he developed by running the family estate.[13] The two new emperors also made it clear that they would respond forcefully to external threats to the empire while addressing the fiscal hangover of Julian's Persian campaign and administrative reforms.[14]

The theme of Roman restoration featured prominently on the brothers' coinage, sharing billing with their boasts to safeguard Roman security and win glory. It is also clear, however, what the emperors believed needed to be restored. Historians at the time noted the financial crisis,[15] but they paid particular attention to the loss of territory to the Persians in the East and the security of the Rhine frontier in the West. In the East, Valens became convinced of the necessity of a new war with Persia that would restore lost Roman prestige. Two officials in Valens's court then wrote brief, propaganda-laden historical works making the case for why a new war with Persia was justified.

In one of these, a court official named Festus penned a narrative of Roman imperial history in which Roman territorial losses are inevitably followed by reconquests of the captured territory. So Trajan's conquests in the East repaired Roman losses of influence over Armenia, Severus's conquests made up for Hadrian's abandonment of Mesopotamia, and the tetrarchic campaigns made good on the Eastern losses in the 250s and 260s.[16] The work then concludes with Jovian's peace treaty and an appeal that God grant Valens a magnificent victory that will "impose the palm of peace upon Babylon."[17]

Eutropius's *Breviarium*, a short history of Rome stretching from the Republic to 364, covered more ground than Festus's narrative but it had a similar objective. Eutropius also marked Roman success according to whether or not an emperor lost territory, but he added to this analysis a historical justification for the renunciation of treaties whose terms were unjust. Unsurprisingly, Jovian's surrender of imperial territory marked him as a failed emperor and the unfair terms of the treaty he signed corresponded to the sorts of treaties that Republican Rome renounced.[18]

Both historians argued that Valens could justifiably abrogate the terms of Jovian's peace treaty and restart the war with Persia if doing so would restore Roman prestige and territory. With this rhetorical groundwork established, Valens broke Jovian's peace treaty and started preparing for a new war with Persia. Even though little came of his efforts, Valens still rewarded both Festus and Eutropius with important governorships.[19]

Valentinian was more successful than his brother on both the administrative and military front. He fought hard against a culture of corruption that often involved the sale of offices and sometimes even outright extortion. He beat back an invasion of the Alamanni, campaigned effectively along the Rhine frontier, and reinforced his military gains with a series of fortifications.[20]

Latin authors who traveled to the region while Valentinan campaigned described the aftermath of his successes in almost idyllic terms. Ausonius, a Gallic rhetorician who tutored Valentinian's two sons, wrote about the beautiful mansions lining the Moselle River valley, a great victory won by the emperor, and "fortresses raised for defense in times of peril now not fortresses but granaries for the unmenaced Belgic people" amid a crowd of "prosperous settlers."[21]

The Roman senator Symmachus praised the emperor for his defeat of the Alamanni, his clemency in not massacring them as they retreated, and his power in getting them to rebuild the destruction they had caused.[22] Symmachus even floated the idea that Valentinian would again restore Roman control over areas across the Rhine "where ancient vestiges of a Roman colony" exist amid faded inscriptions.[23] Roman expansion into

Germany would soon seem utterly absurd. Although no one could imagine it at the time, Valentinian would be the last Roman emperor to successfully maintain the northern frontier.

Valens and Valentinian both saw fit to renew Rome by attacking non-Romans, but neither brother showed a particular interest in targeting Romans so that they might restore the Christian religious order that Julian had overturned. Valentinian intervened tentatively in episcopal succession disputes in the West and Valens acted more aggressively against church leaders in the East, but neither emperor proved particularly interested in ending Julian's restoration of sacrifices and his reopening of temples.[24] They were instead responsible for the continued rehabilitation and reconstruction of pagan temples in areas as diverse as North Africa and Greece.[25] This focus plainly would not do for Christians who expected that Julian's death meant a resumption of Roman progress toward the Christian empire imagined by Constantine and his successors. One bishop even complained that, under the two brothers, "the rites of Jews, of Dionysius, and of Demeter were now no longer performed in a corner, as they would be in a pious reign, but by revelers running wild in the forum."[26]

As long as Valentinian I lived, Romans could believe that their empire continued to be the international power it had been for 500 years. But Valentinian died unexpectedly in November of 375, felled by a stroke while in the middle of a contentious negotiation with barbarians.[27] His sixteen-year old son Gratian had been serving as his co-emperor and designated successor since 367, but Gratian was far away from his father's army when Valentinian died.[28] Fearing a possible rebellion, the army commanders summoned Valentinian's other son, the four-year old Valentinian II, and proclaimed him Augustus.[29]

Gratian and his advisors managed to avoid a civil war, but the empire could ill afford these sorts of problems. In 376, less than a year after Valentinian's death, a group of Goths petitioned Valens for permission to migrate into Roman territory, fleeing, later sources would claim, attacks by the Huns.[30] Valens granted them permission, but the numbers of Goths quickly overwhelmed the Roman administration's capacity to settle and feed them. Then another group of Goths crossed the Danube frontier, this time without Roman permission. The Romans proved unprepared and, amid food shortages and other hardships, the Goths rebelled in the summer of 377.[31]

Rome had dealt with similar situations before. In the aftermath of the Antonine Plague, for example, Marcus Aurelius had settled German refugees in Italy and had put down a rebellion by them in Ravenna. But Valens was more Decius than Marcus Aurelius. Roman forces managed the war with Goths reasonably well across 377 and 378, pinning them down to an area near the city of Adrianople (modern Edirne, located just east of the spot where the borders of Greece, Bulgaria, and Turkey all meet). Valens's forces were nearer to the Goths, but troops commanded by Gratian were marching to meet them. On August 9, a few days before Gratian's forces were to arrive, Valens decided to attack the Goths on his own. He ordered his men to put on their battle gear and march eight miles in the hot summer sun to where the Goths had made camp. Then, compounding his foolishness, the emperor proceeded to negotiate with Gothic emissaries who "deliberately wasted time so that their own cavalry might have a chance to get back."[32]

The Goths also lit fires that forced the dehydrated and exhausted Roman troops to deal with additional heat and smoke. When the battle was joined, the Romans found themselves surrounded by Gothic cavalry and infantry. One contemporary described a "scene of total confusion, the infantry, worn out by toil and danger, had no strength nor sense left to form a plan. . . . The ground was so drenched in blood that they slipped and fell."[33] Perhaps two thirds of the Eastern Roman army died on those fields, their experience and valor rendered useless by the heat, lack of room to maneuver, and incompetent arrogance of their emperor. Following the army's rout, Valens fled to a farmhouse, where the victorious Goths burned him alive.[34] A few days later, Gratian could do no more than survey the destruction.

No one at the time understood the true significance of the catastrophe at Adrianople. Some authors even downplayed the defeat, explaining that Valens's attachment to Arian Christian theological opinions actually meant that he deserved to burn alive.[35] This was a mistake. Valens had lost "at the same time the most brave and numerous portion of his Roman soldiery" and, like the plague losses under Marcus Aurelius and battle deaths seen by the unfortunate emperors of the 250s, the empire could not easily replace these trained and powerful professionals.[36] Furthermore, unlike the Gothic invaders who killed Decius in the 250s, these Goths intended to stay in Roman territory. They were not going back across the Danube unless Romans forced them to do so—and Rome suddenly lacked the capacity to compel them to leave.

Gratian realized the seriousness of the situation after a Gothic attack on Constantinople was beaten back by a band of citizens organized by Valens's widow, Dominica, and a group of Arab auxiliaries who happened to be in the city at the time.[37] This attack is perhaps why he passed over his eight-year-old brother in favor of a thirty-two-year-old Spaniard named Theodosius when Gratian was deciding who could best lead the Roman East.

The emperor Theodosius I understood that he had been selected to defeat the Goths quickly and decisively, so he spent much of 379 rebuilding the eastern field army destroyed at Adrianople. Constantius II's old panegyrist Themistius spoke enthusiastically about how Theodosius "made the fighting spirit return to the cavalry and infantry" while he made "farmers and miners a terror to the enemy."[38] It was, Themistius claimed, "the first turning of the tide" as the "eye of justice leads back to the Romans" and ensured that the "damned villains" would suffer for what they had done.[39]

Themistius's optimism was misplaced. Theodosius tried hard to turn peasants into an army of hardened Roman soldiers, but his new field army was so soundly defeated in Macedonia in 380 that Gratian summoned Theodosius to a meeting in Sirmium late in the year and took control of much of the Balkans back from him.[40]

Theodosius had failed to deliver the sort of Roman military restoration that everyone from Themistius to Gratian assumed to be inevitable. Rome had always maintained its frontiers and punished barbarians who violated them. No longer. When Theodosius slunk back to Constantinople in defeat in late 380, he realized that he could no longer promise a punishing and absolute victory over the Goths.

He could, however, promise a set of religious, administrative, and social reforms that would improve other aspects of Roman life. Ever the ready sycophant, Themistius immediately jumped on board. In mid-January of 381, two months after a humbled Theodosius returned to Constantinople, Themistius dismissed all "reports of wars and battles of men" as irrelevant.

It was, he continued, not a "moment convenient to serenade Ares" but instead to call upon Apollo, whose lyre would bring together Theodosius's subjects and make them "harmonious."[41] Good governance mattered even more than military force because a well-governed empire provides the best "weapons with which men conquer other men."[42] The barbarians would be defeated, of course, but by the emperor's blinding administrative talents rather than his military forces.

Themistius again had to change his approach in October 382 when Saturninus, the commander of imperial forces in Thrace, reached an agreement that ended the Gothic war.[43] The Goths laid down their arms in return for land on which to farm, a degree of political autonomy, and an opportunity to serve in the Roman army.[44] These terms made official what everyone already suspected. Theodosius lacked the capacity to punish the Goths in the fashion Romans expected. The death of Valens and tens of thousands of Romans would remain unavenged.[45]

Themistius somehow needed to again step back from what he had previously told his audiences Theodosius would deliver. The fast and overwhelming victory promised in 379 had become a slow and steady process through which the mature Roman civilization crushed the underdeveloped Goths. Now, as 383 dawned, there was no Roman victory at all.

Themistius again changed course. The peace treaty was now an act of mercy performed because Theodosius "realized that forgiveness toward those who had done wrong was better than to fight it out to the bitter end."[46] In the end, all talk of victory and defeat was irrelevant.[47] The Goths were now settled and, like other peoples the Romans had forgiven, they were well on their way to a future in which they would be "thoroughly Roman."[48]

Theodosius was not foolish enough to think that this argument alone would inspire much confidence. He had promised revenge and renewal. He had delivered neither. The fourth century, however, offered another way for emperors to define their achievements. If Theodosius could not bring about a conventional Roman military recovery or even a genuine victory, he could still use the powers of his office to generate the sort of Christian religious progress that the empire had failed to see since the death of Constantius II. This task is what he set out to do.

Theodosius's pivot from promising a traditional restoration of Roman power to delivering a new Christian future began during those first tense moments after his retreat back to Constantinople in 380. Theodosius first displaced the Arian clergy favored by Valens from the city's main churches and replaced them with clergy who accepted the Council of Nicaea.[49] In May of 381, he summoned the Council of Constantinople, an assembly that reaffirmed the imperial commitment to the Council of Nicaea.[50]

This new direction became even clearer in a series of imperial actions against paganism. In December 381, Theodosius issued a law that prohibited sacrifices, forbade anyone from approaching a temple, and mandated the death penalty for anyone who violated its terms. After twenty years, traditional religion in the Roman Empire had returned to where it was at the death of Constantius II.

Theodosius's new policies claimed victims. They first hit the non-Nicene clergy forced to leave their churches in Constantinople, but the most notorious cases involved organized religious violence against pagan and Jewish sacred buildings in Syria, Mesopotamia, and Egypt.[51] Some Christians cheered the destruction of the "shrines of the idols" that "consigned [traditional rites] to oblivion," but pagans called these attacks "nothing less than war in peace time waged against the peasantry" that left "utter desolation" in their wake.[52] These victims did not matter to Christians, who believed that Theodosius's actions would lead to a Christian future in which worshippers flocked to churches while traditional religion collapsed in on itself.[53] The emperor had successfully shifted the focus from his failed Roman renewal to Rome's accelerating progress toward a fully Christian empire.

Even Gratian seems to have sensed the power of this shift. Although Gratian had far more success as a military leader than Theodosius in the 380s, he too initiated a series of actions against traditional Roman religion in 382 in order to show that he also wanted to move toward this new, Roman Christian future.[54] Gratian sanctioned the removal of the Altar of Victory that had been placed in the Roman senate house by Augustus, removed under Constantius II in the 350s, and restored in the early 360s.[55] He also eliminated imperial funding for public pagan rituals and confiscated the endowments that had funded religious activities and maintained pagan temples for centuries.[56]

The pagan priests, senators, and other devotees of traditional cults victimized by these restrictions pushed back. Traditionalists in the Roman senate tried to appeal to Gratian but failed to even gain an audience with the emperor.[57] Ambrose, the bishop of Milan, later claimed that he had ensured their failure by forwarding a letter of protest signed by the bishop of Rome and a number of Christian senators.[58]

Ambrose merely postponed the inevitable public confrontation between the traditional Roman model of decline and renewal and this new vision of Rome as a state progressing toward an enlightened Christian future. Gratian was killed in the summer of 383 by Magnus Maximus, the governor of Britain.[59] A collection of leading Italian elites led by pagan senators like Symmachus and Christian leaders like Ambrose then created a rival court south of the Alps centered around Valentinian II.

Valentinian II depended upon the support of pagan senators to a degree that Gratian did not. This political reality compelled his courtiers to listen to the objections Symmachus and his colleagues wished to raise concerning Gratian's actions against traditional Roman religion. In the summer of 384, Symmachus forwarded a fresh senatorial motion asking that Valentinian reverse Gratian's policies.[60] He claimed that the Roman state was on the verge of a renewal in which just rule would again prevail.[61] In the spirit of that new age, Symmachus reminded the emperor that it had traditionally been the job of the senate to advise emperors how to promote the welfare of the empire. He asked, "What is more suitable than that the senate defend the institutions of our ancestors and the rights and destiny of our country" by explaining to the emperor how important it was that he restore "the condition of religious affairs which was so long advantageous to the state?"[62]

The senators called for Valentinian II to completely reverse the signature religious measure of his brother and predecessor. Symmachus was adamant that this break with Gratian was necessary. He equated the removal of the Altar to friendship with hostile barbarians,[63] a comment that all of his listeners would understand referred to the recent treaty with the Goths made by the Christian Theodosius. He then compared the present state of affairs with what Rome achieved when it embraced its "ancestral ceremonies." "This worship," the city of Rome might say, "subdued the world to my laws, the sacred rights repelled Hannibal from the walls. . . . Have I been reserved for this, that in my old age I should be blamed" for traditions that worked so well for so long?[64] Symmachus then claimed that pulling support for traditional Roman religion had already tangibly affected the empire.[65] "A general famine followed [Gratian's decision], and a poor harvest disappointed the hopes of all of the provinces . . . because it was necessary that what was refused to religion should be denied to all."[66]

Symmachus implored the new emperor to reverse the anti-pagan policies of the old. He asked that the gods "who in previous ages assisted your ancestors, defend you and be worshiped by us." The recent Roman political, military, and economic decline could be reversed, but only if the religious policies that had shaped the Christian regime of Gratian were scrapped. Roman society could be restored only if it returned to what it once had been.

The vigorous Christian response demonstrates the power of Symmachus's argument. The bishop Ambrose, who, like Symmachus, had been instrumental in helping Valentinian hold on to power the previous summer, framed two different responses to the appeal. The first of these, which offered a general set of points arguing on behalf of Christian anti-pagan measures, anticipated what the bishop thought Symmachus's argument would be. Ambrose later felt compelled to write a second, specific, and nearly point-by-point refutation when he actually saw the powerful rhetoric of decline and renewal that Symmachus's appeal contained.

In that second letter, Ambrose specifically targeted the two biggest proofs of Roman decline that Symmachus offered. The first of these centered on the idea that the ancient gods protected the city of Rome against adversaries like Hannibal. These ancient rites, Ambrose claims, were ineffective even then. If they were so strong, why was it that Hannibal was able to inflict any defeats on the Romans at all?[67] After all, Hannibal too worshipped pagan gods. Why did the worship of the old gods work for Romans and not Carthaginians?[68]

Ambrose then reframed the Roman past in a way that copied the monologue Symmachus placed in the mouth of Roma, his personification of the city of Rome. But Ambrose's Roma was much more optimistic about the new religious world Gratian put in place than the Roma conjured by Symmachus. She had no need for "the rights of ancestors" because she hated "the rites of Neros" and those of the failed "emperors who lasted two months."[69] Ambrose's Roma felt "no shame in passing to better things" and embracing Christian truth.[70] Rome existed on a stronger footing because it now stood on Christian wisdom and practices.[71] Ambrose had answered Symmachus's story of Roman decline with one of Christian progress.

The bishop realized that it was not enough to simply substitute a story of progress for one of decline. Symmachus, of course, also had examples from the recent past that seemed to show tangible, negative consequences of Gratian's decision to act against traditional Roman religion. Ambrose addressed these issues, too. Barbarian incursions, he claimed, could not be evidence of Roman decline, because they happened repeatedly across Roman history.[72] The famine that Symmachus attributed to divine anger at Rome happened because of natural variations in climate.[73]

In the end, the argument between Ambrose and Symmachus centered on the stability of a revolutionary new religious regime put in place in the early 380s. Ambrose agreed that this Christian regime broke with centuries of Roman religious tradition, but that break did not matter to him. It was, as Constantine or Maternus would have argued, a form of genuine Roman progress. The Roman present was indeed different from what came before, but it was better because it was Christian. For Symmachus, however, the dismantling of traditional religion was clear evidence of Roman decline that had already begun. Immediate renewal was essential or the anger of the gods would lead to the collapse of Rome amid barbarian incursions and famine. This centuries-old script offered the new regime of Valentinian II a way to save itself.

In the end, however, Valentinian II's advisors decided to preserve the religious policies of his predecessor, not so much because they were persuaded by the argument of Ambrose but because, in the political dynamics of the moment, Ambrose represented a more important power base.[74] Roman pagans, who also were important to the regime, received other concessions, including permission to lead public processions honoring the old gods and the freedom to remake space around some of the old temples.[75] Gratian's revolution was not undone. It was instead carefully modified so that Ambrose could point to Christian religious progress while Symmachus could claim a sort of Roman renewal.

The empire was nevertheless running out of time to pretend that both visions of the Roman future could coexist. Within a generation, Romans would be forced to choose between embracing Christian progress and mourning Roman decline.

9

THE LOSS OF THE ROMAN WEST AND THE CHRISTIAN FUTURE

THE ALTAR OF Victory controversy previewed a larger argument about progress and decline that would come to dominate the fifth century, a period in which Rome lost most of its Western territories. When Ambrose and Symmachus squared off in 384, they believed that they were having an argument about whether or not attachment to the old traditions of Roman paganism insured protection from barbarians. Both of them certainly thought that the threat from barbarians was limited. It involved damage and disruption rather than the empire's destruction. Rome had, after all, retained control of its western territory for nearly four centuries. No one in the 380s imagined that changing. No one could guess that, within a generation, Goths would sack the city of Rome. A generation later much of Gaul, Spain, and North Africa would fall out of Roman political control. The limited, largely theoretical argument about whether the Roman state should restore the religious traditions it had abandoned or continue progressing to a new Christian future now had very real and very serious implications.

The first serious blow fell when Theodosius I decided to respond to the revolt of Magnus Maximus by mounting a military campaign in which his eastern army, fortified with Gothic troops, defeated the veteran forces of the Roman West in 388. Theodosius then retreated to the East and left Valentinian II in charge of the West, but he found himself forced to return when the usurper Eugenius overthrew and killed Valentinian in 392. Theodosius defeated Eugenius in a horrible, destructive, two-day-long battle along the Frigidus River in September 394, annihilating much of the veteran forces that remained in the West.

The Battle of the Frigidus represents one of the most important turning points in all of Roman history. With Theodosius's victory, the entire Empire came together for the last time under the rule of one emperor.[1] It was also at this moment that, in great part because of the nature of the fighting, the seeds of the eventual breaking apart of the West were sown. Eugenius feared facing Theodosius's larger army in the plains of Italy, so he forced the battle in front of the mountain passes that led to the peninsula. Theodosius elected to sacrifice some of his superior manpower to blunt Eugenius's tactical advantage. A bloodbath ensured. On the first day of the battle, Theodosius ordered his forces to charge Eugenius's lines, with Gothic troops leading the assault. Eugenius's men repelled the initial advance and inflicted heavy casualties on the Goths.[2] At the end of the first day, the fighting remained inconclusive. On the second day, however, Theodosius attacked again, defeated Eugenius, and secured both his surrender and, eventually, that of the western provinces as well.[3]

Christians writing in the aftermath of the battle argued that it affirmed what Ambrose and other Christian leaders had been saying all along. God protected the orthodox Christian emperor Theodosius and ensured that he would be victorious. The Christian historian Rufinus, for example, constructed a narrative in which Eugenius catered to pagans, permitted pagan sacrifices before the battle, and was confident that he would win because pagan augurs assured him as much.[4] Theodosius, by contrast, "fortified by the assistance of the true religion," ordered his troops to attack, scattering the pagan demons. Then, on the battle's second day, Christian sources explain that Theodosius "fought with tears and prayers, not arrows or javelins" as the Christian God sent a powerful wind that blew "the spears of the enemy back onto them." Theodosius's victory "covered him in glory" not just from "the victory alone but from the way that he had won it."[5] Such was the reward for the emperor who embraced the Roman, Christian future.

Christians had a little more than four months to enjoy the unified, orthodox Christian empire that Theodosius had won. He died in January 395 and the empire was then divided between his two sons, Arcadius (age eighteen) and Honorius (age ten). In early March, Ambrose gave a funeral oration for Theodosius before Honorius and the assembled Western court. He already sensed that a new age had dawned.

Ambrose spoke reverently about the emperor who had "departed to receive his kingdom" since he had set aside the Roman Empire "for heavenly Jerusalem" after "his faith removed all worship of images and stamped out all [pagan] ceremonies."[6] Ambrose then, rather desperately, attempted to make the case that good Christians owed it to the pious, deceased emperor to obey his sons.[7]

Appeals like these had little practical effect. Instead the Roman world teetered. When Theodosius marched West, he had entrusted the East to the official control of Arcadius but the effective control of a court official who remained in charge following Theodosius's death. Arcadius remained so weak an emperor that real changes in power in the East came not from the usurpations of imperial pretenders but from the rise and fall of the courtiers who enjoyed the emperor's ear.

The situation in the West was only a little better. Honorius was an even more ineffectual emperor than his brother. The first part of Honorius's reign saw affairs steered by Stilicho, a general of partial barbarian ancestry who married Serena, the niece and adopted daughter of Theodosius. Working collaboratively with his savvy and capable wife, Stilicho deftly managed a series of military and political challenges in the west.[8] But, because Stilicho claimed authority over both the east and the west, he also looked for opportunities to assert control over the court of Arcadius .

As the fifth century dawned, the Western imperial court became centered on the northern Italian city of Ravenna, located on the Adriatic near the delta of the Po River. The Eastern capital remained Constantinople. Thus Illyricum, the area of the Balkans that now includes parts of Croatia, Bosnia, Montenegro, and Albania, formed the key line of approach for any army looking to move between northern Italy and Constantinople. Previous imperial divisions had placed this territory under the control of emperors based in Italy, but Theodosius held on to it during the civil war and elected to entrust much of it to the Eastern court as he moved west to confront Eugenius. If Stilicho wanted to exert authority over Constantinople, he would need this territory.

Stilicho's interest did not exist in a vacuum. Events in the East provided him with a possible ally. Enraged by the sense that Goths had been deliberately sent to their deaths during the initial charge at the Frigidus, the Gothic commander Alaric rebelled in 395, marched on Constantinople, and demanded some sort of military command.[9] The formidable defenses of the capital easily repelled him, but Alaric then set upon a path of destruction through the more poorly defended cities of Greece, sacking Athens in 396. Stilicho countered with a naval attack from the west, forcing Alaric to move north. Before Stilicho could destroy Alaric and take control of Illyricum, however, the Eastern court offered Alaric a military command so that Alaric could keep Stilicho out of the region.[10]

A series of intrigues in the Eastern court and a set of frontier crises in the West prevented either side from forcing a resolution to the standoff. By 401, however, Alaric became convinced that political turnover in the east threatened his position in Illyricum. He moved into Italy before Stilicho again defeated him and pushed him back to Illyricum, perhaps hoping to use him against the East at some point in the future. By 405, Stilicho had given Alaric a military title and, one source claims, planned to reinforce him with Roman troops so that Illyricum might firmly fall under western control.[11] In preparation for this event, Alaric moved his army back down to northwestern Greece.

Stilicho's troops never arrived. Between 405 and New Year's Day of 407, Stilicho faced an unprecedented series of challenges. Barbarians breached the Roman frontier in 405, advancing as far as Florence before Stilicho's army defeated them. A usurper in Britain named Constantine pulled away Britain, Gaul, and Spain from Honorius's control. On December 31, 406, part of the Rhine River froze so solidly that groups of Vandals, Alans, and Suevi all crossed into Roman territory. It was, then, understandable that Stilicho could not send troops to Illyricum, but Alaric had no reason to be understanding. He marched his army to the province of Noricum (which comprised much of modern Austria) and demanded 4000 pounds of gold. If the money was not paid, he would invade Italy.

Stilicho had no good options at that point. If he confronted the Vandals, Alans, and Suevi, Constantine would be able to advance into southern Gaul and, perhaps, forge an alliance with Alaric. If he attacked Constantine, the barbarians would be free to move more deeply into Roman territory—and possibly also make some sort of agreement with Alaric. If he paid Alaric, he would inevitably arouse suspicions from Roman elites that he was too soft on barbarians. After calculating the risks, Stilicho chose to pay Alaric, confront Constantine, and deal with the Vandals, Alans, and Suevi later.

The course of action made sense, but Stilicho had neglected to take into account the unpredictable emperor Honorius. Emboldened by the death of his brother Arcadius in 408 and the hope that he might control the new Eastern emperor, his seven-year old nephew Theodosius II, Honorius ordered Stilicho arrested and killed in August. Honorius then canceled the deal with Alaric and sanctioned a massacre of many of the family members of Stilicho's barbarian soldiers.[12]

He could have done nothing more foolish. In a matter of days, Honorius killed his best general, angered Alaric, and induced segments of the Roman army under his authority to desert. The next two years played out almost exactly as one would expect when a regime as incompetent and capricious as that of Honorius had to manage such complex, overlapping crises. Alaric marched into Italy in the winter of 408 and put Rome's port under siege. After a period of such severe food shortages that Romans might have resorted to burying their many dead outside of the Colosseum, the Roman senate agreed to provide Alaric with money and advise the emperor to make peace with him.[13] When Alaric met with the emperor's envoys, however, they refused to agree to his demands for an imperial position. Perhaps as a negotiating tactic, Alaric stormed out of the meeting. He soon sent word that he would accept grain and land in a frontier province for his men. When this offer too was rejected, Alaric again marched on Rome.

Frustrated by the emperor's unpredictability and general idiocy, Alaric returned to Rome and supported a usurpation against Honorius by a Roman senator named Priscus Attalus.[14] Attalus appointed Alaric his top military commander and began to prosecute a civil war against Honorius, who remained holed up in Ravenna. Attalus failed, however, to secure the province of Africa and its vital grain supply. When Alaric offered to take 500 of his troops to Africa, Attalus and the senate refused to allow "Africa to be entrusted to barbarians."[15]

Sensing yet another betrayal, Alaric turned on Attalus, reopened negotiations with Honorius, and, in early 410, deposed Attalus in favor of a deal with the legitimate emperor. While Alaric waited to finalize negotiations outside of Ravenna, he was attacked by forces under the command of an officer loyal to Honorius. "Impelled by rage and terror at this incident, Alaric retraced his steps, and returned to Rome, and took it by treachery. He permitted each of his followers to seize as much of the wealth of the Romans as he was able, and to plunder all the houses," leaving only some of the churches free from destruction.[16]

Alaric's sack of Rome in August of 410 was the first time an enemy army had entered the city in nearly 800 years. His army remained in Rome for only three days and, while it inflicted damage, the city was immense and Alaric's army could scarcely find, let alone carry, all of its treasures. But the psychological impact of Rome's sack was incalculable. With its capital sacked, the empire that Vergil once described as having "no bounds in space and time, an empire without end," now, for the first time in living memory, looked frail.[17] Someone or something must be to blame.

The tens of millions of Romans around the Mediterranean understandably began to wonder if the Christian progress claimed by emperors and church figures for much of the past century actually masked a creeping Roman decline. Symmachus, for example, had asked who among the Romans "was so friendly with barbarians" that they would turn away from the traditional Roman gods and risk their wrath. Did the warnings of people like Symmachus actually point to oncoming disasters that the Roman focus on progress had ignored?

Pagans certainly felt that they had. Pagan historians writing about Alaric began to make these charges almost immediately. One claimed (falsely) that Athens avoided Alaric's sack because "the old [pagan] traditions of the city" remained alive.[18] Another pagan historian described how some Tuscan priests saved the city of Narnia from Alaric and then offered to protect Rome, but "no one dared to participate in the ancestral rites" in public. They were, he continued, sent away and Rome was left to its fate.[19]

Christians who believed in the ideals of a Christian Roman empire needed to respond—and the responses begin to appear almost immediately. Across 410 and 411, Augustine, the bishop of Hippo, addressed this issue in a series of sermons, some of which were preached in Carthage to refugees who had left Italy to escape Alaric.[20] In one such sermon, Augustine imagined a pagan taunting a Christian. "When we used to sacrifice to our gods," the pagan began, "Rome stood. But now, because the sacrament of your God has prevailed . . . while the sacrifices of our gods are blocked and prohibited, look what Rome suffers."[21]

Augustine at that point lacked a good answer to this pagan charge. He could do no more than to tell his listeners to ignore the pagan and get rid of him quickly. The real concern, Augustine continued, was with Christians themselves. This was indeed a divine punishment, but not one inflicted on Romans by the pagan gods. It was instead a punishment inflicted by the Christian God on his followers who had sinned.[22]

Christian authors working in Constantinople echoed this idea. Writing a generation after the sack of Rome, the church historian Socrates Scholasticus blamed Alaric's sack on divine vengeance prompted by actions the bishop of Rome took against the Novatian Christian sect.[23] Philostorgius, an author affiliated with the Eunomian Christian sect, saw Rome's sack as the fulfillment of a prophesy in the book of Daniel.[24] Echoing both Augustine and the traditional explanations for Roman decline dating all the way back to Cato the Elder, the church historian Sozomen blamed divine anger at the "luxury and debauchery" of the Romans as well as their general "injustice towards each other and foreigners."[25]

All of these authors wrote from the safety of the east. They could allow the sack of Rome to become a morality tale without a detailed explanation for why it had happened. Augustine could not. As the 410s progressed, he fashioned a comprehensive new way to think about Rome's sack and its meaning for Christians. The work that resulted became the *City of God*, a project that he began in 413 but did not complete until 426. As he worked, Augustine asked his pupil Orosius, a Spaniard who had fled to North Africa in order to escape barbarian incursions in the 410s, to write a narrative history that laid out "the passions and the punishments of sinful men, the tribulations of the world, and the judgments of God."[26]

Orosius's rhetorically sophisticated *History against the Pagans* began with the world's creation and ended with the present day.[27] Following in the footsteps of figures like Lactantius and Eusebius, Orosius embedded moments of God's vengeance against persecuting emperors within a fast-moving narrative of Roman history.[28] As he reached the fourth century, the impetus for divine punishment shifted from imperial persecution to Roman sinfulness. The sack of Rome, which formed the most significant of these punishments, arose from "the wrath of God" against "a sinful populace . . . without any evidence of repentance."[29] Even Rome's sack was not as severe as one might imagine. Not only had Alaric given "orders that those who had taken refuge" in churches were to remain safe, but "the more densely the Roman refugees flocked together, the more eagerly their barbarian protectors surrounded them."[30]

Not only did pious Christians escape slaughter, but Orosius also said that the city largely escaped damage. The fire "kindled by the wantonness" of "her own emperor" Nero was far worse than this sack—and the damage from the fire set by the Celts following their sack of Rome around 390 BC surpassed both of those.[31] In fact, Orosius claims that "anyone who saw the numbers of the Romans themselves and listened to their talk would think that nothing had happened . . . unless perhaps he were to notice some charred ruins still remaining."[32]

Christians could then be reassured that the anger of pagan gods had nothing to do with the sack of Rome. The Christian God had orchestrated this disaster so that he could punish the wicked, protect the righteous, and do these things in a way that minimized damage and pious Christian casualties. Rome's sack was, then, necessary to make Roman Christians more pious. It was perhaps not good for Rome in the short term, but it could have a positive effect on Christians if they heeded the lesson God offered. Roman Christian progress continued.

Augustine offered a drearier version of that divine lesson when the completed *City of God* appeared in 426. The decade that had elapsed since the appearance of Orosius's history contained more Roman suffering and more powerful evidence of Roman political collapse.[33] It had become clear to all that Britain was abandoned. Honorius had ceded effective control of the southwest of modern France to the Goths once led by Alaric. The Vandals (who had crossed the Rhine in 406) had established themselves in Spain. Contrary to what Orosius had intimated, the Christian Roman suffering had gotten worse since 410. Better answers were needed.

The *City of God* offered these answers. While a desire "to write against the blasphemies and errors" of pagans who blamed Christians for Alaric's sack sparked Augustine's project, the work evolved over time into an argument that contrasted the worldly *civitas* with that of God.[34] *Civitas* was a key to this formulation. The word means city, but it also describes the larger political community of citizens. Augustine is, then, distinguishing the community of Romans living across the entire empire from the community of Christians that belong to the *civitas* of God. It is to this *civitas* of God that he wants them to turn their attention.

Augustine begins by attacking pagans who blame the Christian prohibition of traditional Roman worship for the sack of Rome. These pagans, Augustine charges, survived Alaric's sack only because they took refuge in Christian churches. If it were not for those churches, these pagan critics "would now be unable to utter a single word" against the Christian God to whom they owe their lives.[35] This is, Augustine continues, completely counter to how war usually proceeds. Enemies do not spare people because of their gods. This stance was true from the very beginning of Rome's mythological history. Troy, the city from which Vergil claims Romans ultimately descend, was sacked and utterly destroyed by Greeks.[36] This pattern of destruction of cities and their gods dominated Rome's pre-Christian history when Romans conquered other cities.

Rome also suffered other serious misfortunes outside of warfare. Drawing upon Sallust and Cicero, Augustine argues that "luxury and avarice" and "cruel and dissolute customs" had "rendered the Republic utterly wicked and corrupt" until it collapsed from its own vices.[37] Sulla, the man most responsible for the horrors of the first Roman civil war, boasted of the favor he enjoyed from the traditional Roman gods even while they incited him to commit massacres.[38] This behavior was to be expected. The traditional Roman gods could not prevent this spreading immorality or the fatal damage it did to the Republic because only the Christian God possesses the power to direct the course of events in the world.[39]

Romans did not just suffer from political calamities before the coming of Christ. Echoing Orosius, Augustine traces the military and political disasters that have afflicted the Roman people across their long history, each getting increasingly severe as the size and complexity of the state grew. The gods failed to help Rome resolve these issues even when Romans did things like build a temple to the goddess Concordia to try to bring civil conflict to an end.[40] They also deserve no credit for the extent or duration of the empire that Rome built because the Christian God alone has the ability to determine these things.[41] This point is shown in the achievements of Constantine and Theodosius, two orthodox Christian emperors whom God favored.[42] Theodosius in particular governed in such a way that he performed "those works for which the reward is eternal happiness . . . though only to those who are sincerely pious."[43]

This discussion of Christian emperors who privileged eternal happiness over worldly concerns sets up a major shift in the work away from the material conditions of this world to the pursuit of eternal life. Pagan gods and pagan thinkers, Augustine argues, have no sense of how one pursues eternal life.[44] This quest instead must come through Christ, the only true mediator between this world and that of God, and through an understanding of Christian Scripture.[45]

Augustine felt that mankind had always been divided between those who pursued the *civitas* of God and those who looked toward the baser *civitas* of Man. From these origins, the two *civitates* have parallel histories and, on some level, parallel aims. The temporal world can, however, only ever offer a shadowy approximation of the peace and goodwill that God can provide.[46] The concerns of this world compete with and distract from the pursuit of eternal life to such a degree that "the two cities could not have common laws of religion." The citizens of the *citivas* of God must, however, still live in this world and take advantage of "the peace of earth" to the degree that they can "without injuring faith and godliness."[47] In the end, though, the residents of the two *civitates* will have different fates. Those who follow God will receive eternal life, while the citizens of the world are doomed to eternal misery.[48] This, Augustine concludes, is all that matters. "For what other end do we propose to ourselves than to attain to the kingdom of which there is no end?"[49]

A work that begins with Alaric's sack of Rome has, by its end, moved completely past it. The sack of Rome belonged to a world that true Christians should care less about. They could take advantage of the peaceful conditions it often provided, but they otherwise should concern themselves with the pursuit of the eternal life that God promised. The Roman Empire would die along with the rest of the world of men, but the *civitas* of God would endure forever—and it is to this *civitas* that Christian citizens owe their primary allegiance.

Augustine's powerful and innovative rhetoric conveyed his sincere belief that Christians needed to focus on a higher purpose than the health of the Roman *civitas*. One cannot discount a significant concession that Augustine made to reality. The "peace of the earth" ensured by the Roman Empire mattered very much in creating the conditions that allowed the citizens of the *civitas* of God to pursue faith and godliness. Even after the events of 410 and the subsequent barbarian occupation of vast territory that had once been Roman, Augustine sat on the other side of the Mediterranean in the relative safety of a North African city that had been Roman for more than 500 years. The peace of the earth still seemed secure there even if it had been shaken severely in Rome's western European territories.

Three years after the conclusion of the *City of God*, the Vandals shattered any remaining illusions Augustine might have had about North Africa's security. Gothic forces pushing into Spain from Aquitaine compelled the Vandals to cross to North Africa in 429. The Vandals then began a rapid advance across North Africa until, in June of 430, their armies put Hippo Regius, Augustine's episcopal seat, under siege. As Vandal forces ranged across the region, Augustine "saw cities overthrown in destruction, and the resident citizens, together with the buildings on their lands, partly annihilated by the enemy's slaughter" while "others were driven to flee and dispersed." He even "saw hymns and praises of God perish from the churches" until, in June of 430, Vandal forces began a fourteen-month-long siege of Augustine's episcopal see of Hippo Regius.[50] Augustine died before the city fell to them in 431, abandoned by its inhabitants and burned by its conquerors.[51]

The Vandal advance meant that Augustine suddenly had to confront a series of very real problems that his theoretical *civitates* of God and Man blurred. What, some priests asked, were they to do in the face of Vandal attacks? The Apostles had, after all, fled persecution and Jesus himself had gone to Egypt to avoid Herod. Augustine told them that they had to remain in their sees so that "those who are in need of others are not abandoned" by the priests because, "without them men could neither live a Christian life nor become Christians." It was all right, Augustine conceded, for Spanish bishops to flee the Vandals after all of their parishioners had fled, been killed, or enslaved, but many more stayed with their people and suffered alongside them. Ultimately, one must not fear death. One must "fear that... the purity of faith may perish rather than that women may be raped" and others "put to torture when overpowered by the attack of the enemy."[52] Even as he stared at the atrocities that accompanied the collapse of Roman authority, Augustine asked Christians to endure the very real horrors of Roman decline that should have, in theory at least, not mattered to Christians focused on spiritual progress.

It would have been interesting to see whether Augustine's views would have changed if he lived to see the Vandal capture of Carthage in 439, an event that completed their conquest of North Africa. By that point, many North African clergy and refugees had fled to Italy. Some of those who remained, including the Carthaginian bishop Quodvultdeus, found themselves forced to endure torture and humiliation before they were, one later author says, put "naked and despoiled on broken ships."[53]

For the Romans who remained in North Africa, the horrors of the initial conquest eventually gave way to a process through which barbarian conquerors and the Roman vanquished moved forward to create something of a functional society in which the distinctions between Vandals and Romans gradually blurred. Roman elites helped the kingdom's administration function and Roman sailors enabled the Vandals, a group that had no significant experience in naval warfare before 429, to become the most powerful naval force in the Western Mediterranean.[54] This transformation happened very quickly. In 455, less than a generation after they completed the conquest of North Africa, the Vandal fleet sacked the city of Rome, plundered it for fifteen days, and returned to North Africa, carrying loot that included the regalia used by the Western Roman emperor.[55] There can be no doubt that many people who were born in the Roman province of Africa as subjects of the Roman emperor participated in this "barbarian" devastation of the eternal city. The empire had become nothing more to them than a competing polity.[56]

Similar processes unfolded in the formerly Roman territories of western Europe. Southern Gaul and Spain came under the control of Goths. The Burgundians established a kingdom centered on the modern city of Geneva. By the late fifth century, the Franks set up a kingdom in northern Gaul. Some Romans who remained in the shrinking empire awaited what Salvian of Marseille would term "its last breath in that part of the world where it appears still to be alive."[57] For Salvian, Rome was the new Israel whose impending doom proved the depth of its sins and the profundity of its abandonment of God.[58]

Others felt that the retreat of the empire was a practical reality that they needed to confront. Large majorities of Romans still inhabited these regions that fell under barbarian control, but these Romans no longer lived in a Roman empire. Instead, they lived in kingdoms run by non-Romans. Like the civil servants and sailors of North Africa, many of these people who were born as Roman citizens quickly adapted to their new status as Roman subjects of non-Roman kings.

No figure embodies this mind-bending transformation better than Sidonius Apollinaris. Born in Lyon around 430, Sidonius emerged as one of the most celebrated orators of the later Roman Empire. A Roman senator and the son-in-law of the emperor Avitus, Sidonius delivered three imperial panegyrics from the mid-450s through the late 460s. The first, which celebrated Avitus as a new Trajan who could allow Rome to rise again from barbarian subjugation, earned Sidonius a bronze statue in the Forum of Trajan.[59] The last, delivered before the emperor Anthemius in 467, proved such a success that Anthemius appointed Sidonius the urban prefect of Rome for 468—the highest office in the city below the emperor himself.[60] As these speeches suggest, Sidonius saw himself as nothing less than a second Pliny for what he hoped to be a new age of Roman imperial restoration.[61]

The Roman restoration for which Sidonius hoped never came. As southern Gaul began to slip away from Roman control, Sidonius's horizons narrowed from the imperial to the local. He took over as bishop of the city of Clermont-Ferrand in the early 470s and his life as an elaborately pedigreed Roman senator ended. By 475, Clermont-Ferrand had fallen to the Gothic king Euric and Sidonius found himself imprisoned for leading the city's defense.

While Sidonius vividly described the horrors of the Gothic conquest and the resulting persecution of Catholic clergy, he also adapted to the new non-Roman political reality as readily as the North African Romans of the mid-400s. He embarked on a second career as a leading member of the

Gallo-Roman aristocracy.[62] He lived until the late 480s, fighting for the interests of his city and its churches while also helping to craft a post-Roman Gallic order in which men like him retained influence. His was a life in which, Sidonius wrote, "he was at times a player in the game, and at others the ball."[63] Roman decline and renewal mattered greatly to Sidonius while he played the Roman imperial game, but it ceased to matter at all once he had passed from Roman to Gothic political control. Rather than recede from the arena, Sidonius moved on and found a way to again become a player in the new, smaller Gothic political game.

Not all elite Gallo-Romans found the transition from Roman aristocrat to Gothic subject so easy. Paulinus of Pella, the grandson of the poet, consul, and imperial tutor Ausonius, shows how precarious the positions of Romans could become in these times of great uncertainty. A generation older than Sidonius, Paulinus was born in 376 to a governor of Macedonia in the thriving Roman Empire of Valens.[64] Although based in Aquitaine, the wealthy family had properties across the Mediterranean. Paulinus grew up a child of privilege, content to spend his time hunting, horseback riding, wearing fancy clothes, and dining on fine silver.[65] Around the age of thirty, Paulinus wed an heiress whose family owned a charmingly decrepit vineyard outside of Bordeaux. Largely ignoring his wife, he instead took to tending the vines so that he might restore their vigor.[66] This was the pampered and protected life of a Roman aristocrat.

That life ended for Paulinus when the Gothic forces that had sacked Rome arrived in Aquitaine in 414. Priscus Attalus, the Roman imperial pretender whom Alaric had backed in 409, was traveling with the Goths when they came to the region. Paulinus agreed to help Attalus just as his grandfather Ausonius had once served Valentinian I and Gratian. But Attalus was not Valentinian, and Paulinus, the distracted dilettante, was certainly no Ausonius. Ausonius's capable service to emperors in the 370s made him richer and more esteemed. Paulinus's incompetence made him so hated that angry Gothic soldiers burned his estate when he could not find the money to pay their salaries.[67] This event began a long slide from privilege to relative penury. By 459, Paulinus was living alone in a townhouse in Marseille, supported by money provided by a Goth interested in purchasing what remained of his land.[68] Paulinus's personal and financial fortunes had fallen in tandem with the loss of Roman control.

Paulinus was not despondent about what he had lost. Instead, he narrated this sequence of personal, political, and financial failures in an autobiographical poem called the *Eucharisticos*—a title best translated as "The Thanksgiving." He begins this tale of worldly woe by contrasting his life with that of "the famous men . . . who, because of their brilliant qualities . . . hand down to posterity a memoir of their deeds." He has no "brilliant achievements" except that he "owed his whole life to God" and has lived a life "subject to his direction."[69]

As the poem progresses, Paulinus emphasizes that his willingness to accept the difficult path God set for him was a more important achievement than anything accomplished by famous Romans of old. All that he suffered, all that he had lost was "ordained by you, Oh Christ, for the strengthening of my faith." The vicissitudes of this world offered Paulinus the opportunity to "win the promise of salvation" in the next. This, Paulinus concludes, was the point of all of his losses and suffering. He needed to learn that, "whatever fate awaits us at the end" the "hope of viewing" Christ "would soothe it."[70] Paulinus was, then, a fifth-century Job facing challenges designed by God to test him in ways that encouraged him to appreciate the true promise of salvation that waited for him after death. And *futurum*, the poem's final word, powerfully turned one's gaze away from the shadowy deeds of this world and toward the eternal future that awaits the faithful with God.

Paulinus points to the radical but logical conclusion of the story of Roman Christian progress that began with Constantine. Its endpoint was not the Christian Roman Empire that fourth-century bishops and emperors imagined. If Roman Christians genuinely thought of themselves as citizens of two worlds, the *Civitas* of Rome and the *Civitas* of God, and the *Civitas* of God was more important, why must the *Civitas* of Rome still exist? What good did it provide?

Paulinus saw none at all. Roman rule in Gaul was not, as Augustine suggested in the *City of God*, a thing that secured peace for Christians seeking God. It was not even, as Salvian of Marseille suggested, a corrupt, late-stage second Israel whose sins had doomed it. It had become a hindrance that prevented one from truly embracing the promise of God's salvation. For

Paulinus, that promise of salvation grew out of "religious self-sufficiency."[71] It was not secured by an emperor, mediated by a bishop, or even pursued in a church. Christ provided that direction to the faithful person. Paulinus learned to listen to Christ's direction only when his life as a Roman nobleman disappeared. Rome was Paulinus's dissolute past. Christ was his blessed and eternal future. One who truly understood Christian progress would not worry about Roman decline. And he certainly would not hope for a Roman recovery. The Roman past was dead. Only the Christian future mattered.

10

JUSTINIAN, ROMAN PROGRESS, AND THE DEATH OF THE WESTERN ROMAN EMPIRE

THE FIRST THREE quarters of the fifth century were disastrous for the western half of the Roman Empire. In 400, the empire controlled roughly the same territory it had for most of the previous 350 years. The Atlantic Ocean bounded its western edges until one reached the Irish Sea. Its northern frontier ran across England and then down the Rhine and Danube Rivers. And its southern frontier lay where the cultivated land of North Africa blended gradually into the mountains of Morocco and the Sahara Desert.

Rome patrolled none of these western frontiers in 475. As the empire's western and southern edges peeled away from Roman control in the fifth century, Rome receded back to its Italian and Dalmatian core. We should not disregard the size and power of the western territory that remained Roman. If the Western Roman Empire of 475 were a modern nation, it would be the third largest country in Europe, roughly the size of modern France. The territory it controlled remained the wealthiest, most populous, and most urbanized parts of the west. This was more land than the Roman Republic controlled at the beginning of its explosive expansion across the Mediterranean in the second century BC. It was more than enough on which to found a vibrant and powerful state. The issue this rump Roman Empire faced was not one of whether it could avoid collapse but how it could make most efficient use of substantial resources it still controlled. If the Western Roman story of the first three quarters of the fifth century was one of the steady erosion of Roman political control back to its Italian core, the period between the 470s and the 520s saw an Italian, Roman recovery in which that Italian state again became the most powerful polity in the Western Mediterranean.

This Roman recovery was real, meaningful, and widely recognized. Ennodius of Pavia described fifth-century Italy as "fruitful land laid waste because of the worthlessness of its governors" and an "impoverished" realm that "put private fortunes in dire straits." By the early sixth century, the same author spoke of the "filth" that was "washed away from the greater part of Italy," taking with it "the dregs of the world" and leaving Rome "living again" as it emerged from "the ashes."[1] Large-scale repairs were made to churches and public buildings throughout the peninsula, including multiple renovations to the Colosseum during which senators proudly inscribed their names and offices on their seats.[2] The great amphitheater, which was approaching its 450th anniversary, again hosted games, and chariot races were organized in the circuses around Italy. Theoderic, the longest-serving leader in the period, "was called a Trajan or a Valentinian, whose times he took as a model" for his own.[3] Like those two great emperors, Theoderic again campaigned effectively beyond the territory he inherited, extending Roman rule back to the old Danube frontier in the northeast and deeply into the southern Rhône Valley in Gaul while, for a time, even creating a Roman protectorate over Spain.[4]

In 507, Ennodius compared Theoderic to Cato and told him that "Rome, the Empress of the world, was demanding you to restore her to prosperity."[5] And, Ennodius continued, Theoderic did just that. With him, "the destruction of Roman reputation together with the wickedness of the times ended." With him, "Rome, the mother of cities, becomes young again" while "the wealth of the Republic grows along with private prosperity." Because Theoderic "considered the empire diminished which does not grow," he pushed the Italian frontier back to the city of Sirmium (the modern Serbian city of Sremska Mitrovica). With this, "the Roman empire has returned to its former boundary" and Theoderic has returned "the culture of our ancestors" to the Sirmians.[6] "The revival of Roman renown brought Theoderic forward" as a credible rival to Alexander the Great[7] because this was, Ennodius concluded, "our Golden Age."[8]

The Romans living in Theoderic's empire had no doubt that they continued to enjoy the superiority that Romans had traditionally enjoyed over the barbarians who lived outside their territory. One of Theoderic's courtiers mocked Gundobad, the king of the Burgundians, by sending him a water clock like the one he "once saw in the city of Rome" because, without such civilized technology, Gundobad would fall back into "the habit of beasts" who "feel the hours by their bellies' hunger."[9] Following the reconquest of southern Gaul, Ennodius spoke about the return of "civilization after the passing of so many years" to Gallic people whose barbarian captivity prevented them from tasting "the flavor of Roman liberty."[10] This reunification of Gaul and Rome was even commemorated by the selection of a Gallic nobleman named Flavius Felix as consul. "Through you," Felix was told, "the consulship returns to a transalpine family . . . so that you might surpass your ancestors, whose honor you restore."[11]

This talk of Roman restoration first in Italy and then across the territories to its north, east, and west neglected to mention one important point. Theoderic, the new Trajan and new Valentinian, was a Goth. He was also an Arian Christian whose beliefs were seen as heretical by many Romans. Indeed, by the time of Theoderic's death in 526, the Roman state based in Italy had not been ruled by a Catholic Roman since the barbarian general Odoacer had taken power in 476.

Matters were even more complicated than that. The five decades before Odoacer's usurpation had seen barbarian generals take on a steadily increasing role in directing the empire's military policy until, in August of 476, Odoacer seized effective control of Italy for himself.[12] He overthrew the puppet emperor Romulus Augustulus and replaced Orestes, the young emperor's father, as the true power governing Italy.[13] Odoacer did not install a new puppet Western emperor. Instead, the Roman senate sent to Constantinople an embassy carrying the Western imperial regalia and bearing the message that there "was no need of a divided rule and that one, shared emperor was sufficient for both territories."[14] Odoacer would serve as the imperial agent governing Italy in the name of the Eastern emperor Zeno. The East grudgingly accepted this reality until, in 488, Zeno encouraged Theoderic to move from the Balkans, invade Italy, and displace Odoacer.

Theoderic's army arrived in 489 and, after four years of brutal fighting, Theoderic and Odoacer agreed to a power-sharing arrangement,[15] which lasted precisely ten days. On March 15, 493, Theoderic personally killed Odoacer at a dinner party and assumed the position of the imperial agent governing Italy.[16] Then, in 497, the Eastern court sent the imperial regalia back to Italy, an action seen in the West as an acknowledgment that Theoderic effectively (though not officially) ruled as a Roman emperor.[17]

Theoderic's regime differed from that of Trajan and Valentinian I, but no one in Italy thought that Roman life had fundamentally shifted following his arrival. The Roman senate continued to meet, Roman consuls continued to be appointed, Roman law continued to bind the land, and coins featuring Roman emperors continued to be minted in Italy. Unlike the early Vandal kings, Theoderic also instituted no persecutions of Roman Christians. All of the things that traditionally marked Rome as Roman continued. In fact, as Ennodius and Cassiodorus both show, Italians very much felt that the regimes of Odoacer and (especially) Theoderic were not only thoroughly Roman but were also actually spearheading a Western Roman revival. Rome had not fallen. It was instead restored after a period of profound decline in the West.

Even the Roman Empire based in Constantinople initially shared this understanding of Italian affairs. When Eastern historians of the late fifth and early sixth centuries speak about developments in Italy, they do not characterize them as the end of Roman power in the West. They focus instead upon relations between the Eastern emperor and the West without challenging the Roman nature of the Italian regime.

The widespread acceptance that Italy remained Roman did not prevent people from trying to define it otherwise. Eastern Romans appreciated the potential power of weaponizing the barbarian backgrounds of Odoacer and Theoderic against Italian Romans and Italian institutions. If one could come to believe that the Western Roman Empire had fallen, all sorts of aggressive Roman actions against the West could be justified as necessary steps in a Roman renewal.

The earliest such claim that Rome fell when Odoacer took power in 476 appears in an attack against Pope Leo and the Council of Chalcedon that is attributed to Timothy Aelurus, an anti-Chalcedonian bishop of Alexandria who died in 477. Timothy assails the orthodoxy of the Pope and those who accept his Christology by offering proof that their ideas have attracted divine disfavor. He wrote, "The Roman Empire has ceased and come to an end, because of the Evil one and the fact that he made appear the abomination that one calls the Tome of Leo. The city that was the mistress and queen of all of the inhabitable world has become captive and placed under the dominion of barbarians."[18]

Although Odoacer is not mentioned by name, it is difficult to understand the statement that Rome has "become captive to barbarians" in any other context. Timothy used the idea of the decline and fall of the Western Roman Empire to call for Christians to stop recognizing the most recent ecumenical council and embrace an anti-Chalcedonian Christological position. Timothy then evoked the old arguments of Symmachus and Socrates Scholasticus that actions against correct religion caused Roman misfortune. This argument was also a call to action. Rome's fall to barbarians was a catastrophe that the East could still avoid if it turned away from the theology of Leo.

Unsurprisingly, the argument met with little success among Chalcedonian Christians. Italian and Constantinopolitan sources all ignore Timothy's claims about Rome's fall. Fifth- and early-sixth-century Constantinopolitans continued to accept the Tome of Leo and, consequently, they had no interest in repeating a narrative of Roman decline that supported Timothy's calls for the Tome to be discarded.

Constantinopolitan receptiveness to the idea of Western Roman decline changed as political tensions with the Italian regime increased in the 510s and early 520s. The East had eyed Italy with some wariness since the time of Odoacer's coup and, as Theoderic pushed western control back to the Danube, his forces bumped up against the Eastern Roman frontier. This move alarmed the East sufficiently that they mounted a few sporadic naval raids on Western territory. Then, after Theoderic's death, the East made an alliance with the barbarian Gepids to push the Western regime back from its borders. The West responded by attacking and capturing the Eastern city of Gratiana, on the south bank of the Danube.[19]

It was in this early-sixth-century climate that the Latin chronicler Marcellinus Comes advanced a novel argument. In his second entry under the year 476, Marcellinus wrote, "Odoacer, king of the Goths, took control of Rome. Odoacer slew Orestes right there. Odoacer condemned

Augustulus, the son of Orestes, with the penalty of exile in Lucullanum, a fortress in Campania. The Western Empire of the Roman people, which the first emperor Octavian Augustus had begun to rule in the 709th year from the foundation of the city, perished with this Augustulus."[20]

It is because of this passage that, for the past fifteen centuries, people around the world have learned that the Roman Empire fell in 476.[21] This is the date that school children memorize, it is the date that historians repeat, it is the date that the popular press uses, and it is even the date with which novelty items like mousepads displaying galleries of Roman imperial portraits end. It is now common knowledge that Rome fell in 476. But this fall of Rome was an illusion. Like the Domitianic decline invented by propagandists working under Trajan and the blissful peace and prosperity of the reign of Marcus Aurelius crafted by historians of the Severan period, the fall of Rome in 476 was manufactured to serve the propaganda purposes of later Romans.

Marcellinus's statement is the earliest of a group of references to the fall of the west, all of which come from a broadly Constantinopolitan environment and suggest a remarkable shift in the historical consensus about what Odoacer's coup meant nearly half a century after it happened. Marcellinus's text also gives away why this shift likely occurred. He mentions that Odoacer was a king of the Goths when he destroyed the Roman Empire. This statement is a fabrication. Odoacer was not a Goth.[22] But Theoderic was a Goth and he had taken power from Odoacer. As the Italian Gothic regime found itself in increasing tension with Constantinople, the fall of the Western Roman Empire emerged as a way to build support for an Eastern Roman intervention in Italy. If Eastern Romans could be convinced that Theoderic's regime was not Roman, they might also be convinced to support an effort by the East to overthrow this barbarian regime and return Italy to Roman control. This plan would be most compelling only if it seemed historically justified. The heretical Gothic king Odoacer then became a useful creation whose violent overthrow of the orthodox Christian Western Roman Empire invited—even required—an Eastern Roman restoration.[23]

Marcellinus did not invent this idea in a vacuum. His project formed part of a larger, imperially sanctioned effort to create Eastern momentum for a campaign to reconquer the West and restore the empire to the Romans living there. Marcellinus was not just any author. He served as a personal aide to the future emperor Justinian during the time when Justinian was the imperial heir apparent. Then, once Justinian had taken power, Marcellinus received several honorific titles as he followed his patron into the inner circles of imperial decision-making.[24] These benefits coincided with the publication of his *Chronicle*, a work that quite deliberately, clearly, and bluntly hammers home its main theme that Old Rome had fallen—and Justinian's Christian Roman Empire was providentially selected to restore it.[25]

Marcellinus's *Chronicle* effectively does the same thing as the histories that Festus and Eutropius wrote to justify the emperor Valens's campaigns against Persia in the early 370s. All three authors had imperial patrons who wanted them to provide historical rationalizations of wars of aggression that they hoped to initiate. All three were then given rewards by their imperial patron following the appearance of their works. Both Valens and Justinian did in fact launch the wars for which these historians laid the intellectual groundwork. But, unlike the claims of Festus, Eutropius, and even Timothy Aelurus, Marcellinus's manufactured fall of Rome fundamentally changed future ideas about the fall of Rome.

This shift occurred because the Roman fall Marcellinus described actually happened—but not because of Odoacer or Theoderic. It happened because Marcellinus helped to create conditions that eventually enabled Justinian to unleash horrifying violence that killed hundreds of thousands, decimated many great Italian cities, and destroyed the prosperity that Roman rule had once created in the West. Future scholars and students could objectively observe that Marcellinus was correct that the Western Roman Empire had fallen, even if they no longer understood that he got both the cause and the date of its fall wrong.

Much of the horror inflicted on the West arose out of Justinian's ideas about a Christian Roman emperor's obligations to his God and his citizens. By the time that Justinian took power in August of 527, Eastern Roman citizens and their emperor both had come to believe that there was a correlation between the personal and Christian virtues of the emperor, the legitimacy of his regime, and the success of the Roman Empire.[26] In Palestine, for example, the ascetic leader Sabas predicted that Justinian would restore the Roman Empire to its size in 395 if he aggressively championed orthodoxy.[27] Justinian himself believed that "there is not much difference between priesthood and imperial power, or between holy and public things."[28]

This framing of imperial power, Christian piety, and Roman success follows an evolutionary path that barbarian invasions had interrupted in the West. Western thinkers like Orosius, Salvian, Augustine, and Paulinus of Pella all had to struggle with the theological implications of a failing Christian Roman Empire whose power declined and borders shrank despite the piety of its emperors. In the East, however, emperors remained empowered to ensure, as Justinian would write, "that the Christian faith is correct and unblemished and that the institution of the most holy Catholic and Apostolic church of God is protected from disturbance everywhere." "It is on account of this," Justinian continued, "that rule over the present world was granted to me by God and I have been entrusted to protect it and subdue the enemies of our state."[29] Roman Christians could see that a strong, Christian empire thriving under pious Roman emperors in Constantinople was still progressing toward a better future. When Justinian looked to the west, he saw what Marcellinus had described. A fallen western order dominated by heretical barbarians. The East could—and should—act to free western Romans from this tyranny. It was their obligation, even if many in the West did not want eastern liberation.

While the most powerful eastern arguments about Rome's fall centered on Italy, Justinian's campaign to reconquer the West began in North Africa. Between 523 and 530, the Vandal kingdom had been ruled by Hilderic, the Chalcedonian Christian grandson of the Roman emperor Valentinian III whom Constantinople recognized as orthodox. When Hilderic was overthrown in 530 by his cousin Gelimer, an Arian Christian, Justinian saw a pretext to launch an attack. Although a significant community of North African Roman exiles had pushed Justinian to order an invasion, the decision was not without its critics.[30] The East had attacked the Vandal kingdom before, most notably in 468 when a massive invasion of Africa ended in disaster.[31] Procopius, whose narrative of Justinian's western campaigns served as a sort of official history, explains that Justinian's advisors reminded him of this failure and the danger that another failure might pose to the empire.[32] Justinian then heard from a bishop that "God had visited him in a dream" and told him to inform the emperor that God himself would "join with [Justinian] in waging war and make him lord of Libya."[33] This was a divinely ordained work of Christian Roman renewal.

Justinian and his generals managed the North African campaign masterfully. Justinian attacked a North African kingdom that was nearly a century old and ruled by a Vandal king who collaborated with local elites to run its affairs. A key part of Justinian's campaign centered on an effort to weaken political cohesion by encouraging North Africans to differentiate themselves again as Roman natives or Vandal invaders. Justinian's agents could then use this recognition to cleave the two groups apart. The Vandal coup in 530 made the task easier because, unlike Hilderic, Gelimer's Arian Christianity put him at odds with many of his subjects.

As 533 began, Justinian fomented revolts in the Vandal provinces of Sardinia and Tripolitania and sent Roman troops to support the rebels. He then launched a fleet against the heart of the Vandal kingdom, surprising the Vandals by landing forces about 150 miles from Carthage. As the Romans marched toward the Vandal capital, Belisarius, the general leading the expedition, instructed his troops not to loot or pillage the land, because "the Libyans, since they are Romans by descent, do not trust the Vandals and are hostile towards them."[34] This was to be a war of Roman liberation and no Romans, either the invaders from the East or the captive Romans of Africa, were to be harmed if it could be avoided.

The strategy worked. Belisarius's army won a victory over the Vandal army ten miles outside of Carthage on September 13. On September 15, his forces entered the city. The general again proclaimed that "the emperor had launched this war against the Vandals" because "all the Libyans are Romans by ancestry, had become subjugated to the Vandals unwillingly, and had suffered greatly under those barbaric men."[35] The Vandals remaining in the city, Procopius wrote, sought sanctuary in churches while Belisarius ensured that the rights of Romans remained intact. The victorious soldiers were then billeted in the homes of these Romans just as they would have been if the city had never fallen from Roman control.[36]

Major combat operations ended soon after the fall of Carthage, with the war itself concluding in March of 534 with the capture of Gelimer. Justinian then celebrated the victory in traditional fashion. He determined that Belisarius "was worthy to receive a triumph which, in times past, had been granted to Roman generals who won the greatest and most remarkable victories." This was, Procopius explained, something that had not been granted in nearly 600 years to a general who did not belong to the imperial family and, even among emperors, it was reserved for "Titus and Trajan and other such emperors who commanded armies that won victories against some barbarian nation."[37]

The procession itself saw the victorious general display the gold, silver, and jewels seized from the Vandal royal treasury, including the "treasures of the Jews that Titus, the son of Vespasian . . . had brought to Rome after the capture of Jerusalem" as well as other items seized by the Vandal raiders in 455.[38] The restoration of Roman treasures to the rightful Roman emperor symbolically reversed the Vandal sack of Rome.

The procession concluded with Gelimer and his family entering the Constantinopolitan hippodrome, the immense chariot-racing stadium that adjoined the imperial palace. Clad in royal purple, the Vandal king and his family were led before the emperor as tens of thousands of Constantinopolitans cheered. The purple garment was then stripped off of him, he and his family bowed, and Gelimer acknowledged his submission to Justinian. In an orchestrated display of imperial philanthropy, Justinian granted Gelimer and his family an estate in Asia Minor.[39] With this well-choreographed act, the entire Vandal kingdom and its ruling structure was again fully reincorporated into the Roman state.

Almost immediately, Justinian began planning an Italian sequel to his successful campaign against the Vandals. As in North Africa, Justinian's Italian campaign would begin by prying apart the orthodox "Romans" of the Italian state from the Arian "Goths" who dominated it. The emperor hoped to exploit these divisions to build Italian Roman support for an Eastern Roman reabsorption of Italy. If all went well, Italy would rapidly fall under Constantinopolitan control, the Gothic leadership would submit to Roman rule, and Justinian could stage another ceremonial public reincorporation of lost Roman territory.

Italian affairs in the 520s and 530s gave the emperor a series of events on which he could capitalize. Ever since the western expansion into Dalmatia of the early 500s, the Western and Eastern Roman regimes had shown only intermittent respect for each other's territorial boundaries.[40] The eastern absorption of the Vandal kingdom opened up another border dispute that Constantinople could exploit. The Vandal kingdom had included the city of Lilybaeum in western Sicily that Theoderic granted to the Vandal regime as a wedding gift when his sister had married the Vandal king Hilderic. Gelimer had retained the town after Hilderic's deposition but, when Constantinople tried to claim Lilybaeum as part of its reconquest, the Italian regime prevented it from taking control.[41]

The pressure on the Western regime did not just come from a belligerent court in Constantinople. Blunders by Theoderic and his heirs made Justinian's efforts easier. One of the biggest such missteps involved Theoderic's decision to order the executions of the philosopher Boethius (in 524) and his father-in-law, Symmachus (in 525), two former consuls and government officials who belonged to the Anicii clan, a powerful family with branches active in both Italy and Constantinople.[42] In good times, the eastern and western Anicii could help authorities in Italy and Constantinople mediate disputes. But, following the murder of prominent western Anicii by Theoderic, the eastern Anicii quickly amplified the outrage felt by their cousins in Italy. Their anger soon blended with that of other Italian senatorial exiles who had fled Italy because of Theoderic.[43] Theoderic had then created a set of Roman senatorial martyrs plucked from a family that was uniquely well positioned to generate Eastern Roman outrage at his act of tyranny.[44] Justinian could now count on a segment of the eastern elite to support the Roman liberation of Italy he would promise.

Justinian finally got his chance to act in the mid-530s. As in the lead-up to the Vandal invasion, the overthrow of a monarch friendly to the Eastern court gave Justinian sufficient cause for war. In 535, eastern forces attacked from two sides with Justinian offering the twin justifications that "the Goths have used force to take Italy, which was ours, and have refused to give it back" and that "the orthodox faith rejects the beliefs of the Arians."[45] A force of 7500 troops commanded by Belisarius landed in Sicily while another Eastern Roman army attacked western holdings in Dalmatia (an area roughly equal to modern Croatia, Bosnia, and Slovenia). Dalmatia would fall to the East by the end of the summer of 536.[46] Sicily fell even faster and, by late 536, Belisarius had advanced as far as the city of Rome.

Procopius records that the response in Italy during the early stages of the war mirrored the Roman-Gothic division that the emperor and his propaganda aimed to create. Outside of Naples, Belisarius was told that he was "acting unjustly by fighting against men who are Romans and have done nothing wrong, . . . for we have over us a guard of barbarians as masters."[47] When he arrived at Rome in December, the city opened its gate, the Gothic garrison retreated, and "Rome became subject to the Romans again after a time of sixty years."[48]

The capture of Rome did not end the war. The Western Roman regime was much larger, more powerful, and more resilient than the Vandal kingdom. It would not collapse simply because eastern forces captured its largest city. Gothic forces regrouped in Ravenna under the new king Vitigis and the war dragged on until Eastern forces seized that city in 540. Justinian then tried to end hostilities through the same choreographed acts of surrender and reconciliation that concluded the Vandal campaign. Vitigis was given an honorific Roman title and a comfortable pension. Even Theoderic's old courtier Cassiodorus moved to Constantinople and tried to integrate himself into Justinian's empire.[49] Some Gothic forces still held out and, after Justinian recalled Belisarius to the East, the war reignited. The second wave of fighting saw Gothic forces sweep down as far as southern Italy. The city of Rome suffered particularly badly in this phase of the conflict. Goths recaptured Rome in 546, lost it in 547, and then retook it again in 549 before losing the city for good in 552. The war did not conclude until the last Gothic holdouts were reduced in 562.

By the end of the war, Justinian had destroyed what many people in 535 believed was the Western Roman Empire and had restored a hollowed-out Italy to the Eastern Roman Empire. Many of the cities of the peninsula were ruined in the fighting. The battles, sieges, and multiple sacks had depopulated the city of Rome and destroyed much of its infrastructure. Residents had even been reduced to eating mice, dogs, and dung during the year-long siege before Rome fell to the Goths in 546.[50] Milan, once the second city of late Roman Italy, fared even worse. When a combined army of Goths and their Burgundian allies captured Milan in 538, Procopius reports that the city was "razed to the ground" with all the male population killed and all women captives presented to the Burgundians as slaves.[51]

Although Justinian's reconquest was successful, it had come at a terrible cost to Italians and the renewal of Roman rule proved ephemeral. An invasion by Lombards in the late 560s soon peeled away large sections of northern and central Italy from Roman control. Romans would hold Ravenna and Rome until the mid-eighth century and they would keep control of parts of the south until the eleventh century, but Justinian's war and the Lombard invasion meant that Italy would not again be unified under a single government until the late nineteenth century.

Justinian's grandiose plans to improve the empire extended into domestic matters. Again claiming a divine mandate to undertake radical and controversial reforms, Justinian and his advisors produced three important texts that completely revolutionized the Roman legal system between 527 and 534. The project purged and invalidated every law that Justinian's advisors found to be outdated or objectionable and, in effect, completely restarted a Roman legal system that had its roots in the early Republic. This sort of radical reform had never been done before. It also cut against the foundational idea that Roman law was a millennium-old living tradition built on layers of legal precedents and juridical interpretations that extended back to the fifth century BC. Justinian did not care. He undertook this reform, he wrote in 534, because he governed an "empire which was delivered to us by the Heavenly Majesty under the authority of God"[52] and "the supreme indulgence of the Deity" charged him with rationalizing "the entire ancient law, which was in a state of confusion for almost 1400 years."[53] This was Christian, Roman progress extending irrevocably into areas of Roman life that had retained structural elements of Rome's pre-Christian past.

Justinian's reform conspicuously destroyed centuries of Roman legal tradition. Roman lawyers had long talked about the *quinquaginta decisiones,* fifty intractable legal questions that involved complicated and often conflicting legal interpretations.[54] These had effectively become exercises in legal reasoning that tested lawyers' ability to frame legally binding arguments and counterarguments. Between 529 and 534, however, Justinian issued laws that resolved them all.[55] These were scholarly exercises rather than active controversies and thus, on one level, completely pointless. But issuing the laws was also a power move by the emperor. By solving the unsolvable, Justinian reinforced his claim that he had removed "every inconsistency from the sacred laws, hitherto inharmonious and confused . . . by the favor of Heaven."[56]

Justinian genuinely believed that his historic legal reform program succeeded because of the intimate involvement of the Christian God. Just as God had a stake in the emperor's successful reform of the Roman legal system, so too did the emperor have a role to play in regulating how Romans worshipped God. This role was by no means a novelty in the 530s—emperors had regulated religious practices since Augustus and had legislated about Christian orthodoxy since the 380s—but Justinian approached religious issues differently. The emperors preceding him had regulated the religious behavior of both Christians and non-Christians and had largely defined Christian orthodoxy either through the bishops with whom one held communion or the active profession of the creeds of ecumenical councils.[57] In legislative terms, one was orthodox if one said orthodox creeds, did orthodox things, and associated with other orthodox people.

For Justinian, however, orthodoxy depended upon both what one did and what one believed—and his laws reflected this view. Beginning with *Codex Justinianus* 1.1.5, a law issued in the first months of his reign in 527, Justinian's legislation related to orthodoxy and heresy contained long doctrinal statements mandating what an orthodox Christian must believe.[58] Justinian continued to do this in subsequent laws, with the statements of correct belief growing in length and complexity.[59] His laws established clear consequences for people who took appropriately orthodox actions but did not adhere to Justinian's ideas about orthodox belief. Justinian resolved to strip imperial offices and social ranks from anyone who "embraced the true and orthodox faith only in pretense" and punished other officials who did not look into the sincerity of another official's religious beliefs.[60]

These restrictions were not mere abstractions. They affected real people. Justinian's laws designed to make a better, more Christian Roman Empire targeted large numbers of actual Romans, Christian and non-Christian, whose beliefs and religious practices he deemed to be insufficiently Christian. Pagans lost their government jobs in 529 and then, a few years later, Justinian launched a round of persecutions in the capital that targeted "famous persons, nobles and others—teachers of grammar, sophists, lawyers, and physicians," who, he believed, had defied the ban on pagans serving in government.[61] He issued an edict that led to the cessation of teaching at the Athenian Platonic school, an action that combined with the emperor's other anti-pagan laws to prompt the Athenian philosophers to seek refuge in Persia.[62] They fled, a contemporary tells us, because "it was impossible for them to live without fear of the laws" in the Roman Empire.[63] In the 540s, widespread anti-pagan actions in the cities of Western Asia Minor led to the forced conversion of, a witness said, 70,000 urban and rural pagans.[64]

Other religious minorities suffered under Justinian as well. Roman Christians who did not agree with the emperor's theological definitions of orthodoxy found themselves sent into exile or killed.[65] Other Christian groups were forbidden from meeting, holding services, appointing priests, and administering baptism.[66] Justinian ordered the destruction of Samaritan synagogues, prohibited their reconstruction, and had imperial forces massacre Samaritans following a revolt in Palestine.[67] Jews saw their legal status dropped so that they were no longer eligible to hold public office, they were not permitted to testify against orthodox Christians engaged in lawsuits, and they were forbidden from inheriting property unless they converted to Christianity.[68] The emperor even prohibited the use of Hebrew in worship.[69]

The early sixth century then offers two very distinctive Roman Empires. The empire run by Theoderic downplayed the religious differences between sovereign and subject while embracing Italy's deep legal and institutional continuity with the Roman imperial past.[70] Evoking comparisons with Trajan and Valentinian, Theoderic catalyzed a Western Roman recovery that stabilized Italy and restored Roman control over territory lost in the fifth century. This was, in many ways, a new imperial dynast pushing a thoroughly conventional story of Roman renewal after a period of decline. Romans from Pliny to Eutropius could recognize the institutions of his empire and the measures it used for success.

Justinian's Constantinopolitan empire was quite different. Justinian continued to embrace the idea of Christian Roman progress that began to be developed in the fourth century. He believed that God had given him control over the empire in order to protect the state by ensuring its Christian orthodoxy and preserving its church from disorder. His empire needed to continue to evolve into a stronger, more perfect Christian state in order to do so. Its greatest days then lay ahead of it. Roman tradition still mattered to Justinian, but progress mattered more. Because of that belief, Justinian upended the Roman legal traditions that Theoderic upheld, invalidating the pieces of nearly a millennium of evolving Roman law. While Theoderic explicitly confirmed the rights of religious minorities like Jews, Justinian did his best to destroy the religious diversity that remained in his empire.[71] Justinian's Roman Empire then did more violence to the long-standing practices of Roman government and principles of Roman society than the Italian regime that he had demoted into a Gothic kingdom.

Justinian could behave in this way because his empire's continued military and political success insulated him from the sort of literary soul searching that Western decline had forced on Orosius, Augustine, Salvian, and Paulinus of Pella. In the East, Romans remained the chosen people of God, citizens of an empire that would subdue its enemies as long as its emperor, his church, and his subjects remained faithful. As part of the process of ensuring Roman faithfulness, the emperor saw it as his duty to push the empire toward his view that orthodoxy involved both religious practices and genuine adherence to specified Christian beliefs. This Roman Empire continually moved forward in a fashion that edited and updated the Roman past to bring it into alignment with an evolving Christian Roman future. In one of history's great twists, the Eastern Roman Empire that shattered so many centuries-old Roman conventions was the Roman state that used the pretext of Roman restoration to provoke a war that devastated the city of Rome, ravaged the cities of Italy, and killed hundreds of thousands of Romans.

Large segments of the West were indeed restored to the Roman Empire of Justinian, but ideas of what Rome was and who Romans were had been fundamentally disrupted. Genuine continuity with the Roman past now mattered less than claims on Christian orthodoxy proven by imperial success. In the sixth century, this shift gave Constantinople the power to attack Rome. But Justinian's success in delegitimizing a self-described Roman regime and attacking a people who saw themselves as Roman also opened up space for the West to try to reclaim its Roman Empire if Constantinopolitan strength and orthodoxy ever faltered. That time would come.

11

ROME, THE ARABS, AND ICONOCLASM

JUSTINIAN BET THAT scrapping many of the assumptions and traditions that had shaped the Roman world would lead to a better Christian Roman future. Many of these bets went bad. By the early seventh century, Eastern Romans confronted undeniable political and military problems across every frontier. Coups rocked the capital while Lombards in Italy, Avars in the Balkans, and Persians in the East broke through imperial frontiers and captured vast amounts of Roman territory. If Romans believed that their successes grew out of imperial virtue and orthodoxy, the crises they confronted must have then grown out of sinfulness and heresy.

The idea that imperial sinfulness caused problems for the empire had long been a part of Christian Roman thought. Salvian of Marseille, for example, saw the corruption and sinfulness of the western aristocracy feeding Rome's long fifth-century contraction. In Constantinople and the East, tales of Roman sinfulness usually worked within narrower chronological and geographic contexts. So, for example, after Justinian killed thousands of Romans in order to suppress the Nika Riot, he branded the riot an act of sinfulness by Romans in Constantinople. God punished the sinners by allowing the destruction of much of the monumental center of the city.[1] The city was saved, the hymnist Romanos the Melode wrote, only because Justinian and others in the city asked God for compassion.[2] When God granted it, the emperor built the magnificent new church of Hagia Sophia to mark the reconciliation of Romans and the Christian God.[3]

Early-sixth-century Romans could see their history as a cycle in which sinfulness and impiety emerged, divine punishment followed, and the punishment then brought repentance and reconciliation—sometimes even a few weeks later. By the 610s, however, it was clear to Romans that God's anger would no longer be easily calmed. That decade saw Romans lose control of much of the Eastern Mediterranean for the first time in nearly seven centuries. The Persian Empire took Damascus in 613, Jerusalem in 614, and Alexandria in 619. Unlike in previous Roman-Persian conflicts, the Persians intended to keep the territories they took. Persian governors assumed control over these areas, extracting onerous taxes from their new subjects to pay for the ongoing war effort.

Accounts of the Persian capture of Jerusalem speak of over 60,000 people killed, sacred buildings destroyed, and floods of refugees fleeing to Alexandria.[4] They also make clear where blame for this disaster lay. A biography of John, the bishop of Alexandria who took in many of the refugees who fled the Persian forces in Palestine, explains that "the Lord allowed His churches in Jerusalem to be burnt down by the heathen Persians because of the multitude of our sins."[5]

Palestinian sources are even more explicit. A composite history attributed to Antiochus Strategos, a monk in the monastery of St. Sabas in the Judean desert outside of Jerusalem, blamed the Persian assault on the supporters of the Blue and Green chariot racing teams, the violence Justinian inflicted on his subjects in the Nika Riot, and the marriage of the emperor Heraclius to his niece.[6] As the Persians approached the walls of Jerusalem, monks they had taken captive informed the Persian army that "because of their sins" Jerusalem had been "given over into the hands of our enemies."[7] All was not lost, however, because God "desires not the death of the sinner, but that he may turn again and live." Thus he "sent on us the evil Persian race as a rod of chastisement and medicine of rebuke."[8]

Antiochus then recalls in great detail the horrors that followed Jerusalem's capture. Scores of Romans were captured and led off to Persia as slaves. Christian nuns were raped, monks were killed, and clergy were taken to Persia and forced to defend their faith. The Persian king even stole the True Cross, taking it from the orthodox in Jerusalem and giving charge over it to Persian Christians, whom the Romans believed to be heretics.

God was merciful once the sinful Romans had been punished. In 628, fourteen years after the capture of Jerusalem, the emperor Heraclius emerged victorious over the Persians. His forces "reached Persia, took possession of many of its cities and royal palaces, killed thousands of Persian soldiers, led back again the Romans[9] who had been carried into captivity, and liberated the Christians from slavery." The culmination of this Heraclian restoration came on March 21, 631, when the emperor entered Jerusalem, looked at "the restoration of the holy places," and "re-established in its own place the glorious and precious tree of the Cross, sealed as before in a chest, just as it had been carried away."[10] With the damage done by the Persians now repaired, the cycle of sin, punishment, repentance, and restoration was now complete. Heraclius, the empire, and the Christians of Palestine could again move forward, reconciled in God.

Roman Christians in Constantinople experienced this period of apparent divine punishment differently. Constantinople never fell to the Persians, but, in 626, it was besieged by the combined forces of Persians to its east and barbarian Avars coming from the north. Constantinopolitan Christians could not know when or whether God would remove his protection from the imperial capital. They could only beg for his mercy.

Heraclius understood how to weaponize their insecurity during these desperate days. Romans in Constantinople knew that their collective sins had pushed the empire to the brink of extinction.[11] They had also come to learn that genuine, sincere, and timely repentance could bring about its salvation. It was during the Avar and Persian siege of Constantinople in August 626 that they were taught to appreciate the true power of divine protection. The siege lasted for ten days. The outnumbered Roman defenders weathered an artillery barrage, blocked the crossing of Persian forces from Asia to Europe, and defeated a simultaneous assault on the city's western land walls and its northern sea walls bordering the Golden Horn.[12] Witnesses at the time reported that God through "the welcome intercession of his unblemished Mother . . . saved the city from the utterly godless enemies who encircled it." One report even described the Virgin Mary herself fighting attackers atop the city walls.[13]

A homily delivered by Theodore Syncellus on the first anniversary of the Roman victory explained how Roman sins prompted this siege and how Romans had emerged victorious.[14] Heraclius had already headed east to attack the Persians when "he entrusted the city . . . to God and the Virgin" and charged Sergius, the patriarch of the city, with preparing this part of the Roman defenses. Sergius posted images of the Virgin along the city's western gates that faced the Avar force and then led a procession of priests atop the walls while Bonus, the city's military commander, marshaled its human defenders.[15] Sergius "beseeched God and the Virgin to keep the city . . . intact" [16] because the fate of Constantinople would determine the survival of both Christianity and the Roman Empire. Neither one, this Roman audience was told, was likely to survive without the other.

Because the stakes were so high, Theodore told his listeners, the Virgin herself defended the city. She beat back an Avar attack on the third day, "present everywhere," spreading "fear and horror upon the enemy and strength to her servants."[17] On the eighth day, the "Mother of God . . . safeguarded the city and all its inhabitants" by sinking enemy boats before they could assault the sea walls.[18] After the Avars retreated from the city, the Persian general across the Bosporus from the city supposedly said that "it is obvious that a divine and superhuman power guards this city and kept it safe and sound. It is impossible for anyone to harm it."[19]

Theodore concluded by telling his audience that the Roman victory in 626 showed the Persians, the Avars, and all the nations of the world how the Christian God protected his chosen people.[20] It also had a clear lesson for Romans. The "multitude of their sins" could have been "the cause of the devastation of this great city, its beautiful buildings, the brilliant houses," but they "received forgiveness" from God and protection from the Virgin. Part of this redemption had to do with Heraclius, whom Theodore calls "another David" and whom he describes as the shepherd of the Roman people. Part too came from the fact that, if the Roman people remained faithful and thankful in the future, they could believe that God and the Virgin would "always save the city and its people."[21]

A narrative of Roman decline and restoration crystallized in the year after the empire's near death. The loss of so much territory and the threat of utter destruction grew out of the sins of ordinary Romans. It was a push for God's chosen people to repent and bring their conduct in line with the piety and devotion of their emperor. God would not let them fail, however. The Romans fought under his protection and, when they recovered from the catastrophes their sins brought upon them, all nations would realize God's true power. Romans in the pulpits of Constantinople now claimed to be sure of this belief.

Heraclius's ultimate victory over Persia in 628 fulfilled this promise. The disasters of the 610s now sat alongside the glorious victories of the 620s—and they could be explained by one narrative. The war had started under Heraclius's predecessor, the sinful emperor Phocas (602–610), and Roman losses piled up as the empire's subjects failed to correct their behavior even after Heraclius took power. The piety of Heraclius, the repentance of the Roman people he led, and the power of God made the empire whole again. As the 630s dawned, Romans began to consider what it actually meant to be ruled by a man who thought that he was "adorned by God with victories" like David and "endowed with the devotion and true faith" of Solomon.[22] Heraclius believed that he owed his life, his kingdom, and his people's freedom to God. Now he would guide his subjects toward the true faith God had empowered him to defend.

The confidence that God had chosen Heraclius to superintend his people proved to be a dangerous delusion. After all, how did one argue against God's chosen sovereign? How did such an emperor now govern territories filled with people who might not agree with his ideas of what constituted true Christian faith? The risks of political miscalculations, military overconfidence, and religious inflexibility born of imperial arrogance loomed, but these dangers were not immediately apparent to Heraclius's enthusiastic supporters. Authors writing soon after Heraclius's Persian victory in 628 compared it to the victory of Christ over Satan.[23] They spoke about how the labors of his Persian campaigns purified Heraclius of his sins and redeemed the Roman world from those of its people.[24] The poet George of Pisidia even framed the Persian victory as something analogous to the world's redemption by Christ.[25]

This redemption proved so short lived that Heraclius himself saw it end. The East again lost all of its territories in Syria, Palestine, and Egypt a little more than a decade after the signing of the treaty ending the long Persian war. Following a series of initial incursions into central Syria in 634 and 635, Arab Muslim armies defeated a large Roman force at the Battle of Yarmouk in Syria during the summer of 636. They completed the conquest of Syria and Palestine in less than four years, with the final Roman fort in Syria falling by 640.[26] The Romans then surrendered Egypt in 642, with Arab armies advancing to within 250 miles of Carthage before retreating in 648.

Cyprus, Crete, and Rhodes were raided. Following two more invasions of North Africa, Muslim Arab armies took Carthage in 698. By 709, their North African domains extended to Tangier and the Atlantic Ocean.[27]

As Arab armies began winning victories in the territories that Heraclius had just reconquered, one could also begin to question whether Heraclius really enjoyed the divinely favored status that he and his backers claimed. These doubts might even have infected some of the ongoing propagandistic projects that Heraclius's supporters had begun in better times.

In the late 620s, Theophlyact Simocatta, an Egyptian probably acting under the supervision of the patriarch Sergius, began a work intended to recount the great Roman wars of the 570s through the 620s.[28] In the heady days of the early 630s, Sergius seems to have been particularly interested in projects updating the story of the empire to emphasize the significance of Heraclius's imperial renewal and the Roman Christian progress that he had resumed.[29] The *Chronicon Paschale*, a universal chronicle extending from the reign of Diocletian to Heraclius's triumphal restoration of the True Cross to Jerusalem in 630 fit into this project, but Theophylact's history served as a much more prestigious capstone.[30] This was to be no mere chronicle. Theophylact intended for his work to fit into the 1000-year-old tradition of classical historical writing that began with Herodotus and Thucydides and climaxed with his story of Heraclius.

Theophylact planned to chart the history of the empire, beginning in 582 with the reign of the emperor Maurice (the endpoint of the history of Menander Protector, the last work of classicizing history before Theophylact).[31] He would then recount Rome's descent into tyranny and dysfunction under Maurice's successor, Phocas, before charting its revival under Heraclius.

A prophecy that Theophylact includes in the history explains more specifically what he believes the work will show. Chosroes, the Persian king, supposedly told an Armenian general that "the Babylonian nation will hold the Roman state in its power" for twenty-one years, that the "Romans will enslave the Persians" for six years, and then a "day without evening will dwell among mortals." In this new Golden Age of man, "the forces of destruction" would dissolve and "those of the better life will dominate."[32] This chronology matches the period of Persian occupation of Roman territories starting under Phocas and the six years of campaigning Heraclius mounted against Persia until 628. The new Golden Age of peace must then begin following Heraclius's victory.

Theophylact's *History* never gets to this promised conclusion. It instead stops abruptly with the death of the emperor Maurice in 602, before the events covered in the prophecy even begin. While Theophylact never explains the reason for his failure to describe the Heraclian renewal that had been predicted, it is not hard to guess why his *History* stopped when it did. The Arab conquests of the 630s showed that Theophylact's entire historical model was wrong. The decline under Phocas was not an ephemeral Roman nadir from which the empire climbed on its way to a new Golden Age. The zenith of 630 was instead ephemeral. Roman decline was real. Heraclian renewal was nothing more than a false promise. Something was clearly wrong with the empire—and it did not seem easily corrected.

The premature termination of Theophylact's narrative encapsulates a wider crisis of confidence that afflicted Romans across the Mediterranean for the rest of the seventh century. Heraclius himself felt it. The Arab victory at the Battle of Yarmouk in 636 and the subsequent Arab Muslim advance through Syria and Palestine broke the emperor. A later Syrian tradition tells of Heraclius leaving Syria "like someone who had given up all hope" as he beat a strategic retreat back into Asia Minor.[33]

A Greek source picks up the story when the emperor reaches the Asian shore across from the capital. He "was afraid of embarking on the sea" so "after a considerable time, the noblemen of the court caused the prefect to collect a great many ships and tie them one next to the other so as to bridge the straits . . . and to make on either side a hedge of branches and foliage so that, as he went by, [the emperor] would not even catch sight of the sea."[34] This tale is probably fictional, but it nevertheless captures a situation in which the emperor who once claimed to be a second David chosen by God suddenly found himself unable to collect taxes, provision armies, or even prevent communities from negotiating their own surrender terms with the Arabs.[35] The Heraclian Golden Age ended before the propagandists chosen to proclaim its advent even finished their work.

Romans believed that they understood why. Sin. Both the emperor individually and the wider behavior of Roman civilians came in for scrutiny.

Constantinopolitan voices revived the old complaints about Heraclius's incestuous marriage that were conveniently disregarded in the early 630s. One even tied the urinary-tract problems of the emperor (that caused his "private parts to turn around and discharge the urine in his face") to this abomination.[36]

Other sources place the blame much more widely. Maximus the Confessor, a prominent opponent of the Monothelete doctrine that Christ had both human and divine natures but acted with one will, attacked Sergius and Heraclius for promoting Monotheletism after the Persian victory. Maximus wrote to a Palestinian associate that the "barbarous desert people overrunning" the empire "happened because of the great number of our sins."[37] In late-seventh-century Egypt, the clergyman John of Nikiu explained that God punished the Romans because, under Heraclius and the Alexandrian patriarch Cyrus, "they defiled the Church by an unclean faith," and they "persecute those who do not agree with them."[38] In Syria during the late seventh century, an unknown anti-Chalcedonian author wrote a poem in Syriac that describes how the sins of the Romans led to conquest by the Persians. Then, "when wickedness has increased in the world . . . a people will go forth from the desert, the sons of Hagar."[39] These Arabs "will plunder the ends of the earth," "countries will be devastated," and "all people will be humbled."[40]

Hope for a Roman renewal still surfaced occasionally, even during the difficult middle decades of the seventh century. The same Syriac work that describes the assault of the sons of Hagar also speaks about how the Arabs will be defeated by peoples from the North and then an angelic host will descend from heaven to lead the chastened Romans back to power.[41] The prophesized renewal might have even seemed plausible if the work was written during the early 680s, a moment when a peace treaty between the Romans and Arabs allowed a large Roman army to attempt to absorb the Slavs and Bulgars who had pushed Rome back from the Danube while the empire's attention was turned to the east. But this Roman recovery was not to be. The Bulgars soundly defeated the Roman force and, in 693, the Roman emperor Justinian II broke the peace with the Arabs as well. The Roman state fell into another twenty-five years of political and military crises.

Christians outside of the empire moved on. By the late 680s, some of them looked to other Christians who would spearhead a revival. A theologically framed response to the Arab conquests written in the Syrian monastery of John Kāmul around 687 looked not to the Romans for deliverance from the Muslim regime but to a group of local rebels called the Shurtē. The author claimed that "the coming of these Shurtē and their victory are also from God . . . for it seems to me that by these ones the [Arabs'] kingdom will come to an end."[42]

By 692, Syriac literature had shifted again. The *Apocalypse of Pseudo-Methodius*, a text that interpreted the book of Daniel in a fashion that related to contemporary times, claimed that the Sons of Ishmael would enslave Christians for seventy years before God raised up a mystical Roman emperor who would overthrow the Arabs, reclaim Golgotha, and bring about the end of times.[43] Pseudo-Methodius here followed the long tradition that the Roman Empire represented the fourth of the four kingdoms mentioned in the book of Daniel and optimistically imagines Rome's return.

By the early 700s, it had become clear that the Arab kingdom was destined to remain in charge of Syrian lands for the foreseeable future. Syrian thinkers understood that, if Roman control of Syria and Jerusalem would not be restored, Rome could not in fact be the fourth and final kingdom prophesized by Daniel. Apocalyptic texts written after 700 then rework the old model, dropping Rome to the third of Daniel's kingdom—and inserting the Arab "kingdom of the South" as the final state in Daniel's prophecy.[44] A Roman return to Syria had now seemed too implausible even for an esoteric prophecy of the end of the world.

Romans still living under imperial control could not walk away from the promise of Roman renewal so easily. They were the ones who would suffer if the empire did not correct its course. As one would expect in a society that had come to link imperial success with the righteousness and orthodoxy of emperors and their subjects, Romans began questioning what they were doing wrong that brought about such unremitting divine disapproval. What, in short, could Romans do to change course, bring about God's mercy, and begin to recover from a century of brutal decline?

Romans cycled through a number of different ideas. In the 640s, figures like Maximus the Confessor and the popes Theodore I and Martin I blamed the heretical Monotheletism of Heraclius and his successor, Constans II.[45] A council convened by Pope Martin in Rome in 649 even equated the Monotheletes "who wage war upon the celestial Jerusalem—that is the Catholic Church" to the Muslims "who have waged war upon the terrestrial Jerusalem."[46] Their opponents, not surprisingly, blamed Maximus and Martin for the empire's troubles.[47] A Maronite Christian author wrote that victorious Arab conquerors followed Maximus wherever he went because "God's wrath punished everywhere that had accepted his error."[48]

The emperor Constans II was less poetic. In 653, he had Martin arrested in Rome and tried in Constantinople. The court convicted the pope of failing to secure imperial approval before his election and sending money and doctrinal documents to the Arabs.[49] Martin was then exiled to the Crimea, where he died in 655 or 656. Maximus for his part was arrested in 653 and put on trial in Constantinople in 655, just after the capital had survived an Arab attack.[50] He was charged with "hating the emperor and his empire," since he "betrayed Egypt, Alexandria, Pentapolis, Tripolis, and Africa to the Arabs" by telling a commander that "God did not deign that the empire of the Romans be assisted under the reign of Heraclius and his kin."[51] Maximus was sent into exile in 658, was tried again for "blasphemies" and "rebellions" in 662, and ultimately had his tongue cut out and hand amputated for his intransigence.[52]

This violence against opponents of imperial Monotheletism did nothing to improve Roman military fortunes. So, from late 680 into 681, the emperor Constantine IV convened a church council in Constantinople that condemned Monotheletism. Still the empire struggled. Monothelete clergy then pointed to the abandonment of the doctrine as a cause for continued Roman military problems in the early 700s. Things did not improve, however, when the emperor Philippicus reinstated the orthodoxy of Monotheletism during his brief reign between 711 and 713.[53]

None of these theological gymnastics seemed to have been particularly effective. The deacon Agathon, who lived through this chaotic period, spoke about "the frightful troubles which had come to pass . . . as a result of our sins." They "caused a weakening and a very great degree of destruction" to both "the body of the God-guarded polity" and "to the head of the empire itself."[54] He was right. The empire teetered precariously amid renewed Arab attacks and the fall of four different emperors between 711 and 717.[55]

Then the last great Arab siege of Constantinople began. The combined Arab land and naval blockade commenced soon after the emperor Leo III took power in March of 717. By the late summer, the Arab army sat outside of the western wall of the city while an Arab fleet sailed the narrow straits to its east. There they stayed for nearly a year despite Roman forces destroying their ships with a napalm-like incendiary called Greek fire and, eventually, cutting the supply lines that kept the Arab army fed.[56] Reduced to eating animals and, one source says, dung in pans, the Arabs finally retreated on August 15, 718, the date that Romans celebrated the Dormition of the Virgin Mary.

Roman sources credited "God and His all-holy virgin Mother" for "fulfilling those who truly call on him" despite their sins.[57] But, unlike the victory in 626, the retreat of the Arab forces did not seem to portend the dawn of a new age of Roman renewal. It did not even really change the Roman-Arab military dynamic. The Romans remained on the defensive into the 720s as Arab strategy shifted from knocking out the empire with one great blow to progressively chipping away at Roman control of Asia Minor. In 727, Arab armies even captured the old provincial capital of Caesarea in Cappadocia and advanced as far as Nicaea, a city less than a hundred miles from Constantinople.[58]

These defeats occurred soon after a massive volcanic eruption in the caldera below Santorini raised a new island in the sea and rained pumice on Greece and Asia Minor.[59] A later Roman source states emphatically that the spectacular natural disaster convinced Leo that "God was angry at him."[60] Other Romans agreed—and they believed that they understood what had angered God. While Nicaea sat under siege in 727, a soldier stationed there "saw an icon of the Mother of God. He picked up a stone and threw it at the icon and, when it fell, he broke it and trampled it."[61] As the emperor undoubtedly noticed, the city did not fall.[62] Icons were suspect.

In some ways, Iconoclasm, as the movement that attacked the use of icons in Roman worship came to be called, reflected another stage in the century-long quest for a theological formula that would end the punishment God seemed to be inflicting regularly on the sinful and disobedient

Romans. Iconoclasm differed from, say, the Monotheletism of Heraclius. Parading images of Christ, saints, and the Virgin had become a normal part of the Roman defensive plan when a city was besieged. Those who could fight did so. Those who could not prayed. Just as Roman weaponry evolved to meet new threats in the seventh century, so too did its spiritual arsenal. Images of Christian holy figures came to adorn city gates. They protected rural shrines. They even became a focus of how individual Romans interacted personally with God. By the late seventh century, some Roman Christians had even taken to bowing deeply when praying before these images.[63] Far more than Monotheletism, Iconoclasm attacked something very fundamental in how Romans sought divine help. But, also unlike Monothelitism, Iconoclasm seemed to work.

The vociferous later Roman reaction against Iconoclasm has obscured the exact path on which Leo pushed the empire.[64] In the main, though, the emperor seems to have attacked what Iconoclasts saw as excessive devotion toward images. Leo instead emphasized the power of the cross, a symbol that he credited with saving Constantinople in 717–718 and that later Iconoclasts would say "turn[ed] the enemy to flight and slaughter[ed] the barbarians."[65] Roman military fortunes began to improve as Leo pushed Romans to increasingly entrust their salvation to the cross. The 730s saw the Roman frontier with the Arabs stabilize somewhat. Then, in 740, Roman troops defeated and destroyed an invading Arab force at Akroinon in Asia Minor, killing thousands of soldiers and two commanders. This victory seemed to vindicate Leo's theological path.

Even greater Roman gains occurred under Leo's son and successor, Constantine V. Constantine's reign began inauspiciously when a revolt by his brother-in-law forced the emperor to flee the capital, but the emperor recovered from this disaster to retake Constantinople, publicly blind the rebel, and force him to retire to a monastery. Many prominent officers were killed, and the patriarch Anastasius, who had backed the coup, is said to have endured public jeering as he was paraded around the hippodrome on an ass.[66]

These events began thirty years of coolly executed Roman recovery that touched nearly every part of Roman life. Ruthless and talented, Constantine engineered a series of administrative, fiscal, and military reforms that greatly improved conditions in the empire. He also catalyzed Constantinople's recovery from an earthquake that damaged large portions of the city in 740 and a plague that ravaged it in 746. He repopulated the capital through forced migrations of Christians from within and even outside of the Roman territory he inherited.[67] He undertook a thorough rebuilding program that repaired Constantinople's massive land walls, reconnected and expanded the aqueduct of Valens (a watersource that had been cut by the Avars in 626), rebuilt the church of Hagia Eirene, and expanded the imperial palace.[68] Despite undertakings that employed thousands of skilled craftsmen and perhaps as many as 10,000 laborers across many years, Constantine left the treasury full.[69] Even his most vociferous opponents admitted that "Constantine made the city prosper."[70]

Constantine V did more than simply repair damage to the empire's cities. He also restored the capacity of the Roman military to mount offensive operations along its eastern and southern frontiers. Since the initial Arab rout of Heraclius's troops in the 630s, Romans had largely conducted defensive operations against Arab invaders. By the late 740s, the civil war that saw the Abbasid dynasty overthrow the Umayyads permitted Constantine to go on the offensive. Constantine capably launched Roman attacks into Arab territory for much of the next quarter century. In 751, his armies captured the cities of Theodosioupolis and Melitene in what is now eastern Turkey. He did not keep many of the Anatolian cities he conquered, however. Instead, Constantine moved their Christian populations to Constantinople and the Balkans, leaving a depopulated wasteland between Roman and Arab territory that made it difficult for Arab armies to provision themselves if they tried to raid Roman lands.[71] This brutal scorched-earth policy of ethnic cleansing nonetheless stabilized Rome's southern and eastern frontiers for much of the next century.

Constantine V also campaigned regularly in the Balkans, launching nine expeditions into Bulgar territory between 759 and 775.[72] The results were equally impressive. Constantine won major victories in 763, 765, and 772 while also rebuilding the Roman populations of the region through the forced transfer of people from the East. Here too his efforts stabilized the Roman frontier while also laying the foundation for the later Roman reconquest of inland Greece.

No emperor since Justinian had done as much to transform the Roman physical and administrative landscape as Constantine V. Perhaps none since Diocletian had so successfully changed the empire's security situation. With this pedigree, one would expect Constantine to be elevated to the very highest tier of Roman emperors. And he was—by some. It is widely acknowledged by even hostile sources that the Constantinopolitan population loved him. Others did as well. An ecclesiastical council he called in 754 "acclaimed him as the 'New Constantine' . . . who had abolished idolatry."[73] But Constantine V is not now remembered as the "New Constantine." He is instead called Constantine Copronymus (Constantine the Manure Named).

Constantine V has received this epithet because he brought the same brutal efficiency to religious matters that he did to the rest of his imperial responsibilities. If civic infrastructure, imperial finances, military structures, and frontier defenses could all be repaired, so too could imperial spiritual life. Even more than his father, Leo III, Constantine became associated with an aggressive, sometimes violent Iconoclasm.

Leo had been interested in restricting the public display and manner of prayer before images of Christ, Mary, and the saints. Constantine went further than this. He did not believe that Christ could be represented pictorially, because Christ was both fully human and fully divine. A picture could represent only his human aspect and thus it heretically ignored his divinity.[74] The emperor personally led a public campaign to persuade his subjects about the correctness of these ideas. He wrote texts against icon veneration and arranged public meetings to discuss them. In 754, he summoned a church council that sanctioned his iconoclastic approaches.[75] This council agreed with the emperor that one cannot "divide the flesh that had been fused with the Godhead" by "painting a picture" of Christ "as if it were that of a mere man."[76] From that point forward "anyone who presumes to manufacture an icon, or to worship it, or to set it up in a church or a private house or to hide it" will be "deemed guilty under imperial law as a foe of God's commands."[77]

Later sources suggest that Constantine ruthlessly enforced these prohibitions. They describe a series of imperial actions against monks, laity, and churches that, in their view, rose to the level of a second Great Persecution.[78]

Constantine's agents covered up or replaced figural mosaics in churches and pulled down other iconographic representations of Christ.[79] They also attacked people who resisted the new policies. In 761 or 762, Constantine ordered a monk whipped to death in the hippodrome for calling him a new Julian.[80] Between 765 and 766, Constantine again tortured a monk to death, compelled his soldiers and officers to publicly swear that they would not make use of icons, and publicly humiliated many of the most prominent Iconophile abbots in the hippodrome.[81] Constantine ordered a monk who lived atop a pillar in the capital to be pulled down, tied up, and left to die in a cemetery. Other monks were supposedly sealed up in bags and thrown into the sea. In October of 767, Constantine publicly tortured the patriarch of Constantinople in front of Hagia Sophia before shaving his face, head and eyebrows. He was then seated backward on an ass and led into the hippodrome to be jeered at and spat upon before the emperor ordered him executed. His head hung for three days at the Milion, the ceremonial center of the city, as an example to the impious.[82]

While anti-Iconoclast sources certainly exaggerate the scope of Constantine's violence, there can be no doubt that the emperor worked to reform the orthodoxy of the empire with the vigor and forcefulness that accompanied other parts of his Roman renewal. The birth of the reformed empire of this "New Constantine" came at a great cost. The material, political, and military success of the empire had become ever more closely tied to the orthodoxy of Roman Christian belief and the relative sinfulness of the Roman population. By the late eighth century, the prosecution and persecution of Christian religious dissenters had become an essential part of how emperors performed their divinely sanctioned task of protecting the state. Roman decline and renewal remained politically potent concepts, but the personal costs Romans now endured to facilitate that renewal continued to grow dearer. For some in the West, they would soon become unbearable.

12

OLD ROME, NEW ROME, AND FUTURE ROME

THE ROMAN RECOVERY begun by Leo III and accelerated by his son Constantine V was real and substantive. These emperors rebuilt and repopulated the capital, reformed the Roman administrative system, and succeeded in stabilizing the empire's frontiers with the Arabs and Bulgars. Their success did not extend to all parts of the empire, however. Both Leo and Constantine struggled to hold on to Roman possessions in northern and central Italy—a struggle they largely lost. Their failure would have profound and unexpected consequences for Romans.

Roman Italy at the turn of the eighth century consisted of a string of centers of power that had held out against principalities set up after the late-sixth-century Lombard invasion of Italy. These principalities included a Lombard kingdom in the north centered on the city of Pavia and two southern Italian Lombard duchies based in Spoleto and Benevento. Roman administration was based in Ravenna, near the mouth of the Po River. The exarch of Ravenna exercised authority over Venetia and the northern Adriatic coast, the city and duchy of Rome, and a strip of central Italian territory that joined Rome with Ravenna. Romans also controlled much of Calabria and Apulia in the south.

As early as the 720s, the duchy of Rome experienced a terrible combination of ineffective political leadership and growing tension with the Lombards. Seven dukes held power between 724 and 743, but all of them ultimately depended upon the exarch of Ravenna, the most important Roman official on the peninsula, for military support.[1] The exarchs of Ravenna had less and less ability to provide this support.

Imperial ineffectiveness had compelled popes to take political affairs connected to the city into their own hands since the late 710s, but a series of imperial actions taken in the early 730s particularly antagonized the bishop of Rome. The bishop and emperor disagreed about the importance of icons (a point underlined by a papal council, convening in 731, that rejected Iconoclasm), but this disagreement does not seem to have been the most significant source of tension. Mid-eighth-century popes and emperors were much more concerned about how reforms of Leo III affected church finances. The Roman bishops had legitimate concerns about the emperor taking direct control of funds generated by papal properties in southern Italy, shifting control over churches in Sicily and southern Italy from the pope to the patriarch of Constantinople, and registering all Italian male children living under Roman imperial control.[2]

All of these things displeased the popes, but they remained policy disagreements that unfolded within a Roman imperial system that had provided security and stability in Italy for much of the past 200 years. By the late 730s, the Roman imperial system began to buckle in the face of Lombard aggression. In 739, Ravenna, the seat of Constantinopolitan control of Italy since the time of Justinian, fell to the Lombards. It was reconquered by the Romans soon afterwards, but this spectacular Roman failure so shocked pope Gregory III that he began looking for military allies beyond the empire.

This was a big step. The pope remained a Roman imperial subject and he lived in an imperially controlled city, but he no longer felt that he could depend on the empire for protection. Gregory's first foray into freelance diplomacy failed badly. Fearing the Lombard king, the pope sought support from the Lombard dukes in Spoleto and Benevento, independent sovereigns who sometimes opposed the efforts of the Lombard king in Pavia. This effort secured no substantial assistance. Even worse, Gregory's appeal signaled the current weakness of Rome's position to the Lombard king Liutprand.

Gregory also apparently did not understand that, by acting independently of the emperor, the papacy had now made itself an unpredictable player in central Italian politics. The Roman Empire posed no existential threat to the Lombard king. He grasped its Italian objectives and capacities. But a pope acting on his own outside of imperial control was new. If a pope ever figured out how to draw more powerful and expansionist allies to his cause, the papacy could potentially become quite dangerous. Liutprand decided that Rome needed to be taken before it learned to activate its latent power.

Gregory soon sensed the situation's urgency. He followed his failed appeal to the southern Italian duchies with another, more desperate appeal to Liutprand's northern neighbors, the Franks. This was the sort of move that Liutprand feared. The Frankish kingdom had developed into northwestern Europe's most powerful Catholic Christian kingdom across the sixth and seventh centuries. By the 730s, Frankish territory extended across much of what is now modern France, Germany, and Switzerland—but the Franks had largely refrained from involvement in affairs south of the Alps.

This remoteness is part of what made Gregory's appeal so extraordinary, but the pope also framed it in an extraordinary fashion. He addressed Charles Martel, the Frankish master of the palace who ran affairs in the kingdom on behalf of the Merovingian king Childeric III, the ceremonial Frankish monarch. The pope understood what he could promise Charles. In two increasingly desperate letters written in 739 and 740, he offered Charles divine blessings if he would help the church but warned that "the Prince of the Apostles" might "shut the Heavenly Kingdom against" Charles if he "despises my appeal or turns deaf ears to my plea."[3] Charles Martel replied in a friendly but noncommittal way that encouraged more dialog but offered no promises. Gregory's overtures to the Franks had failed to produce any tangible, positive effect. But they did set a precedent for his successors.

Gregory died in 741 with Liutprand preparing to move on Rome. The new pope, Zacharias, reached out to the Lombard king and secured an agreement with him to return four towns he had taken from Roman imperial control. In exchange, the pope would not pursue any diplomatic cooperation with the rival Lombard courts in Spoleto or Benevento. Neither side mentioned the Franks. In fact, Zacharias made clear that he still considered himself a subject of the Roman emperor in Constantinople. Upon his appointment, Zacharias sent a letter to Constantinople to inform the new emperor Constantine V of his selection. Zacharias, of course, wanted a direct commitment by Constantine to provide more troops to reinforce the defenses of Rome and central Italy. Constantine had no inclination to do so. His eastern wars meant that the emperor had no trained troops to spare. Italy would have to fend for itself.[4]

This indifference helped deepen the nascent papal alliance with the Franks. In 749, Zacharias responded to a Frankish request that he endorse the plan by Pippin, the son of Charles Martel, to replace the Merovingian Frankish monarchy with one headed by his family.[5] Then, in 752, the Lombard capture of Ravenna and the subsequent moves by their king, Aistulf, against the city of Rome prompted the new pope Stephen II to ask Pippin for help.[6]

Stephen might not have known it at the time, but he stood at the intersection of a millennium-old Roman past and a dawning new Roman future. For much of the past generation, popes had skillfully carved out political control over Rome and its surroundings as imperial authority over central Italy faded. Popes had never declared independence or broken with the empire—but even the emperors were now acknowledging the accumulating papal power.

While Stephen knew he lacked the resources to fight off any Lombard attack, he now had a choice of two different powers who might protect his position. The old empire offered unrivaled historical prestige, but Pippin's Franks pointed to a bright Catholic Christian future. His was a barbarian kingdom, but it was also one willing to send powerful armies into Italy. At that moment, Frankish armies meant more to the pope than Roman history.

A new chapter in European history began when Stephen crossed the Frankish frontier to meet his partners. Accompanied by a growing retinue of Italian and Gallic clergy, the pope was met by a party led by the king's eleven-year-old son, Charles, the boy who would grow up to be called Charlemagne. Stephen spent the winter of 753–754 at the St. Denis monastery outside Paris while he negotiated some sort of Frankish protection for the papacy. In April, an assembly of Frankish nobles agreed to support the pope with a military expedition to Italy, should that prove necessary.[7] Pippin then wrote to Aistulf to demand that Aistulf "return the property of the holy church of God and of the Roman Republic."[8] In July, the pope consummated the papal-Frankish alliance by presiding at a ceremony in which he anointed Pippin both king of the Franks and patrician of the Romans.[9]

Pippin had just recognized the independence of a divinely sanctioned Roman Republic centered on central Italy and run on God's behalf by the pope. There were now two political entities claiming officially to be Roman—the papal Roman Republic based in the city of Rome and the Roman Empire based in Constantinople.[10] Pippin promptly backed up this split by leading a small Frankish force into Lombard territory. He defeated the troops of Aistulf and then besieged the king in Pavia.[11] Aistulf soon sued for peace. The "beloved by God" treaty that resulted bound "Romans, Franks, and Lombards" and compelled Aistulf to "return the city of Ravenna with its other municipalities."[12] Ravenna was to be returned to the Romans—just not the same Romans from which it was originally taken.

It took a second Frankish invasion to really secure this land for Stephen's Roman Republic. By Easter of 756, Pippin's forces had again defeated the Lombard army. Pippin then "made even more sure that the rights of St. Peter would be preserved" by dictating that "Ravenna . . . and the whole exarchate be handed over to St. Peter."[13] Papal sources describe how Pippin "issued a donation in writing" that gave these lands to "St. Peter, the holy Roman church, and the pontiffs of the Apostolic See forever" before turning over to the pope "the keys of the city of Ravenna and the various cities of the exarchate of Ravenna."[14] This document, which has come to be called the "Donation of Pippin," gave the papal Roman Republic the territory that, for much of the next millennium, would comprise the papal states.

With the Lombard threat neutralized, Stephen had to worry about how the Roman Empire and those Italians loyal to it would respond to the birth of his papal Roman Republic. Stephen and his successor, Paul, who held the papacy from 757 until 767, framed a novel counterattack. Popes were the true Roman sovereigns and Pippin remained "their Spiritual Compatriot, King of the Franks and Patrician of the Romans." The emperors of Constantinople and their subjects were no longer Romans, however. Stephen maintained that they had become "the Greeks."[15]

Pope Paul continued this argument, complaining to Pippin how cooperation between the "Greeks" and the Lombards threatened Rome in the early 760s.[16] By the middle of the decade, Paul took to contrasting the "orthodox king (Pippin) . . . our protector and defender" with the "impious wickedness of the heretical Greeks" who "humiliate the holy Catholic and apostolic church" and "destroy the holy orthodox faith and the tradition of the holy fathers."[17]

In 767, a church council held in Gentilly endorsed this framing of the Constantinopolitan Roman Empire as a land of heretical Greeks. Frankish sources described this event as "a great council . . . with Romans and Greeks" involved in a discussion about the appropriate role of icons in worship.[18] The Romans were, of course, the theologians sent by the pope. The Greeks were sent by the Roman emperor. Perhaps not surprisingly, the papal envoys convinced Pippin to endorse a pro-icon position.

By the early 770s, the papal Roman Republic controlled a belt of territory stretching from the Adriatic to the Tyrrhenian Gulf, but the basis on which that control rested was little more than the word of Pippin and the twenty or so city keys he had deposited in the Vatican. Locks could be changed—and so could the minds of Pippin's Frankish successors.

This situation led to a remarkable papal effort to justify its control of this territory. Popes began to claim that their authority over this land was not new. It was very, very old and Pippin and his Frankish armies had merely restored historical powers that the Roman state had once given to popes.

The papacy's proof lay in a document called the *Donation of Constantine*, an imperial law supposedly issued by the emperor Constantine I in the fourth century. The document was forged sometime between the 750s and early 770s and claimed that the pope enjoyed "supremacy" over all the other bishops in the church. It granted him vast properties across the empire, including the Lateran Palace in the city of Rome. It decreed that he should wear the same regalia as an emperor and use the same crown. It also "relinquished" to the pope "the city of Rome and all the provinces, districts, and cities of Italy and of the western regions" of the empire. From that point forward, the document continued, "our empire and the power of our kingdom should be transferred and changed to the regions of the East." In a delightful final flourish, the forged document condemned anyone who doubted the veracity of the document "to eternal damnation" so that "being burned in the deepest hell, he should perish with the devil."[19]

Popes of the 770s and 780s needed the *Donation of Constantine's* powerful support for their temporal power. Pope Paul died in 767 and Pippin died soon after, in September of 768. Then, in 773, the Lombard king Desiderius foolishly inserted himself into a Frankish dynastic quarrel. Frankish forces led by Charlemagne crossed the Alps, invaded northern

Italy, and placed the Lombard capital of Pavia under siege.[20] Charlemagne then traveled to Rome for Easter while his armies blockaded Pavia. Pope Hadrian, who had taken office in 772, organized an entry parade like those that greeted Roman rulers of old. Representatives of all the regions of the city of Rome met Charlemagne a mile outside of the walls, acclaimed him, and then led him into the city alongside crosses, the standards of the papal Roman Republic. They acted "just as if greeting an exarch or a patrician."[21]

On the Wednesday following Easter, Charlemagne and Hadrian held a public assembly in which the sovereigns and their advisors discussed what Italy would look like once Charlemagne had captured Pavia. Papal sources claim that Charlemagne endorsed dividing the Lombard kingdom in half, with the papal Roman Republic receiving all the lands of the old Roman exarchate, Venice, Istria, Tuscany, and all of the Lombard duchies of Spoleto and Benevento. This distribution, the pope claimed, matched what Charlemagne's father, Pippin, had supposedly agreed to in 754.[22] Scribes then drew up three copies of a treaty outlining these terms. Charlemagne received one copy, Hadrian took the second, and the third was placed on the tomb of St. Peter because, officially at least, St. Peter had recovered this territory. Charlemagne soon returned to his armies outside Pavia, captured the city, named himself "King of the Lombards," and then set to work organizing Frankish control of his Lombard kingdom. He also began ignoring the increasingly desperate calls from Hadrian to turn over all of the territory he had promised.

It was in this context that Pope Hadrian I first deployed the *Donation of Constantine*. In a letter to Charlemagne sent in May of 778, Hadrian wrote how, "in the times of the blessed Roman pontifex Sylvester, the Holy Catholic and apostolic Roman Church was elevated and raised and deemed worthy to be granted power over the West by the most pious Constantine, the great emperor." So too, "in your most fortunate age," he continued, "a new most Christian emperor Constantine reigns."[23] Charlemagne was to be this new Constantine. In this role, he was supposed to confirm Constantine's original grant of territory across Italy to the popes. But the pope knew better than to simply make this claim without offering Charlemagne anything in return. So Hadrian asked to reprise Stephen and Paul's role as the king's personal spiritual compatriot by offering to personally baptize Charlemagne's son.[24]

Charlemagne brushed aside Hadrian's offer. No Frankish army came to help the pope take such expansive territory, even after Hadrian threatened to use his own armies to attack the land if Charlemagne did not.[25] So Hadrian stopped asking. In 781, Charlemagne returned to Rome, celebrated Easter with the pope, and worked out a territorial settlement that gave Hadrian a band of land that stretched across Italy and included Tuscany, Campania, the exarchate of Ravenna, and some lands in the Apennines that had once belonged to the duchy of Spoleto.[26] Hadrian had not gotten all that he demanded, but the papal Roman Republic now controlled a substantial part of the Italian peninsula—more than enough to sustain itself politically.

It is then intriguing that further adjustments were made when Charlemagne returned to Rome in 787.[27] At that point, he added territory taken from Benevento and a promise to turn over Calabria to the promised papal lands. But there was a problem. These territorial grants were only aspirational. The Franks did not control Benevento and the Roman Empire still controlled Calabria.

This imbalance pointed to looming conflict between Old Rome and New. A few important things had changed between 781 and 787, many of which grew out of political and religious dynamics in Constantinople. Constantine V died in 775, concluding a thirty-four-year reign that saw dramatic Roman economic, administrative, and theological reforms as well as military successes in just about every arena except Italy. His successor, his son Leo IV, shared his father's prioritization of the Balkans and the East over Italian affairs. But Leo, who suffered from a chronic illness, died in 780, and was succeeded by his young son, Constantine VI. Constantine's mother, Irene, served as regent until the young emperor reached majority.

Irene soon initiated a strong diplomatic push to build an alliance with Charlemagne. She sent ambassadors to meet with Charlemagne when he came to Italy in 781 and proposed that her son, Constantine VI, should marry Charlemagne's daughter Rotrud. Irene even left a Greek teacher behind in Italy so that Rotrud could learn the language of her future husband.[28]

Pope Hadrian reacted with alarm to the Frankish and Constantinopolitan rapprochement. He tried to convince Charlemagne that the Roman Empire was weak by telling the king that an Arab army had penetrated deeply into Roman territory in 781 and 782.[29] Hadrian also began to massage the ego of the Frankish king. He mentioned Charlemagne in official prayers but removed any references to the Roman emperor in Constantinople. He started dating documents not by the regnal year of the Roman emperor but with the year that Charlemagne assumed control of Italy. He also continued to maintain the same friendly stance toward the king in his correspondence.[30]

These papal efforts amplified the impact of a diplomatic breakdown between the Roman Empire and the Franks. By 787, the marriage alliance joining the families of Irene and Charlemagne had ended, with Constantinopolitan sources claiming that Irene broke it off and western sources crediting Charlemagne.[31] Irene then sent a Roman army to intervene in an Italian conflict pitting forces allied with the Franks and those working with a Roman-backed duke of Benevento. Reinforced by a small Frankish contingent, the pro-Charlemagne forces defeated Irene's army and pushed the Romans back to southern Italy.[32] This was the first time that Frankish and Roman forces had fought each other since the reign of Justinian.

This fighting occurred amid theological developments in Constantinople that sidelined the Franks. As the 780s progressed, Irene and the bishops she associated with became increasingly vocal about their objections to Iconoclasm. In 786, they wrote to Rome to ask the papacy to send representatives to an ecumenical council that would condemn Iconoclasm and overturn the pro-Iconoclast council of 754. No Frankish bishops were invited. Indeed, no word of the ecumenical council appears to have been sent to the Franks at all. Instead, Irene intended this to be a properly ecumenical council in the traditional Roman imperial sense. Hadrian's subsequent agreement to send representatives meant that figures dispatched by the bishops of Rome, Constantinople, Jerusalem, Antioch, and Alexandria were all present. None from historically barbarian lands like Francia belonged among the luminaries from these traditional Christian centers.

The Franks reacted angrily when they learned the details of Irene's council, which has come to be known as the Second Council of Nicaea.[33] Frankish bishops complained that Irene's gender should have prevented her from presiding over the council and that there were no biblical grounds to support the use of icons in the fashion it endorsed.[34] Hadrian responded with a work called the *Hadrianum*, but that document only prompted Charlemagne to call a Frankish Synod in Frankfurt in 794. The document that came out of that synod, the *Libri Carolini*, offered the top theologians in the Frankish kingdom an opportunity to answer the Roman and papal claims of ecumenical authority put forward at Nicaea in 787.[35] The synod denied both the authority of the council and its strong endorsement of the use of icons, objects that, the Frankish bishops maintained, should never be prayed to but should, at most, serve only to instruct the unlettered.[36]

The *Libri Carolini* took an even more powerful position against the legitimacy of Nicaea. Its preface describes Charlemagne as a New David who was "anointed by God" to serve as "rector of the Christian people."[37] Because the king and his bishops had no presence at Nicaea in 787, the council could not be considered ecumenical.

The *Libri Carolini* then pressed the case for an entirely new way of thinking about Christian authority. The traditional, Roman imperial notion of an ecumenical Christianity defined by old great cities of the Mediterranean no longer applied in a world where the papacy worked more closely with a Christian kingdom based north of the Alps. Instead, a sort of spiritual universality would take priority. The churches of the East that mattered so greatly in the fourth, fifth, and sixth centuries now sat under Muslim control and presided over shrinking Christian populations. The Frankish church was strong and growing. It, not the old churches of the East, would need to be consulted about theological issues. Because the Franks had not been included at Nicaea, that council represented nothing more than a local, eastern Christian synod that spoke for dwindling Christian populations.

The synod of Frankfurt and its imperial patron had sent a clear message. If Pope Hadrian actually believed that Charlemagne was his "spiritual compatriot" he could no longer ignore the religious concerns of the king and his churches. Hadrian got the message. Neither he nor his successors removed the papal imprimatur of the Council of Nicaea in 787, but Hadrian also decided to endorse the Synod of Frankfurt. This endorsement made little theological sense. Many of the points asserted at Frankfurt were incompatible with things agreed at Nicaea, but that did not matter. Hadrian's wise political pivot away from the old Christian centers of the Mediterranean toward the new ones located north of the Alps aligned the papal Roman Republic even more tightly with its Frankish protector.

Hadrian, who died in 795, did not live long enough to superintend the next, spectacular phase in this transition. It was left to his successor, Pope Leo III, to take the final steps that would transform the European world. In the last years of the eighth century, Charlemagne started construction on an imperial capital in the German city of Aachen, an old Roman spa town once called Aquae Granni.[38] He built an octagonal church decorated with columns and marbles scavenged from the old Roman buildings in Ravenna as well as a massive palace in the city center (see Figure 12.1).[39] The palace itself contained three silver tables, one with a representation of the city of

FIGURE 12.1 CHARLEMAGNE'S THRONE SET WITHIN AACHEN CATHEDRAL DECORATED WITH SPOLIA FROM RAVENNA (PHOTO BY AUTHOR).

Constantinople, another with a likeness of the city of Rome, and a third that represented the entire universe.[40] They hinted strongly at Charlemagne's ambition to be more than a barbarian king—and their location in Aachen suggested that the Frankish capital now looked to claim its place as a third center of Roman authority.[41] So too did the name Charlemagne gave to his new capital: Roma Ventura. Future Rome.

Political disorder in the Roman Empire based in Constantinople and in the papal Roman Republic gave Charlemagne an opening to explore his options. In early 790, Constantine VI pushed his mother, Irene, aside as regent and began to rule in his own right, though without a great deal of success.[42] Then, in 797, Irene staged a coup. She had her son arrested, deposed, and blinded.[43] Irene took power alone, ruling in her own right until she too was deposed in 802. The old Roman Empire looked weak and divided.

So too did Leo III's papal Roman Republic. In April of 799, a group of conspirators led by a nephew of the deceased pope Hadrian attacked Leo and imprisoned him before "the faithful from the various cities of the Romans" helped him flee to Charlemagne.[44] A Frankish escort returned Leo to Rome later that year, where he was greeted by the clergy, "the leading men, the senate, the full militia, and the entire Roman people."[45] Then, in the summer or autumn of 800, Charlemagne decided to travel to Rome himself. The king arrived as winter fell and, on December 23, Charlemagne presided over a public meeting in which Leo swore that he had done nothing wrong.[46] The Frankish king and Roman patrician now stood out as the most powerful Roman figure in the world.

On Christmas Day of 800, Leo made official what the previous years had made clear. Charlemagne had transcended the traditional dignity of a Roman patrician. He deserved a more elevated title. As head of his own sacred Roman Republic, the pope "crowned [Charlemagne] with a precious crown" and "all the faithful Romans . . . cried out with one voice: 'To Charles, pious Augustus crowned by God, great and pacific emperor, life and victory.' . . . And by them all he was established Emperor of the Romans."[47] From this point forward, "the name Patrician was abandoned and he was now called Emperor and Augustus."[48] There were now three Romes: the empire in Constantinople (which traced an unbroken political lineage back to the eighth century BC), the papal Republic in Rome (which was, at best, fifty years old), and the newly born Roman Empire of Charlemagne.

Pope Leo could nevertheless claim that Roman tradition backed his midwifery of this third Roman state. The *Donation of Constantine*, the forgery that had defined the papal Roman Republic in the 770s, also entrusted the popes with the imperial diadem, the imperial palace, and "the crown from [the emperor's] own head."[49] Pope Sylvester supposedly chose not to wear the crown, but it and the Western imperial domains remained papal property. This ownership meant that Sylvester's eventual successor Leo could do what he wanted with both Constantine's crown and the Western Empire. Leo could, then, return the imperial title and the authority it carried to a political figure. None since Constantine had been worthy—until Charlemagne.

The staging of the event in Rome shows that Leo understood the importance of framing Charlemagne's coronation in traditional Roman terms. The city of Rome was much different from that of its imperial heyday. Its population had collapsed from a million to perhaps a few tens of thousands and, as it contracted, large parts of the sprawling city had fallen into ruin. One could still speak of a Roman senate, but, whatever the term meant in 800, that body no longer existed in any form that Cato, Symmachus, or Cassiodorus would recognize.[50] The same was true of the Roman militia and the Roman people. Neither evoked the fearsome, world-changing power of their ancient predecessors. The ghosts of the Roman past still lurked within the shrunken imperial city, however. Leo understood how to summon them to stage a coronation that evoked the traditions of the faded world to which they once belonged. Charlemagne's coronation did not renew the small, weak, but living city of Rome. It resurrected the glorious, powerful, and long-dead Western Roman Empire.

Like many of the Roman renewals that preceded it, the return to Roman greatness that Leo and Charlemagne promised had victims, because Charlemagne's coronation coincided with a new, aggressive assault on the legitimacy of the Roman Empire based in Constantinople. The *Annals of Lorsch*, a text that reflects the earliest Carolingian framing of the imperial coronation, lays out this attack. Its author writes, "Since the title of emperor had become extinct among the Greeks and a woman [i.e., Irene] claimed the imperial authority, it seemed to Pope Leo and to all the holy fathers who were present at the council . . . that Charles, king of the Franks, ought to be named emperor, for he held Rome itself where the Caesars were always accustomed to reside and also other cities in Italy, Gaul and Germany."[51]

This was the same logic that Justinian once used to justify Constantinopolitan Roman attacks on the West, but it was now being used by Westerners against Constantinople. Charlemagne and his associates were saying, effectively, that, like Theoderic's Gothic regime in early-sixth-century Italy, Irene's Greeks in Constantinople had deceived themselves into thinking that they were Roman. But they were Greeks. They did not control Rome. They had no emperor. So they had relinquished their claim on the Roman imperial title. The Roman emperor now resided in the West. His capital was not Constantinople. It was Roma Ventura.

This rhetorical broadside set the stage for something much more nefarious. Charlemagne wanted not just to delegitimize the Constantinopolitan empire. He intended to attack it—in an extremely sophisticated way. Both eastern and western sources speak about diplomats sent from Aachen to the Abbasid court in Baghdad. The caliph granted Charlemagne permission to build a Frankish monastery in Jerusalem, freedom to offer material support to the Christians living under his regime, and—as a sign of his friendship—an elephant.[52] The elephant was nice. A working relationship with Constantinople's most powerful neighbor was better, especially since Charlemagne planned a campaign against Constantinopolitan Roman positions in southern Italy, Sicily, and Dalmatia.[53] This would be like Justinian's Italian campaign, only in reverse—with the Romans of the West now attacking and expelling non-Roman Greeks from land that properly belonged to the Roman Empire.

The war for Italy never came. Irene sent ambassadors to Charlemagne, they agreed to a peace concerning Southern Italy and Sicily. Irene's successor Nicephorus continued negotiating after the empress fell from power in 802. Disagreements still remained about the fates of Venice and Dalmatia, with proxy battles and a series of naval skirmishes breaking out in the region, but neither side gained much from this fighting. They put an end to it in 812 when Charlemagne and the Eastern emperor Michael I agreed to a treaty that defined spheres of influence for each ruler. Most importantly for

Charlemagne, it also contained an explicit recognition of his Roman imperial title by the Eastern Roman emperor. When the treaty was read out in the West, Charlemagne was acclaimed in Greek—and *Basileus*, the Greek word for emperor, was used to refer to him for the first time.[54] It was, of course, a rich irony that this Greek word was apparently what finally and fully satisfied Charlemagne that he had secured true recognition as Roman emperor.

13

THE RETRENCHMENT OF ONE ROMAN EMPIRE, THE RESURGENCE OF ANOTHER

THE TREATY BETWEEN Michael II and Charlemagne in 812 represents a point of inflection for the history of Europe. At that moment, it would be easy to imagine the alliance of the papal Roman Republic and the Frankish Roman Empire continuing to extend its political and military dominance across the Mediterranean. The Roman imperial recovery sparked in Constantinople by Leo III and Constantine V stalled out in the 780s. By the end of that decade, the leadership contests between Irene and her son seemed to be pushing the Eastern Empire into another period of crisis.

Even people in Constantinople felt this way. In 811, the Roman army suffered a horrific defeat at the hands of the Bulgar king Krum during which the emperor Nicephorus I was captured. Krum had the emperor beheaded and then ordered his skull to be clad in silver so that it might be used as a ceremonial chalice.[1] Continued Bulgar successes even prompted a crowd of former soldiers in Constantinople to rig the mausoleum of Constantine V so that it appeared to open spontaneously in 813. They called on the dead Iconoclast emperor to "arise and help the state that is perishing" because of Krum's advances. They then claimed to have seen that "Constantine climbed up on his horse and set off to fight the Bulgarians."[2] Not even Constantine's rumored resurrection could prevent Krum from putting Constantinople under siege later that year. This event prompted the Roman historian Theophanes to conclude his great chronicle with the plea that the Virgin Mary "not allow us to be shamed by the multitude of our sins."[3]

The shaming continued for another generation. Constantine V's reincarnation might have been a mirage, but the reeling empire nevertheless veered back to embrace the Iconoclasm he had once promoted.[4] After some initial successes against the Bulgars in the 810s, military and political defeats again mounted. Civil war gripped the empire in the early 820s. Crete fell to Arab raiders between 826 and 828 and much of Sicily came under Arab control by the early 830s. The Arab presence in Sicily then led to a sustained series of naval attacks on imperial territory in southern Italy and the Adriatic.[5] Along the empire's southeastern frontier, Arab armies inflicted a series of defeats on Roman forces in Asia Minor that resulted in the sacking of the important cities of Ankara and Amorion, the latter of which was the ancestral home of the imperial dynasty itself. Any hopes for a Roman restoration sparked by a new embrace of Iconoclasm soon faded. Soon after his accession in 843, the emperor Michael III abandoned Eastern Roman Iconoclasm for good.

If people in 843 were told that a Roman entity would become the most powerful state in the Mediterranean for much of the next two centuries, it is unlikely they would have guessed that the empire centered in Constantinople would play that role. But, by the 840s, a remarkable reversal had begun. Charlemagne's Frankish Roman Empire, which the emperor had left to his son, Louis, upon his death in 814, proved more brittle and less dynamic than anyone could have anticipated. Louis spent much of his reign in fighting to maintain effective control of its sprawling territory, and his death in 840 marked the end of a unified Frankish imperial structure that joined the kings of the western lands (many of which make up modern France), southern lands below the Alps, and the eastern territory (much of which belongs to modern Germany) under one authoritative and powerful emperor. The imperial title still existed, but it seemed to be more of an emblem of prestige than an actual mechanism for exerting control over subordinate kings.

As Frankish imperial authority waned, the regional kings began fighting one another as equals. A chronicler writing in 862 bemoaned how tedious it had become "to record the dissension between our kings and the desolation caused by the pagans within our kingdoms."[6] The imperial title eventually became so devalued that only two men held it between 900 and 962—and it sat vacant for more years than an eligible emperor claimed it.[7]

The Franks' papal allies were no more successful in managing affairs in the south. As Sicily fell from Constantinopolitan control in the 830s, it opened up the western Italian coast to Arab naval attacks. In 846, Arab raiders sacked Ostia, Portus, and the suburbs of Rome itself.[8] Papal forces repelled an attack on the city walls, and Lombard forces sent by the duke of Spoleto relieved the city.

This event so scared the papacy that papal sources fell back into the old Roman trope of blaming military reverses on moral decline. A serial biography of the popes called the *Liber Pontificalis* declared that the Arab attack arose because church offices were being sold and soldiers of the papal Roman Republic had become lazy under Pope Sergius II.[9] As one would expect from a Roman source, the new Pope Leo IV set about to "restore" the "old and ancient rites and sacred ordinances" which his "predecessors had broken and abolished."[10] "Every day," the *Liber Pontificalis* asserts, he "set his mind to the restoration" of the city surroundings following the Arab attack so that he might "replace everything that their ungodly hands had stolen."[11] Despite these efforts, the pope again had to repel Arab raiders in 848. The decline of what one might call Charlemagne's new Roman West was now clear. It was not until the reign of the great German king Otto I in the 960s that the Western Roman imperial title would again be claimed by someone with the capacity to effectively defend the imperial lands both above and below the Alps.

The troubles in the West developed alongside a gathering Roman resurgence in the East. Starting in the 840s, the emperor Michael III and his uncle Bardas directed Roman armies to attack Arab territories in the central Mediterranean and along the fringes of Asia Minor. This campaign occurred amid a literary and cultural awakening catalyzed in part by Bardas's organization of spaces for secular learning in Constantinople and his establishment of a center of philosophical study housed in the Magnaura within the imperial palace.[12] Bardas's efforts sparked a long cultural and military revival, but neither Bardas nor Michael got much later recognition for it.

The credit went instead to the emperor Basil I, a Macedonian peasant descended from Armenian migrants, whom Michael had taken into his court.[13] Basil personally killed Bardas in 866 and then, in April of 867, he orchestrated the murder of Michael, the patron who had made Basil his co-emperor. So began the Macedonian dynasty.

Despite its disreputable start, the Macedonian dynasty that Basil inaugurated proved the Roman Empire's most enduring to date. Macedonian emperors and empresses would officially rule over the empire until 1056. Those two centuries saw cultural and military achievements unmatched in the East since the time of Justinian. Roman armies captured large swaths of land in Asia Minor, Syria, Armenia, Bulgaria, and the Mediterranean.[14] Roman cultural achievements were no less impressive. Large construction projects like the monastery of Hosios Loukas in Boeotia, spectacular and innovative works of art, a flowering of legal scholarship, and a Greek-language literary renewal have prompted modern historians to call this period the Macedonian Renaissance.[15]

Contemporaries noticed. Even during the life of Basil I, the patriarch Photius wrote works contrasting the dynamism that Basil supposedly embodied with the lethargy and cruelty of Michael. In Photius's works, Basil I became a new David whose humble origins meant little as he overthrew Michael III, a figure who would become equated with Saul.[16] This pattern continued through the reigns of Basil's successor, Leo VI, and Leo's son, Constantine VII Porphyrogenitus.

Leo himself delivered an oration in 888 that praised his father on the anniversary of his death, but the court of Constantine VII emphasized the contrast between Basil and Michael more forcefully than even the figures around Basil himself had done.[17] One mid-tenth-century biography of Basil I written under Constantine VII maintains that the people, army, and senate all loved Basil but hated Michael, Michael broke laws while Basil made them better, God turned away from Michael and embraced Basil, and Michael even behaved so badly that he brought about his own death.[18] By the mid-eleventh century, the historian John Skylitzes could offer a long catalog of Michael's vicious and moronic deeds while commenting how "all the subjects of the Roman Empire rejoiced at the proclamation of Basil as emperor."[19] This was much the same treatment that the supporters of Nerva and Trajan inflicted on Domitian, another reasonably successful emperor with the misfortune of dying so that a new imperial dynasty could be born.

The long-term success of the Macedonian dynasty gave later authors plenty of opportunities to move beyond the propaganda used to justify its origins. One even begins to see texts that evoke the old Antonine way of speaking about Roman restoration as the result of necessary maintenance on an old but thriving polity. To give but one example of this, in late 888 Leo issued the *Sixty Books*, a Greek-language legal text that organized, updated, and translated the Latin-language Justinianic legal codification of the sixth century. The text's preface claimed it would cleanse the cluttered Roman legal landscape by "eliminating the difficulty of studying law" as well as "clarifying the order" of existing laws. It had been three and a half centuries since Justinian's great codification project, and Roman law again needed tidying up. The *Sixty Books* offered "a final answer for any sort of pressing matter" in which "not a single piece of legislation which bears a correct judgement from earliest times until the laws issued now has been omitted."[20] Leo's text explicitly compares itself to the Justinianic codification project but, unlike Justinian, Leo did not invalidate laws or proclaim a new start to Roman law.[21]

A series of new laws issued by Leo takes this comparison with Justianian even further. Justinian, Leo wrote, "perfectly rendered the dispersed substance of the law into one body." But then, as if he were "ashamed by his own efforts," Justinian issued a second work, which introduced confusion and required Leo to act like a physician who treated the disorder of the legal system so that he might prevent future maladies.[22] This was a needed renovation of the existing Roman legal structure, not a legal revolution.

Others agreed that Leo had done a great deal to restore the condition of the empire. Between 901 and 902, Arethas, the rhetorically trained bishop of Caesarea, delivered a series of speeches celebrating Leo VI in terms that evoked Plato's philosopher king and compared his military victories over the Arabs to the campaigns of Alexander the Great.[23] Around 927, an anonymous author celebrated the reign of Leo as the time "when the Race of Gold lived here and all was happiness and enjoyment of divine blessings."[24]

A cluster of texts authored between the mid-940s and mid-960s offer a representative sampling of how authors writing after Leo's death creatively reflected the optimism of a Roman Empire enjoying a military, spiritual, and cultural resurgence. In 944, Roman forces broke off a siege of the ancient city of Edessa in exchange for the Mandylion, an ancient cloth supposedly bearing the impression of Jesus's face.[25] A homily written by the deacon Gregory celebrated the arrival of the relic in the capital on August 15, 944. Gregory describes the role that the image played in earlier Roman history by detailing how it saved the city of Edessa from Persian attack in 544. Now, he called to Jesus, "the day has come when the cloth holding your impression is transferred from Edessa to those whom you esteem." The image of Christ "was conducted with honor to Constantinople," the Roman capital, where it was "reunified with the relics venerated by the chosen people [i.e., the Romans] . . . those by which we receive mercy and by which we are always fortified." If past Roman defeats suggested problems with Christian religious practices or theology, the unexpected capture of so significant a relic showed that God "clearly judged that we now maintain religious observations that accord with tradition."[26] Roman power had returned with Roman orthodoxy and Constantinople again deserved to be the place in which God housed the most important Christian relics.[27]

The mid-tenth century was not just a moment of religious triumph. An anonymous historian writing in the early 960s praised the emperor Constantine VII for a range of activities that rebuilt the infrastructure and cultural life of the capital. He commended the emperor for "his restoration and improvement of all things" after he found them "in a useless and neglected state." Constantine employed the most capable and virtuous advisors, hired the best teachers, and gave public positions to the wisest philosophers and compelling rhetoricians. His educational reforms brought to the capital teachers who "adorned and enriched the Roman state with their wisdom" while giving the emperor an opportunity to meet students and give them stipends so that they could focus on their studies. He "restored" the imperial garments and diadems that had begun to show their age, rebuilt one of the quarters of the capital, and expanded a charitable hospital first built in the sixth century. He "treated his subjects like an eagle hovering over its nest," worked hard to punish corruption, and reformed rural life by restricting the ability of the wealthy to compel poor people to sell them property. He even built a home for the elderly on property that had once belonged to a corrupt church official. All this happened while the emperor's generals won a series of victories in theaters ranging from Italy to the borders of Syria.[28] The Golden Age of Leo could be said to have continued under his son.

Constantine VII died in 959, but the Roman successes continued under his son, Romanus II. In 961, Roman forces recaptured Crete more than 130 years after it fell under Arab rule.[29] This victory inspired a remarkable poem by Theodosius the Deacon.[30] The poem begins by calling on "Old Rome" to "not feel ill will towards [our] ruler" when you recognize that neither Scipio nor Sulla nor Caesar nor Pompey could compare to Romanus. "Caesar had no boldness" and "Sulla was a dictator in vain." Instead of honoring them, "be in awe of Romanus." Indeed, Theodosius continues, "I have read many books of many learned men," including those of "Plutarch extolling the Romans' might" and Cassius Dio, but "I have not found such a beacon of military leadership" as Romanus, who was "elevated with God's cooperation" to conquer widely. His great qualities ensured that "the city of the Cretans" is "again a Roman city."

The great Anatolian city of Tarsus, Theodosius continues, "heard [about the conquest of Crete] and is digging moats and raising towers . . . foreseeing in others' misfortunes the burden coming upon her." It is not just Tarsus who should fear Roman reconquest. Theodosius also warns Sicily, Africa, and Syria that the Roman "sovereign will soon free you" because "God is our ally and travels with us." Theodosius writes that his fellow Romans have been "fortunate in your crowned [sovereigns] as you have extended your ancestral land, as you have conquered those who were conquered in the past."[31]

According to Theodosius, Romanus had sparked a genuine, extensive, and lasting Roman territorial recovery that began in Crete but would spread across all of what was once the Roman world. Romanus's peers were not emperors like Justinian or Heraclius, who had recovered lost Roman territory. They were instead the dashing and charismatic Republican generals like Scipio, Julius Caesar, and Pompey, who had conquered vast new territories for Rome. The empire was returning to lands it had once controlled, but these divinely favored campaigns of the 960s were wars of expansion that effectively incorporated new territory into a powerful Christian empire. The dynamism of the Republic rather than the stability of the high empire or the fluidity of the sixth and seventh centuries now seemed to offer the best parallels for this new era of Roman history.

This mid-tenth-century celebration of widespread Roman renewal still had its victims. Some of these, like the soldiers and civilians impacted by Roman wars or the wealthy Roman families whose property Constantine VII redistributed, were obvious. Others arose from the strange political dynamics of the moment. Constantine VII, Romanus II, and Romanus's son Basil II together held the imperial office from 913 until 1025—the longest combined reigns of any three consecutive emperors in all of Roman history. But this snapshot gives the misleading impression of imperial stability during this time. All three men began their reigns as child emperors. Constantine officially took power at age eight and often served merely as an imperial figurehead alongside a series of regents and unrelated co-emperors until he was in his early thirties. Romanus took the title of emperor around age seven and reigned alongside his father until he was twenty-one. Basil II assumed the imperial title in 960 when he was one year old. He too first served as a junior emperor alongside his father before serving as a dynastic figurehead to two co-emperors who were not blood relations until Basil finally took effective control of imperial affairs in 976.[32]

These tenth-century Roman co-emperors shared the credit for their triumphs with their colleagues who belonged to the Macedonian dynastic line, but they often had the troubles of the time pinned exclusively on them rather than on the Macedonian with whom they served.[33] So Romanus I, co-emperor with Constantine VII from 920 until 944, was said to have caused the economic inequality and corruption that Constantine repaired after Romanus's fall from power. Although he shared power with Constantine at the time, Romanus was also blamed for canceling the Broumalia, an ancient autumnal festival of Dionysius that marked the arrival in the capital of the year's new wine. Constantine then was praised for restoring the Broumalia and "making it extraordinarily popular."[34] One contemporary author even framed Romanus's removal from office and forced exile to a monastery as God "chastening" him and making him "cognizant of his own sins."[35] Constantine required no such divine punishment.

The emperor Nicephorus II Phocas, who ruled alongside Basil II from 963 until 969, offers an even more interesting example. Nicephorus, not Romanus II, actually led the campaign that reconquered Crete. As Theodosius promised, Nicephorus also led a series of offenses that reconquered Tarsus and then pushed Roman control deeply into Syria between 963 and 969. These later campaigns were expensive, however, and Nicephorus, not the child emperor Basil II, bore the brunt of the popular frustration at tax increases, currency devaluations, and overly aggressive efforts at riot suppression.[36] Nicephorus was eventually assassinated by conspirators led by his own nephew, John Tzimiskes, the man who then took his spot as co-emperor. Some mourned Nicephorus, others criticized Tzimiskes, but the child Basil II was held effectively blameless.[37]

This series of events points to a new way of talking about Roman decline and renewal that identified problems in the empire, offered ways to punish the people deemed responsible for them, and still affirmed Macedonian dynastic continuity. The empire could change course, remove problematic co-emperors, and still maintain a sort of baseline political stability by ensuring that emperors of the Macedonian dynasty remained in place. This way of talking about change simultaneously offered rhetorical support for a long-standing dynasty and for the political churning a dynamic state sometimes required.

This model broke down somewhat after Basil II consolidated effective control of the government for himself in the 970s and 980s, but the empire continued to thrive under his leadership.[38] Indeed, as the Macedonian dynasty neared its end, some of the texts written in the capital again began to resemble works from the Antonine Age that saw emperors repairing natural decay rather than correcting problems caused by a vicious or incompetent predecessor. In the 1040s, for example, the emperor Constantine IX Monomachus patronized a set of rhetorically skilled intellectuals. The polymath Michael Psellus, the most prominent member of this group, wrote that "philosophy was moribund" and the "golden [literary] streams and baser silver streams of the past" were "so blocked up" that there was no one, "not even in the two Romes, the ancient and lesser Rome and the newer, more powerful city," who practiced these ancient arts effectively.[39]

Psellus does not say who is responsible for the dispersal of the best philosophers and rhetoricians that Constantine VII employed in the 950s or even the exceptional "crop of philosophers and orators" that he says were active under Basil II in the early 1000s.[40] It is clear, though, that the quality of philosophy slipped not because of the vicious attacks of dissolute emperors but through a gradual, unplanned neglect that required active restoration. Under Constantine IX's patronage, Psellus restored these decayed arts. He taught rhetoric and philosophy to all who wished to learn while inducing the emperor to sponsor the re-emergence of a court culture that involved regular rhetorical performances and rewarded skilled young orators with prizes.[41]

Psellus enjoyed this moment of cultural flowering at the time, but it did not last. Psellus later compared the empire that Constantine IX ruled to "a healthy animal with a thoroughly strong constitution which is not altered by the first sign of illness . . . until, by slow degrees the sickness grew until it reached a crisis that threw the patient into utter confusion and complete disorder."[42] Unfortunately for Psellus, that moment of crisis arrived within a generation of Constantine IX's death. In 1070, the Roman Empire centered on Constantinople was the most powerful state in the Mediterranean. In 1080, it was reeling toward collapse.

A devastating defeat suffered by the emperor Romanus IV outside of the eastern Anatolian city of Manzikert in the year 1071 caused this deterioration. While this Seljuk Turkish victory over the Romans would become a historical turning point of massive significance, it did not seem so at the time. Romanus was captured in battle but quickly released so he could implement a peace agreement. Unfortunately, a new emperor, Michael VII, had been chosen in his absence and Romanus returned to Roman territory not as an emperor secure in his power but as an imperial contender who needed to overthrow his own replacement.[43]

The decade that followed saw the Roman nobility seemingly try their best to destroy their empire. Instead of accepting the Seljuk peace terms or rallying to avenge the defeat at Manzikert, the empire descended into a series of civil wars that distracted its leaders and sapped its strength. Roman Italy fell to the Normans in 1071 and Norman raiders then began attacking Corfu and territory on the eastern side of the Adriatic, including the vital port city of Dyrrachium.[44] The Roman civil wars of the 1070s also left the imperial heartlands of Asia Minor open to Turkish raids and, eventually, Turkish settlement. In many of these areas, Romans would never return to the lands they lost in the 1070s. Like the Roman losses of northwestern Europe in the fifth century and the Arab conquests of the mid-seventh century, the struggles of the 1070s prompted a slowly dawning sense that something had gone very wrong with the empire.

This period saw a series of increasingly strained attempts to fit contemporary Roman problems within the reassuring old model of Roman decline and recovery. Each new emperor's supporters blamed his predecessor for Rome's current problems, but now, with the Macedonian dynasty extinct, no figure remained who embodied imperial stability. The unmoored empire instead bounced chaotically from one short-lived regime to the next. Each emperor promised to reverse the decline his predecessor caused. None delivered.

Writing under Romanus's rival and successor Michael VII Ducas, Psellus blamed the defeat at Manzikert on the "vainglory" of Romanus that caused him "to rely on no counsel or guidance but his own" and an "insolence" that caused him to "lose respect for everything." The victory of Michael over Romanus brought Psellus hope. Michael, Psellus wrote, possessed "a human nature of such divinity that it far surpasses all others we have known before" and renders him "a prodigy of our generation." "At a time when our affairs . . . were at their lowest ebb," Psellus writes, "the tide of misfortune was checked by Michael's steadfast spirit, and his unshakeable resolve" so that the ship of state "is riding the storm."[45]

If only it were so. By the late 1070s, Michael's regime had faltered and then fallen to the usurper Nicephorus III Botaniates, an elderly general who seized the throne with the help of Turkish troops. Nicephorus arranged for Michael to live out his life as a monk and then fought off another usurper in the Balkans. Even amid signs of growing Roman political breakdown, the historian Michael Attaleiates looked rather optimistically toward a renewal he hoped Nicephorus would spark.

As Attaleiates builds his narrative up to the career of Botaniates, he includes a remarkable digression that compared the "emperors of the Romans" of his day and their ancient Roman predecessors. Unlike Theodosius's favorable comparison of Romanus II to ancient Romans like Scipio and Caesar in the 960s, Attaleiates sees the Romans of the 1070s as far inferior to their Roman predecessors. Contemporary Romans, he writes, "do not seek to learn the causes behind all the misfortunes that befall their empire" but instead "distance themselves from any decision that would please God, honor the divine, and restore the ancestral laws." Emperors now "commit the worst crimes and God-detested deeds under the pretext of public interest" but the ancient Romans, even though they were not Christian, "investigated matters, often found the causes of their calamities, took corrective action, and ensured that they had placated the divine." Now Romans should do the same. Everyone across the empire in the 1070s, Attaleiates writes, "prayed to God" to "return the fortunes of the Romans to a happier state." "Their prayers were not long left answered" because God chose Nicephorus Botaneiates to rule the state. [46]

Attaleiates's embrace of Botaneiates had no better outcome than Psellus's endorsement of Michael VII. Nicephorus's reign proved an utter failure, spawning a number of serious revolts around the empire while failing to check further Turkish advances. In 1081, Alexius Comnenus, the masterful general whose military exploits had kept Nicephorus's regime afloat, took power for himself.

The biography of Alexius written by his daughter, Anna, speaks about how "he was considered by Romans to have attained the summit of the general's art." Again evoking the great Roman past, she wrote that "he was another Aemilius [Paullus], the famous Roman, or a Scipio [Aemilianus]," figures from the Roman Republic who blended personal virtue and effective military leadership.[47] The Roman Empire at his time, Anna wrote, suffered from a series of "mortal plagues" as "pretenders" within and outside the empire fought for the throne. But "God preserved Comnenus, like some precious object, for a greater destiny since [God] wished for him to revive Roman power."[48]

Alexius managed to arrest the deterioration of Roman power in the 1080s. In order to counter Norman naval attacks on Greece, Alexius ordered many of the Roman forces based in Asia Minor to campaign in the West. When these proved insufficient, the emperor made a treaty with the Venetians. The treaty had great immediate benefits—Venetian and Roman naval forces broke the Norman navy and recaptured Dyrrachium in 1085—and terrible long-term consequences. In return for the naval support, the Venetian Doge received a Roman title and a state pension, the churches of Venice received annual payments of gold, and Venetian merchants could trade everywhere in Roman territory without paying any taxes or custom duties. "They were," Anna wrote, "completely free of Roman authority."[49] Although several of Alexius's successors tried to walk away from this deal, the Venetians tenaciously fought to preserve the privileges Alexius granted them—at times going to war in order to get them reinstated.[50]

Even this costly treaty with the Venetians addressed only one of the many threats the empire faced. Alexius's decision to pull troops from Asia Minor less than a generation after Manzikert also proved extremely damaging. Perhaps fearing a return to the infighting that had so weakened the empire in the 1070s, Alexius chose to rely heavily on non-Romans to garrison the empire's remaining cities and fortresses in the region. This plan worked initially but, in 1085, his most trusted Turkish commander died on campaign in Syria and the commander's son, to whom the emperor had entrusted the defense of the well-fortified city of Nicaea, rebelled. He seized Nicaea for himself and then began a campaign to reduce other Roman cities.

By the early 1090s, the empire had lost much of its territory in northwestern Asia Minor—including the city of Nicomedia, less than a hundred miles from the capital. Antioch, Edessa, and other cities in the southeast fell, too. On the Aegean coast, the empire saw Smyrna pass out of Roman control for the first time in 1200 years. After an alliance with the Turkish sultan of Baghdad failed to stem the attacks, Roman clerics in the capital began openly speaking about Alexius's failures and seemingly imminent divine punishment.[51]

The restoration Alexius promised now seemed as if it might have been just as illusory as those of his predecessors in the 1070s. It remained uncertain whether the Roman Empire still retained the capacity to gather the considerable resources it possessed to meet the many military challenges it now faced. As the next chapter will show, Alexius decided it could not. The results set in motion a process that would result in catastrophe.

14

THE CAPTURES OF CONSTANTINOPLE

THE EMPEROR ALEXIUS I Comnenus spent the first few years of the 1080s in struggling to restore some of the immense power that the Roman Empire had exercised for most of the preceding century. By the early 1090s, his efforts looked to be on the verge of failure. Fearing imperial collapse, Alexius sent envoys to Pope Urban II in 1095 and "implored his lordship the Pope and all the faithful of Christ to bring assistance against the heathen . . . who had conquered as far as the walls of Constantinople."[1]

Alexius's appeal came at a wonderful time for the pope. The previous two decades had seen Urban and his immediate predecessors fall into a violent and protracted conflict with Henry IV, the German who held the title of Roman emperor of the West. This feud culminated in Henry's armies attacking the city of Rome in 1083. Urban, the bishop of the old Roman port of Ostia, was appointed to the papacy in 1088 but, aside from a brief furtive visit to Rome in 1089, Urban could not even enter the city over which he supposedly presided. The pontiff was an extremely skilled political actor, however. He made his papal court a refuge for people fleeing Henry—including the emperor's son, Conrad. In a reversal of the state of affairs in the eighth century, the pope then established a relationship with Alexius and the Eastern Roman Empire that he headed in order to offset German imperial power in the West.

This alliance required considerable finessing. The Catholic church broke communion with the emperor and patriarch of Constantinople in 1054 because of a combination of procedural and theological disagreements.[2] In the late 1080s, both Alexius and Urban worked to minimize these issues so that they might bring the churches back into union. Their collaboration came to work so well that Alexius and Urban together issued a call for king

Zvonimir of Croatia to send knights to fight on behalf of the Roman Empire in the early 1090s.[3]

Alexius's call for help in 1095 drew upon the emperor's well-established cooperative relationship with Urban, but Alexius framed his request so that it would also resonate widely among eleventh-century Western Europeans who had become increasingly fixated on the holy city of Jerusalem.[4] Urban followed the Constantinopolitan emperor's lead, preaching about the threats to Jerusalem while distributing large numbers of religious relics sent from the Eastern Empire to the West—including a suspiciously large quantity of fragments of the true cross.[5]

Both sides had something to gain. Alexius, of course, hoped the west would give him military support that included knights, the heavily armored cavalry that effectively supplemented the emperor's own powerful infantry. Urban, who had recently crowned Henry's son, Conrad, as Western Roman emperor in opposition to his father, now had a way to rally Western Christians around a cause that only he could champion. If Western Christians heeded his call, Urban could even undercut the temporal authority of Henry.

Urban's call succeeded beyond anyone's expectation. The pope himself recruited knights and administered oaths that bound them to the expedition, but so many other Europeans headed east that their numbers far outstripped the supplies available for them.[6] The first wave of Crusaders that arrived at the Roman frontier looked much different from what Urban or Alexius expected. Anna Comnena described "warriors who came with a host of civilians . . . carrying palms and bearing crosses on their shoulders."[7]

This group, the so-called People's Crusade led by Peter the Hermit, was ill supplied and not terribly useful as a fighting force. They massacred Jews across Germany and then, when Peter's undersupplied followers crossed the Roman frontier, they began plundering Roman towns and villages to feed themselves. Alexius had the good sense to send Peter's crusade quickly into Asia Minor, but the militants persisted in killing both Christians and Muslims who stood in their path. Until October of 1096. Then a much larger and more capable Turkish force defeated the soldiers who followed Peter, captured most of the civilians, and either killed or forced the conversion of the survivors.[8] Many in the West soon came to believe that Alexius "rejoiced greatly" when he learned of this defeat.[9] So began a narrative of "Greek" treachery that wove itself ever more deeply into Western European tales of the Crusades.

Urban played a role in selecting the more capable and disciplined second wave of Crusaders, but these figures brought Alexius a different set of problems. Some encountered bandits. Others found themselves inadvertently provoking conflict with Roman imperial naval or land forces.[10] As the petty nobility and royal second sons of Europe began arriving in Constantinople in 1096, Alexius received many of them with the honors they expected—and even managed a civil conversation with the Norman Bohemond, against whom he had fought in the 1080s.[11] Their overbearing arrogance grated on their host's patience, but nearly all of the Crusaders eventually swore to return any captured territory to the emperor before they left the capital.[12]

The imperial and Crusader armies successfully fought alongside each other in the initial phases of the campaign. In early 1097, their combined forces set out for Nicaea. The city surrendered to Alexius that June as Crusader siege engines battered its walls. Alexius then used the Crusader progression through central Asia Minor as a shield behind which he could recapture most of the western coastal cities he had recently lost.

The cooperation between Crusaders and the emperor broke down by the end of the summer. As the Crusaders reached southeastern Anatolia, they began taking territory for themselves and refusing to return it to the emperor. Then, in the autumn of 1097, the Crusader forces put Antioch under siege. The attack proved difficult, the imperial assistance they requested did not materialize, and, when the Crusaders finally captured the city in June of 1098, they kept it.

The consequences of Alexius's decision to request Western military aid in this way now became clear. He had done well fighting behind the Westerners. By the end of 1098, the empire had recovered Smyrna, Ephesus, and nearly all of the cities along the coast because of their advance. But his invitation had also introduced Catholic, Western European–ruled kingdoms into the Eastern Mediterranean. After the Crusaders succeeded in capturing Jerusalem in July of 1099, they controlled four Crusader kingdoms occupying territory stretching from Edessa in southeastern Anatolia to the Egyptian border.

Some of these Crusader states abutted the empire and comprised territory that had very recently been Roman. The inevitable border tension only increased western animosity toward and suspicion about Alexius and his Roman Empire. The Norman Bohemond, who had taken control of Antioch after its capture, even arranged an attack on Roman territories in 1107. In an ominous turn, he received the endorsement of Urban II's successor as pope.[13] Alexius beat the attack back and reduced the principality of Antioch to a Roman vassal, but this violence prefigured more than a century of growing tension between the Crusader states, the empire, and Western Christians.

Three more Crusades set out from the West between 1146 and 1203. Alexius's grandson, Manuel, avoided conflict by ferrying the warriors of the Second Crusade by sea from Roman territory to the Crusader port of Acre without serious incident. The next wave of Crusaders proved far more difficult to handle. The city of Jerusalem fell in 1187 to the Muslim general Saladin and the West launched the Third Crusade to take the city back. Led by the German emperor Frederick Barbarosa and including the kings of France and England, the soldiers of the Third Crusade arrived in Roman territory in 1189.

They found an empire in crisis. Following the death of Manuel Comnenus in 1180, the short reign of Alexius II and the incompetence of Andronicus Comnenus had caused Roman central authority to collapse. Bulgaria and Serbia both threw off Roman control in the 1180s and, as Frederick approached the capital, negotiations began for the Serbs and Bulgars to support him in an attack on Constantinople. The Roman emperor at the time, Isaac II Angelus, narrowly avoided this attack by agreeing to help Frederick's progression to the Levant. Frederick drowned in the Saleph River in Asia Minor later that summer without causing further damage to the empire, but the English king Richard did seize Cyprus from a grandson of Alexius Comnenus in 1191.

The tensions between Constantinople and the West finally exploded during the ill-fated Fourth Crusade. The Third Crusade was a well-funded and well-organized affair that included three European kings. The Fourth

Crusade was a mess. Instead of traveling by land through Roman territory, this group of Crusaders contracted with Venice to ferry them to Egypt. When far fewer Crusaders turned up than the organizers had expected, they found themselves owing the Venetians a significant sum of money.[14] The Venetians then convinced the Crusaders to pay off their debts by fighting on Venice's behalf. The Crusaders first captured the Croatian city of Zadar for the Venetians, but the plunder proved insufficient to pay what they owed.[15]

The Crusaders then summoned a Roman exile named Alexius Angelus. The son of the deposed and imprisoned former Roman emperor Isaac II Angelus, Alexius had spent much of the past few years trying to induce Western Christians to provide troops to back his bid for the Roman throne.[16] He told a compelling story of parricide "through which the imperial throne was occupied and polluted" by an "unprecedented tyranny" that restricted Rome's "ancient public freedom."[17] Pope Innocent III had earlier prohibited any Crusader actions against Constantinople on behalf of Alexius, but the Roman pretender promised the Crusaders large cash bonuses and pledged he would bring about a union of the Orthodox and Catholic churches.[18] These promises were enough to persuade the desperate Crusaders to ignore the pope's injunction.

Alexius, of course, had no capacity to bring these things about. He almost certainly had no idea of the imperial budget and had little capacity to force papal supremacy on the Orthodox church. While Alexius hoped to rule alongside his father, Isaac's imprisonment had enfeebled a man who, even at the peak of his powers, was one of the least capable Roman emperors in centuries. But the Roman armies were far away from the capital, Isaac was a former emperor, Alexius belonged to an imperial line, and the Crusaders were thus able to put the two of them on the Roman throne late in 1203. This was, the Crusaders explained to the pope, an action through which "liberty had been restored to the city."[19] And this was, of course, the same language that new Roman autocrats had used since the time of Augustus.

Then reality dawned. The Greek-speaking residents of Constantinople resented the growing community of Western Europeans who lived in their capital. Constantinopolitan anger at Western Europeans had even led to a massacre in 1182. Soon after the Crusaders installed Alexius, another violent conflict erupted that saw much of the center of the city burn and resulted in 15,000 Western European residents of Constantinople fleeing to safety with the Crusader army.[20]

Alexius and Isaac also soon realized that they lacked the money to pay the Crusaders what Alexius had promised. The result was that they could count neither on the support of the army that had installed them nor that of the Roman population they governed. Alexius then pivoted away from the Crusaders and endorsed a Roman attack on the Crusader fleet. This effort failed, however, and, in January of 1204, Alexius was deposed, thrown in jail, and murdered. Isaac supposedly died of shock when he learned of his son's death. The Crusaders suddenly found themselves locked out of a well-fortified city controlled by a hostile Roman emperor. Under these conditions, the Crusaders began a siege that, in April of 1204, resulted in their capture of Constantinople.

The Crusaders initially described their conquest of Constantinople as the seamless restoration of Eastern Christianity to the Catholic fold after Christians in the empire had descended into vice. The first line of argument grew out of the empire's failure to implement the promised union binding the Greek and Latin churches. Pope Innocent himself had framed this agreement as a restoration of an earlier state in which "the Catholic emperors rendered, from ancient times, [devotion] to the orthodox fathers, the Roman Pontiffs."[21] But the empire never really returned to the Catholic fold. Because the Greeks (as the Crusaders called the Romans of Constantinople) "had formerly been obedient to the law of Rome but now were disobedient," Robert of Clari wrote, "one must certainly attack them" and such an attack "is not a sin but an act of great charity."[22]

Crusaders also highlighted the immorality of the arrest and murder of Alexius. Geoffrey of Villehardouin, a knight who participated in the capture of Constantinople, explained that "all the clergy" agreed that this "war is just and lawful" because "anyone guilty of such a murder [as that of Alexius] had no right to hold lands, while those who consented to such a thing were accomplices in the crime."[23] Robert of Clari agreed. The Greeks, he wrote, "are traitors and murderers, and they are disloyal because they have killed their lawful sovereign."[24]

In their letter to the pope explaining their actions, the Crusaders gave even more examples of the supposed moral decline of Constantinopolitans. They "had deviated into worldly arrogance by providing arms, ships, and foods" to "infidels." They had "forgotten to honor Christ in paintings of and by themselves." They had even "deemed all Latins worthy of being called not humans but dogs"[25] and "almost reckoned the shedding of their blood among works of merit." "The Lord himself" administered "Divine Justice through our ministry and, with fitting vengeance, punished such absurdities."[26] Constantinople then deserved to fall because its rulers were murderers, their subjects were accomplices, and all were not to be considered truly Christian, because they had broken with the papacy.

The Crusaders emphasized the necessity of restoring Greeks to the authority of the pope but, in their initial communications, they said little about the victims this restoration created. This reticence caused the papacy, which had consistently argued against the Crusader attacks on Constantinople in 1203 and early 1204, to quickly change course after Rome learned that Constantinople had fallen. In November of 1204, Innocent agreed that "the kingdom of the Greeks" had "turned away from obedience to the Holy See." It had "continuously descended from evil to worse evil until, by the just judgement of God, it was transferred . . . from the disobedient to the obedient . . . so that it might rise" again.

The Christians of Constantinople had declined from virtue and now they had fallen. The Crusaders offered them redemption and the papacy would "assist [the Crusaders] prudently and mightily in defending and holding onto the empire of Constantinople."[27] "Surely," the pope wrote to clergy traveling with the Crusaders, "this was done by the Lord and is wondrous in our eyes."[28] Innocent even came to attach an almost eschatological significance to the city's capture and the "transfer of the empire of Constantinople from the Greeks to the Latins." Innocent came to believe that this transfer marked a dawning age of Christian concord and purification that would precede the Apocalypse.[29]

The pope did soon learn that the Crusaders facilitated this "transfer of empire" through horrific bloodshed that included the mass killing of Constantinople's Greeks. Baldwin of Flanders eventually confessed to him that "our men were occupied with killing" Greeks until they were exhausted, as one would expect when "a populous city is captured."[30] The Venetian Doge Enrico Dandolo told the pope that "a great massacre of Greeks had taken place" once the city had been captured but before his forces had begun to plunder it.[31] Another Crusader who participated in the sack reported that "a massive killing of Greeks ensued" when the city fell because "we set fire" to every Greek who stood in our way.[32]

The human death toll tells only part of the story. The Crusaders devastated large quarters of an already ravaged city. In 1203, Crusader catapults had damaged the Blachernae Palace at the northwest corner of the city walls, battering rams had punctured the wall in other places, and fires set by the Crusaders burned houses along the Golden Horn, the city's majestic harbor.[33] In August of 1203, they burned a mosque within the city, unleashing a firestorm that came close to torching Hagia Sophia.[34] Then, when they stormed the city in 1204, the Crusaders set another fire that again burned along the Golden Horn for more than a mile.[35] The horrible scene, the Crusader Geoffrey of Villehardouin wrote, suggested that "more houses had been burnt in [Constantinople] than there are in any of the three greatest cities of the kingdom of France."[36]

Then the looting began. After the fall of Constantinople, the Crusaders ransacked palaces, private homes, churches, and monasteries. The treasure was brought to a designated location, where it was divided among the Venetians, the papacy, and the Crusaders themselves, property to which they believed they were entitled for their participation in the city's "liberation."[37] Despite a papal injunction against taking any "ecclesiastical possessions" of the church of Constantinople, many of the most powerful relics and impressive artistic treasures now found in Venice were stolen from Constantinople during those days.[38] Other relics and artistic masterworks flowed out across Catholic Europe, with Crusaders like Nevelon de Chérisy directing large hauls to their hometowns.[39]

After the looting ceased, the Crusading leaders elected Baldwin, a count from Flanders, as the new Latin emperor of Constantinople. He celebrated his coronation on May 16, hoping to rule over the "Greeks" of the newly created empire, Greeks who still called themselves Romans. Along with his fellow Crusaders and their Venetian backers, Baldwin began a partition of the rest of the imperial territory—an area that the Crusaders themselves called Romania (the land of the Romans). Baldwin tried to claim the title of Roman emperor, marching out from the city and expecting that the people of Romania would "proclaim him emperor of the Romans."[40]

The treachery, brutality, and rapacity of the Crusaders and their new Latin emperor when Constantinople fell made impossible Baldwin's widespread acceptance by Romans. The truth of what the Crusaders had done shocked even the pope when he finally received a full report. In July of 1205, Innocent wrote to one of his cardinals, "How will the Greek Church, thus afflicted by persecutions, return to unity and devotion to the Apostolic See" when it sees in the Crusaders "nothing except an example of affliction and the works of Hell, so that now it rightly detests them more than dogs?" He then warned, "Divine Retribution now begins to scourge [the Crusaders'] sins and already rages upon them."[41] The pope thought restoration of the East was wonderful—until he learned about the mass of victims it had created.

The violence of the Crusaders sparked an energetic Roman resistance to Latin imperial rule in the months following Constantinople's fall. For many Romans, the fall of their capital was simply inconceivable—until it actually happened. Nicetas Choniates, a Roman historian who lived through the conquest, had already set to work on a history that traced the decline of Roman central administration over much of the empire's territory from the death of Alexius Comnenus until sometime before 1204.[42] It details some of the incidents one would expect to find in a Roman historical narrative of decline—like pirate attacks resulting from Alexius's son John's failed naval policies, Turkish conquests of cities in Asia Minor, and the foolish destruction of critical infrastructure by Isaac II Angelus.[43] The renewal was to come with the reign of Alexius III Angelus, the figure on whose behalf the work was apparently written and whose triumphs its last parts celebrate.[44]

But the second part of the text, which Choniates began after fleeing Constantinople and, eventually, trading his palace there for a refugee settlement in Nicaea, speaks to the reality that the empire was not in the midst of the traditional Roman cycle of decline and renewal.[45] It had fallen. In a long lament for the lost city, Choniates combined biblical descriptions of the end of the Israelite state, Persian attacks on Greece in the fifth century BC, and discussions of how the Crusader actions made even the Arab conquest of Jerusalem look moderate.[46] Crucially, Choniates also emphasized that the fall of the Roman Empire did not mean the end of the Romans.

Choniates described an assembly held in Hagia Sophia after the Constantinopolitan walls were breached and the emperor had fled the city. Two leading notables, Constantine Ducas and Constantine Lascaris, both spoke in bids to assume leadership over the Roman resistance. After listening to them, the patriarch of Constantinople selected Constantine Lascaris as the new leader. The patriarch offered him the imperial insignia, but Constantine Lascaris declined to take them. Instead, he walked with the patriarch to the Milion, the great assembly point at which all roads in the empire begin, and "exhorted the assembled populace, cajoling them to put up resistance . . . and reminding them that they should not fear destruction any less than the Romans should fear the Roman Empire falling to another nation."[47]

No one listened at this moment, but Choniates used the supposed address of Constantine Lascaris to emphasize that the Roman nation would survive without its empire. "Since God both kills and restores life," Choniates suggests that Roman resistance to the Latin Empire might result in the rebirth of a genuinely Roman Empire centered again in Constantinople. The last part of his *History* records the stirrings of this great Roman resistance as well as the first defeats the Latin Empire suffered at its hands.

Choniates did not live long enough to see the Roman renewal he predicted, but he did survive to see Constantine Lascaris plant its seed.[48] After Constantinople fell, formidable Roman commanders remained alive and the Crusaders proved unable to take the lands where these men regrouped. Three centers of power successfully resisted the advance of the Crusaders. One, based in Epirus, comprised lands on the eastern shore of the Adriatic. Another, the so-called Empire of Trebizond, was based along the southeastern coast of the Black Sea. The third, the Empire of Nicaea in northwestern Asia Minor, became the largest and most powerful survivor.

It was to Nicaea that Constantine Lascaris traveled. He there joined his brother, Theodore, and together they organized an armed Roman resistance to the Latin Empire in Asia. It was not immediately successful. Henry of Flanders, the brother of the Latin emperor Baldwin, won significant victories over resistance forces in Asia in 1205. Constantine Lascaris, for example, disappears from the historical record, apparently dying following a defeat outside of the city of Adramyttion.[49] But Crusader defeats in the West and an invasion of Latin imperial territory by the king of Bulgaria forced Henry to withdraw and permitted Theodore to consolidate power in Asia Minor.

The Empire of Nicaea expanded its territory for much of the first half of the thirteenth century. By the early 1230s, the Nicene Empire included territory in Europe. By 1240, Thessaloniki had fallen under Nicene control. By 1248, the emperor John III Lascaris had pushed the Bulgarians out of Thrace. The Nicene Empire now surrounded the shrunken Latin Empire of Constantinople.

These events set the stage for the last great Roman imperial restoration, a renewal sparked by Michael Palaeologus, the founder of the Roman Empire's last dynasty. His full name was Michael Ducas Angelus Comnenus Palaeologus, a name that marked his connections to each of the last three families to hold power in Constantinople before the Latin conquest.[50] Born around 1225 in territory controlled by the Empire of Nicaea, Michael began his military career in the mid-1240s.[51] In 1253, he was accused of plotting against the emperor John III Lascaris, barely avoided having to prove his innocence in a trial by ordeal, and then fled to serve in the military of the Turkish Sultan of Rum.[52] He returned to Roman imperial service in 1258 and soon afterwards led a coup that secured him guardianship of the young emperor John IV Ducas Lascaris. Then, on January 1, 1259, Michael was proclaimed co-emperor with John.[53]

Michael had even larger ambitions. In the winter and early spring of 1260, Michael mounted an unsuccessful attack on the city of Constantinople.[54] Then, after making an alliance with Genoa that could secure him robust naval support, Michael prepared to attack Constantinople again in 1261.[55] Before the Genoese fleet arrived, however, Michael's general Alexius Strategopoulus took a small Roman exploratory force to Constantinople. He might have intended nothing more than a probe of the city's defenses but, as the Roman troops came near the city on July 24, people loyal to Michael helped Alexius's army through the walls. The Latin emperor Baldwin II fled to Athens on a Venetian galley. Alexius then prevented any sort of organized resistance from the Venetian and other Latin residents of the city by burning their houses.[56] While the Latin Constantinopolitans panicked, Alexius mobilized the city's Greek-speaking population and the Genoese within its walls to prevent a Venetian fleet from coming to their aid. Constantinople was Roman again.

Michael entered the city on August 15, crossing through the Golden Gate as a pious Roman Christian emperor re-establishing the orthodox and Roman character of the capital. Once he had entered the city, Michael marked the end of Catholic Constantinople by listening to prayers of Thanksgiving delivered in Greek by a Greek Orthodox priest.[57] He then processed through the city to Hagia Sophia, marching behind the holy icon of the Virgin that had long protected Constantinople.

When the emperor reached Hagia Sophia, the cathedral hosted a Greek-language, Orthodox Christian service in the presence of a Roman emperor for the first time since 1204. Not long afterwards, Arsenius, the new patriarch of Constantinople, arrived from Asia and presided at a ceremony in the refurbished cathedral that crowned Michael as Roman emperor in Constantinople.[58] This was his second coronation—the first had happened in Nicene territory in 1259 when he became co-emperor with John IV—but this coronation meant something very different. Michael was crowned alone, in Hagia Sophia, as Roman emperors had been for centuries before 1204.

The next five years saw Michael work hard to rebuild the recaptured capital. It needed the work.[59] Writing decades later under Michael's son, Andronicus II Palaeologus, Nicephorus Gregoras described the recaptured Constantinople as an "enormous desolate city, full of ruins" because "it had received no care from the Latins, except destruction of every kind."[60] He exaggerates, but only somewhat. Constantinople had once housed perhaps 500,000 people but, at the time of Michael's reconquest, the population was 35,000 or less.[61] The great churches of the city leaked following decades during which the Latin emperors had taken the lead sealings off their roofs so that they could sell the metal they scavenged.[62] Michael repaired the lesser churches, restored the monasteries in the city, and lavishly redecorated the reconsecrated Orthodox church of Hagia Sophia.[63] The new regime repaired and improved the city walls and public buildings, including theaters, stoas, law courts, colonnades, and even retirement homes.[64]

Michael also lavished attention on Constantinopolitan cultural life. He refounded the University of Constantinople, reintroduced the position of official rhetorician, and restarted the tradition of an annual panegyric given by the official rhetorician in honor of the emperor.[65] A contemporary, the orator Gregory of Cyprus, portrayed Constantinople telling Michael, "Because of you, I am a city again," for he had "restored to my head the crown" that the evil Latins "had thrown down to the ground."[66]

Michael himself strongly encouraged the idea that he restored both the city and its empire.[67] Mere days after taking the city, Michael began calling himself a "new Constantine" and styling himself the second founder of Constantinople. By 1266, this title became the central defining feature of his reign.[68] Manuel Holobolos, the official court rhetorician, declared that Michael was "judged the new Constantine before the entire Roman world" because he restored "the city of Constantine, the thrice blessed city, the queen of cities, and the most beautiful of all beautiful cities across the world." He was also "a new Moses" because he had "freed us from the slavery of the Latins, those other Egyptians," just as Moses had liberated the Israelites from Pharaoh.[69]

Michael ordered a series of visual commemorations marking his achievements. Outside of the Church of the Holy Apostles Michael had erected a column showing his namesake, the Archangel Michael. Below it stood an image of the emperor himself holding a representation of Constantinople in his hand and offering it to the Archangel.[70] Within Hagia Sophia, the patriarch Germanus ordered a tapestry hung that showed the emperor and described him as "The New Constantine."[71]

Romans paid a high price for the achievements of their new Constantine. Although Michael would eventually put in place a set of policies that governed the Latins who remained in Constantinople after the reconquest, the fires that Alexius had used to burn them out of their houses when he entered the city prompted an exodus of refugees.[72] Michael showed even greater brutality when, in late 1261, he decided to break firmly and fully with the old legacy of the Nicene Empire. His co-emperor John IV Lascaris had remained behind in Nicaea. On Christmas of 1261, John's eleventh birthday, Michael ordered the boy blinded, exiled and imprisoned in a fortress.[73] Then Michael ordered the mutilation of the orator Manuel Holobolos because Holobolos expressed distress at the boy's blinding.[74] The patriarch Arsenius, who had been placed in office by John's father, excommunicated Michael because of this brutality. Michael responded by deposing Arsenius and replacing him with Germanus, an action that prompted a schism that lasted until 1315.

Michael returned the Roman Empire to Constantinople and ended its Nicene exile. He proved a masterful diplomat, dancing and maneuvering around a host of western, northern, and eastern adversaries to maintain Roman control of the city. He repaired the decaying capital, renewed Roman cultural and court life, and helped to catalyze a literary flourishing that came to be called the Palaeologian Renaissance. These achievements were real. They were substantial. And they came at a great cost. Like Augustus, Septimius Severus, Justinian, and Basil I, Michael's Roman restoration required murder, brutality, and warfare.

Michael was as ruthless as others who had claimed to restore Rome over the preceding 1300 years, but he differed from them in one important way. Michael's sins were so great that even his successors hesitated to embrace his legacy too closely. Although his family had constructed a mausoleum in Constantinople, Michael's body never made it back to the capital after he died in Selymbria in 1282.[75] Instead, he was buried at a monastery near where he died—with his body bloating grotesquely over time, supposedly because of his excommunication.[76] The Palaeologian dynasty he founded would last until the end of the empire—the longest lasting of all Roman imperial dynasties. Unlike the founders of the other great Roman dynasties, Michael was never an unequivocally heroic figure. Even the Palaeologian dynasty's long duration could not wipe away the stains of its founder's misdeeds.[77]

15

THE FALL OF ROMAN CONSTANTINOPLE AND THE END OF ROMAN RENEWAL

THE ROMAN RECAPTURE of Constantinople in 1261 resonated across the restored empire's artistic, literary, and cultural life. For a time, Michael Palaeologus's savvy and skill even seemed to produce a sustainable military and political revival. By 1265, the empire again controlled a large swath of territory that extended from the Adriatic coast of Albania to the middle of the Black Sea coast of modern Turkey and down across the eastern shore of the Aegean as far as Rhodes. It was a large state, but Michael's empire was far more brittle than what a map of his lands might suggest.

Michael himself understood as much. While the reconquest of Constantinople had been surprisingly easy, Michael's empire and Constantinople, its new crown jewel, attracted the attention of a wide range of ambitious Christian powers across Europe.[1] The neighboring Serbian and Bulgarian kingdoms both eyed Michael's empire eagerly. Even greater threats lurked to the west. The Roman reconquest of Constantinople represented a serious symbolic defeat for the papacy. The Latin Empire of Constantinople was a failed imperial enterprise in which Catholics tried to extend political and ecclesiastical control over Eastern Orthodox Romans who had been separated from the Western church since 1054.[2] Michael's reconquest of the old Roman imperial capital ended this effort.

Charles of Anjou, a brother of King Louis IX of France, the king of Sicily and Naples, and the collector of many other important-sounding royal titles, became the lynchpin of a western effort to retake Constantinople.[3] A man of grandiose ambition who possessed considerable military and diplomatic skill, Charles built a coalition of Roman adversaries that included

Bulgaria, Serbia, and even the former Latin emperor of Constantinople to attack Michael's empire.[4]

Michael proved Charles's match. He crafted an opposing alliance that included the king of Hungary, the Tatars of Russia, and the Mamluk leaders of Egypt. Michael then reached out to pope Gregory X and negotiated an agreement to bring Eastern and Western churches back into union, an overture that prompted the pope to block Charles from attacking the empire. The agreement sparked fierce resistance in the East and fell apart in the early 1280s, but it had served its short-term purpose.[5] Charles died in 1285 without ever being able to launch his attack.

Charles of Anjou was not the only outsider eyeing the overextended Roman state. Serbia and Bulgaria, the same neighbors who once allied with Charles, continued to covet Roman territory. Soon after the fourteenth century dawned, the empire saw another serious rival emerge on its eastern frontier—the Ottoman Turks. Over the next century these rivals chipped away gradually at Roman territory, with a set of devastating Roman civil wars in the 1320s and 1340s making their jobs easier. The Serbian king Stefan Dušan expanded his domains deeply into Macedonia, Epirus, and Thessaly by the mid-1340s while, in the East, the Ottomans captured important Asian cities like Nicaea and Nicomedia.[6] By the 1360s, the Ottomans had crossed into Europe and taken control of much of Roman Thrace. The next generation saw Ottoman expansion in Europe accelerate further. Serbia was reduced to vassalage following the Battle of Kosovo in 1389 and Bulgaria became an Ottoman province in 1396. By that point, the Roman Empire retained only small slivers of territory around Constantinople and in the Peloponnese. Constantinople had effectively become a Roman island in an Ottoman sea.

The erosion of Roman territorial control across the fourteenth century was both profound and undeniable. In the winter of 1391, the emperor Manuel II Palaeologus found himself compelled to campaign in Asia Minor alongside the Ottoman sultan Bayezid I. In one of his letters, the Roman emperor wrote back to Constantinople about the desolate state of land that "had some name once when it was fortunate enough to be inhabited by Romans." Now one sees only the ruins of cities, "a pitiable spectacle for people whose ancestors once possessed them," whose "magnificent remains" offer ghostly honors to the great Romans like Pompey for whom they were once named.[7]

The haunting power of Manuel's prose underlines a Roman cultural and literary vitality that persisted amid political and military decay.[8] Indeed, the fourteenth century saw the flourishing of gifted authors and breathtaking artistic projects like the mosaic and fresco work done between 1315 and 1321 at the Church of the Holy Savior in the Country (better known as the Chora Church). The very name of that church underlines the dimming of Roman fortunes. The Church of the Holy Savior in the Country lay within the walls of the capital, a once teeming metropolis whose city limits now contained farms, orchards, and "country" monastic retreats (see Figure 15.1).[9]

It seemed only a matter of time before the empire succumbed entirely. In 1394, the Ottoman sultan Bayezid I put Constantinople under siege in an effort to extinguish the Roman state. This was not Bayezid's only campaign at that moment, however, and Ottoman actions on other fronts meant that the siege dragged on for years. Manuel did what he could to save the city. The emperor's Venetian and Genoese allies provided ships that evaded the Ottoman navy and periodically resupplied the city. In 1395, Manuel agreed to contribute forces to a Western Crusade against the Turks—a Crusade that resulted in a devastating defeat for the Crusaders at the Battle of Nicopolis in 1396. Then, in 1399, a French relief force of 1200 troops led by

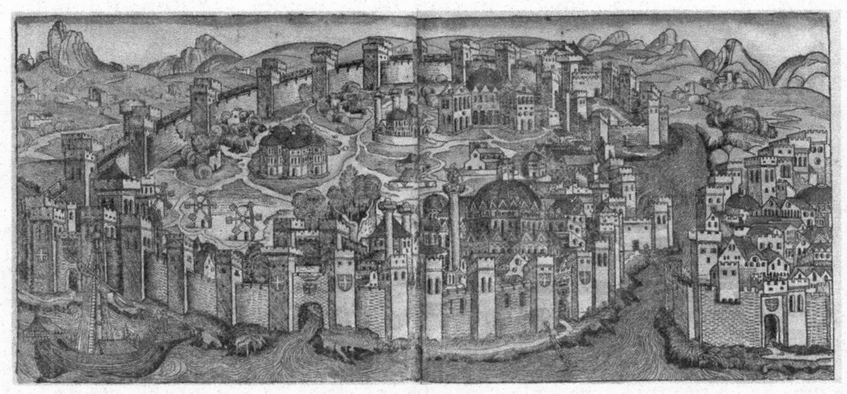

FIGURE 15.1 CONSTANTINOPLE IN THE FIFTEENTH CENTURY, *NUREMBERG CHRONICLE* (WIKIMEDIA COMMONS).

Marshal Charles Boucicaut, a veteran of Nicopolis, broke through the Ottoman blockade. Realizing that the depopulated city still lacked troops, Boucicaut suggested that Manuel seek more reinforcements from the West.

In December of 1399, more than five years into the Ottoman siege, the emperor Manuel did something extraordinary. He left the capital, sailing first to Italy and then to the courts of the great Christian kingdoms of Western Europe. He was received with a mixture of fascination and pity.[10] An observer of the emperor's Christmas-time visit to king Richard II of England wrote, "I thought to myself how sad it was that this great Christian prince from the far east should be compelled violently by unbelievers to visit the distant islands of the West and seek aid. Oh God! What has become of you, oh ancient glory of Rome? The greatness of your empire is shorn today."[11]

Despite the curiosity that Manuel attracted in Italy, France, England, and Germany, very little came of the trip. Constantinople continued to suffer in the emperor's absence. Apparently wanting to take the city intact, Bayezid mounted no armed assault on the capital. He instead simply surrounded its land walls with 10,000 troops and prevented supplies from entering. The Romans within "suffered a terrible dearth of grain, wine, oil and other provisions" and were forced to tear down the ancient, abandoned buildings so that they could use their wooden beams for firewood.[12] The City, the historian Ducas later wrote, "was distressed by the magnitude of the famine and about to throw away its soul."[13] Romans did as they had done during the great sieges of 626 and 717. They again turned to prayer in hopes that "perhaps God, overlooking our sins, will show us mercy as He did in the past."[14]

Their prayers were answered in a most unexpected way. Relief for Constantinople came not from the Christian West but from the Islamic East. In 1402, with Constantinople still under siege, the Turko-Mongol general Tamerlane inflicted a serious and humiliating defeat upon Bayezid and the Ottomans at Ankara. Bayezid was captured and soon died in captivity. Tamerlane's forces advanced as far as the Aegean, and, in sudden disarray, the Ottomans broke off the siege of Constantinople as their empire fell into a prolonged civil war.[15] The empire had received what seemed like another miraculous reprieve.[16]

The empire had escaped destruction in 1402, but its survival had little to do with a resurgence of Roman power or with Manuel's personal leadership. In fact, the emperor took his time returning to Constantinople after the Ottoman defeat at Ankara, tarrying in Paris and Italy before finally arriving back in the capital in the middle of 1403. As the Ottoman civil war dragged on, however, the empire began to make some significant territorial gains. It retook Thessaloniki and the monasteries at Mt. Athos, consolidated Roman authority over much of the Peloponnese, and even rebuilt the Hexamilion, a wall across the Isthmus of Corinth originally constructed during the reign of Theodosius II as a defense against attackers trying to penetrate the Peloponnesian peninsula.[17]

These gains were modest by Roman historical standards, but, in the limited way that the weakness of the state permitted, they represented a comprehensive catalog of the sorts of achievements a Roman emperor ought to have. The recapture of Thessaloniki, long the second most important city in the empire, served as a genuine military triumph. The resumption of control over Mt. Athos, the financial privileges the emperor extended to the monasteries there, and the close relationships that Manuel had with monastic leaders placed him firmly in a tradition of Roman Christian imperial piety that stretched back to Constantine I.[18] Even intellectuals who disliked monastic "leeches" praised Manuel as a genuine fiscal reformer for his efforts to ensure that regular Romans no longer bore the burden of supporting the "swarms of laggards" in the monasteries.[19] The Hexamilion restoration tied Manuel's new security priorities to the deeper Roman past while, he claimed, providing renewed prosperity again for his subjects who lived behind the "ancient walls which had been raised up."[20]

Romans responded to these real and unexpected achievements as they had for centuries. They celebrated Manuel in some of the same terms used to praise real and imagined Roman restorations for the past 1600 years. Indeed, Manuel himself advanced some of these themes. In a funeral oration that the emperor composed for his brother, Theodore, around 1410, Manuel describes Theodore's successful tenure as the Roman official in charge of the Peloponnese.[21] When Theodore took office, the peninsula had been "totally destroyed" and was on the verge of an Ottoman takeover as local Roman leaders began to ally with the Turks.[22] The defeat of the western alliance at Nicopolis in 1396 only made matters worse.[23] Following the efforts of Theodore and the support of Manuel, "a lasting peace [was] signed" and "within a short time, the fields of the Peloponnese were waving with grain and the trees were laden with fruit."[24]

Manuel here echoed a wider sense that, following its narrow escape from the Ottomans, the Roman Empire was rebounding. Other imperial panegyrists praised the emperor even more fulsomely in the two decades after 1402. One author framed Manuel's movements through central and southern Greece as those of a great liberator.[25] Another, the Platonist teacher George Gemistus Pletho, mused to Manuel about a massive social reorganization that would restore the austerity and virtue of ancient Sparta to the fifteenth-century Peloponnese, though for Pletho the result would be a Hellenic and not Roman restoration.[26] Demetrius Chrysoloras framed the reassertion of Roman power in northern Greece and the Peloponnese as actions that placed Manuel alongside Alexander the Great.[27] Chrysoloras emphasized that this recovery involved more than just military affairs. Manuel also "restored the private and public affairs of cities which had often fallen into decay" by permitting the free and open expression of political opinions.[28]

As in other Roman restorations, there were victims. Manuel's *Funeral Oration for Theodore* makes clear that Roman forces violently suppressed many leading Peloponnesians who had allied with the Ottomans.[29] Both Manuel and Chrysoloras speak about the annoying and sometimes violent resistance of people in the Isthmus of Corinth to the emperor's efforts to build his defensive wall.[30] The pace of construction, the use of forced labor, and the effective confiscation of private land soon prompted an armed revolt led by local notables.[31] Their army was defeated in July of 1415, but it took Manuel's troops another few months to reduce all of their fortresses.

In the end, it all mattered very little. As Manuel reached old age, he turned more of the administration of the empire over to his son, John VIII. Acting against his father's advice, John VIII intervened in the Ottoman succession struggle that followed the Sultan Mehmet I's death in 1421. Mehmet's son Murad II defeated John's favorite, a son of Bayezid named Mustafa, and then turned against the Romans to punish what he saw as their unprovoked aggression. Constantinople came under siege in June of 1422—and remained blockaded until that September. At the same time, Ottoman forces began attacks across Greece. Thessaloniki came under siege again in 1423, with the Romans handing it over to the Venetians so that it might better hold out. When the city finally fell to the Ottomans in 1430, the population had dropped from 40,000 to perhaps as few as 2000.[32] Roman gains in central Greece proved similarly ephemeral. Even the Hexamilion failed to do much to protect the Peloponnese; the Ottomans breached it four times between 1423 and 1452.

In the end, the wars, diplomacy, and social unrest of Manuel's reign produced nothing more than a final blip of Roman power. It lasted less than twenty years—and then it was gone. Manuel and John confirmed its loss when they signed a humiliating treaty with the Ottomans in 1424 that effectively gave back nearly all of the gains Manuel had secured after 1402.

John assumed full control over the empire upon Manuel's death in 1425, but, by 1430, the empire had been reduced to Constantinople, some coastal lands around it, the Peloponnese, and a few Aegean islands.[33] John VIII then began looking for a way to secure outside help. In 1432 he began negotiations with the papacy to call a church council that would arrange a union of the Roman Catholic and Constantinopolitan imperial churches in return for western military aid. As these negotiations began, Constantinopolitan and Peloponnesian thinkers held out hope that John would be like a second Constantine who would restore the church to orthodoxy by getting the churches to agree not to "abandon anything they thought right" nor add to "what had been sanctioned by the holy fathers."[34] This would be a union, but a union on Constantinopolitan terms that maintained the same ostensible fidelity to apostolic Christian tradition that had dominated eastern theological discussions for nearly a millennium. John would maintain the orthodoxy of the Eastern church and restore that of its Roman Catholic cousin.

This hope proved unrealistically optimistic. Unlike Michael VIII, who agreed to a church union in the 1270s as the sovereign of a relatively large state looking to consolidate its recent gains at the expense of the West, John initiated negotiations in 1432 out of extreme desperation. He had little leverage and, by the time that the churches agreed to return to communion at the council of Ferrara-Florence in July of 1439, Romans knew that John was not a second Constantine, nor was Florence another Nicaea.[35]

Instead of bringing the Roman church back to orthodoxy, the emperor had compromised theologically in exchange for the promise of military support. The perception that John had betrayed Christian orthodoxy split Roman public opinion. Figures who had once supported the idea of a union with the Catholic church reacted viscerally against the reality. Pletho, who had attended the council as one of the eastern representatives, turned against it, as did others who had once offered the emperor their fulsome support.[36] By the 1440s, it was openly stated that God would exclude from the "heavenly church" any monarch who supported the "innovation" or "accommodation" required to accept union.[37]

Opposition to union also offered a powerful platform for members of the fractious Palaeologian family, who looked to oppose, replace, or succeed the emperor. John had no sons and, as he grew older, his younger brothers each jostled for the chance to replace him. Demetrius Palaeologus proved the most aggressive. Not only did critics of the church union gather in his court and give orations praising his defense of orthodoxy, but Demetrius himself also foreshadowed what would become an anti-unionist line of thinking when he allied with an Ottoman commander to briefly besiege his brother in Constantinople in 1442.[38] This effort was, in some ways, a tangible manifestation of the idea shared by many Romans that "it would be better to see the turban of the Turks ruling in the midst of the city than the staff of the Latins."[39] Both Pletho and John Doceianus said as much when they later praised Demetrius for working with the Ottomans as allies rather than treating them as enemies.[40]

John's compromise seemed even less palatable when the Ottomans continued their advance in the northern Balkans while the West slowly organized a response. It was not until 1443 that western forces set off from Hungary, after Belgrade and much of Transylvania had fallen to the Ottomans. Making matters worse, the Ottomans then defeated the western army outside of Varna in 1444. Constantinople and what was left of its empire would have to effectively fend for itself.

John died in October of 1448. His brother Constantine XI, who was governing the Peloponnese at the time, had himself proclaimed emperor there in January of 1449. He entered Constantinople that March. Then, in February of 1451, the Ottoman sultan Murad died, leaving the Ottoman throne to his nineteen-year-old son Mehmet II.

The last act of the Eastern Roman Empire commenced with this changing of the Roman and Ottoman regimes. In the years since the failure of Manuel's Roman revival, Roman authors and thinkers had come to see the empire and the city of Constantinople as effectively one and the same thing. Much of the Peloponnese and some northern Aegean islands remained under Roman control, but the city towered above them in symbolic importance. To one Roman, Constantinople was "the leader and eye of the inhabited world." To another it was "a link between the Eastern and Western parts of the world" whose capture would lead to "the complete ruin of our affairs." A third spoke about it as "the common hearth" of the empire's Greek language, culture, and people .[41]

Mehmet shared the Roman fixation on the capital. Following a foolish Roman attempt to back an Ottoman pretender in 1451, Mehmet began planning a massive and sophisticated campaign to capture Constantinople.[42] The preparations unfolded across the year 1452. They began that spring with the construction of a fort, Rumeli Hisar, that clung to the hills along the European side of the Bosphoros. Packed with cannons and set opposite an older fort on the Asian coast, Rumeli Hisar gave the sultan's forces the ability to blow out of the water any unauthorized ship traveling south to Constantinople.[43] The Roman historian Ducas bitterly noted that the building materials for the fort that would help kill the empire were "taken from the ruins of the great dedicatory monuments of antiquity strewn around Byzantium" and included "columns from the ruins of the Church of the Archangel Michael."[44] The remains of the glorious Roman past would now help destroy what remained of Rome's empire.

The sultan's attack commenced on the morning of April 6, 1453, when Turkish artillery began bombarding the great Constantinopolitan land walls. More Turkish forces continued to arrive until, by early May, Mehmet's army seemed too large to count. One observer estimated the sultan had a force of 200,000. Another imagined 400,000. All agreed that it far outnumbered the approximately 5000 Romans and 2000 foreigners defending the city and its nearly five miles of walls.[45] Still the Roman defenses held for more than a month, reinforced by the procession of "holy, revered icons and sacred emblems along the walls" and tearful prayers "begging God to not deliver us, on account of our sins, to the hands of an enemy," icons and prayers that had delivered the city many times in the past.[46]

This defense worked for only so long. The sultan's troops breached Constantinople's walls on the morning of May 29 and soon were pouring east as panicked Romans ran toward Hagia Sophia, propelled by rumors of Turkish troops looting homes and slaughtering civilians. The Romans' last hope, Ducas wrote, was a prophecy:

The City was fated to be surrendered to the Turks, who would enter with great force and that the Romans would be cut down by them as far as the Column of Constantine the Great. Afterwards, however, an angel, descending and holding a sword, would deliver the empire and the sword to an unknown man, extremely plain and poor, standing at the Column.... Then the Turks would take flight and the Romans would follow them, cutting them down. They would drive them from the City and from the West and from the East as far as the borders of Persia.[47]

In their desperation, the Romans believed that their Christian, Roman Empire would not die. As had happened in 626 and 717 and even 1204, the Roman Empire would rise again, pardoned for its sins and fully restored to its ancient glory through God's mercy. For 1700 years, Roman decline had always been followed by a renewal. Why was this to be any different?

But 1453 was different. As the Turkish forces advanced through the city, the emperor Constantine XI died in the fighting. When the Turkish troops reached Hagia Sophia, it was clear no angel of the lord was going to appear. "Within an hour," Ducas wrote, "they had bound everyone, the male captives with cords and the women with their own veils" and then led them out of the church "like sheep."[48]

By 2 p.m. it was all over. The city of Constantine was no longer controlled by Romans. Hagia Sophia soon became a mosque. Many of the Roman residents in the city were enslaved and those who could not be ransomed were then dispersed across the Ottoman Empire. Husband was separated from wife and mother from child. This was, Ducas concluded, the new Jerusalem fallen like the old—with the new Israelites of Constantine's Roman Empire deported not to Babylon but all over the world.[49]

It may seem as if Ducas were leaving a crack open for an eventual Roman renewal. The Israelites, after all, did return from the Babylonian captivity. Ducas believed that the Romans would come back, too. He says that he wrote his history because he trusted that the reign of the Ottomans would end soon after that of the Palaeologan dynasty and, when it did, a Roman restoration would follow.[50] Perhaps for this reason, Ducas's history does not end with the fall of Constantinople. He goes on to describe how Mehmet swept up the final fragments of Roman territory over the next decade, taking the Roman Peloponnese in 1460 and the Roman splinter empire of Trebizond in 1461.

Ducas never saw the renewal he hoped to chronicle. Instead, his history ends in midsentence as he describes the Ottoman capture of the island of Lesbos—an event that seems to have either ended his dreams or his life.[51] When Ducas put down his pen, he certainly understood that the Roman Empire had finally expired. For the first time in their recorded history, Romans had no state to call their own. It is hard to imagine how incomprehensible this desolation must have been. The Roman state had survived Hannibal in the third century BC, the fall of the Republic, the plagues and invasions of the second and third centuries AD, the evolution of the empire into a majority Christian state, and the territorial contractions that remade the empire in the fifth through eighth centuries. It had even rebounded from the Crusader capture of Constantinople in 1204.

In each of these previous moments of crisis, Romans saw their state and its institutions revitalized after a crisis that many at the time saw as evidence of Rome's decline. But now, in the 1460s, the people who called themselves Romans no longer had a state—and they had no real hope that a Roman Empire under their control would return. Their Roman Empire had not just declined; it had fallen. Unlike in 1204, the Roman people no longer had the capacity to renew it.

16

ROMAN RENEWAL AFTER THE FALL

MANY OF THE Romans who lived through the fall of Constantinople ceased to dream about a renewal of their empire. They began processing their new reality as Roman subjects of the Ottomans. In the new Ottoman capital, an Athenian student of Pletho named Laonikos Chalkokondyles composed a history of the events leading up to and immediately following the conquest of Constantinople. He wrote in a literary Greek styled to resemble that used by Thucydides nearly 2000 years before. His work was, in a sense, a post-Roman history that evoked the ancient notion of a conflict between East and West to reframe the Turkish conquest of Greek-speaking lands as an Asiatic defeat of European Hellenism.[1]

Chalkokondyles deliberately constructed his work to be a history of Greeks that began before the Roman conquest of Greece and pointed to a Hellenic, non-Roman future. The millennium of Christian Roman Hellenism now served as a temporary interlude in a fundamentally Greek story.[2] Indeed, Constantinople's fall was not really the fall of the Roman Empire, because the people living in the city were Greeks, whose "language and customs prevailed but they changed their name" to Romans so that they "no longer called themselves by their hereditary" name of Greeks.[3]

The Ottoman capture of Constantinople then was "the fall of the Greeks and the events surrounding the end of their realm."[4] Chalkokondyles did not envision Greeks staying in this fallen state forever. When Greeks rose again, they would do so not as Romans but as Greeks. In the future, Chalkokondyles wrote, there will be "a king who is Greek himself" and he "will rule over a substantial kingdom."[5] This new, Greek kingdom would allow "the sons of the Greeks" to be "gathered together and govern themselves according to their own customs . . . and from a position of strength with regard to other peoples."[6] This was not a Roman renewal. It was instead a restoration of the vitality of the pre-Roman Hellenic world.

Other Greek speakers who lived through the conquest were far more pragmatic. One such figure, Michael Critobulus, wrote a history of the period between 1451 and 1467 that was dedicated to "the king of kings" Mehmet II, whom he describes as "the most mighty emperor" whose deeds are "in no way inferior to those of Alexander the Macedonian."[7] A native of the island of Imbros, Critobulus was born as a Roman subject of the emperor Manuel II, but he later negotiated the handover of Imbros, Thasos, and Lemnos to the Ottomans in 1456.[8] He then served as the Ottoman governor of Imbros until at least 1460 before fleeing to Constantinople at some point before the island fell to the Venetians in 1466.

Critobulus's history reflects his own biography. His project recounted both a history of Roman failure under Constantine XI and a story of Constantinopolitan renewal under Mehmet. This was, Critobulus claimed, an age of great men and dramatic historical shifts. On the one hand, Mehmet's deeds were so "excellent and in every respect surpassing those of his predecessors" that "they should not go unrecorded for subsequent generations." This was also a time when "a very great government, that of the Romans (which is the oldest we know), has been destroyed after a struggle of no long duration."[9]

Critobulus chooses not to "grieve as others do over our misfortunes, or be burdened by the sufferings of our nation."[10] "There is," he continues, "nothing astonishing" when the Romans, like the Assyrians, Persians, and Greeks before them, "lose their empire and prosperity, which pass on and are transferred to others, just as they came from others to them." One cannot "possibly condemn our nation, with any justice, because it has not been able to preserve its happiness forever or to guard its supreme power and good fortune."[11] Instead, Critobulus claims, he will follow the Jewish historian Josephus, a leader of the Jewish revolt in the 60s AD who switched sides in the war and went on to serve under the Roman emperor Vespasian. In his history of the Jewish war, Josephus "praises the skill and valor of the Romans, and exalts them very truthfully" while he also "reproaches the evils which appeared within his own nation."[12]

While Critobulus does narrate the horrors of the capture of Constantinople in wrenching detail, he also speaks about Mehmet's restoration of the city.[13] Following the sultan's entry into the city, "almost his very first care was to have the City repopulated" so he sent "an imperial command to every part of his realm, that as many inhabitants as possible be transferred to the City."[14] Mehmet also repaired the parts of the walls damaged by cannon and began the construction of new monumental buildings "so that it should be a worthy capital for him."[15]

Critobulus explained how Mehmet displayed mercy and justice in the years following his victories over the Romans. He set up a scheme so that the enslaved Romans in Constantinople could buy their freedom by working on construction projects.[16] The patriarch Gennadius, who had been marginalized under Constantine XI because of his opposition to the church union, received from Mehmet both recognition as the head of the imperial church and substantial properties to support the patriarchate.[17] The death of the empire and the devastation of the Romans that accompanied it were quite real to Critobulus, but so too was the path forward. Romans were no longer masters of the Mediterranean. Their empire was not coming back. They were now the subjects of a sultan whose great achievements and personal virtues offered Romans a path toward reconciliation, renewal, and rewards in a new post-Roman imperial order. Critobulus believed that they would be wise to embrace it.

If many Greek-speaking Romans had given up hope of a restoration of their empire, Catholic leaders in Europe still believed that they could roll back the Ottoman conquest of Constantinople. After all, they still had their own version of the Roman Empire. The entity born under Charlemagne had been called the Holy Roman Empire since the mid-1200s, but the nature of that empire and the powers of its emperor differed dramatically from that of the old Roman Empire of the East.[18] It based its Roman identity on the idea that the Roman Empire had been translated from Constantinople to the West in the ninth century when the pope, drawing upon the temporal authority granted to him by the *Donation of Constantine*, crowned Charlemagne in Rome.[19] This origin story led some fifteenth-century Catholic theorists to speak about the Holy Roman Empire as a Christian commonwealth in which the pope and the emperor enjoyed complementary but universal power.[20]

While the Holy Roman Empire idealized its emperor as the temporal power supporting Western Christianity, the imperial state and its emperor were actually quite weak. Fifteenth-century emperors were elected by a group of seven Prince Electors based in German regions of the empire and ruled over an extremely decentralized confederation in which electors and other stakeholders exercised significant checks on imperial initiatives.[21] While the popes remained conceptually quite important to emperors, few emperors were actually crowned by them. In fact, for much of the period between the mid-1200s and the early 1500s, the empire existed without any papally crowned monarch at all.[22]

Despite these very real limitations on imperial power, western thinkers still turned toward the Holy Roman Empire as the entity that could best respond to the fall of Constantinople. The emperor Frederick III understood that the end of the Eastern Empire presented him with a new opportunity to reaffirm his symbolic status as the wielder of the West's only legitimate Christian, Roman temporal power. Soon after news of Constantinople's capture reached the west, Frederick's allies held a series of councils in the German cities of Regensburg (in May of 1454), Frankfurt (in October of 1454), and Wiener Neustadt (in March and April of 1455) to organize a new Crusade in which Catholics would combine forces to wrest Constantinople back from the Turks. Enea Sylvio Piccolomini, who was then bishop of Siena and an advisor to the emperor, stood out as the star of these councils. Piccolomini, who would become Pope Pius II in 1458, eloquently argued that the Ottomans represented a serious threat to the West that could be confronted only through collective action led by the Holy Roman Emperor Frederick, the universal Christian sovereign in the West.

To make this case, Piccolomini passionately framed the loss of Constantinople as "a great victory for the Turks, a total disaster for the Greeks, and a complete disgrace for the Latins" for "we have never lost a city or a place equal to Constantinople."[23] He then detailed the horrors of the conquest, the bloodshed that accompanied it, and the death of the emperor.[24] "Christians," he proclaimed, "had two emperors, one Latin, the other Greek" but now, with the Greek emperor gone, it is as if "one of the two eyes of Christians has been ripped out, one of their two limbs amputated."[25]

The West, he continued, needed to raise itself up to follow the examples of Moses, Fabius Maximus, and those who gave their lives for Rome, as well as Charles Martel and Roland who battled for the Franks.[26] It had to recapture Constantinople on behalf of all Christendom. This moving performance grabbed the attention of conference attendees, but it secured no firm troop commitments. With the emperor lacking the authority to compel German princes to mobilize, the Crusade never happened.

Piccolomini had no more success in generating a Crusade after his selection as pope. So, late in his life, the pope probed a different way in which the West might protect itself from the victorious sultan.[27] After his death in 1464, a letter appeared that Piccolomini had composed for Mehmet. In it, the pope offered Mehmet papal recognition as the eastern emperor in exchange for his conversion to Christianity. "A little thing," he wrote, "can make you the greatest, most powerful and illustrious man alive today." It is just "a little bit of water by which you will be baptized" and "the same affection of the Holy See will be extended to you as to other kings," but it will be more intense "because you are higher than they."[28] There is no evidence that Piccolomini ever sent this letter and no clear idea of any other audience he might have imagined for it, but the approach he took in it opened a possible path toward restoring the Christian East that did not involve Crusading armies.

By the middle of the 1460s, the papacy decided to pursue this approach more aggressively. In 1464, the new pope, Paul II, sent his former tutor George of Trebizond to Constantinople to convert the sultan.[29] A native of Crete, George migrated to Italy in 1416 and worked as a teacher of Greek in a number of Italian cities before he joined the papal curia in the 1440s. A talented and gifted translator of ancient Greek texts, George evidently decided that he might gain the sultan's patronage—and then perhaps his conversion—by dedicating translations of ancient texts to him. So he dedicated a translation of the Hellenistic Greek geometrician Ptolemy to Mehmet, calling the sultan "the greatest emperor of the Romans" to whom God granted "the throne of Constantine" because "his nature surpasses those of all the emperors" who preceded him.[30]

George expanded on this point in a second letter that accompanied a philosophical work comparing Plato and Aristotle. In this, he argued that the true seat of the Roman Empire is Constantinople and, since Mehmet holds Constantinople, he is "the rightful emperor of the Romans."[31] This claim to Roman imperial power, however, depended upon God. Mehmet could become a new Constantine and a universally empowered Roman emperor if he "restored unity to . . . the faith, the church, and the empire" by converting to Catholicism.[32] If he did convert, Mehmet would rule a revived Roman Empire based in Constantinople that could again extend Roman Christian rule across both the West and the East.

George's alchemical transfiguration of the Muslim Ottoman Empire into a Catholic Roman state proved no more realistic than the angel-led Roman military restoration that the residents of Constantinople hoped for in 1453. Indeed, there is no record that Mehmet ever read or responded to this proposal, a scheme that no clear-headed person could see as anything more than a desperate dream. But, as the fifteenth century progressed, the weak Holy Roman emperors began to embrace a different path toward restored Roman rule in Constantinople. This restoration would not happen through a pan-European Crusade or a miraculous conversion of the sultan. The recovery of Constantinople would instead be accomplished through military forces commanded by the Holy Roman Emperor. He would reunify the empires, ruling both East and West as a genuinely ecumenical Roman emperor.

Frederick's son, the emperor Maximilian I, embraced this idea wholeheartedly. Maximilian was the first western emperor born after the fall of Constantinople—an important distinction. While people like Piccolomini and Frederick III sought first to preserve and then to restore the Roman Empire of the East that existed when they were young, Maximilian never knew anything but an Ottoman-ruled Constantinople. When he wrote in his autobiography that it was his destiny to recover "the Constantinopolitan kingdom," he was using the idea of Roman restoration to justify his violent destruction of an existing political order.[33] This notion was aggression dressed up as renewal.

Maximilian nevertheless faced real constraints on his ability to move against the Ottoman capital. He took over as emperor after his father's death in 1493, but Maximilian, like all Holy Roman emperors of his era, understood that his imperial title and his position as the leader of the Habsburg house placed two separate and sometimes competing obligations upon him. As emperor, he had to work to maintain imperial power in the face of resistance from the regional princes and dukes who controlled much of the empire's territory. As a Habsburg, he also needed to build up family power both within and outside the empire—often in competition with some of the same people over whom he ruled as emperor. The empire was, in effect, an institution that Maximilian superintended on behalf of a large group of nobles. There was no guarantee that Maximilian's descendants would run it. The Habsburg lands belonged to his family—and his heirs would get whatever territories Maximilian could string together. The empire was, in a sense, a common good. The Habsburg lands were family possessions.

Maximilian succeeded wildly in building up the power and lands controlled by the Habsburg family.[34] He engaged in what a contemporary called "matrimonial imperialism" through which he used a series of dynastic marriages to position his grandson Charles to become the most powerful man in Europe. Maximilian's maneuverings made Charles simultaneously heir to the Spanish crown, the Kingdom of Naples, Sardinia, Sicily, the Habsburg central European lands, and the lands in the Netherlands and eastern France that belonged to the old Burgundian royal family. This was, the king of Hungary would observe, an empire won not through the virtues of Mars but those of Venus.[35]

Maximilian defended his status as emperor much less effectively. Although he had hoped to be crowned by the pope in Rome, Maximilian never managed to make his way into central Italy—even though much of the land through which he would need to pass theoretically belonged to the empire.[36] This failure to get to Rome particularly galled Maximilian because his bitter rival, the French king Charles VIII, had also begun toying with his own Roman imperial trappings. Unlike Maximilian, Charles marched freely into the imperial lands of northern Italy. And, when he entered Florence in 1494, Marsilio Ficino, the Florentine Platonist and intellectual heir of Pletho, gave an address that favorably compared the French king to Julius Caesar.[37]

Charles was also rumored to have purchased the title of Eastern Roman emperor from one of the surviving members of the Palaeologus family. When Maximilian learned of this purchase, he wrote to Rome immediately that he had heard "the king of the Franks" might "assume the title of the emperor of the Greeks." This would, Maximilian claimed, "bring enormous harm upon him and the whole Christian religion" because there would "not be one Christian emperor" but two who make the claim.[38] Other reports from Italy that Charles "sought to usurp not just the name but the genuine power of Roman emperor" by purchasing the "right to the empire of Constantinople" further fanned Maximilian's fears.[39]

Maximilian responded to this challenge on two different levels. He did not shy away from military conflict. Quite the contrary. He and the French kings Louis XI, Charles VIII, Louis XII, and Francis I frequently fought one another over various Habsburg and Burgundian possessions in Burgundy, Italy, and the Low Countries. He launched these wars primarily in defense of Habsburg claims to the sprawling constellation of lands his marriage and that of his son had put under the control of the family.[40] Much of this land over which he fought sat within imperial boundaries, but much of it did not—and the coalitions that Maximilian assembled to confront the French sometimes included non-imperial actors like king Henry VIII of England. These were, at their heart, dynastic but not imperial wars.

Maximilian also fought a public relations battle to defend his exclusive claim to the Roman imperial legacy. To this end, Maximilian commissioned a series of artistic and literary projects that emphasized his place in an unbroken Roman imperial succession stretching back to Julius Caesar. These works included an engraved representation of an imperial triumphal procession executed in a series of woodcuts that, had it been completed, would have included more than 200 engravings and extended more than 50 meters.[41]

Another series of woodcuts topped this one. Underpinned by the work of the imperial genealogist and propagandist Jakob Mennel, Maximilian commissioned Albrecht Dürer to create a massive engraved triumphal arch featuring his exploits alongside images of his Roman imperial and Habsburg familial ancestors.[42] (See Figure 16.1.)The arch included images of exemplary emperors like Constantine and Charlemagne, but also somewhat surprising figures like Aurelian and Heraclius.[43] When the printings are

FIGURE 16.1 ALBRECHT DÜRER, *THE TRIUMPHAL ARCH OF MAXIMILIAN I* (WIKIMEDIA COMMONS).

assembled, the entire composition stands more than 3 meters tall. Maximilian designed a similar artistic program depicting the deeds of his life amid busts of his familial, heroic, and imperial ancestors for a massive tomb.[44]

Maximilian did not just let his historical connection to the Roman past stand as an inert defense of tradition. This connection was meaningful to him because, as a Holy Roman Emperor, he could follow in the path of institutional ancestors like "Aurelian the revivor" and spark a Roman imperial renewal through the use of the military power of the West to reclaim Roman territory lost in the East.[45]

This aspiration caused the Christian reconquest of Constantinople to figure prominently in Maximilian's public profile. As early as 1490, Maximilian floated the idea of heading a Christian army assembled by the pope against the Ottomans.[46] He often repeated his desire to capture Constantinople, even going so far as to include Constantinople among the kingdoms existing under his imperial authority.[47] The French could purchase the Roman imperial title from the Palaeologans, but, as the Holy Roman Emperor, Maxmilian alone had the right to actually restore the fallen eastern capital to Christian Roman rule. He could, like Aurelian and Constantine more than 1200 years earlier, recover the Roman East by attacking from the West.

Maximilian's Roman restoration of the East nevertheless remained entirely rhetorical because he lacked the capacity to campaign against the Ottomans. But Maximilian's imperial successor, his grandson Charles V, had far more resources at his disposal. Unlike his grandfather, he sought to use them not only to further the objectives of his family but also to spur a Christian Roman reconquest of lands lost to Muslims.

Charles benefited the most from Maximilian's "matrimonial imperialism"—and the benefits began to accrue very early in his life. He took control of the Netherlands in 1506 (when he was six years old) and secured the Spanish throne when he was sixteen. Then, in a final act of Habsburg grandfatherly piety, Maximilian bribed the imperial electors so that Charles succeeded him as Holy Roman Emperor.[48]

Maximilian also passed along to Charles his idiosyncratic view of what it meant to be a Roman emperor. Charles's education featured daily reading about "the battles and victories of Caesar, Augustus, and Charlemagne," but the Roman past about which he learned also included both Maximilian's Holy Roman Empire and the fallen, Constantinopolitan east.[49] As Nate Aschenbrenner has shown, at roughly the same time that Charles received his education about the heroic figures of the Roman past, the Viennese scholar Johannes Cuspinianus composed for Maximilian a history of the Caesars stretching from the first century BC to Maximilian himself. Published along with it was an oration urging "Caesar Augustus Charles" to rouse the forces of Germany, Spain, England, and France to fight the Turks so that he might recover Greece, "ascend the other imperial throne," and rule both "the East and West together."[50]

Charles did not get the idea of restoring the East to Christian Roman imperial rule just from his paternal grandfather. Similar ideas circulated in Spain as well. His maternal grandparents Ferdinand and Isabella also very much desired to undertake campaigns in the southern and eastern Mediterranean against Muslim-held, formerly Christian territories.[51] For much of the latter part of his reign, Ferdinand mounted attacks and settled Spanish Christians at Presidios along the North African coast. Ferdinand also eyed the Levant, planned an attack on Alexandria, and hoped to assert the dynastic claim to the long-dead Crusader kingdom of Jerusalem that had passed to his family.[52]

An oration given in praise of Charles by the Spaniard Pedro Ruiz de la Mota at the Cortes of Santiago in 1520 shows how contemporaries framed Charles's decision to embrace the imperial legacies of both of his grandfathers. Mota rose to support Charles's request that the Spanish nobles approve funds to support his travel to Germany to accept the imperial title.[53] With his election as emperor, "the glory of Spain has returned" because, "whereas other nations sent tribute to Rome, Spain sent emperors" like Trajan, Hadrian, and Theodosius. "And now," Mota continued, "the Empire has come to Spain in search of an emperor."

Charles's response to Mota's evocation of the ancient Roman imperial past showed that the new emperor also understood his position in contemporary terms. The empire, Charles responded, "comes from God alone" and, while he would have been content with the Spanish possessions across Europe, the Mediterranean, and the Americas, the Turkish "enemy of religion has expanded so much that neither the repose of Christendom nor the dignity of Spain" would be able to withstand it "unless I link Spain with Germany and add the title of emperor to king of Spain."[54]

This exchange previewed a public image that Charles would continue to embrace for much of his reign. Charles blended ancient Roman imperial tradition, medieval notions of the Holy Roman Emperor as the temporal leader of Western Christianity, Maximilian's recent ideas of Roman imperial restoration through the conquest of Constantinople, and Ferdinand's interest in a Christian reconquest of the Mediterranean. He played all of these roles well, at least initially. After word got out that the emperor had read the writings of Marcus Aurelius while ill with a fever, Charles adopted Marcus's hairstyle and beard for his imperial coronation.[55] When he first visited Aachen in 1520, Charles prostrated himself before the reliquary containing the skull of Charlemagne.[56] The emperor often promised that "after annihilating the powerful Turks" he would "recover the imperial city of Constantinople."[57] The idea of a Roman recovery of the East remained very much alive.

Like his grandfather, Charles fancied himself a direct institutional descendant of Augustus, Trajan, and Constantine, but Charles ruled in a very different fashion from that of any of these distinguished imperial predecessors. The emperors of old ruled an empire won by the Roman people. They were its stewards but, in the old tradition of the Republic, the Roman Empire belonged to the people, not the emperor.

This was not the case for Charles. He was the Roman emperor, but the vast majority of his lands did not belong to the empire, as people like Hernán Cortés, the conqueror of Mexico, understood. When writing to the emperor as he pacified Mexico in 1520, Cortés promised Charles that he "could call himself emperor of it, with no less title than that of Germany."[58] Cortés was not alone in differentiating the conquests of the emperor as an individual and the success of the Holy Roman Empire he headed. In 1528, when Cortés arrived back in Spain, the German artist Christoph Weiditz painted his portrait and captioned it thus: "This is the man who won almost all America for Emperor Charles V."[59] Weiditz knew that Cortés had not won the land for Rome. He had won it for Charles. The difference, which everyone understood, mattered greatly. Charles's successes were his own—and the language of imperial renewal he used was designed not to reflect improved conditions within the Roman Empire. It instead served simply as another way to communicate Charles's achievements as an individual who happened to be the Holy Roman Emperor.

The German electors who chose Charles in 1519 also understood these differences. Writing in German (a language that Charles did not yet speak), they compelled him to agree to conduct all administrative business in either German or Latin, employ only Germans as administrators, never bring foreign troops into the empire, never bring the empire into any foreign alliance, and never allow a German to come to trial in a foreign jurisdiction.[60] Charles could be emperor only if he agreed to keep the empire administratively sealed off from the rest of the territory he controlled.

There was even resistance to the theoretical claim that Charles, as Holy Roman Emperor, served as the temporal leader of Western Christians against the Ottomans. As Charles dreamed of an attack on Constantinople, his sister, Mary of Hungary, wrote to Charles that "although your majesty is the foremost Christian prince in honor and the number of your dominions, you are not obliged to defend Christendom alone."[61] Her words reflect the reality that, despite his immense power, Charles no longer occupied the position of Christian temporal leadership in which figures like Piccolomini had once placed the Holy Roman Emperor.

No one could. Because, on April 18, 1521, in the German city of Worms, Martin Luther stood before Charles and defiantly exploded the old ideal of a papally and imperially guided Holy Roman Empire. Luther had followed up the publication of his *Ninety-Five Theses* in 1517 with a series of increasingly aggressive criticisms of the conduct of the papacy. Written in German, Luther's 1520 *Open Letter to the Christian Nobility of the German Nation* drew on growing German frustration with what he called "the shameful and devilish rule of the Romans."[62] Although Luther acknowledged that the popes "robbed" the "emperor at Constantinople, who was the genuine Roman Emperor" and turned his title "over to the Germans . . . as a fief" under papal control, Luther felt that this wickedness was part of a divine plan to "give such an empire to the German nation."[63] Luther explicitly affirmed his loyalty to the emperor and complained about how "the good emperors Frederick I and II and many other German emperors were shamefully oppressed and trodden under foot by the popes."[64] Instead of allowing these "princes of hell" to "steal from us," he wrote, German kings, princes, and all the nobles should throw the corruption of the Roman church out of German lands.[65] The empire could then serve its true purpose by putting the needs of Germans above those of the papacy.

By the autumn of 1520, Luther had attracted the support of the imperial Elector of Saxony, a very powerful backer who ensured that Luther would receive safe passage to give a defense of his conduct before the emperor and the imperial Diet in Worms. It was at that assembly, attended by Charles and other leading figures in the empire, that Luther rose. Speaking first in German and then switching to Latin at Charles's request, Luther told the emperor that it was "a duty that I owe to Germany" that he expose the Roman tyranny over the German nation. [66]

The war of words at Worms in 1521 previewed a growing rebellion within the empire against papal dictates that culminated in the 1527 sack of Rome by an imperial army of German and Spanish troops. They plundered the city for ten days, killing perhaps 8000 Romans and doing such damage that a contemporary opined that "Rome will not be Rome again in our lifetimes, or in 200 years."[67] The contemporary observer Paolo Giovio wrote that there was never any "greater ferocity either among the barbarians who are inflamed with the sect of Mohammad nor in any of the enemies or adversaries from the past." They allowed no refuge to any Romans they caught and even destroyed churches and shrines that "Totila the Goth and Geiseric the Vandal" respected.[68] When news reached Charles of his troops' capture and sack of Rome, the Florentine ambassador at his court reported "instead of inducing piety and sympathy in the emperor . . . he laughed and joked so much . . . that he scarcely found time to eat."[69]

The barbaric imagery and references to the late-antique Germanic Arian kings in Giovio's text resonated because many of the German troops who sacked the city were Lutherans, followers of a man whom a papal spokesman at Worms in 1521 had already compared to Arius.[70] These Germans did not hide their eagerness to take revenge on the "tyrannical Rome" that Luther had described. As the army advanced into Italy, one of their commanders even took to boasting that he looked forward to hanging the pope with a golden noose he carried with him.[71] This impression of Charles's army as a group of heretical, anti-papal fanatics became so dangerous that the Spanish Franciscan Quiñones warned the emperor that he needed to mend relations with the pope or he might "no longer be styled Emperor but Luther's Captain, as the Lutherans, in his name and under his flag perpetrated their atrocities."[72]

The sack of Rome did profound damage to both the city of Rome and the reputation of the emperor, but it occurred amid a decade and a half that produced some of the most extensive conquests that anyone claiming the

Roman imperial title ever achieved. The Spanish domination of much of the Americas had begun under Ferdinand and Isabella, but it expanded greatly in the first two decades of Charles's regime.[73] In 1518, Charles agreed to sponsor Magellan's voyage around the world. In 1519, he signed off on Cortés's expedition to conquer Mexico, a conquest that was completed with the establishment of Spanish control over Tenochtitlan in the late summer of 1521.[74] Then, in 1529, Francisco Pizarro secured permission from Charles to scout Peru, an expedition that led to Pizarro's seizure of the Incan empire in 1532. The conqueror of Peru quickly sent six tons of gold and twelve tons of silver back to Spain as the emperor's share of the booty.[75] All told, by the middle of the 1530s, Charles had gained control of nearly 2 million square kilometers of new territory in the Americas.[76]

The gold and silver that Charles stole from the Americas funded a long series of European and Mediterranean wars. There were three wars with France between 1521 and 1536, largely centered on securing Charles's possessions in Italy and his family's inheritance in the Low Countries. Charles also fought frequently with the Ottoman sultan Suleiman the Magnificent, prompted first by an Ottoman victory in 1526 that led to the conquest of much of Hungary and then intensified by the Ottoman siege of Vienna in 1529. The Ottomans also worked with naval commanders based in North Africa to attack Spanish and Italian ships and ports.

It was this last concern that prompted one of Charles's most spectacular campaigns. In 1535, Charles attacked the city of Tunis in order to capture a base of operations used by the admiral Hayreddin Barbarossa to raid Charles's Spanish and southern Italian possessions. This war, a contemporary observed, offered an "opportunity for the emperor to attend not only to everything required for Africa" but the "greater and more honorable enterprise" of the conquest of Constantinople.[77] Funded in large part by gold coming in to Spain following Pizarro's recent capture of the Incan king Atahualpa, the emperor assembled a fleet of nearly 400 ships and an army of perhaps 30,000 troops in Sardinia. He landed in North Africa in June of 1535, and captured Tunis on July 21.[78]

Charles's campaign against Tunis produced some of the most marvelous monuments illustrating the emperor's particular fusion of the ancient Roman past, the Holy Roman Empire, and the contemporary influences of his grandfathers. The new pope Paul III celebrated news of the victory with a mass in Santa Maria Maggiore held amid breathless speculation that "God will give such grace to the Christian people that the pope . . . will say a Mass in Hagia Sophia in Constantinople the following year."[79] When Charles returned to Sicily, he was greeted as a second Scipio Africanus. Sicilians staged re-enactments of Scipio's defeat of Hannibal for the emperor and erected triumphal arches celebrating Charles's victory. The city of Cosenza dedicated a statue of Charles with an inscription calling him "Charles Africanus" along with two other statues honoring Scipio and Marius, the two greatest Republican Roman victors in African wars.[80]

Charles then capped his grand victory tour in the spring of 1536 with a triumphal procession into Rome modeled on ancient imperial practices. He entered on the southeast side of the city, passing the Circus Maximus and the Colosseum before heading to the arches of his imperial predecessors. He first reached the Arch of Constantine, entered the Forum beside the Arch of Titus, exited it via the Arch of Septimius Severus, and approached the Capitoline hill. The emperor continued through the Campus Martius, crossed the Tiber at Ponte San Angelo, the bridge linking the Campus Martius to the western bank on which the Mausoleum of Hadrian sat, and then arrived at St. Peter's basilica to meet Pope Paul III.[81]

The triumphal emperor who marched into Rome that spring controlled more territory than any Roman emperor ever. More than Charlemagne. More than Justinian. Even more than Trajan. And yet the centripetal forces that continually threatened to pull apart Charles's diverse realms remained a problem. Pope Paul III had undertaken some repairs to spruce the city up for Charles's triumph, but doing so could not hide the fact that many of the Romans who lined Charles's triumphal parade route had lived through the trauma of the imperial sack of the city. They could, at best, have had mixed feelings about the German-Spanish king who came to their city to dress up as an ancient Roman emperor after his anti-Roman, Lutheran soldiers had done so much damage nine years earlier. In any event, Romans did not long pretend to love Charles. A few months after his triumph, Charles suffered a defeat at the hands of the French near the Rhône River. Placards then began appearing in Rome that showed Charles retreating on horseback with the caption "PLUS RETRO" (Retreat further), a line that mocked his personal motto "PLUS ULTRA (Further Beyond)."[82]

This display hinted at the dramatic turn that Charles's fortunes would take across the last decade and a half of his time as emperor. From the earliest point in his career, Charles had been warned that he lacked the time and attention necessary to attend to the needs of the many diverse lands joined together only by the identity of their sovereign.[83] These problems had barely been manageable when Charles was successful, but he saw far fewer successes as the 1530s became the 1540s. The failures and near failures following the Roman triumph of 1536 are almost as striking as the successes that preceded them. The emperor nearly lost control of Peru in the mid-1540s following a revolt of Spanish settlers led by Pizarro's brother. In 1539, his birthplace, the city of Ghent, rebelled against the high taxes it had to pay to support yet another war in Italy. Charles was forced to go personally to the city and punish his countrymen by hanging some of the rebellion's leaders while compelling others to parade through the city with nooses tied around their necks.[84] A campaign against Barbarossa's new base in the city of Algiers resulted in an expensive failure in 1541. And the Protestant Reformation proved a persistent source of instability in Germany across the 1530s and 1540s.

Charles did not just have to deal with insurrections within the territory over which he was nominally sovereign. He also confronted an open fracturing of the unified front that Christian Western Europe had pretended to hold against the Ottomans. After more than a decade of intermittent discussions, Charles's two most powerful European adversaries, the French king Francis and the Ottoman sultan Suleiman, entered into a formal alliance in 1536.[85] Backed by this Ottoman support and a constellation of other allies around western Europe, Francis then launched a set of coordinated military actions against Charles's territories. These actions included a joint Ottoman-French naval attack on the city of Nice in 1543 and French troops and artillery fighting alongside the Ottomans in Hungary in 1543 and 1544.[86]

The serious threats posed by the Franco-Ottoman alliance also had implications for religious life within the empire. Charles's need for Lutheran troops in these conflicts and his inability to compel Lutheran princes to enforce bans on Luther's ideas forced him into a series of compromises that prevented him from taking any lasting actions against German Protestants.[87] Eventually, his hostility against Protestants proved so intolerable that, in both 1546 and 1552, some German Protestant princes began to work with the king of France to fight their emperor.[88]

Charles eventually relented. At the end of his reign, he agreed to a settlement with the Schmalkaldic League (a military alliance of Lutheran princes) that permitted rulers within the empire to choose whether their domains would practice Lutheranism or Catholicism. Signed in September of 1555, the so-called Peace of Augsburg laid the foundations for an Empire that now had two co-existing, legally sanctioned Christian confessions—one of which the pope condemned as heretical.[89] As rumors circulated that the pope intended to order Charles deposed for legalizing Lutheranism, the emperor wrote to his brother that he had decided "to no longer be enveloped by this religious point."[90] This retreat finally and fully ended the idea that the Holy Roman Empire served as the epicenter of Catholic Christian military and political life.

This long and frustrating political career took a serious toll on Charles's health. Afflicted with gout, arthritis, and many other ailments, Charles announced to his subjects on October 27, 1555, that he was "not feeling in himself the vigor which the government of so many states requires," and stated that he intended to dedicate "the remainder of his life to the service of God" and the Catholic faith.[91] He then began the process of disentangling the motley collection of territories he ruled. Naples, Sicily, the Netherlands, Spain, and the Spanish territories in the Americas went to his son, Philip. Austria and the empire went to his brother, Ferdinand. Charles spent the last years of his life in the Spanish monastery of Yuste, dying of malaria in 1558.

Ultimately, amid his many successes and spectacular failures, the reign of Charles V marks an important endpoint in any consideration of the power of Roman renewal. From the very beginning of Rome's historical record, Romans spoke about the decline of their society and called for its renewal. For more than 1700 years, their history had taught them to believe that decline would be followed by renewal sparked by contemporary Romans whose virtues paralleled those of the great Romans of the past. This belief is why, for example, figures as diverse as Charles V, Alexius

Comnenus, and Romanus II could evoke the legacy of Scipio Africanus. He belonged to a Roman past they all shared, a past that could uniquely inform and inspire the Roman present.

As the history of Critobulus showed, the powerful idea that the Roman resilience of the past guaranteed Rome's restoration in the present had largely disappeared in the East by the end of the 1460s. The rhetoric of renewal continued to echo across the West for more than a century after the fall of Constantinople. People as diverse as Piccolomini and Charles V believed that a living, dynamic connection with the Roman past remained in the Holy Roman Empire of the West. In part because of this belief, the Holy Roman Emperor could (and should) restore Roman, Christian rule over Constantinople. By the time of Charles's abdication, however, this idea seemed unrealistic to the West as well. Not only was the Ottoman Empire now firmly in control of Constantinople but also the Ottoman alliance with the French had made united Christian action against the Ottomans impossible. The West now embraced its own post-Roman pragmatism.

It had also become clear that the Holy Roman Empire no longer could exclusively claim the Roman legacy. Among the many titles used by Ottoman sultans from Mehmet II onward was Kayser-i Rum (Caesar of the Romans), a title that marked their sovereignty over those Greek speakers who called themselves Romans.[92] Venice styled itself as a new and improved version of the Roman Republic with its Doge Andrea Gritti embracing the legacy of the deliberate Roman Republican general Fabius Maximus in implicit contrast with Charles's dashing Scipio.[93] Even the grand duke of Moscow was now bidding for papal recognition as Roman emperor.[94] In a century in which Lutheran imperial troops had sacked Rome, imperial coronations no longer took place in the eternal city, and Lutheranism was legally permitted within the Holy Roman Empire, the German emperor struggled to press his exclusive claim on the Roman legacy. The idea of Rome remained resonant, but its use had been democratized. Rome was no longer a living polity with an illustrious past that joined to a singular Roman present. It had become a powerful metaphor to speak about the present and future that was now open to all who wished to evoke it.

17

A DANGEROUS IDEA

THE SIXTEENTH-CENTURY PATTERN of European kings, emperors, and republics claiming a connection to the Roman past continued over the next two centuries. This was an age of republics, monarchies, and empires that borrowed Roman images and traded upon Roman historical legacy. Russian czars trafficked in their own version of the translation of empire that joined Roman Constantinople and Moscow. Between 1780 and 1800, France whiplashed between various invocations of the Roman past. It first had a king who evoked the symbols of the Catholic Roman West, then a consular-led secular republic patterned on that of Rome that destroyed those symbols, and, finally, an Empire headed by Napoleon, a sovereign who erected triumphal arches and monumental columns while placing his laureled bust on coins just like Roman emperors of old. By the end of the eighteenth century, this behavior had even spread to the new world as the founding fathers of the nascent United States drew heavily upon models of the Roman Republic while they fashioned their own, expansive form of representative democracy.[1]

The Roman legacy particularly energized nineteenth- and early-twentieth-century Italian politicians. Giuseppe Mazzini, one of the leaders of the revolution that briefly forced Pope Pius IX out of Rome in 1848, believed that a Roman state "alone could rise, die, and then rise again with a new mission."[2] Rome, he wrote, was "the verb of History" that had twice unified the world—first in the Rome of the Caesars and again as the Rome of the Popes. In Mazzini's mind, "the descendants of Brutus and Cato" would create a third Rome, a "Rome of the People," which would unify Italy and, eventually, birth a world governed by the people and founded on freedom and equality. The city of Rome would again be the beating heart of an Italian—and world—historical project. "The liberty of Rome," he wrote, "is the liberty of the world."[3] If this liberation required bloodshed, so be it.

Even though Mazzini countenanced violent revolution, he could not have imagined the level of violence that the idea of a revivified Rome would later inspire from Benito Mussolini and other Italian fascists. Mussolini saw the fall of the Roman Empire as temporary and reversible. The vigor of Rome could be brought back through tangible actions like imperial conquests in Africa and the Mediterranean, but its ghosts could also be roused to actively participate in shaping the great Italian future.[4] The ancient past then continued to exist in what Claudio Fogu called a "historical present" in which Rome's imperial past and Italy's fascist future coexisted, blended, and reinforced each other.[5] This vision is why the fascists reorganized the Italian military into centuries and gave them legionary standards like the Roman armies of antiquity. It is also why, following Italy's brutal conquest of Ethiopia, Mussolini told the new "legionaries" to "salute, after fifteen centuries, the re-appearance of the Empire on the predestined hills of Rome."[6] (See Figure. 17.1.) Nearly 800,000 Ethiopians are estimated to have died in the conflict that created this reborn empire.[7]

Mussolini agreed with Mazzini that the city of Rome was again to be the beating heart sustaining a new future, but the future was fascist rather than liberal. Rome became the place where the ideology of fascist empire was displayed, most notably in a series of five giant black-and-white maps hung on a wall abutting the Via dell'Impero, the great road Mussolini had cut next to the Roman Forum so that the "monuments of Imperial Rome could be liberated from the filthy huts that suffocated them."[8] The first four maps, all of which are still displayed beneath the Basilica of Maxentius, showed the expansion of ancient Rome from a city state into the empire of Trajan. The fifth map, which now sits broken and in storage, showed the Fascist Italian empire as it stood in 1936.

That fifth map was a key visual component of Mussolini's imperial program. The Via dell'Impero served as a military parade route that stretched from the ancient Roman Colosseum to the modern Italian monument to King Victor Emmanuel II at the Piazza Venezia. The maps hanging along it visually reinforced the link these parades made between the ancient imperial capital and Mussolini's revived empire. The map of the Fascist Italian

FIGURE 17.1 ***LA RIVISTA ILLUSTRATA DEL POPOLO D'ITALIA*, NOVEMBER, 1933 (CREATIVE COMMONS).**

empire was also placed in the background of a poster distributed around Italy. In addition to the map, the poster showed the Capitoline Wolf and Roman legionary standards and bore the caption: "Rome must appear marvelous to all the people of the world: vast, organized, and powerful just as it was in the times of the first empire of Augustus."[9] Mussolini's Rome was to be made great again, both as a city and as the center of a renewed empire.

The renewal of the city became a particular concern for Mussolini. His planners hoped Rome would become a "school of that great humanity which our Roman fathers called virtue" by excavating and then setting apart ancient monuments so that "someone going about his business" would "stop for a moment, in spite of himself, before the great memories of the past" and ponder their "lessons, warnings, and rules for life."[10] That city needed to be allowed to emerge like "the trunk of a great oak liberated from all that still constrains it."[11]

The fascist liberation of ancient Rome destroyed large quarters of the old city. The Circus Maximus, Forum, and Capitoline hill were "sanitized" of houses, shops, and factories, "annulling the centuries" so that the exposed monumental spaces could "point toward better times with greatness and constructive clarity."[12] The Mausoleum of Augustus, which had housed the city's symphony, was made physically distinct from the buildings around it and gutted down to what remained of its ancient core. This process destroyed 120 houses—and left the once-functional building an overgrown, vacant eyesore that Romans called "the rotten tooth."[13] Fascist planners also cleared a vibrant market district around the Theater of Marcellus, houses and other buildings covering the Forum of Trajan, and even the remains of ancient monuments built by Nero and the Flavians that blocked the sight lines to the Arch of Constantine.[14] This was, one of the men involved in the plan's execution maintained, a process that made Romans' memories of how these newly cleared districts once looked "seem ancient, relics of a seemingly distant epoch."[15] The recent disorder of the city had become ancient history while Rome's antique ruins were now simultaneously ancient and modern monuments that offered "magnificent manifestations . . . and unequivocal proof which the regime has given of its powerful, renewing vitality."[16]

Part of the power in what Mussolini did to the Italian capital came from his sustained attack on an idea of Rome that both Italians and others had long shared. As Joshua Arthurs describes, outsiders loved to come to Rome and gape at the "half-buried columns of the Roman forum filled with grazing cattle" and see in them "metaphors for the frailty of human creation."[17] Despite the fascist efforts, these ideas never went away.

Their continued strength prompted a swift and powerful reaction against the fascist rhetoric of Roman revivification after Italy's defeat in World War II. With Italy's empire lost and monuments like Augustus's "rotted tooth" Mausoleum covered in sandbags to protect them from errant bombs, the ancient imperial Roman past again seemed quite distant. The map of the "Second Roman Empire" came down, Mussolini's Via dell'Impero was renamed the Via dei Fori Imperiali, and Italian intellectuals turned aggressively against the fascist idea of *romanità*. The idea of Rome was, Paolo Nalli wrote, "a cancer" whose malignancy should be acknowledged and combated.[18] Many agreed with Nalli that no one should again try to revive an ancient Rome that all now clearly understood had declined, had fallen, and was not coming back.

Nineteenth- and twentieth-century Italians had a unique, tangible connection to the remains of the Roman past, but most of the rest of the world had long accepted the idea of a fallen, extinct Rome. The glory of Rome's Republic and its Empire still awed them, but the process through which it declined, fell, and expired fascinated them even more.

No figure was more responsible for fixing this idea of the decline and fall of the Roman Empire in the public mind than an Englishman named Edward Gibbon. Gibbon, of course, did not invent the idea of Roman decline and fall. Romans had been identifying signs of decline and debating its causes for as long as our literary record stretches. By the early sixth century AD, Romans as diverse as the anti-Chalcedonian bishop Timothy Aelurus of Alexandria and the Constantinopolitan historian Procopius had already used the idea of a decline and fall of Roman control over the West to justify aggressive actions against people perceived to have caused that fall. Western figures like Charlemagne and Charles V similarly drew on ideas about the decline and fall of the Eastern Roman Empire to justify Western aggression against the East. In all of these cases, however, the fall of Rome served as an invitation for a Roman outsider to step in and spark a renewal that disrupted, often through massive loss of life, the postlapsarian Roman world. The decline, fall, and restoration of the Roman Empire represented a call to arms.

Beginning in the fifteenth century, a different way of thinking about Roman decline began to emerge. Starting with the work of Renaissance Florentines like Leonardo Bruni, the completed story of the empire emerged as a tool that enabled contemporaries to understand the particular moment in which they were living. Fifteenth-century Florentines saw the fall of Rome as an event that distanced their small, "modern" Republic from a vast and ancient Roman world that was "unlike their own and yet illuminated it."[19]

Unlike the Romans, popes, and German emperors who preceded them, these Florentines embraced the chronological distance that separated them from Rome while revering Rome's deep, classical literary and cultural legacy. For Bruni in the first half of the fifteenth century, Rome's fall was a necessary precondition to Florence's rise. When Rome was strong, Bruni wrote, "her grandeur limited Florence" like "mighty trees overshadow young seedlings." Later, "as Roman domination ceased," Florence flourished because "that which Rome's rise took away, its decline restored."[20] Bruni then offered a Tuscan history covering both what came before Roman domination and what came after barbarians ended it. Bruni did not just point to the moment when the empire ended; he also identified the onset of its decline. "The decline of the Roman Empire," Bruni explained, "ought to be placed at the time when, giving up its liberty, Rome began to serve the emperors . . . and, when liberty departed, so did virtue."[21]

Bruni wrote before Constantinople fell in 1453, but, as a historian of Florence, he also had no interest in a universal history of the Roman Empire that included the small, Greek-speaking Roman imperial sliver that lived on in his day. He was instead pointing toward a way of thinking about Roman history as a complete story whose beginning, middle, and end offered markers that his readers could use to observe and diagnose the conditions in their "modern" polities. Thus Bruni emphasized that the liberty of the Republic catalyzed Rome's startling rise to power and that the loss of liberty under the emperors initiated Rome's slow decline and fall. Fifteenth-century Florentines understood liberty to be both precious and precarious. Bruni's Roman story helped reassure them that this concern was well founded by giving them a historical context in which to appreciate why liberty and its loss mattered so profoundly.

Other Italians writing after the fall of Constantinople followed Bruni in assigning an end to Roman history and meditating about its contemporary significance. Flavio Biondo, who lived through the fall of Constantinople, expanded Bruni's model of decline and fall to include both Western and Eastern components in what amounted to a long, multi-book preface to his history of fifteenth-century Italy. Unlike Bruni, however, Biondo struggled to articulate exactly why this Roman story mattered to his Italian contemporaries.[22]

Nicolò Machiavelli took a different approach. He thought deeply about the lessons that contemporary Italian states could take from the organization of the Roman Republic and the processes through which its institutions later decayed. He wrote in a fashion that "compared ancient with modern events" so that "those who read that which I write may more easily see what utility there is . . . from the understanding of history."[23] These lessons did not, however, appear as components of a long and developed narrative about how Roman decay unfolded. They emerged instead across Machiavelli's commentary on the first ten books of Livy's massive Roman history, a work that Livy completed in the first century BC. Machiavelli's discourses on Livy mixed discussions of events in Livy's texts with observations about their contemporary relevance. The success of this project depended upon the idea that Machiavelli's world was distant from the ancient Roman past, but not so distinctive that it prevented one from using the concluded narratives of the Romans to understand unfolding modern events. This was, in a sense, a better developed application of Bruni's notion of Roman decline and fall.

It was not until the early eighteenth century that a thinker emerged who nearly combined the narrative talents of Bruni and the acute political insights of Machiavelli. This was the French political philosopher Charles-Louis de Secondat, baron de la Brède et de Montesquieu, better known now as Montesquieu. Montesquieu was closer to a political theorist than a historian in his intellectual orientation. His *The Spirit of the Laws* (*L'Esprit des lois*), which attempts to explain human laws and social structures, stands out as one of the most consequential works of political analysis in history. Among other things, it helped to inspire the thinking of eighteenth-century revolutionaries in both America and France.[24]

The Spirit of the Laws developed in conversation with another work, Montesquieu's *Considerations on the Causes of the Greatness of the Romans and of their Decline*. Montesquieu would write thus about the *Considerations*: "I had at first thought I would not write more than a few pages on the establishment of the monarchy of the Romans, but the greatness of the subject won me over. I rose imperceptibly to the first moments of the Republic and then descended until I reached the decline of the Empire."[25]

Like Bruni, Montesquieu came to Roman history out of a concern to better understand how decadence had, in his conception, caused Romans to choose the monarchy of Augustus over the liberty of the Republic. He soon appreciated that Roman history could point to a much larger and important story. To tell it, he embarked upon a discussion of the Roman state, an account that stretched from the traditional founding of Rome in 753 BC until the fall of Constantinople in 1453. The work, which is around 200 pages in its modern edition, offers a set of chronologically organized "considerations" rather than a detailed narration. It began in a familiar way. The Roman successes, in Montesquieu's view, derived from laws that "sagely divided public power across a large number of magistracies that support, arrest, and temper one another."[26] Echoing figures like Cato the Elder and Sallust, Montesquieu explained that territorial expansion in the Republic introduced a decadence that undermined traditional Roman civic virtues.[27] Beginning under Sulla, however, the system changed as voters gave the most powerful Romans "extraordinary commands that negated the authority of the people and the magistrates and placed all of the most important business of the state in the hands of one man or a few men."[28]

Eventually, civic virtues became so debased that Romans welcomed the autocracy of Augustus as a cure to the "anarchic space of the Republic." Augustus's regime tolerated public crimes that a legislature of fellow citizens would have prevented, a first step in a process that saw him systematically corrupt the people, the courts, and the armies.[29] Montesquieu held too that the virtues Augustus destroyed were never restored. His successors instead further strangled the surviving elements of the Republic, though great emperors like Antoninus Pius, Marcus Aurelius, and Julian did arrest Roman decline temporarily.[30] By the third century, the army had come to "exercise supreme authority" just as it began to lose the ability to effectively confront barbarians.[31]

Rome became increasingly alienated from its past greatness following the move of the capital to Constantinople. Emperors became more "attached to their palaces and more separated from their empire."[32] The East now took resources from the West, shifting the privileges the Republic had established for Romans away from Italy. The domination of the state by

Christianity, the end of religious toleration, and the increasing barbarization of the army further diluted the virtues the Republic once nurtured until Rome succumbed to barbarians, Arabs, and, eventually, Turks.[33]

The *Considerations* used Roman history to demonstrate Montesquieu's theory that political vitality grew out of a liberty tinged with virtue and decline set in when this liberty dissipated. The Roman successes under the Republic derived from the tremendous creative tension produced by the controlled chaos that the Roman mixed constitution generated. Decline began when autocratic generals and emperors progressively shackled the political and legal institutions of the Republic. Rome still persevered for a long time. It first enjoyed the long afterglow of the immense power it had once earned. Later, the favorable geography of Constantinople and lucky circumstances like the discovery of Greek fire long insulated it from its final collapse.[34]

The *Considerations* also performed another important function for Montesquieu's larger intellectual project by offering empirical evidence that seemed to prove the theories he laid out at length in the *Spirit of the Laws*. Montesquieu had, in a way, wedded Bruni and Biondo's narratives of Roman decline and fall with Machiavelli's concern for the contemporary relevance of ancient Roman events. Together, Montesquieu's *Considerations* and *Spirit of the Laws* intertwined the story of Rome's decline and fall with analysis about why the entire trajectory of the Roman state across 2200 years mattered to those living in a post-Roman world. All that was left was for someone to take this resonant, illustrative Roman story and present it clearly, powerfully, and memorably to a wider public.

Edward Gibbon was the man to do this. In one sense, Gibbon's project offered a mirror image of Montesquieu's *Considerations*. Montesquieu foregrounded his observations about the elements of Roman society and political life that made Rome strong as well as those which eroded that strength. He then hung these observations around a rudimentary narrative of Roman history. Gibbon, by contrast, offered a masterful, 4000-page-long monumental history that was narrative driven with observations and connections to the contemporary world either subordinated to the discussion of the Roman past or, in many cases, buried in the wonderfully insightful footnotes.

In some important ways, Gibbon offers a late-eighteenth-century distillation and rehydration of the ancient Roman ways of thinking about their own decline and renewal. Like thinkers going back at least to Sallust, Gibbon saw Roman power deriving from a civically engaged class of citizen warriors living in a polity governed well by civilians.[35] In other ways, however, Gibbon broke radically from the models of his predecessors. Unlike Sallust, Tacitus, Bruni, Biondo, Machiavelli, and Montesquieu, Gibbon does not situate the beginning of Roman decline in the late Republic. Instead he followed third-century authors like Dio and Herodian in marking the Antonine Age as Rome's peak.[36] Roman decline then begins not with the loss of Republican freedom. It started instead with the gradual onset of two processes that emerge under the emperors, processes that led to what Gibbon will call "the triumph of barbarism and religion."[37]

The first of these processes involved the barbarization of the Roman military and, eventually, the Western Roman lands. In Gibbon's view, barbarization progressed in a relatively straightforward fashion. As the Roman Empire of the second and third century moved away from citizen soldiers and started embracing the recruitment of barbarian mercenary troops, it became less robust. The brittle Roman military could not then resist the waves of German invaders that flooded across Roman frontiers in the third, fourth, and early fifth centuries.

The story of religious triumph proved more complicated to tell. Gibbon had a famously hostile view of Christianity's influence on the empire. He saw a sort of religious harmony existing in the pagan empire that gradually gave way to an inflexible, dogmatic, and intolerant Christian polity focused on imposing religious uniformity.[38] Christianity became a source of division and, ultimately, an agent of the disintegration of the empire. Perversely, Gibbon sees the Eastern Empire as an entity that withered across a millennium of "premature and perpetual decay" as the somnolent Greeks endured "passive connections" with more active peoples from both the West and the East.[39] To Gibbon, the toxic combination of Christianity and Eastern influences deprived the empire that remained of the dynamism that Rome at its peak had once possessed.

Gibbon's *Decline and Fall* did, however, have a larger, contemporary goal. In an idea evocative of Bruni's creation of the medieval world, Gibbon saw that the twin paths of barbarization and Christianization led to the emergence of a new, post-Roman, Christian Europe that was chronologically distinct from the classical past and geographically distinct from what had been the Roman East and South. Gibbon did not idealize this "medieval" Europe, but he did see it as a necessary precursor to the emergence of Gibbon's own "modern" Europe in which the great eighteenth-century European kingdoms lived in a sort of balance with one another. This modern Europe consisted of a system of states strong enough to prevent any one king's dominance over the continent and a religious order of Catholic and Protestant polities capable of checking the Christian tendency to violently enforce orthodoxy. It was a coherent and dynamic political system founded on disunity rather than homogeneity and the singular control of an emperor.[40]

The last installment of Gibbon's *Decline and Fall* appeared in 1788, less than a year before the French Revolution blew up the European Republic of States that Gibbon idealized. It is not surprising, then, that most people have forgotten that Gibbon's *Decline and Fall* set out both to narrate Rome's history and to offer a way to explain the present. *Decline and Fall* has suffered this fate because the present it explained, to borrow Gibbon's own terms, had a "premature" demise. In fact, it died so quickly that one could barely have time to read and process Gibbon's views about the European present before reality rendered them irrelevant. Thus readers were left to focus only on the narrative and the explanations for Rome's fall it provided.

What a narrative they found! It was gripping, powerful, and, once the French Revolution had stripped the relevance from its origin story for a modern European Republic of States, timeless. At this moment, Gibbon's *Decline and Fall* still sits among the top hundred Roman history books on Amazon.com's bestseller list—nearly 250 years after it first appeared.[41] The great genius of Gibbon's work and its afterlife grows not out of what the work says across its 4000 pages but what it represents. People know its title, they know what it is about, and many of them have a beautiful leather-bound copy of the book on their shelves. But few of those who own it ever read it. Even fewer read the entire work.

At the same time, Gibbon's title has an undeniable power. Because of it, a huge portion of the English-speaking world knows that the Roman Empire declined and fell. Although the dates, people, and details of the story are much less widely understood, they are not meaningless. At the outset of this book, I suggested that a powerful claim about a society's decline required nothing more than a snapshot and a story. Roman history has shown over and over again that this is true. In the Republic and early empire, the story of Rome's decline from a virtuous past offered figures as diverse as Cato the Elder, Tiberius Gracchus, Sulla, and Augustus a ready-made narrative they could tailor to justify taking the lives, rights, and property of rivals. In the high empire, Roman decline and renewal became the basic rhetorical cadence to which the birth of new imperial dynasties moved. As barbarian kings took the Western Mediterranean from the empire and Muslim conquerors gradually reduced the East, various "falls of Rome" were invented to justify wars of reconquest. In each case, people used a story of Roman decline to refashion how Romans understood an aspect of their world so that they could disrupt an existing political order. But the impact of these stories was limited to Romans. They did not resonate with non-Romans, who either did not know or did not appreciate their power.

Gibbon's *Decline and Fall* was different. Its success made the story of Roman decline and fall ubiquitous while liberating its power from the Roman context that once confined its disruptive potential. Roman decline and fall now offered a ready-made narrative to which one could attach just about any snapshot. Everywhere could now be Rome—and everyone could now be warned to avoid its fate.

CONCLUSION: ROMAN DECLINE AND FALL IN CONTEMPORARY AMERICA

A WONDERFUL LITTLE article recently published by the historian Hal Drake traces the diverse ways in which the story of Rome's decline and fall has been used in the United States since the late 1960s. This is, Drake writes understatedly, "a time-honored game" in which one can "take whatever problem is bothering you today, add the word Rome" and then claim that "if we want to avoid Rome's fate, we had better act."[1]

Perhaps the most absurd example of this came from Joan Collins who, in an interview with *Playboy* magazine in 1984, attacked what she saw as the libertine culture of the early 1980s by claiming that AIDS appeared "to teach us all a lesson." "It's just like the Roman Empire," she said. "Wasn't everyone just covered in syphilis? And then it was destroyed by the volcano."[2] Neither was true, of course. Syphilis is believed to have originated in the Americas and there was no volcano, but these details did not matter to Dame Collins. She knew Rome fell—and that was enough to use its fate as a weapon against a culture that seemed to be falling out of control.

Joan Collins's attack was offensive and absurd, but innocuous. Others used Rome's fall in much more careful and consequential ways. In 1969, Ronald Reagan delivered a speech at Eisenhower College in which he referenced "the observations of historians such as . . . Gibbon" about how the "pioneer heritage" of the Roman Empire led first to "two centuries of greatness" before "going into decline and collapse in its third."[3] But, Reagan claimed, "the signs of decay were becoming apparent in the latter years of that second century." It was, he said, an age "of the idle rich and the idle poor" with the poor "put on a permanent dole, a welfare system not unlike our own." As emperors catered to them, "the great, solid middle class—Rome's strength as ours is today—was taxed more and more to support a bureaucracy that kept growing larger" until eventually the "government engaged in deficit spending" that led to spiraling inflation.

At the same time, "the young men of Rome began avoiding [military] service . . . they took to using cosmetics and wearing feminine like hairdos and garments until it became difficult, the historians tell us, to tell the sexes apart." "Among the teachers, there was a group called the Cynics, whose number let their hair and beards grow, and who wore slovenly clothes, and professed indifference to worldly goods as they heaped scorn on what they called middle class values." Over time, "all these forces overcame the energy and ambition of the middle class." Ultimately, Reagan concluded, "Rome fell" before adding ominously "we are now approaching the end of our second century."

The rest of Reagan's speech launches into what he would later call "conservative principles" that address both issues of government and the "turmoil on the campuses."[4] "All the ferment and rebellion," Reagan claimed, "is in reality a cry for help" by young people rebelling against a society that no longer lives "by the standards we've tried to teach them." The young see a society in which people ignore the laws. This thought leads Reagan to wonder about "a gradual and silent erosion of our own moral code." America, Reagan said, began as a city on a hill. It risked suffering the same slow decline and fall as Rome unless it addressed the creeping moral, financial, and educational decay that had begun to surface on the government-subsidized campuses of the 1960s.

Reagan's Eisenhower College speech was a piece of genius. It evoked Gibbon's *Decline and Fall of the Roman Empire* and then used Rome to diagnose a hidden, but fatal, disease whose symptoms included many of the cultural, economic, and social ailments that budding conservatives sensed lurked beneath the American prosperity of the late 1960s. Reagan admitted that he had not read Gibbon himself, but this admission did nothing to disperse the power of the comparison he made.[5] With its proto-hippie Cynics and its ancient welfare recipients who destroyed middle-class values and wealth, Rome provided Reagan with villains that one could see appearing again in 1960s America. Roman high taxes, expansive bureaucracy, and waning commitment to military service also pointed ominously to the hidden but inevitable unsustainability of the Great Society.

Reagan did not support any of these claims about Rome with historical analysis. He could not have—many of them were false or misleading—but no matter. He mocked academics who dismissed as "cliché" the "almost eerie" parallels Reagan saw between "the rise and fall of Rome and our own Republic." They did, after all, work at the modern American "diploma factory" that caused students to "lose their identity" before they were "spewed from the assembly line in four years, stamped 'educated.' "[6] What of consequence could such people possibly say? In any event, the details of Roman decline did not matter. Rome had declined, it had fallen, and Reagan knew what he could do to prevent America from doing the same. Cut taxes, trim bureaucracy, clip the wings of campus rebels, and eliminate the welfare benefits that transferred wealth from the hard-working middle class to the indolent poor.

Reagan's use of Rome to diagnose and offer cures for 1960s-era social ills resonated strongly in certain segments of American conservative thought. In the July 1973 issue of *Ensign* magazine, Ezra Taft Benson, the former US Secretary of Agriculture and future president of the Church of Jesus Christ of Latter-Day Saints, quoted Reagan's summation of Roman history at length. He followed up with five bullet points offering what he claimed to be a concise summary of Gibbon's work, and then concluded that "even during the hour of our great prosperity, a nation may sow the seeds of its own destruction. . . . The lessons of history stand as guideposts to help us safely chart the course for the future." Heed Rome, in other words, so that America can avoid its fate.[7]

Subsequent decades saw many other Americans use Gibbon's title to opine about elements of the contemporary world that they disliked. Like Reagan, they used the decline and fall of Rome to claim a disastrous endpoint if the subtle and unnoticed signs of contemporary American decline went unheeded. In 1977, Phyllis Schlafly blamed Rome's fall on "the liberated Roman matron, who is most similar to the present day feminist" and "helped bring about the fall of Rome through her unnatural emulation of masculine qualities, which resulted in a large-scale breakdown of the family and ultimately of the empire."[8] Stop feminism now, in other words, before the nascent American decline it had initiated reached a point that could not be stopped.

The 1990s and early 2000s saw the same line of attack directed against new targets. In 1994, Republican congressman Frank Cremeans opposed the recently enacted "Don't Ask, Don't Tell" policy by opining that AIDS and homosexuality might have been responsible for the collapse of the Roman Empire.[9] Then, in 2012, Ben Carson, a prominent neurosurgeon and the future United States Secretary of Housing and Urban Development, argued that gay marriage represented "a slippery slope with a disastrous ending, as witnessed in the dramatic fall of the Roman Empire."[10]

The clumsy claims of people like Cremeans and Carson have as much basis in fact as Joan Collins's volcano, but the absurdity of their points should not hide the danger of the game they are playing. As Hal Drake says, they take what bothers them at that moment and attribute Rome's fall to that issue. The position they are taking is neither historical nor based on evidence anyone can examine. It is prophetic. The decline and fall of Rome offers "eerie parallels" to the present that permit people to take on faith a set of conclusions that reasonable analysis would not support.

The 2010s have seen a particular focus across the West on the fall of Rome and its purported lessons about immigration. In 2014, Phyllis Schlafly sat for an interview with Alex Jones in which she agreed with Jones that America was "going the way of Rome" by "bringing in the giant third-world populations, and it seems to be an accelerated collapse-of-Rome timetable now."[11] Other figures speak about things like the "the suicide of the West" by comparing recent immigration to the actions of an unnamed "weak-willed, greedy emperor" who "wanted cheaper soldiers to expand his political reach" and so "began the collapse of the Roman Empire."[12]

Some contemporaries have pushed this idea into even more dangerous territory. While Schlafly and Alex Jones are reacting to prevent a prophesized American decline modeled on Rome, white nationalists have begun planning a Roman restoration along the lines of what Mussolini tried to create in Italy during the 1930s. In a 2013 speech, the white supremacist Richard Spencer envisioned a racially pure "White Ethno-State on the North American continent" that would represent "a reconstitution of the Roman Empire." It would be, Spencer envisions, "an Altneuland—an old, new country" that would serve as a home for "Germans, Latins, and Slavs from around the world" and "could rival the ancients" by restoring an order in which "the globe itself [is] administered by a central elite."[13] The similarities to Mussolini's rhetoric are surely not accidental.

It is here, at long last, that the story of Roman decline and renewal reaches the present. Spencer is not the first to imagine a Roman Empire resurrected through a recommitment to basic values that supposedly once propelled its expansion—figures from Napoleon to Mussolini got there long before Spencer. All of them draw upon the same basic rhetoric used by Sulla, Augustus, Justinian, Charlemagne, Michael Palaeologus, and Charles V. It is a rhetoric that uses the decline and fall from an idealized Roman past to destabilize existing orders. It is also a rhetoric that has been used to support actions that have cost millions of people their lives, property, and rights over the course of two millennia.

So why does it work?

On one level, each individual across the 2200 years we have examined felt the power of ideas of Roman decline and renewal differently. Romans in the first century BC and Americans in the twenty-first century AD can both admire Scipio Africanus, but they do so for very different reasons. It is impossible to recapture each of these individual reactions over so long a period of time.

We can, however, identify some elements of ancient, medieval, and modern life that encourage a broader and more systematic identification with these Roman ideas and their champions. During the Republic, Romans interacted with their past by listening to eulogies, singing songs, and attending plays that celebrated the virtues and condemned the follies of their ancestors. Under the empire, institutions like the imperial cult and regular festivals for divinized emperors in Roman calendars sustained popular awareness of the men like Augustus, Vespasian, and Trajan who had restored Rome after real or imagined crises.[14] Medieval Romans also regularly commemorated historical events like the Roman victory over the Avars and Persians in 626 that saved Constantinople and reversed the tide of Heraclius's Persian war.[15] These public events collectively reinforced the idea of Rome as a uniquely resilient society and credited those responsible for its recovery.

Roman schools did the same, but even more effectively. Students learned about momentous events in the Roman past and read aloud speeches written by some of the people involved in them. They were taught to see models of virtuous behavior in men like Fabius Maximus, who fought to save Rome from the threat of Hannibal.[16] Students were even encouraged to write their own speeches that addressed historical controversies in the voices of their ancient predecessors. Augustine wrote that this was a system in which a student was "most worthy of praise" when his composition "reproduced the emotions of anger and sadness in a fashion most similar to persona of its subject and who dressed this up in the most appropriate words."[17]

These later Romans identified so closely with the achievements of their predecessors because their education rewarded them when they most effectively inhabited that Roman past themselves. Students imagined the experience of living through crises, they spoke in the voices of the Romans who had resolved them, and they shared in the exhilaration of the Roman recovery.[18] The heroes who saved ancient Rome came to feel very real to students trained to imitate them and inhabit their personae. The casualties of Rome's salvation seldom merited much student attention. A student might imitate Cicero as he spoke to the senate about the conspiracy of Catiline in 63 BC, but he would not be asked to inhabit the persona of one of the Catilinarian conspirators whom Cicero ordered killed without trial.

Events and celebrated figures from Christian Roman history resonated across even wider segments of Roman society. Much of this influence had to do with the particular way in which Christians were taught to interact with the Christian Roman imperial past. For nearly two millennia Christian churches have offered liturgical commemorations of Roman saints, church fathers, and Christian Roman emperors spread regularly across the year.[19] Mosaics and paintings depict martyrs, theologians, and exemplary emperors like Constantine and Justinian. Sermons explain who these figures were and why they mattered. Hymns encourage Christians to speak in the voice of these ancient Roman figures and experience the Roman past as participants in it.[20]

The sixth-century poet Romanus the Melode shows how Roman Christians could be invited to experience the past. Around 537, Romanus penned a hymn that celebrated the building of Hagia Sophia as part of the Roman recovery from the Nika Riot. The hymn spoke of Roman sins, Justinian and his wife, Theodora, begging God for forgiveness on behalf of their subjects, and their subsequent promise to build the great church. In the hymn, Romanus blends the present and past to such a degree that he links Solomon, Constantine, and Justinian.[21] Romanus's work then joins the sixth century to the fourth—and to the Old Testament—but it also invites future singers to experience this moment as he did.

Romans accepted this invitation and others like it for centuries. Constantinopolitan congregations continued to sing Romanus's hymns well into the Macedonian dynasty. As they did, Justinian's city seemed as close to ninth-century Christians as the Roman Republic did to someone like Augustine. But Romanus's age of Justinian did not include any mention of the tens of thousands of civilians Justinian massacred in the hippodrome before work on Hagia Sophia began. Like schoolchildren in the high empire, Roman Christians also had a selective understanding of what the restorations they celebrated had actually entailed.

Rome's physical presence in cities across Europe and the Mediterranean gave added immediacy to these historical evocations. Both Rome and Constantinople were so stuffed with monuments, artwork, and buildings dating back centuries that people could easily enjoy the illusion of experiencing the same physical space as Romans who came before them. Many of the later visitors might have had an experience similar to that of the Roman philosopher Seneca. He found the old Baths of Scipio inspiring in the 60s AD because the person entering them "knows that in that space your hero Cato or Fabius Maximus . . . once warmed the water with his own hands."[22] Merely being in that building transported Seneca from the reign of Nero back to the glories of the Republic.

Roman spaces could have this effect even after the empire retreated from them. An eighth- or ninth-century Old English poem called "The Ruin" describes a visitor to Roman ruins who communes with the past. It describes "the work of giants decaying" as their "buildings grow desolate, and the red-curved roof parts from its tiles of the ceiling vault." Although "the grasp of the earth possesses the mighty builders, perished and fallen," the author can still imagine their world of "gold bright splendor" that produced magnificent structures that no one of his time could match.[23] Everyone from Charlemagne to Charles V to Mussolini shared his exhilaration when interacting with Roman materials that, in the right circumstances, could seem to come alive again. This emotion arose, the Italian fascist Carol Cecchelli wrote, because Roman ruins offered "signs of a millennial nobility that has become current again and will develop itself further in the future" when properly revived.[24] These physical remains still invite the seductive possibility of another Roman renewal long after Rome's fall.

This response suggests something even more fundamental that lies beneath the pull of the Roman past. Roman stories of decline and renewal have resonated so deeply for so long because Rome is unique among European and Mediterranean states. Rome still remains the only state to ever control the entire Mediterranean basin—and it maintained that control for over 400 years. Its physical, religious, and cultural legacy deeply influences significant aspects of life in many of the countries whose lands Romans once inhabited—and in many, many more places Romans never imagined. Rome also endured far longer than any other state in history. Rome declined many times, it recovered many times, and, therefore, it seems to offer lessons to people facing similar challenges in less successful or durable states.

Like the schoolchildren of the empire and the Christian congregations of Constantinople, we often look for Rome's lessons in stories of Roman decline and recovery that leave out the people whom Roman renewal victimized. This omission is a mistake. The people killed by Sulla or Augustus or Justinian or Mussolini were the victims of actions taken under the cover of a dangerous idea. All of them were real. All of them suffered. And the rhetoric of decline and renewal is no less dangerous now.

But Rome also offers us different ways to think about change. Opposite Sulla and Justinian stand men like Antoninus Pius and Leo the Wise, emperors who took credit for restoring and revivifying their empire, but who refused to blame others for the problems they were correcting. The twenty-first-century world faces a host of problems that include political instability, environmental degradation, wealth inequality, and climate change. Two approaches are open to us. We can follow the path of Sulla or

Augustus by assigning blame to the people who caused these problems, destroying the structures they created, and creating a new class of victims. Or we can follow the path of the later Antonines. We can take credit for what we restore as part of a collaborative process that rebuilds and renews, bringing society together rather than tearing it apart through recrimination and violence. The past that we choose to describe can ultimately shape the future we experience. One of these paths can make our society stronger. The other will tear it apart. It is up to us.

NOTES

INTRODUCTION

1. Decline and renewal were also themes in Barack Obama's first inaugural (e.g., "Starting today, we must pick ourselves up, dust ourselves off, and begin again the work of remaking America." Accessed at https://obamawhitehouse.archives.gov/blog/2009/01/21/president-barack-obamas-inaugural-address).
2. "Every decision on trade, on taxes, on immigration, on foreign affairs, will be made to benefit American workers and American families." Accessed at https://www.whitehouse.gov/briefings-statements/the-inaugural-address.
3. For the "Hacer España grande otra vez" slogan see https://www.youtube.com/watch?v=RaSIX4-RPAI, accessed on February 28, 2020.
4. So, for example, #1–5 (aimed at eliminating aspects of regional autonomy), #9 (revocation of the "Ley de Memoria Histórica" condemning the Franco regime), #70 (revocation of the gender violence law and end of public support for "organismos feministas radicales"). The full list of proposals can be found at https://web.archive.org/web/20190501100029/https://www.voxespana.es/biblioteca/espana/propuestas-memes/100medidasngal_101319181010040327.pdf, accessed on February 28, 2020.
5. For the number of extrajudicial killings see https://www.hrw.org/tag/philippines-war-drugs.
6. Quoted in R. Bernstein, "The Paradox of Rodrigo Duterte," *The Atlantic*, February 22, 2020, accessed at https://www.theatlantic.com/international/archive/2020/02/philippines-rodrigo-duterte-china/606754/.
7. D. Thompson, "The Richest Cities for Young People: 1980 vs. Today," *The Atlantic*, February 15, 2015, archived at https://www.theatlantic.com/business/archive/2015/02/for-great-american-cities-the-rich-dont-always-get-richer/385513.
8. Ps. Galen, *De Theriaca, ad Pisonem* 16 (14.280-1K).
9. Effects: K. Harper, *The Fate of Rome: Climate, Disease, and the End of an Empire* (Princeton, 2017), 99–100.
10. Aristides's experience: *Or.* 48.38.
11. Generally: Harper, *Fate of Rome*, 99–100. Settlement of Germans: Dio 72.11.
12. Dio is less complimentary of the Roman response during the massive plague outbreak in 189 AD, under Marcus's son Commodus (73.14).
13. Dio 72.35.2.

CHAPTER 1

1. Dating: N. Slater, “The Dates of Plautus’ *Curculio* and *Trinummus* Reconsidered,” *AJP* 108 (1987), 264–69. Themes: T. Moore, *The Theater of Plautus: Playing to the Audience* (Austin, 1998), 81–90.
2. Plautus, *Trin.* 13.
3. Plautus, *Trin.* 28–38, translation from Moore, adapted for clarity.
4. W. Anderson, “Plautus’ ‘*Trinummus*’: The Absurdity of Officious Morality,” *Traditio* 35 (1979), 333–45, at 338–39.
5. Livy, 25.2.6–7; 26.18.8–9. For discussion see B. Straumann, *Crisis and Constitutionalism* (Oxford, 2016), 38–39.
6. For the tensions in Rome before Scipio’s election as consul see Livy, 28.38; Cassius Dio, 17.57.5–6; Valerius Maximus, 2.8.5 and, before the invasion, see Livy, 29.16–22.
7. The most notable of these was the *lex Oppia*, a law passed in 215. Discussion: Livy, 34.1–8;P. Johnston, “Poenulus 1.2 and Roman Women,” *TAPA* 110 (1980), 143–59, at 145–48.
8. Livy, 31.49.4–5.
9. Livy, 37.3.7.
10. E.g., Livy, 40.59.3, on triumph of Fulvius Flaccus.
11. Twenty-five pairs of gladiators: Livy, 31.49.9; 120 gladiators: Livy, 39.46.
12. E.g., the cases of M. Acilius Glabrio (Livy, 40.34.5; Valerius Maximus, 2.5.1) and L. Aemilius Regillus (Livy, 40.52.4; *SEG*[2] 588.104).
13. Livy, 39.46.
14. Livy, 39.6.7–9. Discussion: A. Lintott, “Imperial Expansion and Moral Decline in the Roman Republic,” *Historia* 21 (1972), 626–38, at 628–29.
15. Livy, 39.6–7; Calpurnius Piso, *Historiae* fr. 34.
16. Cato’s family: Plutarch, *Cato Maior* 1.1; A. E. Astin, *Cato the Censor* (Oxford, 1978), 2–4.
17. Spanish command: Plutarch, *Cato Mai.* 10–11; Astin, *Cato*, 28–50. Fortune: Plutarch, *Cato Mai.* 21.5; P. Kay, *Rome’s Economic Revolution* (Oxford, 2014), 230–31.
18. Aulus Gellius, *NA* 11.2.2.
19. Aulus Gellius, *NA* 11.2.5.
20. Pliny, *HN* 29.1.13–14; Plutarch, *Cato Mai.* 22–23.
21. Plutarch, *Cato Mai.* 16.
22. Plutarch, *Cato Mai.* 17.
23. Plutarch, *Cato Mai.* 18.
24. Criticism of Scipio: Plutarch, *Cato Mai.* 3.6; Livy, 29.19. Greek philosopher expulsions: Plutarch, *Cato Mai.* 22.1–23.3.
25. Pliny, *HN* 7.30.112; Plutarch, *Cato Mai.* 22. Discussion: K. E. Wilkerson, “Carneades at Rome: A Problem of Sceptical Rhetoric,” *Philosophy and Rhetoric* 21 (1988), 131–44, at 134–36.
26. Plutarch, *Cato Mai.* 19.
27. Plutarch, *Cato Mai.* 19.
28. R. Stem, “The First Eloquent Stoic: Cicero on Cato the Younger,” *Classical Journal* 101 (2005), 37–49.

29. Economic developments: J. Tan, *Power and Public Finance at Rome, 264–49 BCE* (New York, 2017), 61–64; Kay, *Rome's Economic Revolution*; E. Watts, *Mortal Republic* (New York, 2018), 45–67; S. Roselaar, *Italy's Economic Revolution* (Oxford, 2019).
30. Plutarch, *Cato Mai.* 21.5–6.
31. Family background: D. Stockton, *The Gracchi* (Oxford, 1979), 23ff.
32. Plutarch, *Tiberius Gracchus* 8; Appian, *Civil Wars* 1.1.7.
33. Plutarch, *Ti. Gracch.* 8.
34. Plutarch, *Ti. Gracch.* 8.
35. N. Rosenstein, *Rome at War: Farms, Families, and Death in the Middle Republic* (Chapel Hill, 2004), 141–69.
36. Campaign topic: C. Steel, *The End of the Roman Republic, 146 to 44BC* (Edinburgh, 2013), 16. Slogans: Plutarch, *Ti. Gracch.* 9. Speech: Appian, *Civil Wars* 1.9.
37. Five hundred *iugera*, the legal limit, equates to about 350 acres.
38. K. Bringmann, *A History of the Roman Republic* (Cambridge, 2007), 151.
39. Plutarch, *Ti. Gracch.* 10.
40. Plutarch, *Ti. Gracch.* 10.4–6.
41. Plutarch, *Ti. Gracch.* 11–12; Appian, *Civil Wars* 1.12.5; Stockton, *The Gracchi*, 65–67.
42. Cicero, *Laws* 3.24.
43. Constitutional problems raised by Titus Annius: Plutarch, *Ti. Gracch.* 14–15; Straumann, *Crisis*, 119–22.
44. Plutarch, *Ti. Gracch.* 13.
45. Plutarch, *Ti. Gracch.* 14–15. Livy, *Per.* 58 suggests that Tiberius proposed gifting the money to the urban poor who did not receive land allotments. Senate role in finance and foreign relations: Polybius, 6.13.
46. V. Arena, *The Practice of Politics in the Late Roman Republic* (Cambridge, 2012), chap. 3.
47. Cicero, *Laws* 3.24, *Mil.* 72; Straumann, *Crisis*, 16, 199.
48. Plutarch, *Ti. Gracch.* 13; Appian, *Civil Wars* 1.1.13.
49. Appian, *Civil Wars* 1.2.14; Plutarch, *Ti. Gracch.* 16.
50. Plutarch, *Ti. Gracch.* 16; Appian, *Civil Wars* 1.2.15.
51. Tiberius's murder: Plutarch, *Tiberius Gracchus* 18–19; Appian, *Civil Wars* 1.2.14–17; Dio, 24.83.8.
52. Plutarch, *Ti. Gracch.* 20.1.
53. Plutarch, *Ti. Gracch.* 21.3.
54. Celebration of the murder: *Mil.*72. Tiberius dividing people: *Republic* 1.31.
55. Appian, *Civil Wars* 1.1.2 (first to die in civil strife); 1.2.17 (polarization).
56. Appian, *Civil Wars* 1.2.17.
57. Appian, *Civil Wars* 1.2.17, lines 9–11.

CHAPTER 2

1. Gaius Gracchus's death: Cicero, *De oratore* 2.132–34; Plutarch, *Gaius Gracchus* 13–18; Appian, *Civil Wars* 1.3.25–26; Stockton, *The Gracchi* 176–205.
2. Sallust, *Jugurtha* 41.9.

3. Saturninus: Appian, *Civil Wars* 1.32; Plutarch, *Marius* 30; J. Lea Beness and T. W. Hillard, "The Death of Lucius Equitius on 10 December 100 BC," *Classical Quarterly* 40 (1990), 269–72; E. Badian, "The Death of Saturninus," *Chiron* 14 (1984), 101–47.
4. The term is first used quite late—by Julius Caesar in *Civil Wars* 1.5—but the institution took shape in the second century. On the SCU see Straumann, *Crisis*, 57–60, 89–92.
5. E.g., Cicero, *In Catilinam* 1.4; Livy, 6.19.3; and Sallust, *Bellum Catilinae* 29.3.
6. Plutarch, *Sulla* 1.
7. Plutarch, *Sulla* 3 (depicted on a signet ring); 6 (gold statue of Sulla accepting the surrender of Jugurtha).
8. Outbreak of Social Wars: Appian, *Civil Wars* 1.38; Velleius Paterculus 2.15; H. Mouritsen, *Italian Unification* (London, 1998), 142–55.
9. Plutarch, *Sulla* 6.
10. 80,000 killed: Valerius Maximus, 9. 2 ext. 3; Memnon, *FGrH* 3 B 434. F. 22. 9. 150,000 killed: Plutarch, *Sulla* 24.4.
11. Sulla's greed: Plutarch, *Sulla* 2.
12. Sulpicius: T. Mitchell, "The Volte-Face of P. Sulpicius Rufus in 88 BC," *CP* 70.3 (1975), 197–203; Steel, *End of the Republic*, 87–93.
13. Illegality of Sulpicius's actions: Cicero, *Orationes Philippicae* 8.7; Diodorus Siculus, 37.29.2; Straumann, *Crisis*, 77–79
14. Asconius 64 C.
15. Appian, *Civil Wars* 1.57.
16. Sulla's capture of Rome: Appian, *Civil Wars* 1.58; Plutarch, *Sulla* 9; Velleius Paterculus 2.19.
17. Appian, *Civil Wars* 1.59.
18. List of dead: Appian, *Civil Wars* 1.72–74; Steel, *End of the Republic*, 97. Heads on the speaker's platform: Appian, *Civil Wars* 1.73; Cicero, *De or*. 3.8–10.
19. Battle at the Colline Gate: Velleius Paterculus 2.27.1–3; Appian, *Civil Wars* 1.93; Plutarch, *Sulla* 29.
20. Sallust, *Bellum Catilinae* 28; Appian, *Civil Wars* 1.96.
21. Plutarch, *Sulla* 30.
22. Reforms: Watts, *Mortal Republic*, 140–42; H. Flower, *Roman Republics* (Princeton, 2010), 117–34.
23. Dionysius of Halicarnassus, 5.77.4 (trans. Cary). Discussion: Straumann, *Crisis*, 74.
24. Watts, *Mortal Republic*, 166–67.
25. SCU against Lepidus (77 BC): Sallust, *Historiae* 1.77.22. Catilinarians (63 BC): Sallust, *Bellum Catilinae* 29.2; Cicero, *Cat*. 1.4. Metellus Nepos (62 BC): Cassius Dio, 37.43.3.
26. Romans as *hostes*: Straumann, *Crisis*, 96–99.
27. Asconius 45C, 65C–66C.
28. Context: Watts, *Mortal Republic*, 170–75; Straumann, *Crisis*, 101–12.
29. Dio, 36.34.4.
30. F. Drogula, *Cato the Younger* (Oxford, 2019), 102–28.
31. Dio 37.57.1.
32. Discussion: Watts, *Mortal Republic*, 200–209.

33. Dio 40.49.5; Appian, *Civil Wars* 23.84; Cicero, *Pro Milone* 23, 61.
34. Burning the Senate House: *Mil.* 13. Pompey's SCU: *Mil.* 70.
35. Cannot restrain: *Mil.* 77. Justifies violence: *Mil.* 14.
36. Cicero, *Republic* 3.41; Straumann, *Crisis*, 263–64.
37. Cicero, *Laws* 3.42; Straumann, *Crisis*, 32.
38. E.g., Suetonius, *Divus Iulius* 30.3; Caesar, *Civil War* 1.pref. 1.7.
39. Caesar, *Civil War* 1.5.
40. Caesar, *Civil War* 1.7, trans. McDevitte and Bohn, adapted for clarity. Although the text was not written by Caesar himself, it does purport to capture the main ideas of his statements to the troops.
41. Implied at *Republic* 3.41. For this reading: Straumann, *Crisis*, 263.
42. Sallust, *Bellum Catilinae* 3.3–5.
43. Sallust, *Bellum Catilinae* 3.4. Similar ideas: Polybius, 36.9.5–7; Piso fr. 36 = Pliny, *Naturalis historia* 34.14.
44. Appian *Civil Wars*, 4.17–29 and 4.36–51; Valerius Maximus 6.8.6; J. Osgood, *Caesar's Legacy: Civil War and the Emergence of the Roman Empire* (Cambridge, 2006), 63–81.
45. Appian, *Civil Wars*, 4.19–20; Dio 47.8, 11; Plutarch, *Cicero* 47–48, *Antony* 20.
46. Appian, *Appian Civil Wars* 5.12.
47. Josephus, *Jewish Antiquities* 14.272 (extortion of Judaea); Appian 4.64–81 (fining of Tarsus, plundering of Rhodes, sacks of Xanthus and Patara). For discussion see Osgood, *Caesar's Legacy*, 88–89.
48. For discussion see Osgood, *Caesar's Legacy*, 326–32.
49. E.g., *ILS* 8393, the so-called *Laudatio Turiae*, 2.1–19. A. Gowing, "Lepidus, the Proscriptions, and the *Laudatio Turiae*," *Historia* 41 (1992), 283–96.
50. Livy, *Periochae* 130; Plutarch, *Antony* 37–38.
51. Dio. 49.40; Plutarch, *Antony* 50.4 (pseudo-triumph); 54.3 (territory distribution).
52. Dio 50.4.1; Osgood, *Caesar's Legacy*, 354–55.
53. Dio 50.3, 50.20; Suetonius, *Divus Augustus* 17.2; Plutarch, *Antony* 58.4.
54. Antony degenerating: Suetonius, *Aug.* 17.1; "judged an enemy": Suetonius, *Aug.* 17.2.
55. Augustus, *Res Gestae* (hereafter *RG*) 25.2.
56. Dio, 51.21.4.
57. *RG* 34.
58. Dio, 53.18.2.
59. Vergil, *Georgics* 1.489–97; Osgood, *Caesar's Legacy*, 97.
60. Livy, Preface.9.
61. Dio, 53.33.3, 54.1.3–4; *RG* 34.
62. Dio 54.6.1–4; 54.10.1–5.
63. Dio, 54.10.5.
64. Horace, *Carmen Saeculare*, lnn. 57–59.
65. Augustan Age: B. Breed, "*Tua, Caesar, Aetas*: Horace *Ode* 4.15 and the Augustan Age," *AJP* 125 (2004), 245–53. Dating: J. Benario, "Book 4 of Horace's Odes: Augustan Propaganda," *TAPA* 91 (1960), 339–52, at 341.
66. Horace, *Odes* 4.15.9–14. Discussion: C. Edwards, *The Politics of Immorality in Ancient Rome* (Cambridge, 1993), 58 n.84

67. Augustus, *RG*.Pr; for the location in Rome see Suetonius, *Aug.* 4.
68. *RG* 1.1–3.
69. *RG* 8.13–14. There is a lacuna in the Latin text, so this reading is based on the Greek translation from Ancyra.
70. *RG* 16.22–27.
71. *RG* 17.34–39.
72. *RG* 18.
73. *RG* 19.21.
74. *RG* 27.31–34.
75. *RG* 29.39–43.
76. *RG* 24.49–54. For Antony taking these precious items and giving them to Cleopatra see Dio, 51.17.
77. *RG* 25.1–3.

CHAPTER 3

1. Tacitus, *Dialogue on Oratory*, 36–42. On the *Dialogus* see C. van den Berg, *The World of Tacitus' "Dialogus de Oratoribus"* (Cambridge, 2014).
2. Courtroom oratory: e.g., Tacitus, *Dial.* 1; Pliny, *Epistulae* 5.8.6. Historical themes: Philostratus, *Vitae sophistarum* 481.
3. E.g., Pliny's *Panegyricus*, a published oration praising the virtues of Trajan. About it: Pliny, *Ep.* 6.27.1; C. Noreña, "Self-Fashioning in the *Panegyricus*," in *Pliny's Praise: The Panegyricus in the Roman World*, ed. P. Roche (Cambridge, 2011), 29–44.
4. E.g., Tiberius (who shared Augustus's powers from 13 AD and was marked as his successor on coins like *RIC* 1.Augustus 237–41, 245–48, 356, and 469–70) and Nero (marked on coinage as future emperor as early as 50, e.g., *RIC* 1.Claudius 82–83, *RPC* 4169 [Antioch]).
5. J. Osgood, *Claudius Caesar* (New York, 2012), 56–62.
6. The clearest evocation of Augustus occurs on Galban coinage that featured images of Livia, Galba's friend and Augustus's wife (e.g., the denarius and aureus issues at *RIC* 1.Galba 142–43, 150–53, 184–89, 223–24).
7. Plutarch, *Life of Galba*, 16.1–3 (ostentatious frugality), 17.1–4 (execution of Neronian associates).
8. LIBERTAS RESTITVTA and ROMA RENASC legends appear on coins from the Spanish mint that first issued Galban coinage (e.g., *RIC* 1.22–24, [LIBERTAS legend] and *RIC* 1.25–29 ROMA legend]). ROMA RENASC legends later: *RIC* 1.87, 95 (Gallic mint); *RIC* 1.229–30 (Roman mint).
9. Plutarch, *Life of Galba*, 18–19, 22.
10. Legislative act: Dio, 53.18; Gaius, *Institutes* 1.5. Text itself: *CIL* VI.930 and M. H. Crawford et al., *Roman Statutes*, vol. 1 (London, 1996), 549–53.
11. In one case (extending the border of the *pomerium*), only Claudius is mentioned—presumably because he was the first emperor to claim that power.
12. For the Flavian attempts to classify the reign of Nero as a time of decline see D. Hurley, "Biographies of Nero," in *A Companion to the Neronian Age*, ed. E. Buckley and M. Dinter (Chichester, 2013), 29–44, at 30–31.

13. Cluvius Rufus: Pliny, *Ep.* 9.19.5; B. Levick, "Cluvius Rufus," in *The Fragments of the Roman Historians, Vol. 1*, ed. T. Cornell (Oxford, 2013), 549–60. Four fragments of his history survive, two of which recount Nero's drunkenness (fr. 2) and his incestuous relations with his mother (fr. 3).
14. Plutarch, *Life of Galba* 1.
15. Plutarch, *Galba* 1; *Otho* 9.
16. P. Stadter, "Plutarch and Rome," in *A Companion to Plutarch*, ed. M. Beck (Chichester, 2014), 13–31, at 18–19.
17. Suetonius, *Domitian* 5 and 17; Eutropius 7.23. In a cruel twist, the expanded Forum is now called the Forum of Nerva, Domitian's successor.
18. J. D. Grainger, *Nerva and the Roman Succession Crisis of AD 96–99* (London, 2003), 22–23; 106–8.
19. Vespasian had issued denarii with an average purity of 90% and an average weight of 2.87 grams. Domitian increased both the weight and purity of the coin, first to 98% pure coins of 3.26 grams and then, from 85–96, coins of 3.04 grams at 93.5% purity.
20. Grainger, *Nerva*, 77–88.
21. Suetonius, *Domitian*, 14–17.2; Dio, 67.17.
22. *RIC* 2.Nerva.7, a denarius with the reverse LIBERTAS PVBLICA dated between September 19, 96, and late autumn of the same year.
23. Suetonius, *Domitian* 23; Grainger, *Nerva*, 4.
24. Grainger, *Nerva*, 29–31.
25. *Lex agrarian*: Dio, 68.2.1.
26. Dio, 68.1.3.
27. Crassus: Dio 68.3.2. Praetorian riot: Dio, 68.3.3.
28. Negotiations: Aurelius Victor, *de Caes* 13; C. P. Jones, "Sura and Senecio," *JRS* 60 (1970), 98–104, at 99; J. Bennett, *Trajan: Optimus Princeps* (Bloomington, 1997), 46.
29. Ammianus, 16.10.15.
30. Cato: *RIC* 2.Trajan.775; Pompey: *RIC* 2.Trajan.811; Aemilus Paullus: *RIC* 2.Trajan.788; Brutus: *RIC* 2.Trajan.797.
31. Trajan's restitution issues: B. Woytek, "Trajan's Restoration of the Denarius RRC 343/1b," *Numismatic Chronicle* 164 (2002), 227–33.
32. Tacitus, *Histories* 1.1–2.
33. Campaigns: Tacitus, *Agricola* 10–38; Dio, 66.20; A. R. Birley, *The Roman Government of Britain* (Oxford, 2005), 71–95.
34. Tacitus, *Agricola* 40.
35. Tacitus, *Agricola* 41.
36. Tacitus, *Agricola* 44.
37. Tacitus, *Agricola* 3.
38. Tacitus, *Histories* 1.1.
39. Inscription commemorating Domitian's restoration: *SIG*[3] 821, Dessau, *ILS* 8905; Plutarch's possible role: Stadter, "Plutarch and Rome," 16.
40. Plutarch, *Publicola* 15.3–5.
41. Plutarch, *De Pythiae oraculis* 408 C, 409A.

42. Pliny, *Ep.* 9.13.2. Context: R. Gibson, *Man of High Empire: The Life of Pliny the Younger* (Oxford, 2020), 102–5.
43. Execution of Helvidius Priscus the younger: Suetonius, *Domitian* 10 and, indirectly, Tacitus, *Agricola* 45.
44. Pliny, *Ep.* 9.13.21.
45. This thought is Pliny, *Ep.* 9.13.
46. C. Noreña, "Self-Fashioning in the *Panegyricus*," 29–44.
47. C. Noreña, "The Social Economy of Pliny's Correspondence with Trajan," *AJP* 128 (2007), 239–77, at 245–46.
48. Pliny, *Ep.* 10.97.2.

CHAPTER 4

1. Eutropius, *Brevarium* 8.5.3.
2. Edward Gibbon, *The Decline and Fall of the Roman Empire* (London, 1781), vol. 1, chap. 3.
3. Fronto, *Ep.* 5.8.
4. Aelius Aristides, *Orationes* 14.74–75; Dio, 69.9; *Historia Augusta, Hadrian*.10–11 (hereafter *SHA*); *RIC* 2.Hadrian 908–37 (series of coins showing Hadrian addressing regional armies).
5. E.g., the cities of Italica (Spain), Aelia Capitolina (Palestine), Gerash (Arabia—though this expansion may predate Hadrian), Cyrene (Libya), and Athens. For discussion see M. Boatwright, *Hadrian and the Cities of the Roman Empire* (Princeton, 2000), 144–203. Structures: Temple of Augustus in Terragona (*SHA Hadrian* 12) and the tomb of Pompey in Pelusium (*SHA Hadrian* 14.4).
6. W. MacDonald, *The Pantheon: Design, Meaning, and Progeny* (Cambridge, MA, 1976), 12–13.
7. *RIC* 2.Hadrian 938–66. Discussion: C. Ando, *Imperial Ideology and the Provincial Loyalty in the Roman Empire* (Berkeley, 2000), 319, 410.
8. E.g., in Italica, where a temple to Trajan seems to have been part of his expansion of the city (L. Revell, *Roman Imperialism and Local Identities* [Cambridge, 2009], 91–92).
9. Dio, 68.17–32.
10. Withdrawal: Fronto, *Principia Historiae* 8–9; Eutropius, 8.6; Festus, 14.3; *SHA Hadrian* 5.1–8, 9.1; Ando, *Imperial Ideology*, 317. Executions: Dio, 69.2.5; Fronto, *Princ. Hist.* 8.
11. Dio, 68.32; Appian, *Civil Wars* 2.90, 380, *Liber Arabicus* fr. 19; Eusebius, *Historia ecclesiastica* 4.2.2. Discussion: M. Pucci Ben Zeev, *Diaspora Judaism in Turmoil 116/117 CE* (Leuven, 2005).
12. *SHA Hadrian* 5.5–9.
13. Rebuilding of Rhodes: Aelius Aristides *Or.* 25. An inscription (Bull. Ép. 1946/7.156) refers to Antoninus Pius as the "savior and restorer" of Rhodes following this event. *SHA Antoninus* 8.11 (famine), 9.1–3 (other disasters).
14. Smyrna: Dio, 72.32; Aelius Aristides, *Or.* 18 and 19; Philostratus, *VS* 582. Sack of Eleusis: G. Mylonas, *Eleusis and the Eleusinian Mysteries* (Princeton, 1961), 156 n.6.

15. *SHA Marcus* 17; Zonaras, 12.1, Dio, Book 72 unplaced fragment=*Excerpta Salmasiana* N. 117, a story that echoes a less positive anecdote about Nerva (Dio 68.2).
16. Dio 72.33. Cf. *SHA Marcus* 1.
17. Dio 72.22; *SHA Marcus* 24–26; *SHA Avidius Cassius* 9.5–10 = Marius Maximus, fr. 13.
18. *SHA Marcus* 21.1.
19. Egyptian revolt under Pius: *SHA Antoninus* 5. Bucoli revolt against Marcus: Dio 72.4, *SHA Marcus* 21, Marius Maximus, fr. 11a and b.
20. Outbreak of plague: *SHA Verus* 8.1–2. Description of symptoms: Galen, *Methodus medendi* 5.12 = Kühn 10.360ff, *De atra bile* 4 = Kühn 5.115. Identification with smallpox: R. J. Littman and M. L. Littman, "Galen and the Antonine Plague," *AJP* 94 (1973), 243–55. Mortality estimates: K. Harper, *The Fate of Rome: Climate, Disease, and the End of Empire* (Princeton, 2017), 18, 115; W. Scheidel, "A Model of Demographic and Economic Change in Roman Egypt after the Antonine Plague," *JRA* 15 (2002), 97–114; J. Haldon et. al., "Plagues, Climate Change, and the End of an Empire," *History Compass*, November 9, 2018 (https://onlinelibrary.wiley.com/doi/full/10.1111/hic3.12506).
21. Lucian, *Alexander the False Prophet*, 36.
22. *SHA Marcus* 18.2.
23. K. Harper, "People, Plagues, and Prices from the Roman World: The Evidence from Egypt," *Journal of Economic History* 76 (2016), 803–39; P. Van Minnen, "*P. Oxy.* LXVI 4527 and the Antonine Plague in the Fayyum," *ZPE* 135 (2001), 175–77; P. Temin, *The Roman Market Economy* (Princeton, 2013).
24. *SHA Marcus* 21.6–9.
25. Dio 72.11.
26. Herodian 1.5.5. For this continuity see the discussion of A. Kemezis, *Greek Narratives of the Roman Empire under the Severans* (Cambridge, 2014), 48–49.
27. Joint emperor: *SHA Marcus* 37.5; coins of 177 marking Commodus as Augustus: *RIC* 3.Marcus Aurelius 1554–1587. Joint campaign: *CIL* 2.4114, 6.8541, 10.408 = Dessau *ILS* 1117, 1140, and 1573. Joint triumph: *SHA Commodus* 2.5.
28. E.g., *RIC* 3.Marcus Aurelius 1260.
29. Dio 73.2; Herodian 1.6–7.
30. Kemezis, *Greek Narratives of the Roman Empire*, 50–51.
31. Dio 73.21.
32. E.g., *RIC* 3.Commodus 221, 253, 254, 427.
33. Dio 73.15.2.
34. Dio 73.14.3.
35. Fire: Herodian, 1.14.2–6; Galen, *On the Avoidance of Grief* 8, 18, and 23, *De Compositione Medicamentorum per Genera* 1.1, and *De antidotis* 1.13; Dio 72.24; S. Lusina, *Creating Severan Rome: The Architecture and Self-Image of L. Septimius Severus (AD 193–211)* (Brussels, 2014), Appendix II.
36. Dio 73.22.
37. Dio 74.1.
38. Dio 74.8; Herodian 2.4.2.
39. Herodian 2.4.4.

40. Dio 74.5.
41. Dio 74.7 and *SHA Pertinax* 6.9; Herodian 2.4.9 implies as much. Epigraphical evidence shows a more complicated picture, with Pertinax's son carrying the title of Caesar in at least a few places (e.g., Dessau, *ILS* 410, 5842, 5845). For discussion see Kemezis, *Greek Narratives*, 54 n.69.
42. Dio 74.11; Herodian 2.5; *SHA Pertinax* 11.6–7.
43. Herodian, 2.14.3; cf. Dio 75.2, *SHA Severus* 7.5.
44. Described at length in Dio. 75.4–5. Note too *SHA Severus* 7.7–9.
45. *SHA Severus* 10.3–6; Kemezis, *Greek Narratives*, 58–65. Dio 76.7.4 places this claim after the war but the numismatic evidence shows that coins of Caracalla bearing the name Marcus Aurelius Antoninus appeared in 196 (e.g., *RIC* 3.Caracalla 1–5).
46. Divinization of Commodus: Dio 76.7, *RIC* 3.Severus 72A. Commodus as his brother: *CIL* 6.1031, ln. 2. The renaming of Caracalla: *SHA Severus* 10.6.
47. This break seems to coincide with his eleventh acclamation as imperator, in late 198 or early 199 (beginning with *RIC* 3.Severus 122).
48. *CIL* 6.954 = Dessau, *ILS* 418.
49. Allowing soldiers to marry: Herodian 3.8.5; S. Phang, *The Marriage of Roman Soldiers (13 BC–AD 235)* (Boston, 2001), 115–38. Increased compensation: Dio 75.2.3; Herodian 3.9.2.
50. F. Millar, *The Roman Near East 31 BC–AD 337* (Cambridge, MA, 1993), 121–41.
51. T. D. Barnes, "Aspects of the Severan Empire, Part I: Severus as a New Augustus," *NECJ* 35 (2008), 251–68.
52. Dio 77 [76].16.4; Tertullian, *Apologeticus*. 4.8; Ulpian, fr. 1834 = *Fragmenta Vaticana* 158; Barnes, "Aspects of Severan Empire," 256–58.
53. *CIL* 6.1033. On the arch see Lusina, *Creating Severan Rome*, 75–84; R. Brilliant, *The Arch of Septimius Severus in the Roman Forum* (Rome, 1967), 101–18.
54. Herodian 3.8.10. Barnes, "Aspects of Severan Empire," 264; Lusina, *Creating Severan Rome*, 105–16.
55. For these aspects of the games see M. Beard, J. North, and S. Price, *Religions of Rome, Vol. 1* (Cambridge, 1998), 201–6.
56. Lusina, *Creating Severan Rome*, 117–33.
57. *CIL* 6.1031 (Theater of Pompey) and *CIL* 6.896 = Dessau, *ILS* 129 (Pantheon).
58. Rebuilding: *SHA Severus* 23; *CIL* 6.938 = Dessau, *ILS* 255 (Temple of Vespasian), *CIL* 6.935 (Temple of Peace), *CIL* 6.1034 (Porticus Octaviae). Analysis: Lusina, *Creating Severan Rome*, 17–21.
59. Lusina, *Creating Severan Rome*, 148–54 as well as the digitized fragments at https://formaurbis.stanford.edu/docs/FURmap.html.
60. Lusina, *Creating Severan Rome*, 154.
61. E.g., *RIC* 3.Severus 288.
62. Damage caused by age: *CIL* 6.1031 (Theater of Pompey), *CIL* 6.896 = Dessau, *ILS* 129 (Pantheon), *CIL* 6.1259 = *ILS* 424 (Aqua Claudia), *CIL* 6.31555 = Dessau, ILS 5934 (Tiber Banks).
63. E.g., *CIL* 6.1024 (Porticus Octaviae) and an inscription commemorating his work rebuilding the Forum of Trajan following fire damage, published in G. Pani, "Gerontius

v(ir) s(pectabilis)-Horatius Rogatus proc(urator) Aug(usti) n(ostri): Nuova documentazione sull'epigrafia del Colosseo e dei Mercati di Traiano," *ArchLaz* 12 (1995), 173–80.

64. Kemezis, *Greek Narratives*, 68.
65. Dio 78.9.
66. C. Ando, *Imperial Rome, 193–284 AD* (Edinburgh, 2012), 52–57; A. Bryen, "Reading the Citizenship Papyrus (*P. Giss.* 40)," in *Citizenship and Empire in Europe 200–1900* (Stuttgart, 2016), 29–45; F. Millar, "The Date of the *Constitutio Antoniniana*," *Journal of Egyptian Archeology* 48 (1962), 124–31.
67. E.g., Justinian, *Novellae* 78.5 (Antoninus Pius); Aurelius Victor, *Caesares* 16.12 (Marcus).
68. External threats: Herodian, 6.7.2–5; D. Potter, *The Roman Empire at Bay* (New York, 2004), 217–36. Submissiveness: Herodian 6.7.9–10.
69. Herodian 6.8.2, 4–7.
70. Dio, 72.36.4; Herodian. 1.3.1–5.
71. Dio 73.23
72. The process culminates in 75.3, just before the long narration of the funeral of Pertinax.
73. Dio 72.35.
74. Dio 80.4.1–5.3.
75. Herodian, 6.8.5–6.9.5; Kemezis, *Greek Narratives*, 88–89.
76. Herodian, 1.1.4. On Herodian's declinism see Kemezis, *Greek Narratives*, 229–39.
77. Kemezis, *Greek Narratives*, 271–72.
78. Herodian, 8.8.8.

CHAPTER 5

1. Summaries: Potter, *Empire at Bay*, 233–53; C. Ando, *Imperial Rome, AD 193–284: The Critical Century* (Edinburgh, 2012), 146–60.
2. The eight Augusti were Maximinus I (235–238), Gordian I (238), Gordian II (238), Balbinus (238), Pupienus (238), Gordian III (238–244), Philip I (244–249), and Philip II (Augustus from 247 to 249). The three failed dynasties were those of Maximinus (whose son Maximus served as his Caesar and designated successor), the Gordians, and Philip.
3. Eutropius 9.4; *Epitome de Caesaribus* 29.1; Aurelius Victor 29.1 (near Sirmium). *Oracula Sibyllina* (hereafter *Sib. Or.*) 13.83 says he was Dacian, which is incorrect.
4. Moesia Inferior (*CIL* 3.12519, 13724, and 13758) in 234 and Hispania Terraconensis (*AE* 1951.9) in 238.
5. Reflected in *Sib. Or.* 13.82; *Epit. de Caes.* 29.2; Aurelius Victor 29.5.
6. *RIC* 4C.Trajan Decius 77–98. Discussion: S. Dmitriev, "'Good Emperors' and Emperors of the Third Century," *Hermes* 132 (2004), 211–24.
7. Dmitriev, "Good Emperors," 220.
8. *SHA Valerian* 5–7.
9. Dessau, *ILS* 8922.

10. C. L. Babock, "An Inscription of Trajan Decius from Cosa," *AJP* 83 (1962), 147–58; U. Marelli, "L'Epigrafe di Decio a Cosa et l'epiteto di 'Restitutor Sacrorum,'" *Aevum* 58 (1984), 52–56.
11. J. B. Rives, "The Decree of Decius and the Religion of Empire," *JRS* 89 (1999), 135–54, at 146.
12. Rives, "Decree of Decius," 150–51.
13. Rives, "Decree of Decius" offers a good starting point for the immense literature on this persecution.
14. M. Kulikowski, *Rome's Gothic Wars* (Cambridge, 2007), 18; D. Potter, *Empire at Bay*, 240–42, on the basis of Jordanes, *Getica* 101–2.
15. Reckless to fight without a general: Dexippus, *Scythica*, Fr. 26.7. Decius as commander: Dexippus, *Scythica*, Fr. 26.9–10. Discussion: C. Davenport and C. Mallan, "Dexippus' 'Letter of Decius': Context and Interpretation," *Museum Helveticum* 70 (2013), 57–73.
16. Zosimus 1.23; Zonaras 12.20.
17. Zonaras 12.21.
18. *Res Gestae Divi Saporis* 9–17 (Greek text, troop figures, and list of captured places) in P. Huyse, *Die dreisprachige Inschrift Šabuhrs I. an der Ka'aba-I Zardu: Corpus Inscriptionum Iranicarum 3; Pahlavi Inscriptions 1.1* (London, 1999), 22–64.
19. *Sib. Or.* 13.119–29, trans. Potter. For these events see Potter, *Empire at Bay*, 243–45.
20. Harper, *The Fate of Rome*, 136–39.
21. Captives: Philostorgius, *Historia ecclesiastica* 2. 5 (Family of Ulfila, future bishop of Goths) *Chronicle of Seert*, PO 4.222 (bishop Demetrianus of Antioch, taken to Persia). Discussion: G. Downey, *A History of Antioch in Syria* (Princeton, 1961), 258–59.
22. Censorship: *SHA Valerian* 5–7. *Princeps senatus*: *SHA Gordian* 9.7.
23. Potter, *Empire at Bay*, 248.
24. Zosimus, 1.32.3. Downey, *A History of Antioch*, 259.
25. E.g., *RIC* 5A.Valerian 286 and 287.
26. Army ravaged: Zosimus, 1.36. 5000 people a day: *SHA Gallieni* 5.5. Alexandrian population: Eusebius, *Hist. eccl.* 7.21. Plague's effects under Valerian: Harper, *Fate of Rome*, 136–45.
27. Eusebius, *Hist. eccl.* 7.21 (trans. Schott), quoting Dionysius of Alexandria.
28. Tacitus, *Annals* 15.44.
29. Cyprian, *Ad Demetrianum* 5.2–3.
30. Eusebius, *Hist. eccl.* 7.10.2–6, quoting Dionysius of Alexandria.
31. Eusebius, *Hist. eccl.* 7.10–12; *Acta Proconsularia Sancti Cypriani* 1.1–6. Discussion: P. Keresztes, "Two Acts of the Emperor Valerian," *VC* 29, no. 2 (1975), 81–95.
32. Large numbers of dead: Porphyry, fr. 36 [ed. Harnack]. Few casualties: Cyprian, *Epistles* 9–12, 19, 20, 22, 24, 38–40.
33. Cyprian, *Liber de lapsis* 5–6.
34. Cyprian, *De lapsis* 12.
35. Lactantius, *De mortibus persecutorum* 5.
36. Potter, *Empire at Bay*, 256, following *SHA The Two Gallieni*, 1.3.
37. *SHA V. Tyranni Triginta* 9.1, 10.1.

38. Gallic command: Zosimus, 1.38.2; *SHA V. Trig. Tyr.* 3.9; Aurelius Victor 33.8; Eutropius 9.9. Revolt: J. Drinkwater, *The Gallic Empire* (Stuttgart, 1987), 24–28.
39. Dating of the text: F. Millar, "P. Herennius Dexippus: The Greek World and the Third-Century Invasions," *JRS* 59 (1969), 12–29, at 23–26. Idea of partnership: C. Mallan and C. Davenport, "Dexippus and the Gothic Invasions: Interpreting the New Vienna Fragment (*Codex Vindobonensis Hist. gr.* 73, ff. 192v–193r)," *JRS* 105 (2015), 203–26.
40. L. Bakker, "Das Siegesdenkmal zur Juthungenschlacht des Jahres 260 n. Chr. aus Augusta Vindelicum," *Das Archäologische Jahr in Bayern. Jahrgang 1992* (1993), 116–19.
41. Drinkwater, *Gallic Empire*, 28.
42. *RIC* 5B.Postumus.82, adapting both *RIC* 2.Hadrian.325 and *RIC* 5a.Gallienus, joint reign.27–35 (a coin type Gallienus stopped issuing after his father's capture).
43. Reign of Uranius: *Sib. Or.* 13.147–53; Malalas 12.26; H. R. Baldus, *Uranius Antoninus* (Bonn, 1971); D. Potter, *Prophecy and History in the Crisis of the Roman Empire*, (Oxford, 1990), 323–28.
44. N. Andrade, *Zenobia: Shooting Star of Palmyra* (Oxford, 2019), 127–32; Potter, *Prophecy*, 381–94.
45. Zonaras, 12.24.
46. Zosimus, 1.39.2; *SHA Gallienus* 10.3–6, 12.1; *Sib. Or.* 13.155–71. Discussion: Andrade, *Zenobia*, 133; Potter, *Prophecy*, 341–46.
47. Zosimus 1.41, Zonaras 26.1 and Drinkwater, *Gallic Empire*, 145f.
48. John of Antioch, *fr.* 152.2.
49. Following Claudius's brother, Quintillus. For the circumstances see Potter, *Empire at Bay*, 265–66.
50. Potter, *Empire at Bay*, 265–66.
51. *SHA Aurelian* 32.1–3; *SHA Firmus* 3.1.
52. Aurelian's Syrian campaign: Andrade, *Zenobia*, 199–209.
53. Narrated in Drinkwater, *Gallic Empire*, 34–44.
54. *SHA Aurelian* 33.3; *SHA Tyr. Trig.* 24.1–2 both speak about Tetricus betraying his troops before Châlons. Drinkwater (*Gallic Empire*, 42–43, 90–91) offers an alternative reconstruction.
55. Zenobia: *SHA V. Tyr. Trig.* 30.27. Tetricus I's governorship and Tetricus II's senatorial rank: Aurelius Victor 35.5, Eutropius 9.13.
56. Andrade, *Zenobia*, 217.
57. G. Fowden, "City and Mountain in Late Roman Attica," *JHS* 108 (1988), 48–59, at 53.

CHAPTER 6

1. Diocletian took power in 284 following the premature death of the emperor Numerian, a son of the recently deceased emperor Carus. He secured it after the defeat of Carus's other son Carinus in 285. On the battle against Carinus see T. D. Barnes, "Emperors, Panegyrics, Prefects, Provinces, and Palaces (284–317)," *JRA* 9 (1996), 532–52, at 535–37.
2. Maximian was initially appointed as a Caesar, but was elevated to co-Augustus in April of 286 (S. Corcoran, *The Empire of the Tetrarchs*, 2nd ed. , [Oxford, 2000]), 273–74.

3. J. C. S. León, *Los Bagaudas: Rebeldes, demonios, mártires; Revueltas campesinas en Galia e Hispania durante el Bajo Imperio* (Jaén, 1996), 31–80.
4. "Inexperienced farmers . . . barbarian enemy": *XII Panegyrici Latini* (henceforth *Pan. Lat.*) 10.4.3, trans. Nixon and Rodgers in C. E. V. Nixon and B. Saylor Rodgers, *In Praise of Later Roman Emperors: The Panegyrici Latini* (Berkeley, 1994),. "Ravaged countryside . . . assailed many cities": Eutropius, *Caes.* 39.17 (trans. Bird).
5. Aurelius Victor, *Caes.* 39.20; Eutropius, 9.21–22; Nixon and Rodgers, *In Praise of Later Roman Emperors*, 107.
6. For a short (albeit confused) summary of all of these challenges see Aurelius Victor, *Caes.* 39. Diocletian's devastation in Egypt: J. McKenzie, *The Architecture of Alexandria and Egypt, 300 BC-700 AD* (New Haven, 2007), 209.
7. *Pan. Lat.* 10.1.5 (trans. Nixon and Rodgers).
8. *Pan. Lat.* 10.4 (Bagaudae), 10.5–7 (barbarians), 10.12 (Carausius).
9. *Pan. Lat.* 10.14.2.
10. Dessau, *ILS* 617, from Hieraconpolis.
11. *Pan. Lat.* 11.3.1.
12. *Pan. Lat.* 11.5.1–4.
13. Pan. Lat. 11.15.1–4.
14. Dating: Nixon and Rodgers, *In Praise of Later Roman Emperors*, 105–6. "Miracle of valor:" *Pan. Lat.* 8.1.1.
15. *Pan. Lat.* 8.1.5 (trans. Nixon and Rodgers).
16. *Pan. Lat.* 8.9.3.
17. *Pan. Lat.* 8.9.4.
18. *Pan. Lat.* 8.21.2.
19. *Pan. Lat.* 8.19.2.
20. *Pan. Lat.* 8.10.1–4.
21. S. Corcoran, *The Empire of the Tetrarchs*, 2nd ed. (Oxford, 2000) remains the definitive English-language study.
22. This process of imperial subdivision had begun in the third century (e.g., *Corpus Inscriptionum Latinarum* [hereafter *CIL*] 3.6783, which dates a division to the reign of Gordian III), but Diocletian got particular credit for creating smaller, more efficiently administered provinces (e.g., Lactantius, *De mort. pers.* 7.4). Discussion: T. D. Barnes, *The New Empire of Diocletian and Constantine* (Cambridge, MA, 1982), 195–225. Separating of military and civilian offices in early fourth century: Eusebius, *Martyrs of Palestine* 13.1–3; *Hist. eccl.* 9.5.2. Discussion: F. Millar, *The Roman Near East, 31 B.C.–A.D. 337 AD* (Cambridge, MA, 1993), 191–92
23. This reform is best seen in the decree describing the new system issued by the prefect of Egypt in 297. On it see A. E. R. Boak and H. C. Youtie, *The Archive of Aurelius Isidorus in the Egyptian Museum, Cairo and the University of Michigan (P. Cair. Isidor.)* (Ann Arbor, 1960), no. 1.
24. R. Bagnall, *Currency and Inflation in Fourth Century Egypt, Bulletin of the American Society of Papyrologists Supplement*, No. 5 (1985), 19–25, dating to 296. Alternative date of 293: K. Harl, *Coinage in the Roman Economy* (Baltimore, 1996), 148–51.

25. Nixon and Rodgers, *In Praise of Later Roman Emperors*, 115–6, n.16 and 172–74 nn.81–82.
26. This edict is preserved in at least forty different locations. On it see S. Lauffer, *Diokletians Preisedikt* (Berlin, 1971). The translation follows that of R. Rees, *Diocletian and the Tetrarchy* (Edinburgh, 2004), 139.
27. *Coll. leg Mos. et Rom.* 15.3, trans. Rees, *Diocletian and the Tetrarchy*, 174–75.
28. Lactantius, *De mort. pers.* 12.3.
29. E.g., *P. Flor* 171; *P. Oxy.* 1357; Eusebius, *Hist. eccl.* 8.1.4 and 8.6.2–4.; Lactantius, *De mort. pers.* 15.2.
30. *SHA Elagabalus* 35.4.
31. Eusebius, *Hist. eccl.* 8.2.3–4 and Lactantius, *De mort. pers.* 13.1. Discussion: Potter, *Empire at Bay*, 337; Corcoran, *The Empire of the Tetrarchs*, 179–81.
32. Eusebius, *Hist. eccl.* 8.6.8.
33. Eusebius, *Martyrs of Palestine* 3.1. Discussion: Corcoran, *Empire of the Tetrarchs*, 181–82.
34. Breakdown: Corcoran, *Empire of the Tetrarchs*, 181–88.
35. Lactantius, *De mort. pers.* 15.1–7; Eusebius, *Hist. eccl.* 8.6–13.
36. *P. Oxy.* 2673.
37. Lactantius, *De mort. pers.* 13.2; cf. Eusebius, *Hist. eccl.* 8.5.1.
38. Lactantius, *De mort. pers.* 18–20.
39. Lactantius, *De mort. pers.* 23.6.
40. Lactantius, *De mort. pers.* 42.
41. Lactantius, *De mort. pers.* 29–30.
42. Lactantius, *De mort. pers.* 33–35.
43. Lactantius, *De mort. pers.* 52.
44. Overlap: A. Louth, "The Date of Eusebius's *Historia Ecclesiastica*," *JTS* 41 (1990), 111–23, at 116; R. Burgess, "The Dates and Editions of Eusebius' '*Chronici Canones* and *Historia Ecclesiastica*,'" *JTS* 48 (1997), 471–504, at 502–3.
45. For the dating and the basic chronological structure of this text see Burgess, "Dates and Editions," 471–97.
46. D. Potter, *Constantine the Emperor* (Oxford, 2013), 111–14; T. D. Barnes, *Constantine: Dynasty, Religion and Power in the Later Roman Empire* (London, 2011), 62–64.
47. Barnes, *Constantine*, 71 speaks aptly of the "dismal" alternative of ruling only the territory he inherited from his father.
48. Lactantius, *De mort. pers.* 44.3–5. See too H. Drake, *Constantine and the Bishops* (Baltimore, 2002), 180; N. Lenski, "The Reign of Constantine," in *The Cambridge Companion to the Age of Constantine*, ed. N. Lenski (Cambridge, 2006), 59–90, at 69.
49. Battle of the Milvian Bridge: R. Van Dam, *Remembering Constantine at Milvian Bridge* (Cambridge, 2011); W. Kuhoff, "Die Schlacht an der Milvischen Brücke: Ein Ereignis von weltgeschichtlicher Tragweite," in *Konstantin der Große: Zwischen Sol und Christus*, ed. K. Ehling and G. Weber (Darmstadt 2011), 10–20.
50. *Pan. Lat.* 12.2.3–4.
51. *Pan. Lat.* 12.2.5.
52. Lactantius, *De mort. pers.* 44.5, 44.9, trans. Rees, adapted.

53. Eusebius, *Hist. eccl.* 8.9.1–11, trans. Schott.
54. M. Hollerich, "Religion and Politics in the Writings of Eusebius: Reassessing the First Court Theologian," *Church History* 59 (1990), 309–25, at 311.
55. J. Schott, *Christianity, Empire and the Making of Religion in Late Antiquity* (Philadelphia, 2008), 79–109 and 112–13 for the text's influence on Constantine.
56. *Or.* 1.3; cf. Schott, *Christianity, Empire, and the Making of Religion*, 113.
57. Discussion: Schott, *Christianity, Empire and the Making of Religion*, 113–14.
58. Constantine, *Or.* 16–17. Discussion: Schott, *Christianity, Empire and the Making of Religion*, 114–15.
59. *Or.* 22; cf. Schott, *Christianity, Empire and the Making of Religion*, 116.
60. *Or.* 24 (Decius and Valerian). Constantine includes Aurelian in this group on the basis, presumably, of the (probably false) rumor that he intended to launch a persecution. *Or.* 25 (Diocletian). Discussion: Schott, *Christianity, Empire and the Making of Religion*, 116–17.
61. *Or.* 22.
62. The letter to the Eastern Provincials is preserved in Eusebius's *Life of Constantine*. This passage is from <AQ: add ok?>> *Life of Constantine* (hereafter *VC*) 2.57.
63. H. Drake, "The Impact of Constantine on Christianity," in *The Cambridge Companion to the Age of Constantine*, 2nd ed., ed. N. Lenski (Cambridge, 2010), 111–36, at 128; Barnes, *Constantine*, 113–20.
64. *Cod. Theod.* 16.2.2.
65. Eusebius, *VC* 2.46. For discussion see Barnes, *Constantine*, 135–36; P. Brown, *Power and Persuasion* (Madison, WI, 1992), 90;P. Brown, *Poverty and Leadership in the Later Roman Empire* (Hanover, NH, 2002), 26–32.
66. *Cod. Theod.* 1.27.1 and 2; *Sirmondian Constitution* 1. Discussion: Drake, *Constantine and the Bishops*, 322–25; C. Rapp, *Holy Bishops in Late Antiquity* (Berkeley, 2005), 242–44; J. C. Lamoreaux, "Episcopal Courts in Late Antiquity," *JECS* 3 (1995), 143–67.
67. *VC* 2.60.2.
68. Eusebius, *VC* 2.45; see Barnes, *Constantine*, 109–10.
69. Eusebius, *VC* 2.45.
70. S. Bradbury, "Constantine and the Problem of Anti-Pagan Legislation in the Fourth Century," *CP* 89 (1994), 131–32; note though A. D. Lee, "Traditional Religions," in *The Cambridge Companion to the Age of Constantine*, 2nd ed, ed. N. Lenski (Cambridge, 2010), 159–80, at 172–74.
71. Eusebius, *VC* 3.54; Sozomen, *Hist. eccl.* 2.5 Palladas, 10.90 may refer to this confiscation, though see E. Watts, *The Final Pagan Generation* (Oakland, 2015), 48–51.
72. Schott, *Christianity, Empire and the Making of Religion*, 128–35.

CHAPTER 7

1. E.g., Eusebius, *VC* 1.12. Discussion: F. Damgaard, "Propaganda against Propaganda: Revisiting Eusebius' Use of the Figure of Moses in the *Life of Constantine*," in *Eusebius of Caesarea: Tradition and Innovations*, ed. A. Johnson and J. Schott (Washington, DC, 2013), 115–49.

2. *Deuteronomy* 12.2 (New Revised Standard Version translation). I thank Jeremy Schott for calling my attention to this similarity to Deuteronomy.
3. Watts, *The Final Pagan Generation*, 48–51.
4. Zosimus, 4.36.
5. E.g., *Cod. Theod.* 16.10.1.
6. *CIL* 11.5265. Constantine did set the condition that "this temple dedicated to our name should not be defiled by the deceits of any contagious superstition," probably a reference to sacrifices. See N. Lenski, *Constantine and the Cities: Imperial Authority and Civic Politics* (Philadelphia, 2016), chap. 5.
7. E.g., J. Baillet, *Inscriptions grecques et latines des Tombeaux des Rois Syringes à Thebes* (Cairo, 1920–1926), no. 1265. Discussion: G. Fowden, "Nicagoras of Athens and the Lateran Obelisk," *JHS* 107 (1987), 51–57.
8. Analysis: R. Burgess, "The Summer of Blood: The Great Massacre of 337 and the Promotion of the Sons of Constantine," *DOP* 62 (2008), 5–51.
9. On Arius: R. Williams, *Arius: Heresy and Tradition*, 2nd ed. (Grand Rapids, MI, 2002).
10. Watts, *Final Pagan Generation*, 84–86.
11. Gallus's unpopularity: Ammianus, 14.7; J. Matthews, *The Roman Empire of Ammianus* (Ann Arbor, 2007), 406–8. Execution: Ammianus, 14.11.
12. *Cod. Theod.* 16.10.2.
13. *Cod. Theod.* 16.10.6. There is no evidence that this penalty was ever inflicted on anyone.
14. The manuscripts of the *Theodosian Code* date this law, *Cod. Theod.* 16.10.4, to 346 but its addressee, the praetorian prefect Taurus, held office from 355 through 361. The dating of the addressee is more convincing based upon the evident contextual relationship to *Cod. Theod.* 16.10.6.
15. Sacrifices continuing: Ammianus, 19.12. Implementation challenges: Bradbury, "Anti-Pagan Legislation," 137.
16. Caesareum transfer: C. Haas, *Alexandria in Late Antiquity* (Baltimore, 1997), 210. Other transfers: Rufinus, *Hist. eccl.* 11.22; Sozomen, *Hist. eccl.* 7.15.
17. Six are known (temples at Cyzicus, Aegae, Arethusa, Heliopolis, Gaza, and Alexandria). Discussion: T. D. Barnes, "Christians and Pagans in the Reign of Constantius," in *L'Eglise et l'empire au IVe siècle*, ed. A. Dihle (Geneva, 1989), 301–43, at 325–28; P. Heather and D. Moncur, *Politics, Philosophy and Empire in the Fourth Century* (Liverpool, 2001), 52 n.26.
18. No surviving Constantian legislation encourages this sort of activity, but private possession of temple property was retroactively criminalized and punished by Constantius's successor, the pagan emperor Julian. E.g., Libanius, *Epistles* 724, 763, 1364.
19. Maternus, *De Errore Profanarum Religionum*, a work dated between 343 and 350. Discussion: J. Lössl, "Profaning and Proscribing: Escalating Rhetorical Violence in Fourth Century Christian Apologetic," in *The Purpose of Rhetoric in Late Antiquity: From Performance to Exegesis*, ed. A. J. Quiroga Puertas (Tübingen, 2013), 71–90.

20. Maternus, *De Errore* 16.4.
21. Maternus, *De Errore* 20.7.
22. Maternus, *De Errore* 28, 29.4.
23. E.g., Italica (expanded by Hadrian), Lepcis Magna (expanded by Septimius Severus), and Philippopolis (modern Shabha, Syria, expanded by Philip I).
24. Themistius, *Or*. 3.47c.
25. Shoddily built structures: Zosimus, 2.31–32. Discussion: Heather and Moncur, *Politics*, 134 n.278.
26. Themistius, *Or*. 3.48a.
27. Themistius, *Or*. 3.47c.
28. Themistius, *Or*. 3.48a.
29. Themistius, *Or*. 3.43a.
30. Themistius, *Or*. 3.43c–d.
31. Date of death: Jerome, *Chronica* 361; Aurelius Victor, *Epitome de Caesaribus* (hereafter *Epit.*) 42.17. Ammianus (21.15.3) wrongly dates it to October 3.
32. Ammianus, 21.15.6.
33. Julian, *Epistle to the Athenians* 284; cf. Ammianus, 20.5.
34. For discussion see Watts, *Final Pagan Generation*, 106–9.
35. His guiding principles seem to have derived primarily from a Neoplatonic interpretation of Plato's *Laws*. On this see J. Marvin, "Curing Folly: Reforming the Roman Empire in the Reign of Emperor Julian," PhD Diss., UC San Diego, forthcoming.
36. Libanius, *Or*. 18.130; Ammianus, 22.4. On his unkemptness see Julian, *Misopogon*, 338–39c.
37. Philosophical character of Julian's court: S. Elm, *Sons of Hellenism, Fathers of the Church* (Oakland, 2015), 88–143.
38. Objection to executions: Julian, *Letter to the Athenians* 272B–D. Trials at Chalcedon: Ammianus, 22.3.
39. Ammianus, 22.5. For Julian's interest in traditional religion while a student see also Eunapius, *Vitae sophistarum* 473.
40. Watts, *Final Pagan Generation*, 110–12.
41. *Letter to a Priest*, 288D. Discussion: Marvin, "Curing Folly," chap. 1.
42. Julian, *Letter to the Athenians* 278C–279D.
43. Julian, *Letter to the Athenians* 280B–D.
44. *Pan. Lat*. 3.3.
45. *Pan. Lat*. 3.4.1–3.
46. *Pan. Lat*. 3.4.4–6.
47. *Pan. Lat*. 3.9.1.
48. *Pan. Lat*. 3.9.2–4.
49. *Pan. Lat*. 3.10.1–2.
50. *Pan. Lat*. 3.23.4–5.
51. *Pan. Lat*. 3.30.2–3.
52. Julian's response is *Oration* 7. Discussion: Elm, *Sons of Hellenism*, 108–18.
53. *Or*. 7.228B.

54. *Or.* 7.234C. Discussion: Elm, *Sons of Hellenism*, 115; M. P. García Ruiz, "Julian's Self-Representation in Coins and Texts," in *Imagining Emperors in the Later Roman Empire*, ed. D. Burgersdijk and A. Ross (Leiden, 2018), 204–33, at 222–23.
55. Julian, *Epistulae* 8.415D.
56. Julian, *Contra Galilaeos* 193C–197C.
57. Julian, *Contra Galilaeos* 206A–B.
58. Julian, *Misopogon* 360D.
59. Gregory Nazianzen, *Or.* 4.1. Discussion: Elm, *Sons of Hellenism*, 336–77.
60. Ammianus, 22.10.7.
61. Elm, *Sons of Hellenism*, 271–23.
62. Ammianus, 25.3. Persian campaign more generally: Matthews, *Roman Empire of Ammianus*, 140–79.
63. Ammianus 25.7; Themistius, *Or.* 5. 66a. Treaty details: J. W. Drijvers, *Jovian*, chap. 2 (forthcoming); Matthews, *Roman Empire of Ammianus*, 185–87; N. Lenski, *Failure of Empire: Valens and the Roman State in the Fourth Century* (Berkeley, 2002), 167–85.

CHAPTER 8

1. J. W. Drijvers, *Jovian*, chap. 2 offers an extensive analysis of the actual status of the territories Jovian ceded, many of which, he argues, were already under de facto Persian control.
2. Discussion: K. Smith, *Constantine and the Captive Christians of Persia* (Oakland, 2016), 84–93.
3. E.g., Ephrem, *Contra Julianum* (hereafter *Against Julian*), 2.19; 3.3.
4. *Against Julian* 3.11 (all translations follow those of Lieu).
5. Ephrem, *Against Julian* 2.20–21. For discussion see Smith, *Captive Christians*, 87.
6. Ephrem, *Against Julian* 3.1.
7. Ephrem, *Against Julian* 3.1.
8. Themistius, *Or.* 5.66.
9. Eutropius, 10.18; Ammianus, 25.10.13; Sozomen, *Hist. eccl.* 6.6 (among many others). Discussion: Lenski, *Failure of Empire*, 19.
10. Matthews, *Roman Empire of Ammianus*, 188–89; Lenski, *Failure of Empire*, 20.
11. Ammianus, 26.1.7–14.
12. Reflected in Symmachus's *Oration* 1 and 2. Discussion: C. Aull, "Imperial Power in the Age of Valentinian I, 364-375 CE," PhD diss., Indiana University, 2013, chap. 1; C. Sogno, *Q. Aurelius Symmachus: A Political Biography* (Ann Arbor, 2006), 9–17.
13. Themistius, *Or.* 8.113d; echoed in Ammianus, 31.14.
14. External threats: Ammianus, 26.5; Lenski, *Failure of Empire*, 159–63. Fiscal issues: Watts, *Final Pagan Generation*, 130–33.
15. Ammianus, 30.8; Eutropius, 10.16.
16. Festus, *Breviarium* 20 (Trajan), 20–21 (Hadrian and Severus), and 23–25 (Gallienus and the tetrarchs).
17. Festus, *Brev.* 30.2.
18. Loss of territory marking an unsuccessful emperor: *Brev.* 7.14 (Nero); 8.6 and 9.15 (Hadrian); and 10.17 (Jovian). Rome ignoring bad treaties: *Brev.* 2.9 (post Caudine

Forks); 2.12–13 (Pyrrhus); 4.17, 26 (Numantia and Numidia). Implications for Valens's Persian policies: *Brev.* 10.17. Discussion: Lenski, *Failure of Empire*, 190–95.

19. This was the proconsulship of Asia that Eutropius held in 371–372 (*Prosopography of the Later Roman Empire, vol. 1)* Eutropius 2; Ammianus, 29.1.36) and Festus between 372 and 378 (*PLRE* Festus 3).
20. Lenski, *Failure of Empire*, 375–79 provides a fortifications catalog.
21. Ausonius, *Mosella*, 454–60.
22. Symmachus, *Or.* 2.10 (clemency); 2.15 (rebuilding what was destroyed).
23. Symmachus, *Or.* 2.16.
24. They did act against people suspected of practicing divination and magic. See Aull, "Valentinian," chap. 5 and Lenski, *Failure of Empire*, 211–13.
25. Aull, "Valentinian," chap. 5; G. Sears, "The Fates of the Temples in North Africa," in *The Archeology of Late Antique Paganism*, ed. L. Lavan and M. Mulryan (Leiden, 2011), 229–62, at 232–36.
26. Theodoret, *Hist. eccl.* 4.21; cf. Epiphanius, *Adversus haereses* 51.22.9–11.
27. Ammianus, 30.6.
28. Ammianus, 30.10; Zosimus 4.19; *Epit. de Caes.* 46.10.
29. Ammianus, 30.10.
30. Ammianus, 31.3–4; Eunapius, fr. 42; Socrates, *Hist. eccl* 4.34; Sozomen, *Hist. eccl.* 6.37. Discussion: P. Heather, *Goths and Romans 332–489* (Oxford, 1991), 128–35; Kulikowski, *Rome's Gothic Wars*, 123–38.
31. Discussion: Heather and Moncur, *Politics, Philosophy, and Empire*, 200. Kulikowski, *Rome's Gothic Wars*, 131–32; J. Matthews, *Western Aristocracies and Imperial Court, A.D. 364-425* (Oxford, 1975), 89.
32. Ammianus, 31.12.
33. Ammianus, 31.12.
34. Ammianus, 31.7–13; Heather, *Goths and Romans*, 143–47; Kulikowski, *Rome's Gothic Wars*, 139–43.
35. E.g., Theodoret, *Hist. eccl.* 4.32, admittedly a much later source.
36. Philostorgius, *Hist. eccl.* 9.17.
37. Socrates, *Hist. eccl.* 5.1.
38. Themistius, *Or.* 14.181b.
39. *Or.* 14.181b–c.
40. Heather and Moncur, *Politics, Philosophy, and Empire*, 207, on the basis of Themistius, *Or.* 15; N. McLynn, "Moments of Truth: Gregory Nazianzus and Theodosius I," in *From the Tetrarchs to the Theodosians*, ed. S. McGill, C. Sogno, and E. Watts (Cambridge, 2010), 215–39, at 226–27.
41. *Or.* 15.185c.
42. *Or.* 15.197b.
43. For the full career of Saturninus see *PLRE* I Flavius Saturninus 10.
44. Treaty terms: H. Wolfram, *History of the Goths* (trans. Dunlap) (Berkeley, 1988), 133–35; G. Wirth, "Rome and its Germanic Partners in the Fourth Century," in *Kingdoms of the Empire: The Integration of Barbarians in Late Antiquity*, ed. W. Pohl (Leiden,

1997), 13–56; Heather and Moncur, *Politics, Philosophy, and Empire*, 259–64; Kulikowski, *Rome's Gothic Wars*, 152–53.

45. The modern estimates of Roman dead range from 10,000 to 20,000 (e.g., P. Heather, *The Goths*, 135). Ammianus reckons that only Hannibal's great victory at Cannae saw more Romans killed in one battle (31.13.14).
46. *Or*. 16.208a–b.
47. *Or*. 16.210a.
48. *Or*. 16.211c.
49. *Cod. Theod.* 16.1.2 is often seen as a key moment in this replacement. For a thorough discussion of how the handover worked in practice see McLynn, "Moments of Truth," 222–31.
50. Council of Constantinople: McLynn, "Moments of Truth," 232–39.
51. Arian displacement: Socrates, *Hist. eccl.* 5.7; Marcellinus Comes, *Chronicle* 380; Discussion: McLynn, "Moments of Truth," 222–24. Anti-pagan violence: Libanius, *Or*. 30; Brown, *Power and Persuasion*, 107 (on campaigns of Cynegius); Libanius, *Or*. 1.255 (sacred grove at Daphne); Ambrose, *Ep*. 40 (synagogue at Callinicum).
52. Oblivion: Theodoret, *Hist. eccl.* 5.20. War against the peasantry: Libanius, *Or*. 30.13–14.
53. Prudentius, *Peristephanon* 2.473–84, John Chrysostom, *In Babylam* 13; Gregory Nazianzen, *Carmina* II. 11.1292–1304.
54. N. McLynn, *Ambrose of Milan: Church and Court in a Christian Capital* (Berkeley, 1994), 151–52.
55. The Altar of Victory removal and replacement: C. P. Jones, *Between Pagan and Christian* (Cambridge, MA, 2014), 70, 109; J. Harries, *Imperial Rome, AD 284–363: The New Empire* (Edinburgh, 2012), 278. Note, however, J. H. W. G. Liebeschuetz, *Ambrose of Milan: Political Letters and Speeches* (Liverpool, 2010), 72 n.7.
56. Symmachus, *Relationes* 3.7 and Ambrose, *Epistulae* 17.3 (Altar of Victory); *Rel*. 3.11–12 and Ambrose, *Ep*. 18.13 and 18.18 (Vestals); *Rel*. 3.12–14 and Ambrose, *Ep*. 18.13–16 (public funding). Discussion:M. Salzman, *The Letters of Symmachus, Book 1* (Atlanta, 2011), xxxii; A. Cameron, *The Last Pagans of Rome* (Oxford, 2013), 33–48; Sogno, *Symmachus*, 45–46; R. Lizzi Testa, "Christian Emperor, Vestal Virgins, and Priestly Colleges: Reconsidering the End of Roman Paganism," *Ant. Tard.* 15 (2007), 251–62.
57. *Rel*. 3.1.
58. Ambrose, *Ep*. 17. Discussion: Salzman, *Letters of Symmachus*, xxxii; McLynn, *Ambrose*, 151–52.
59. *PLRE* I Magnus Maximus 39. Revolt: Gregory of Tours, *Historia Francorum* (hereafter *HF*)1.43; *Chronica Minora* 1.646.7.
60. *Rel*. 3.1–2. Discussion: Matthews, *Western Aristocracies*, 206.
61. *Rel*. 3.1.
62. *Rel*. 3.3.
63. *Rel*. 3.4.
64. *Rel*. 3.9.
65. *Rel*. 3.14.
66. *Rel*. 3.14.
67. Ambrose, *Ep*. 18.4.

68. *Ep.* 18.6.
69. *Ep.* 18.7.
70. *Ep.* 18.7.
71. *Ep.* 18.23.
72. *Ep.* 18.7.
73. *Ep.* 18.17–21.
74. McLynn, *Ambrose of Milan*, 167.
75. *Carmen contra Paganos*, 103–14.

CHAPTER 9

1. The emperor Theodosius II would briefly control all of Roman territory in 425, but at that point significant chunks of the West had already been abandoned (i.e., Britain) or effectively surrendered to barbarian leaders (i.e., Aquitaine).
2. Zosmius, 4.58.2–3; Socrates, 5.25.
3. Selection of sources for battle: F. Paschoud, ed., *Zosime: Histoire Nouvelle, vol.* 2 (Paris, 1979), 474–500. Discussion: Cameron, *The Last Pagans*, 93–131.
4. Rufinus, *Hist. eccl.* 11.33. As Cameron has shown (*Last Pagans*, 100–110), most Christian narratives about the battle derive from Rufinus.
5. John Chrysostom, *Patrologia Gracae* (hereafter *PG*) 63.491 (trans. Cameron, adapted). Discussion: Cameron, *Last Pagans*, 107–8.
6. Ambrose, *De obitu Theodosii*, 2, 5.
7. *De obit.* 11–12.
8. On the relationship between Serena and Stilicho, see C. Sogno, *Serena and Stilicho*, forthcoming.
9. Zosimus, 5.5.4. For the plausibility of Alaric's grievances after the Frigidus, see Kulikowski, *Rome's Gothic Wars*, 164–65.
10. Claudian, *In Eutropium* 2.211–18; Discussion: Kulikowski, *Rome's Gothic Wars*, 167.
11. Sozomen, 9.4.
12. Olympiodorus, fr. 5.1; Sozomen, 9.4. Discussion: Kulikowski, *Rome's Gothic Wars*, 173.
13. Sozomen, 9.7. Colosseum burials: M. Salzman, *The Falls of Rome: Crises, Resilience, and Resurgence in Late Antiquity* (Cambridge, 2021), chap. 3.
14. Giovanni Cecconi argues the Attalus was chosen as a result of a senatorial rebellion against Honorius: G. A. Cecconi, "Gruppi di potere, indirizzi politici, rapporti tra Goti e Romani: La vicenda di Prisco Attalo," in, *Potere e politica nell'età della Famiglia Teodosiana (395–455)*, ed. I. Baldini and S. Cosentino (Bari, 2013), 141–62.
15. Sozomen, 9.8.
16. Sozomen, 9.9. For a reconstruction of the path Alaric took through the city, see M. Salzman, *The Falls of Rome*, chap. 3. Salzman shows that, contrary to the claims of Christian sources, the sack did lead to the theft of some church property.
17. Vergil, *Aeneid* 1.278–79. On this passage in this context see M. Salzman, "Memory and Meaning: Pagans and 410," in *The Sack of Rome in 410 AD: The Event, Its Context and Its Impact*, ed. J. Lipps et al. (Wiesbaden, 2013), 295–310, at 300; P. Van Nuffelen, *Orosius and the Rhetoric of History* (Oxford, 2012), 53–61.
18. Zosimus, 5.5.8.

19. Zosimus, 5.41.3, a passage that draws upon Olympiodorus. Discussion: Salzman, "Memory and Meaning," 304–6.
20. Salzman, "Memory and Meaning," 297–301.
21. Augustine, *Sermon* 296.9. Discussion: Salzman, "Memory and Meaning," 295.
22. Augustine, *Sermon* 296.12. Discussion: Salzman, "Memory and Meaning," 298 and *Falls of Rome* (forthcoming).
23. Socrates, *Hist. eccl.* 7.10. Discussion: E. Watts, "Interpreting Catastrophe: Disasters in the Works of Pseudo-Joshua the Stylite, Socrates Scholasticus, and Timothy Aelurus," *Journal of Late Antiquity* 2, no. 1 (2009), 79–98, at 83–87.
24. Philostorgius, *Hist. eccl.* 12.3. Discussion: Watts, "Interpreting Catastrophe," 87–92.
25. Sozomen, *Hist. eccl.* 9.6. Discussion: Salzman, "Memory and Meaning," 306.
26. Orosius, *History against the Pagans*, 7.43. On this larger work see P. Van Nuffelen, *Orosius and the Rhetoric of History*. See *Hist.* 3.20.6–7; 5.2.1; 7.41.4–6 for Orosius's flight. This most likely occurred in 411, around the time the Suevi occupied his home region (Hydatius, *Chronicle* 17.49).
27. Orosius, *Hist.* 1.1.
28. Orosius, *Hist.* 7.7–28.
29. *Hist.* 7.39.
30. *Hist.* 7.39.
31. *Hist.* 7.39.
32. *Hist.* 7.40.
33. The last datable event in Orosius's *History* happened in 417, giving a likely date of composition for the work.
34. Augustine, *Retractionum* 2.69.
35. Augustine, *De civitas Dei* (henceforth *De civ. D.*) 1.1.
36. *De civ. D.* 1.4.
37. *De civ. D.* 2.19, cf. 2.18 (Sallust) and 2.21 (Cicero).
38. *De civ. D.* 2.23–25.
39. *De civ. D.* 2.23.
40. *De civ. D.* 3.25–26.
41. This is the larger argument of books 4 and 5.
42. *De civ. D.* 5.25 (Constantine) and 5.26 (Theodosius).
43. *De civ. D.* 5.26.
44. This point is discussed at length in books 6–10.
45. *De civ. D.* 11.2.
46. E.g., *De civ. D.* 19.12.
47. *De civ. D.* 19.17.
48. *De civ. D.* 19.28; 21.1–4, 9–11; 22.3.
49. *De civ. D.* 22.30.
50. Possidius, *Vita Augustini* 28.
51. Possidius, *Vit. Aug.* 28. He cannot be giving a complete picture because Hippo actually became the Vandal capital until the capture of Carthage in 439. Discussion of the siege: J. Conant, *Staying Roman: Conquest and Identity in Africa and the Mediterranean, 439–700* (Cambridge, 2012), 68.

52. Possidius, *Vit. Aug.* 30, quoting a letter of Augustine.
53. Victor of Vita, *Historia persecutionis* 1.5. Refugees and their religious impact: J. Conant, "Europe and the North African Cult of the Saints, circa 350–900," *Speculum* 85 (2010), 1–46, at 1–3.
54. A. Merrills and R. Miles, *The Vandals* (Chichester, 2010), 116–24. See the case of Masties (discussed in Merrills, "Kingdoms of North Africa," 277) for an example of a Roman military official who continued in this capacity under the Vandals.
55. Sack of 455: Procopius, *Wars* 1.5.4; J. Moralee, "Commemorating Defeat: Cultural Memory and the Vandal Sack of Rome in 455," in *The Fifth Century: Age of Transformation*, ed. J. W. Drijvers and N. Lenski (Bari, 2019), 307–20.
56. P. Brown, *Through the Eye of a Needle* (Princeton, 2012), 433–53.
57. Salvian of Marseilles, *De gub. Dei* 4.6.30; Brown, *Eye of a Needle*, 434.
58. Salvian, *De gub. Dei* 4.1.4; Brown, *Eye of a Needle*, 442.
59. Roman restoration and Avitus as a new Trajan: Sidonius, *Carmina* 7.115–138. Statue: Sidonius, *Ep.* 9.16.3.
60. Urban prefecture: Sidonius, *Epp.* 1.9.6–8, 9.16.3. Larger context: J. M. O'Flynn, "A Greek on the Roman Throne: The Fate of Anthemius," *Historia* 40 (1991), 122–28.
61. Sidonius makes this aspiration clear by explicitly modeling his letter collection on that of Pliny (*Epp.* 1.1.1; 9.1.1.). S. Mratschek, "The Letter Collection of Sidonius Apollinaris," in *Late Antique Letter Collections*, ed. C. Sogno, B. Storin, and E. Watts (Oakland, 2017), 309–36.
62. Most vividly in *Ep.* 7.6, a letter to bishop Basilius.
63. *Ep.* 5.17.6.
64. Date of birth: Paulinus, *Eucharisticos* 472–75. Place of birth: *Euch.* 24–25. Family background: Brown, *Eye of a Needle*, chap. 23.
65. Dissolute youth: *Euch.* 141–75. Discussion: J. Osgood, "The Education of Paulinus of Pella," in *From the Tetrarchs to the Theodosians*, ed. S. McGill, C. Sogno, and E. Watts (Cambridge, 2010), 135–52.
66. *Euch.* 180–82.
67. Service under Attalus: *Euch.* 293–96; N. McLynn, "Paulinus the Impenitent: A Study of the Eucharisticos," *JECS* 3 (1995), 461–86, at 470–72 (service under Attalus) and 468–75 (context of burning of his home).
68. *Euch.* 489–515.
69. *Euch.* Pref. 1–2.
70. *Euch.* 610–16.
71. McLynn, "Paulinus the Impenitent," 484.

CHAPTER 10

1. Ennodius, *Life of Epiphanius* (hereafter *VE*) 141 and *Panegyric of Theoderic* (*PanThe*) 23–24 (impoverishment), 47 (dregs), 56 (Italy living again). The translations of the *Panegyric* follow those of Haase, adapted for clarity. Discussion: J. Arnold, *Theoderic and the Roman Imperial Restoration* (Cambridge, 2014), 2, 33–36; S. Bjornlie, *Politics and Tradition between Rome, Ravenna, and Constantinople* (Cambridge, 2013), 153.

2. E.g., Ennodius, *VE* 101–5. Colosseum repairs: *CIL* 6.31957, commemorating the repairs of the urban prefect Decius Marius Venantius Basilius, variously attributed to the consul of 484 and to his son, consul in 508.
3. *Anonymous Valesianus Pars Posterior* (henceforth *Anon. Val.*) 60.
4. Ennodius, *PanThe* 60–69. Gallic campaign: Arnold, *Theoderic*, 262–94. Protectorate over Spain: Procopius, *Wars* 5.12.54–57.
5. *PanThe* 30. On this speech and its context see Arnold, *Theoderic*, 33–36.
6. *PanThe* 52 (wickedness of times), 57 (senate), 58 (wealth), 60–69 (Sirmium).
7. *PanThe* 79.
8. *PanThe* 93.
9. Cassiodorus, *Variae* 1.46.
10. Ennodius, #447.6, trans. Arnold, *Theoderic*, 274.
11. Cassiodorus, *Variae* 2.2.5. Discussion: Arnold, *Theoderic*, 293; Bjornlie, *Politics and Tradition*, 193–94.
12. On the career of Ricimer, the most notable of these generals see P. MacGeorge, *Late Roman Warlords* (Oxford, 2002), 167ff.
13. Rebellion of Odoacer: Procopius, *Wars* 5.1.4–8; Ennodius, *VE* 95–100; *Anon. Val.* 8.37; Eugippius, *Vita Sancti Severini (Epistola ad Paschasium)* 4; Marcellinus, *Chron*. s.a.476; Jordanes *Getica* 242 and *Romana* 344. Discussion: J. Moorhead, *Theoderic in Italy* (Oxford, 1992), 6–8; B. Croke, "A. D. 476: The Manufacture of a Turning Point," *Chiron* 13 (1983), 81–119, at 83–87.
14. Quotation: Malchus, fr. 14 (Blockley). Imperial insignia: *Anon. Val.* 12.64.
15. *PanThe* 26–34 recounts the migration. For the warfare see the summary of Arnold, *Theoderic*, 57–60.
16. Killing of Odoacer: *Anon. Val.* 55, 57; John of Antioch, fr. 214a; Agnellus of Ravenna, 39. Theoderic as an imperial agent: Procopius *Wars* 6.6.23–24; Jordanes, *Get.* 291 and *Rom.* 348–49; *Anon. Val.* 49.
17. *Anon. Val.* 12.64. For discussion see Arnold, *Theoderic*, 70–71.
18. John Rufus, *Plerophories* 89.
19. Capture of Gratiana: Procopius, *Wars* 5.3.14–18. Larger context: A. Sarantis, "War and Diplomacy in Pannonia and the North-west Balkans during the Reign of Justinian," *DOP* 63 (2009), 15–40, at 21–22.
20. Marcellinus Comes, *Chronicle* 476.2.
21. The tradition can be traced from Marcellinus to Evagrius Scholasticus (*Hist. eccl.* 2.16, possibly based upon the lost history of Eustathius), Jordanes (*Get.* 243; *Rom.* 345), Theophanes (*Chronicle*, AM 5965), Paul the Deacon (*Historia Romana* 15.10), and, in modern times, Edward Gibbon, *Decline and Fall of the Roman Empire*, 1.36. The interdependence of these various sources has been discussed, e.g., by Croke, "A. D. 476," 90–103 as well as W. Goffart, *The Narrators of Barbarian History (AD 550–800)* (Princeton, 1988), 22–47, 357–69 and, on Marcellinus in particular, B. Croke, *Count Marcellinus and His Chronicle* (Oxford, 2001), 190–96.
22. His father, Edeco, was a Hun (father of Odoacer: *Anon. Val.* 10.45; John of Antioch, fr. 209.1; Hunnic background: Priscus, fr. 8). His mother is variously identified as a Scirian (John of Antioch, fr. 209.1) or a Rugian (Jordanes, *Rom.* 344) in contemporary sources.

One ninth-century Constantinopolitan source does say she was a Goth (Theophanes AM 5965), but this view may reflect a tradition influenced by Marcellinus.

23. Heretical character of the Italian Gothic regime: Marcellinus Comes, *Chron.* 525, among many examples. Discussion: Bjornlie, *Politics and Tradition*, 93 nn.49–51.
24. Honorifics including *comes* and *vir clarissimus*: Marcellinus Comes, *Chron.* Praef.
25. Marcellinus's position: Cassiodorus, *Instit.* 1.4.3. Reward for writing: Bjornlie, *Politics and Tradition*, 90–91.
26. On this note, for example, the public acclamations greeting new emperors recorded by Constantine Porphyrogenitus, *De Ceremoniis* 1.91–93.
27. *Vita Sabas* 72.175.20–23. Discussion: A. Hasse-Ungeheuer, "Das palästinische Mönchtum und der Streit um Origenes im 6. Jahrhundert im Spannungsfeld zwischen Jerusalem und Konstantinopel," in *Verurteilung des Origenes: Kaiser Justinian und das Konzil von Konstantinople 553*, ed. A. Fürst and T. Karmann (Münster, 2020), 69–84.
28. *Novellae* 7.2.
29. Justinian, *Liber Adversus Origenem*, *PG* 86.1.945–47.
30. North African pressure groups in Constantinople: Merrills and Miles, *Vandals*, 196–223; Procopius, *Wars* 4.5.8; Aeneas of Gaza, *Theophrastus* 66.15–67.1.
31. Procopius, *Wars* 3.6.
32. These doubts, which Procopius explains were widely held, are expressed in the text by John the Cappadocian (*Wars* 3.10.8–17).
33. *Wars* 3.10.21.
34. *Wars* 3.16.3.
35. *Wars* 3.20.17.
36. *Wars* 3.21.10.
37. *Wars* 4.9.1–2.
38. *Wars* 4.9.6.
39. *Wars* 4.9.12–14.
40. G. Greatrex, "Roman Frontiers and Foreign Policy in the East," in *Aspects of the Roman East*, ed. R. Alson and S. N. C. Lieu (Turnhout, 2007), 103–73.
41. Procopius, *Wars* 4.5.11–25.
42. For a summary of the events and their consequences see Bjornlie, *Politics and Tradition*, 138–41.
43. Exiles: Priscian, *In laudem Anastasii Imperatoris*, 239–45; Lydus, *De magistratibus* 3.28.4 as well as Croke, *Marcellinus*, 86–88; M. Maas, "Roman Questions, Byzantine Answers," in *The Cambridge Companion to the Age of Justinian*, ed. M. Maas (Cambridge, 2005), 1–27, at 11.
44. For this as an act of tyranny see *Anon. Val.* 86–87.
45. Procopius, *Wars* 5.5.8–10. This justification appears in a letter that Justinian supposedly sent to the Catholic Franks, asking for their alliance against the Italian regime.
46. The Dalmatian campaign met with a reverse leading to the death of the first commander, but the newly appointed commander quickly completed the reconquest (*Wars* 5.5–7).
47. *Wars* 5.8.7.

48. *Wars* 5.14.14.
49. Cassiodorus's time in Constantinople: Vigilius, *Epistulae* 14; Jordanes, *Get.* Pre.1
50. *Wars* 7.17.12–14.
51. *Wars* 6.21.39–40
52. *Constitutio Deo Auctore*. Pro. (trans. Watson).
53. *Constitutio Deo Auctore*. 5.
54. T. Honoré, *Justinian's Digest: Character and Compilation* (Oxford, 2010), 22; Humfress, "Law and Legal Practice in the Age of Justinian," in *The Cambridge Companion to the Age of Justinian*, ed. M. Maas (Cambridge, 2005), 161–84, at 165–66.
55. *De emendatione* 1.
56. *Institutes*. Proemeium (trans. J. B. Moyle).
57. E.g., *CJ* 1.1.1 = *Cod. Theod.* 16.1.2, a law of 380 defining orthodoxy as agreement with specific bishops, though with a brief credal statement is included; *CJ* 1.5.8, a law of 455 defining orthodoxy as professing what was held at the ecumenical councils of Nicaea, Constantinople, Ephesus, and Chalcedon. One exception to this law is the Henotikon of the emperor Zeno, a document that affirmed the faith agreed to at Nicaea, Constantinople, and Ephesus while offering a vague anathema of those who held a different belief at Chalcedon. On the text of the Henotikon see Zacharias, *Hist. eccl.* 5.8 and Evagrius, *Hist. eccl.* 3.14; cf. Liberatus, *Breviarium* 17; Nicephorus Callistus, *Hist. eccl.* 16.12.
58. *CJ* 1.1.5.
59. E.g., *CJ* 1.1.6.1–6 and *CJ* 1.1.7.6–11, both laws of 533.
60. *CJ* 1.5.18.5 (pretense); 1.5.18.10 (investigation).
61. Persecutions in 529: Malalas, 18.42; John Lydus, *De mag.*, III.73–76. Later persecution: Pseudo-Dionysius of Tel-Mahre, p. 76 (trans. Witakowski).
62. E. Watts, *City and School in Late Antique Athens and Alexandria* (Berkeley, 2006), 128–42.
63. Agathias, 2.30.3–4.
64. Pseudo-Dionysius of Tel-Mahre, *Chronicle*, p. 72; M. Whitby, "John of Ephesus and the Pagans: Pagan Survivals in the Sixth-Century," in *Paganism in the Later Roman Empire and Byzantium*, ed. M. Salaman (Cracow, 1991), 111–31.
65. On this process and the resulting separation of the Coptic and Syrian churches from that of Constantinople see V. Menze, *Justinian and the Making of the Syrian Orthodox Church* (Oxford, 2008).
66. *CJ* 1.5.20.
67. Prohibition: *CJ* 1.5.17. Samaritan rebellion: Procopius, *Anec.* 11.24–31, 18.34; Cyril of Scythopolis, *Vita Sabae* 70–72.
68. *CJ* 1.5.12.
69. *CJ* 1.5.21.
70. Legal continuity is evidenced by Cassiodorus's *Variae* and the *Edictum Theoderici*. On the latter see S. Lafferty, *Law and Society in the Age of Theoderic the Great: A Study of the "Edictum Theoderici"* (Cambridge, 2013).
71. Theoderic on Jewish rights: *Edictum Theoderici* 143; *Variae* 2.27 (conferring permission to Jews in Genoa to rebuild and use their synagogue).

CHAPTER 11

1. For this part of the city, see B. Croke, "Justinian's Constantinople," in *The Cambridge Companion to the Age of Justinian*, ed. M. Maas (Cambridge, 2005), 60–86, at 66–68 and J. Herrin, *Byzantium: The Surprising Life of a Medieval Empire* (Princeton, 2007), 55.
2. *Hymn* 54.14. Discussion: J. Koder, "Imperial Propaganda in the *Kontakia* of Romanos the Melode," *Dumbarton Oaks Papers* 62 (2008), 275–91, at 280–82. The translations of *Hymn* 54 are those of Schork, with the modifications of Koder.
3. *Hymn* 54.18.
4. Death total of 66,509: Antiochus Strategos, *Capture of Jerusalem* (translations follow those in F. C. Conybeare, "Antiochus Strategos's Account of the Sack of Jerusalem in A. D. 614," *English Historical Review* 25 [1910], 502–17, at 516). Destruction of buildings: Antiochus Strategos, p. 510, *Life of John the Almsgiver*, 9, suppl. 20; Refugees: *Life of John the Almsgiver* 9–13. For a more realistic view of the destruction see G. Avni, "The Persian Conquest of Jerusalem (614 c.e.)—An Archeological Assessment," *Bulletin of the American Schools for Oriental Research* 357 (2010), 35–48.
5. *Life of John the Almsgiver*, suppl. 20.
6. Antiochus Strategos, p. 503 (Blues and Greens, Justinian); p. 516 (Heraclius and Martina).
7. Antiochus Strategos, pp. 505–6.
8. Antiochus Strategos, p. 503.
9. Conybeare translates this term (*Berdzen* in Georgian) as Greeks, but the term's meaning in this period is more accurately rendered as Romans.
10. Antiochus Strategos, p. 516.
11. E.g., Theodore Syncellus, *Homily on the Siege of Constantinople*, chap. 9 in *Analecta Avarica*, ed. L. Sternbach (Krakow, 1900), 298–320, reproduced in F. Makk, *Traduction et commentaire de l'homélie écrite probablement par Théodore le Syncelle sur le siège de Constantinople en 626* (Szegad, 1975).
12. Sources: *Chronicon Paschale* (hereafter *CP*), 626 (pp. 715–76); Theodore Syncellus, *Hom.* chaps. 18–36; George of Pisidia, *Bellum Avaricum*; Theophanes, *Chronographia* 6117. Reconstruction: J. Howard-Johnston, "The Siege of Constantinople in 626," in *Constantinople and Its Hinterland*, ed. C. Mango and G. Dagron (Aldershot, 1995), 131–42.
13. Welcome intercession: *CP* 626 (p. 716). Virgin manning walls: *CP* 626 (p. 725).
14. Dating: Howard-Johnston, "Siege," 132 n.2. Sins: Theodore Syncellus, *Hom.* chap. 9.
15. Theodore, *Hom.* chap. 18.
16. Theodore, *Hom.* chap. 15.
17. Theodore, *Hom.* chap. 19.
18. Theodore, *Hom.* chap. 24.
19. Theodore, *Hom.* chap 39.
20. Theodore, *Hom.* chap. 40, referring to Ezekiel 38.16.
21. Theodore, *Hom.* chap. 52.
22. Theodore, *Hom.* chap. 52.

23. George of Pisidia, *Hexaemeron*, 1766–1852. Discussion: M. Whitby, "The Devil in Disguise: The End of George of Pisidia's *Hexaemeron* Reconsidered," *JHS* 115 (1995), 115–29, at 118.
24. His sins: George of Pisidia, *In Bonum Patricium* 160–61. Those of wider world: George, *Expeditio Persica* 3.407–20.
25. George, *Hex.* 767–882. See Whitby, "Devil in Disguise," 128–29; D. Olster, "The Date of George of Pisidia's *Hexaemeron*," *DOP* 45 (1991), 159–72, at 160–68.
26. Raqqa, the last major Syrian city in Roman control, fell between 638 and 640 (W. Kaegi, *Byzantium and the Early Islamic Conquests* [Cambridge, 1992], 172). The Romans held Tripoli (in modern Lebanon) until 645 or 646.
27. W. Kaegi, *Muslim Expansion and Byzantine Collapse in North Africa* (Cambridge, 2010).
28. On Theophylact: M. Whitby, *The Emperor Maurice and His Historian: Theophylact Simocatta on Persian and Balkan Warfare* (Oxford, 1988), 28–54.
29. Suggested in Theophylact, *Hist.*, Dia. 8–10.
30. For the *Chronicon Paschale* see Whitby, *Emperor Maurice*, 40; M. Whitby and M. Whitby, *Chronicon Paschale, 284–628 AD* (Liverpool, 1989), xi–xii.
31. On Menander: R. Blockley, *The History of Menander the Guardsman* (Liverpool, 1985).
32. Theophylact, *Hist.* 5.15.6–7.
33. *Chronicle of AD 1234* (in M. Penn, *When Christians First Met Muslims* [Oakland, 2015], xix).
34. Nikephorus, *Short History* 24–25. Translation and discussion: W. Kaegi, *Heraclius, Emperor of Byzantium* (Cambridge, 2003), 288–89.
35. Discussion: Kaegi, *Heraclius*, 265–90.
36. E.g., Nikephorus, *Short History*, 27.
37. Maximus Confessor, *Letter* 14. See P. Booth, *Crisis of Empire: Doctrine and Dissent at the End of Late Antiquity* (Oakland, 2017), 278–79.
38. John of Nikiu, *Chronicle* 117.5–7.
39. *Apocalypse of Pseudo.-Ephrem* 61 (trans. Penn).
40. *Apocalypse of Ps.-Ephrem* 63 (trans. Penn).
41. Chronological setting in mid-680s: Penn, *When Christians First Met Muslims*, 38–39.
42. John bar Penkāyē, *Book of Main Points*, Bk. 15.167, trans. Penn, *When Christians First Met Muslims*, 107.
43. *Apo. Ps-Meth.* 44. Context: L. Brubaker and J. Haldon, *Byzantium in the Iconoclast Era, c. 680–850: A History* (Cambridge, 2011), 31,
44. E.g., *Apocalypse of John the Little*, 18. For the first mention of the "kingdom of the Arabs" in a Syriac historical work see the *Chronicle of 705*.
45. Discussion: Booth, *Crisis of Empire*, 282–300.
46. *Acts of the Lateran Council* [Riedinger 142]. See Booth, *Crisis of Empire*, 294–95.
47. E.g., Constans II, described by Brubaker and Haldon, *Iconoclast Era*, 18–20.
48. *Syriac Life of Maximus the Confessor*, 311 (trans. Penn).
49. Theodore Spudaeus, *Narrations* 3.
50. Dating and context: Booth, *Crisis of Empire*, 305–7.
51. *Record of the Trial* 1 in P. Allen and B. Neil, *Maximus Confessor and His Companions* (Oxford, 2002), 48–50. See Booth, *Crisis of Empire*, 307; Brubaker and Haldon,

Iconoclast Era, 19–20; W. Brandes, "Juristische Krisenbewältigung im 7. Jahrhundert? Die Prozesse gegen Martin I und Maximos Homologetes," *Fontes Minores* 10 (1998), 141–212, at 161.

52. Punishment: *Greek Life of Maximus* (*PG* 90), 104D–105C, Theophanes, *Chron.* 6160, Anastasius Apocrisiarius, *Letter to Theodosius* 1. See Booth, *Crisis of Empire*, 323–26.
53. Brubaker and Haldon, *Iconoclast Era*, 20.
54. *Acta conciliorum oecumenicorum*, eds. E. Schwartz and J. Straub (Berlin, 1914) (hereafter *ACO*) vol. II.2, 898.30–5, quoted in Brubaker and Haldon, *Iconoclast Era*, 32.
55. Summary: Brubaker and Haldon, *Iconoclast Era*, 70–73.
56. Greek sources: Theophanes, *Chron.* 6209–10, Nikephorus, 53–54. Syriac: *Chronicle of Zuqnīn* AG 1028; Ḍionysius of Tel Mahre, AG 1028.157–63.
57. Theophanes, *Chron.* 6210.399. See too the homily given by patriarch Germanos on the anniversary of the victory (V. Grumel, "Homélie de S. Germain sur la délivrance de Constantinople," *REB* 16 [1958], 188–205).
58. Capture of Caesarea: Theophanes, *Chron.* 6218. Context: J. Herrin, *The Formation of Christendom* (Princeton, 1987), 321–22; Brubaker and Haldon, *Iconoclast Era*, 75–76.
59. Eruption: Theophanes, *Chron.* 6218.404–5.
60. Theophanes *Chron.* 6218.405. Theophanes then continues that this "still more shamelessly incited him to fight against the blessed, holy icons."
61. Theophanes, *Chron.* 6218.406.
62. The iconophile Theophanes does emphasize that the soldier in question died (*Chron.* 6218.406).
63. Herrin, *Formation of Christendom*, 307–12. For *proskynesis* as a focal point of initial Iconoclastic complaints see Brubaker and Haldon, *Byzantium in the Iconoclast Era*, 139 and Mansi xiii.116C–117B.
64. See Brubaker and Haldon, *Byzantium in the Iconoclast Era*, 79–155.
65. On this later inscription and its possible connection to sentiments of Leo III see Brubaker and Haldon, *Byzantium in the Iconoclast Era*, 140.
66. Rebellion and its context: P. Speck, *Artabasdos, der rechtgläubige Vorkämpfer der göttlichen Lehren* (Bonn, 1981); Brubaker and Haldon, *Byzantium in the Iconoclast Era*, 156–61. Coup's aftermath: Theophanes, *Chron.* 6235.419–21, Nikephoros, 136.
67. Theophanes, *Chron.* 6237.422, 6247.429.
68. Hagia Eirene: R. Ousterhout, "The Architecture of Iconoclasm: Buildings," in *Byzantium in the Iconoclast Period*, ed. L. Brubaker and J. Haldon (Aldershot, 2001), 3–19, at 5–8.
69. Theophanes records 1000 builders, 200 plasterers, 500 tile makers, 200 potters, and 5000 workers employed on the aqueduct of Valens alone (*Chron.* 6258.440). Treasury full: Theophanes, *Chron.* 6262.449.
70. Theophanes, *Chron.* 6259.443.
71. E.g., Theophanes, *Chron.* 6237.422. Policy objective: Brubaker and Haldon, *Byzantium in the Iconoclast Era*, 166.
72. Brubaker and Haldon, *Byzantium in the Iconoclast Era*, 163–66.
73. P. Magdalino, "The Distance of the Past in Early Medieval Byzantium," in *Ideologie e pratiche del reimpiego nell'alto medioevo* (Spoleto, 1999), 115–46, at 141.

74. This belief is expressed most clearly in Constantine's *Peusis,* accessible through H. Hennephof, *Textus Byzantinos ad iconomachiam pertinentes in usum academicum* (Leiden, 1969), frr. 141–87. Discussion: Brubaker and Haldon, *Byzantium in the Iconoclast Era,* 180–82.
75. Council of 754: Theophanes, *Chron.* 6245.427–28; Brubaker and Haldon, *Byzantium in the Iconoclast Era,* 189–97.
76. Mansi xiii.257E.
77. Mansi xiii.328B–C, following C. Mango, *The Art of the Byzantine Empire, 312–1453* (Toronto, 1986), 165–68.
78. Theophanes, *Chron.* 6267.448.
79. Discussion: Brubaker and Haldon, *Byzantium in the Iconoclast Era,* 201–12.
80. Theophanes, *Chron,* 6253.432.
81. Theophanes, *Chron.* 6257.437–38.
82. Details of tortures: Theophanes, *Chron.* 6259.441–43.

CHAPTER 12

1. Turnover in duchy of Rome: Herrin, *Formation of Christendom,* 347.
2. Theophanes, *Chron.* 6224.410. Discussion: Herrin, *Formation of Christendom,* 349; W. Brandes, "Das Schweigen des Liber Pontificalis: Die 'Enteignung' der päpstlichen Patrimonien Siziliens und Unteritaliens in den 50er Jahren des 8. Jahrhunderts," in *Fontes Minores XII,* ed. W. Brandes et al. (Frankfurt, 2014), 97–204. Theophanes's mention of the male-children registry equates Leo to Pharaoh, an exaggeration that obscures the measure's real intent.
3. *Codex Carolinus* (henceforth *CC*) 1 (pp. 476–77 in the *Monumenta Germaniae Historica* edition) and 2 (pp. 477–79). The quoted section is *CC* 2.478.25–31. Context for collection creation: D. van Espelo, "A Testimony of Carolingian Rule? The *Codex epistolaris carolinus,* Its Historical Context, and the Meaning of *imperium,*" *Early Medieval Europe* 21 (2013), 254–82.
4. On the relationship between Zacharias and Constantine see Herrin, *Formation of Christendom,* 354–56.
5. *Royal Frankish Annals* 749, trans. Scholz, edited for clarity.
6. Appeal for help: *Liber Pontificalis* (hereafter *LP*) 1.444. The precise dating of the fall of Ravenna is unknown, though Aistulf issued an edict from the city on July 7, 751. For this work see C. R. Brühl, ed., *Codex Diplomaticus Langobardiae* 3.1, no. 23 (Rome, 1973), 111–15.
7. *LP* 1.448–49, *Royal Frankish Annals* 753. Discussion: T. Noble, *Republic of St. Peter* (Philadelphia, 1984), 82–86.
8. *Propria sanctae Dei ecclesiae reipublice Romanorum reddidisset* (*LP* 1.449).
9. Described in *Clausula de unctione Pippini regis* (*Monumenta Germaniae historica, Scriptores=MGH SS* Merov 3.465), *Royal Frankish Annals* 754. For discussion see Noble, *Republic of St. Peter,* 87.
10. On the powerful contrast made here between the real Catholic, Roman state in Italy and the heretical one in Constantinople, see Noble, *Republic of St. Peter,* 95–97.
11. On this campaign see Noble, *Republic of St. Peter,* 88.

12. *LP* 1.450–51. Cf. Einhard, *Vita Karoli* (henceforth *VC*) 6; *CC* 6.489.
13. *Royal Frankish Annals* 756.
14. *LP* 1.454.
15. CC 11.506.
16. Greek and Lombard cooperation: *CC* 15, 17.517, cf. 20.521.12–14.
17. *CC* 32.539.
18. *Royal Frankish Annals*, 767, cf. *Annals of Einhard* 767; *CC* 37.549
19. The translation follows that of E. Henderson, *Select Historical Documents of the Middle Ages* (London, 1910), 319–29. For the likely context of the forgery within the period stretching between the papacies of Stephen II and Hadrian I see the summary of Noble, *Republic of St. Peter*, 132–34.
20. Fall of Pavia: *Royal Frankish Annals* 773, *Ann. Lauren.* 1.150, *Pauli continuato Romana*, in *Monumenta Germaniae historica, Scriptores rerum Langobardicarum et Italicarum saec. VI–IX=MGH SSrL* 201. Discussion: Noble, *Republic of St. Peter*, 131–32.
21. *LP* 1.497.
22. *LP* 1.498.
23. *CC* 60.587.9–18.
24. *CC* 60.586.30–36.
25. *CC* 61.589.8–10.
26. These terms are reconstructed from the *Ludovicianum*, a donation from Charlemagne's son Louis to Pope Paschal I in 817. Clauses 1–3 related to Tuscia and Campania, 4–5 speak about Ravenna and the Pentapolis, 6 speaks about Sabine land, and 7 speaks about additional coastal territory added to Tuscia. Discussion: R. Davis, *Lives of the Eighth Century Popes* (Liverpool, 2007), 112–13.
27. *Ludovicianum*, clause 10.
28. Theophanes, *Chron.* 6274.455; cf. Einhard, *VC* 19. Context: Noble, *Republic of St. Peter*, 165; Brubaker and Haldon, *Byzantine Iconoclasm*, 256–59.
29. Campaign: Theophanes, *Chron.* 6274.456. Hadrian's Letter: CC 74.605.10–18. Discussion: Brubaker and Haldon, *Byzantine Iconoclasm*, 254.
30. Herrin, *Formation of Christendom*, 414.
31. Irene: Theophanes, *Chron.* 6281.463. Charlemagne: *Annales qui dicuntur Einhardi*, 786.
32. Discussion: Brubaker and Haldon, *Byzantine Iconoclasm*, 258.
33. For the council, its findings, and the reaction see Brubaker and Haldon, *Byzantine Iconoclasm*, 262–86.
34. These criticisms are known primarily from the *Hadrianum*, the response sent by pope Hadrian. Objection to Irene: *Had.* 53. Biblical grounds for icons: *Had.* 19.
35. Full Title: *Libri Carolini sive Caroli Magni Capitulare de Imaginibus* (hereafter *LC*). On this document see Herrin, *Formation of Christendom*, 427ff; Brubaker and Haldon, *Byzantine Iconoclasm*, 281–84.
36. *LC* 2.13, 30.
37. *LC*, Preface 2.3, 7; 1.17, 19. Discussion: Herrin, *Formation of Christendom*, 436–40.
38. Roman site: H. Cüppers, *Aquae Granni: Beiträge zur Archäologie von Aachen* (Cologne, 1982).
39. Ravenna materials: D. Deliyannis, *Ravenna in Late Antiquity* (Cambridge, 2010).

40. Silver tables: Einhard, *VC* 39; D. Deliyannis, "Charlemagne's Silver Tables: The Ideology of an Imperial Capital," *Early Medieval Europe* 12 (2004), 159–77.
41. Aachen as a New Rome: *Karolus Magnus et Leo Papa*, ed. H. Beumann et al. (Paderborn, 1966); Moduin of Autun, *Ecloga*, 192.24–31; Herrin, *Formation of Christendom*, 448 n.5.
42. Constantine's actions: Theophanes, *Chron*. 6282.465–66
43. Sources and dating of Irene's coup: Brubaker and Haldon, *Byzantine Iconoclasm*, 291 n.173.
44. *LP* 2.4.
45. *LP* 2.6.
46. L. Wallach, "The Roman Synod of December 800 and the Alleged Trial of Leo III: A Theory and the Historical Facts," *Harvard Theological Review* 49 (1956): 123–42.
47. *LP* 2.7, trans. Davis, adapted.
48. *Royal Frankish Annals*, AM801.
49. *Donation of Constantine*, trans. E. Henderson, p. 315.
50. E. Hlawitschka, "Karl Martell, das Römische Konsulat und der Römische Senat: Zur Interpretation von *Fredegarii Continuatio* cap. 22," in *Die Stadt in der europäische Geschichte*, ed. W. Besch (Bonn, 1972), 74–90.
51. *Annales Laureshamenses* xxxiiii.801.
52. Einhard, *VC* 16 (elephant, cf. *Royal Frankish Annals* a. 801), 27 (Christians under Abbasid rule).
53. Ambitions in Italy and Dalmatia: Einhard, *VC* 15. Sicilian campaign: Theophanes, *Chron*. 6293.475.11–32.
54. *Royal Frankish Annals*, a. 812.

CHAPTER 13

1. So, at any rate, says Theophanes, *Chron*. 6303.491.
2. Theophanes *Chron*. 6305.501. In part to prevent a repeat, Constantine's tomb was later destroyed. P. Grierson et. al., "The Tombs and Obits of the Byzantine Emperors," *DOP* 16 (1962), 1–63, at 53–54.
3. Theophanes, *Chron*. 6305.503.
4. Iconoclasm and military success: Nicephorus, *Antirrhetikos* 3.70–2; Theophanes, *Chron*. 6304.496. Analysis: Brubaker and Haldon, *Byzantine Iconoclasm*, 366–85.
5. Discussion: Brubaker and Haldon, *Byzantine Iconoclasm*, 406–7.
6. *Annales Xantenses*, s.a. 862.
7. The two emperors in this span were Louis III (who ruled effectively as emperor from 901 until he was blinded in 905) and Berengar I (916–924). The title then sat vacant until Otto I took it in 962. See P. Wilson, *Heart of Europe: A History of the Holy Roman Empire* (Cambridge, MA, 2016), 693.
8. T. P. Lankila, "The Saracen Raid of Rome in 846: An Example of Maritime ghazw," *Studia Orientalia Electronica* 114 (2015), 93–120.
9. *Liber Pontificalis* 2.98.
10. *Liber Pontificalis* 2.109.
11. *Liber Pontificalis* 2.108.

12. On the Magnaura and Leo, its first chair of philosophy, see Ioannis Skylitzes, 101–2.
13. Basil's family background: Skylitzes, 115–17; Genesios, *On the Reigns*, Book 4.24.
14. Nature of the Roman imperial regime: A. Kaldellis, *Romanland* (Cambridge, MA, 2019), 233–68. Texts celebrating expansion: A. Kaldellis, "The Discontinuous History of Imperial Panegyric in Byzantium and Its Reinvention by Michael Psellos," *GRBS* 59 (2019), 693–713, at 706–8.
15. On this term see, for example, K. Weitzmann, *The Joshua Roll: A Work of the Macedonian Renaissance* (Princeton, 1948); P. Magdalino, "The Bath of Leo the Wise and the 'Macedonian Renaissance' Revisited: Topography, Iconography, Ceremonial Ideology," *DOP* 42 (1988), 97–118.
16. Photius's *Hymns* for Basil: *PG* 102, col 581c and 582b–584a. An anonymous laudatory poem he may have written: A. Markopoulos, "An Anonymous Laudatory Poem in Honor of Basil I," *DOP* 46 (1992), 225–32. More balanced portrait of Michael: E. Kislinger, "Michael III—Image und Realität," *Eos* 77 (1987), 389–400
17. Leo's text: A. Leo and I. Hausherr. *Oraison funébre de Basile I* (Rome, 1932) and T. Antonopoulou, *The Homilies of the Emperor Leo VI* (Leiden, 1997). Materials from reign of Constantine: L. van Hoof, "Among Christian Emperors: The *Vita Basilii* by Constantine VII Porphyrogenitus," *JECS* 54 (2002), 163–83.
18. *Vita Basilii* 18 and 19 (love of Basil, hatred of Michael); 20, 26, 31, 33 (contrasting law breaking and law making); 24 (divine rejection and protection); 20 (Michael bringing about own death). Rhetorical strategy: Van Hoof, "Among Christian Emperors," 169.
19. Skylitzes, 107–14, 131–33 (Michael's foolishness and treachery), 130 (Basil's proclamation).
20. *Sixty Books*, Pro. 15–17 (eliminating difficulty), 28–31 (nothing omitted). The translation follows that of Z. Chitwood, *Byzantine Legal Culture and the Roman Legal Tradition* (Cambridge, 2017), 33–35.
21. Chitwood, *Byzantine Legal Culture*, 34–35.
22. Leo, *Novels*, Novel 1.22–34, translation Chitwood, *Byzantine Legal Culture*, 38.
23. Arethas, *Op.* 61–65. *Op.* 61 compares Leo to Plato, *Op.* 62 to Alexander. Discussion: Kaldellis, "Discontinuous History," 703.
24. I. Dujčev, "On the Treaty of 927 with the Bulgarians," *DOP* 32 (1978), 217–95. The passage quoted is chap. 11.
25. Skylitzes, 231–32.
26. Text: A.-M. Dubarle, "L'homélie de Grégoire le référendaire pour la reception de l'image d'Edesse," *REB* 55 (1997), 5–51. Legend itself: Averil Cameron, "The History of the Image of Edessa: The Telling of a Story," *Harvard Ukrainian Studies* 7 (1983), 80–94. Specific references: 14 (Persian siege), 17–18 (conducted to city), 19–20 (procession).
27. Similar ideas are developed in another text, Ps. Constantine Porphyrogenitus, *Narratio de Imagine Edessena* (*PG* 113 col. 423–54), e.g., chap. 16–17 = col. 437–41 (Persians); chap. 27 = col. 448 (Constantinople as new home); chap. 28 = col. 450 (procession).
28. Theophanes Continuatus, 444 (eagle overhead), 445 (neglected state), 446 (best teachers), 447–48 (diadems, fishtanks, and legal reforms), 449 (hospital and home

for the elderly). Translations follow those of D. Sullivan, *The Rise and Fall of Nikephoros II Phokas* (Leiden, 2018).

29. Capture of Crete: Theophanes Continuatus, 473–477, 480; *Revised Chronicle of Symeon the Logothete* 18, 21; Skylitzes 249–50; Leo the Deacon, *Hist.* 2.4.
30. The poem and its translation now appear in Sullivan, *Rise and Fall of Nicephorus*, 136–91. These quotations follow Sullivan, with adaptations for clarity.
31. *Capture of Crete*, 1.1–17 = pp. 263–64, 1.256–59 = p. 273 (Republican generals and Romanus); 3.220–30 = p. 294 (Plutarch and Dio); 5.115–122 = p. 306 (God's cooperation); 2.166 = p. 281 (Syria, Tarsus, etc.); 5.75–79 = p. 304 (ancestral land).
32. Basil still had to fight civil wars in 979 and 989 before his hold on the empire became fully secure.
33. Sharing credit: e.g., the presence of both Constantine and Romanus I at the Mandylion arrival (discussion at Dubarle, "L'homélie," 10–11). This blame shifting happened despite public gestures of loyalty: e.g., Romanus I affirming the senior status of Constantine VII (Theophanes Continuatus 435); Nicephorus II Phocas pledging no insurrection against Basil II (*Revised Chronicle of Symeon* 23).
34. Theophanes Continuatus, 457. For the festival itself see Constantine Porphyrogenitus, *De Cer.* 2.18.
35. Theophanes Continuatus, 435.
36. Skylitzes 274–77. Fiscal situation: P. Magdalino, "The Byzantine Army and the Land," in *To empolemo Buzantio (Byzantium at War, Ninth to the Twelfth Centuries)*, ed. N. Oikomides (Athens, 1997), 15–36. Coinage: M. Hendy, "Light-weight solidi, tetartera, and the Book of the Eparch," *BZ* 65 (1972), 57–80.
37. Death of Nicephorus: Skylitzes 279–81; forced repentance of John: Skylitzes, 285–86. Reconstruction of events: R. Guilland, *Études de topographie de Constantinople Byzantine* (Amsterdam, 1969), 334–67. Nicephorus remained so beloved in some devout religious circles that a surviving text (published in Sullivan, *Rise and Fall*, 191–237) celebrates him as a saintly martyr.
38. Basil continued to reign with a co-emperor, but it was his brother, Constantine VIII.
39. Michael Psellus, *Chron.* 6.41 (philosophy), 6.43 (rhetoric). Discussion: A. Kaldellis, *Hellenism in Byzantium* (Cambridge, 2007), 193–95. Psellus and his career: S. Papaionnou, *Michael Psellos: Rhetoric and Authorship in Byzantium* (Cambridge, 2013). Translations of Psellus follow those of E. R. A. Sewter, *Fourteen Byzantine Rulers: The Chronographia of Michael Psellus* (New York, 1979), with adaptations for clarity.
40. Michael Psellus, *Chron.* 1.30 (exceptional crop under Basil II). Psellus does speak about the rise of a "whole new race of philosophers and orators" in the 1030s who lacked genuine understanding of the Platonic tradition (*Chron.* 3.2–3) and blames the emperor Romanus III (1028–1034) for failing to discern this lack. He also speaks about the attachment that Michael IV (1034–1041) had to Christian ascetic philosophers rather than conventional scholars of Plato and Aristotle, though ostensibly this attitude is to Michael's credit (*Chron.* 4.34).
41. Michael Attaleiates, *History* 21. Discussion: Kaldellis, "Discontinuous History," 711–12.

42. Psellus, *Chron*. 6.48.
43. Narration: Psellus, *Chron*. 7. Romanus chap. 22–43.
44. Anna Comnena, *Alexiad* 1.16.
45. Psellus, *Chron*. 7. Romanus chap. 5 (vainglory), chap. 9 (insolence); Psellus, *Chron*. 7. Michael chap. 1 (divine nature), chap. 4 (prodigy of our age), chap. 7 (riding the storm).
46. Attaleiates, *History*. Chap. 24.1–2 (comparison), 27.1 (choice of Botaneiates). Translations follow Kaldellis and Krallis.
47. Anna Comnena, *Alexiad* 1.1. Translations follow Sewter.
48. *Alexiad*, 1.6.
49. *Alexiad* 6.5.
50. Later consequences: M. Lau, "Rewriting the 1120s: Chronology and Crisis under John II Komnenos," *LIMESplus* 2 (2016), 87–107.
51. Passing of Nicaea out of Roman control and subsequent campaigns: P. Frankopan, The First Crusade: The Call from the East (Cambridge, MA, 2012), 49–59. Clerical complaints: see P. Gautier, "Diatribes de Jean l'Oxite contre Alexis Ier Comnène," *Revue des études byzantines* 28 (1970), 5–55, at 35.

CHAPTER 14

1. Bernold of Constance, *Chronicle* 520 (ed. Robinson).
2. The most difficult point of contention concerned the western addition of the term *filioque* to the Nicene Creed. For discussion and bibliography see Frankopan, *The First Crusade*, 17–18.
3. F. Sisic, ed., *Letopis Papa Dukljanina* (Belgrade, 1928), 413–16. Discussion: P. Frankopan, "Co-operation between Constantinople and Rome before the First Crusade," *Crusades* 3 (2004), 1–13.
4. Ideas captured by, among others, Robert the Monk, Lucus Protospatharius, and Gilbert of Mons. Discussion: P. Frankopan, *First Crusade*, 92–93.
5. Frankopan, *First Crusade*, 95.
6. Papal involvement: Frankopan, *First Crusade*, 111–12.
7. *Alexiad* 10.5.
8. People's Crusade: Frankopan, *First Crusade*, 117–23.
9. *Gesta Francorum* 1.5.
10. E.g., *Alexiad* 10.8–9 (naval encounter near Epirus), *Alexiad* 10.9 (conflict outside Constantinople).
11. *Alexiad* 10.11.
12. E.g., *Alexiad* 10.10, an account of a western knight who sat on Alexius's imperial throne.
13. On Bohemond see J. Flori, *Bohémond d'Antioche* (Paris, 2007).
14. Geoffrey of Villehardouin, *Conquest of Constantinople*, chaps. 1–4.
15. The attack on Zadar also led to a papal sanction excommunicating the Crusaders, though the pope soon offered them readmittance to communion (Innocent III *Register* 5.161 [162], a letter of February of 1203).
16. Robert de Clari, xvii, in C. Hopf, *Chroniques Gréco-Romanes Inédites ou Peu Connues* (Berlin, 1873), 12. On his activities in the west: A. J. Andrea, *Contemporary Sources for*

the Fourth Crusade (Leiden, 2008), 32–35. Against the legitimacy of Alexius's claims see Innocent III's letter of November 16, 1202 (*Reg.* 5.121 [122]).

17. Laid out by Alexius in *Reg.* 6.209, a letter of August 25, 1203, and echoed almost verbatim in a letter from the Crusaders themselves (*Reg.* 6.210). Translations of letters from this collection follow those in Andrea, *Contemporary Sources*.
18. Papal prohibition: *Reg.* 6.48; 6.101. Promise of union from Alexius: *Reg.* 6.209, 6.210. Cash bonuses: *Reg.* 6.210.
19. *Reg.* 6.210.
20. Numbers: Villehardouin, chaps. 51–2. Fire: *Devastatio Constantinopolitana,* p. 11 in Hopf, *Chroniques,* 89–90.
21. *Reg.* 6.28 [229], a letter of February of 1204 to Alexius Angelus.
22. Robert de Clari, lxxii, in Hopf: *Chroniques,* 57.
23. Villehardouin, chap. 56. Translations of Villehardouin follow those of M. Shaw, *Joinville and Villehardouin: Chronicles of the Crusades* (New York, 1963), adapted for clarity.
24. Robert de Clari, lxxiii, in Hopf: *Chroniques,* 58.
25. *Reg.* 7.152, echoed in Robert de Clari, lxxii.
26. *Reg.* 7.152, a letter written from occupied Constantinople after May 16, 1204.
27. *Reg.* 7.153, a letter from Rome to Constantinople, dated November 7, 1204.
28. *Reg.* 7.154.
29. Transfer of Empire: *Reg.* 7.203 (letter of January 21, 1205). Eschatology: *Reg.* 7.154, with extensive quotations of Joachim of Fiore's *Exposition on the Apocalypse*. On this see Andrea, *Contemporary Sources,* 116, 131.
30. *Reg.* 7.152.
31. *Reg.* 7.202, a letter to the pope written in June of 1204.
32. *Devastatio Constantinopolitana* 12 in Hopf, *Chroniques,* 92.
33. Analysis of the damage done by the Crusaders: A.-M. Talbot, "The Restoration of Constantinople under Michael VIII," *DOP* 47 (1993), 243–61, at 243–45.
34. Choniates, *Historia* 553–54, describing the loss of his own house in this fire.
35. Choniates, *Historia* 570.33–35.
36. Villehardouin, chap. 64. For discussion see Talbot, "Restoration," 245.
37. A claim made in *Reg.* 7.205, a description of the so-called March Pact.
38. Venetian plunder: D. M. Perry, *Sacred Plunder: Venice and the Aftermath of the Fourth Crusade* (University Park, PA, 2015). Papal prohibition: *Reg.* 7.208.
39. Robert of Clari, lxxxii–lxxxiii, catalogues plundered relics. On plunder sent by Nevelon de Chérisy to Soissons see Anonymous of Soissons, *De terra Iherosolimitana et quomodo ab urbe Constantinopolitana ad hanc ecclesiam allate sunt reliquie,* 172–74 in the discussion and translation of A. J. Andrea and P. Rachlin, "Holy War, Holy Relics, Holy Theft," *Historical Reflections* 18 (1992), 147–75.
40. Choniates, *Historia* 597.
41. *Reg.* 8.127 (128).
42. A. Simpson, "Before and after 1204: The Versions of Niketas Choniates' *Historia,*" *DOP* 60 (2006), 189–221.
43. Choniates, *Historia* 55 (pirates), 124 (Turks), 329–30 (infrastructure).

44. Simpson, "Before and after," 203–4.
45. *Historia* 645.
46. *Historia* 573–82.
47. Choniates, *Historia* 572. Quotations from Choniates follow those of H. Magoulias, *O City of Byzantium: Annals of Niketas Choniates* (Detroit, 1984), with adaptations for clarity.
48. The last we hear about him, Choniates and his family are still living in squalid huts with other Constantinopolitan refugees in Nicaea in 1214 (*Historia* 645).
49. Villehardouin (83–84) and Choniates (*Historia* 603–4) give conflicting accounts of this battle, with each source describing a different Roman commander.
50. D. J. Geanakoplos, *Emperor Michael Paleologus and the West, 1258–1282* (Cambridge, MA, 1959), 17.
51. George Akropolites, 83–84, in A. Heisenberg, *Georgii Acropolitae Opera* (Leipzig, 1903).
52. Trial by ordeal: Akropolites, 95–96. Service under Sultan: Manuel Holobolos, 34–35 in M. Treu, ed., *Manuelis Holoboli orationes,* I–II (Potsdam, 1906–1907); Akropolites, 134.
53. Geanakoplos, *Emperor Michael,* 36–46.
54. Holobolos 43–44; Pachymeres, *Corpus scriptorum historiae byzantinae=CSHB* 1, 110–11, 119, 122–24. For this incident see Geanakoplos, *Emperor Michael,* 76–81; R. Macrides, "The New Constantine and the New Constantinople—1261?" *Byzantine and Modern Greek Studies* 6 (1980), 13–41, at 33.
55. Alliance with Genoa: *Annales Ianuenses* 4.41–42; Holobolos, 45–47. Discussion: Macrides, "New Constantine," 33–36.
56. Accounts of the capture: Akropolites, 182; Gregoras, 83–85; Pachymeres, 138; Holobolos, 74; Marino Sanudo Torsello, *Fragmentum* (in Hopf, *Chroniques,* 172) and *Istoria del Regno di Romania* (in Hopf, *Chroniques,* 114); Bar Hebraeus, *Chronicle* I.428.
57. Akropolites, 11.13ff.
58. The coronation fell between August and Christmas (Macrides, "New Constantine," 14, n.6).
59. Deterioration of city: Talbot, "Restoration," 245–48.
60. Gregoras, *Hist.* 81–88. Cf. Pachymeres, I, 161.
61. P. Magdalino, *Studies on the History and Topography of Byzantine Constantinople* (London, 2007), 36, 61.
62. This scavenging became such a problem that the Nicene emperor John III had even sent money to the Latin emperor to prevent him from continuing the practice. Scutariotes, 509. For discussion see Geanakoplos, *Emperor Michael,* 124.
63. Churches: Gregoras, 88. Monasteries: Pachymeres, 164.5–12. Hagia Sophia: Pachymeres, 172–73.
64. Holobolos, 58.31–34.
65. Macrides, "New Constantine," 25–31.
66. Gregory of Cyprus, *Laudatio,* in Migne, *Patrologiae Cursus, series Graeca* 142, col 377. Cf. Geanakoplos, *Emperor Michael,* 136–37.
67. E.g., Michael Palaeologus, *Typikon for St. Michael,* 771.

68. New Constantine: *Annali Genovesi di Caffaro d de' suoi continuatori = Annales Ianuenses*, IV.45.
69. Holobolos, 57.4–25. This allusion echoes Eusebius's description of Constantine I, nine centuries earlier.
70. Gregoras, 202.10–13; Pachymeres, II, 234.16–22.
71. Pachymeres, II, 614. Discussion: Macrides, "New Constantine," 23 n.53.
72. For these terms see Pachymeres, I, 162–63; Gregoras, 97.
73. Pachymeres, I, 190–92.
74. Pachymeres, I, 193.
75. Gregoras, 153, 159; Pachymeres, I, 530–32. A.-M. Talbot, "Empress Theodora Palaiologina, Wife of Michael VIII," *DOP* 46 (1992), 295–303 at 303; A. Laiou, *Constantinople and the Latins: The Foreign Policy of Andronicus II, 1282-1328* (Cambridge, MA, 1972), 30–31.
76. Macrides, "New Constantine," 20–21, n.41, citing Philotheos of Selymbria.
77. E.g., Doukas, *Historia Turcobyzantina* 6.2.

CHAPTER 15

1. Constantinople's symbolic status: Manuel Chrysoloras, *Comparison between the Old and New Rome* and Isidore of Kiev, *Encomium on John VIII Palaiologos*, in *Παλαιολόγεια καὶ Πελοποννησιακά*, ed. S. P. Lampros (Athens, 1926), vol. 3.202–203. Discussion: D. Angelov, *Imperial Ideology and Political Thought in Byzantium, 1204–1330* (Cambridge, 2007), 114.
2. On the ebb and flow of relations see G. Demacopoulos, *Colonizing Christianity: Greek and Latin Religious Identity in the Era of the Fourth Crusade* (New York, 2019).
3. By the time of his death in 1285, Charles was the king of Naples and Sicily, king of Albania, prince of Achaea, count of a number of French lands, and owner of a claim to the nearly defunct Kingdom of Jerusalem.
4. Charles's career: J. Dunbabin, *Charles I of Anjou: Power, Kingship and State-Making in Thirteenth-Century Europe* (London and New York, 2014).
5. The election of Pope Martin IV doomed the agreement. On Martin's election see R. Brentano, *Rome before Avignon: A Social History of Thirteenth Century Rome* (Berkeley, 1990), 96–125.
6. Serbian expansion: G. Soulis, *The Serbs and Byzantium during the Reigns of Tsar Stephen Dusan (1331–1355) and His Successors* (Washington, DC, 1984). Roman imperial context: D. Nicol, *The Reluctant Emperor: A Biography of John Cantacuzene, Byzantine Emperor and Monk* (Cambridge, 2002).
7. Manuel II Palaeologus, *Ep.* 16.21–45, trans. G. Dennis, *The Letters of Manuel II Palaeologus* (Washington, 1977).
8. In some cases, the literary products engage directly with this decay. See, for example, I. Ševčenko, "The Decline of Byzantium Seen through the Eyes of Its Intellectuals," *DOP* 15 (1961), 167–86.
9. Made clear in, among other things, travelers' accounts. See M. Angold, "The Decline of Byzantium Seen through the Eyes of Western Travelers," in *Travel in the Byzantine World*, ed. R. Macrides (Aldershot, 2002), 213–32.

10. Ducas, *Historia Turcobyzantina*, 14.5.
11. *Chronicon Adae de Usk*, fol. 169, p. 57 in E. M. Thompson, *Chronicon Adae de Usk* (London, 1904). See D. Nicol, "A Byzantine Emperor in England: Manuel II's Visit to London in 1400–1401," in *Byzantium: Its Ecclesiastical History and Relations with the Western World*, ed. D. Nicol (London, 1972), 204–25.
12. Siege: Ducas, 13.7–14.5; P. Gautier, "Un récit inédit du siège de Constantinople par les Turcs (1394–1402)," *REB* 23 (1965), 106.
13. Ducas, 13.7. All translations from Ducas follow those of Magoulias.
14. Ducas, 14.1.
15. Ottoman civil war: D. Kastritsis, *The Sons of Bayezid: Empire Building and Representation in the Ottoman Civil War 1402–1413* (Leiden, 2007).
16. E.g., Demetrius Chrysoloras's *Oration to the Mother of God*, 47.21–34, on which see P. Gautier, "Action des graces de Démétrius Chrysoloras à la Théotocos pour l'anniversaire de la bataille d'Ankara (28 julliet 1403)," *REB* 19 (1961), 340–57.
17. Manuel, *Ep*. 68.44–45. The Hexamilion, whose construction was once dated to the reign of Justinian (on the basis of Procopius, *Buildings* 4.2.27–28), is now thought to have an earlier phase dating to the early fifth century. Earlier date: T. Gregory, *The Hexamilion and the Fortress* (Princeton, 1993). Justinianic phase:R. Hohlfelder, "Trans-Isthmian Walls in the Age of Justinian," *GRBS* 18 (1977), 173–79.
18. Relations with Athos: "Patriarch Matthew I's Testament," in *Byzantine Monastic Foundation Documents: A Complete Translation of the Surviving Founders; Typika and Testament*, ed. A. Constantinides Hero (Washington, DC, 2000), 1662.
19. Discussion: N. Aschenbrenner, "Reframing Empire: Byzantium and the Transformation of European Identity, c. 1400–1520," PhD Diss., Harvard University, 2019, 120. Leeches: Alexandrian Anonymous, *Anonymous Panegyricus ad Manuelem et Joannem VIII Palaeologum*, in *Παλαιολόγεια καὶ Πελοποννησιακά*, ed. S. P. Lampros (Athens, 1926), vol. 3, 208.29–209.1. Laggards: George Gemistus Plethon, *Oratio ad Manuelem Palaeologum de rebus in Peloponneso* in *Παλαιολόγεια καὶ Πελοποννησιακά*, ed. S. P. Lampros (Athens, 1926), vol. 3, 246–265, at 259.16–19, trans. Aschenbrenner, 120.
20. Manuel, *Ep*. 68.80.
21. J. Chrysostomides, *Manuel II Palaeologus, Funeral Oration on His Brother Theodore* (Thessaloniki, 1985]: 75–259. Discussion: F. Leonte, "Rhetoric in Purple: The Renewal of Imperial Ideology in the Texts of Emperor Manuel II Palaiologos," Diss., Central European University, 2012, 244–93.
22. Totally destroyed: *Fun. Or*. 115.7–10; locals allying with Ottomans: *Fun. Or* 133.6–12.
23. *Fun. Or*. 193.33–195.2.
24. *Fun. Or*. 207.1–7 (trans. Leonte, "Rhetoric in Purple," p. 272). Manuel's guiding role: *Fun. Or*. 113.13–16.
25. *Anonymous Panegyricus ad Manuelem et Joannem*, 164.3–6.
26. *Oratio ad Manuelem Palaeologum de rebus in Peloponneso* in S.P. Lampros, *Παλαιολόγεια καὶ Πελοποννησιακά*, vol. 3.246–265.
27. Successes around Greece: e.g., Demetrius Chrysoloras, *Synkrisis*, 238.21–5; Alexander comparison: *Synkrisis*, 222.8.

28. Demetrius Chrysoloras, *Synkrisis*, 229.11.
29. *Fun Or.* 157.23–159.30;
30. E.g., Chrysoloras, *Synkrisis*, 241.27–30. Context: J. Barker, "On the Chronology of the Activities of Manuel II Palaeologus in the Peloponnesus in 1415," *BZ* 55 (1962), 39–55; J. Barker, *Manuel II Palaeologus (1391–1425): A Study in Late Byzantine Statesmanship* (New Brunswick, 1969).
31. Mazaris (*Journey into Hades*, 177–8) names two of the leaders as Krokondylis and Eleavourkos. Text and context: L. Garland, "Mazaris's Journey to Hades: Further Reflections and Reappraisal," *DOP* 61 (2007), 183–214.
32. Fall of Thessaloniki: Ducas, 29.1–5.
33. Chalkokondyles I, 1.8. Discussion and context: Aschenbrenner, "Reframing Empire," 135–36.
34. *Anonymous Panegyricus ad Manuelem et Joannem VIII Palaeologum*, in Lampros, *Παλαιολόγεια καὶ Πελοποννησιακά* (Athens, 1926), vol. 3, 208.15–18 (trans. Aschenbrenner). Discussion: Aschenbrenner, "Reframing Empire," 139–43.
35. On the council: J. Gill, *The Council of Florence* (Cambridge, 1959).
36. Aschenbrenner, "Reframing Empire," 145–50.
37. Eugenikos, *Oratio ad imperatorem Constantinum Palaeologum*, in Lampros, *Παλαιολόγεια καὶ Πελοποννησιακά* (Athens, 1912), vol. 1, 124.21–22. (Discussion and trans.: Aschenbrenner, "Reframing Empire," 149.
38. Sphrantzes, 25.1–3; Chalkokondyles, 2.6.32.
39. Ducas, 37.10.
40. Pletho: *Prosphonematium ad Demetrium despotam Porphyrogennitum*, in Lampros, *Παλαιολόγεια καὶ Πελοποννησιακά* (Athens, 1930), vol. 4, 209.5–15; Doceianus: *Address to Demetrios Palaiologos from Elena*, 290.21–23. Discussion: Aschenbrenner, "Reframing Empire," 146–47.
41. The speakers are Macarius Macris (in C. Dendrinos, "An Unpublished Funeral Oration on Manuel II Palaeologus [† 1425]," in *Porphyrogenita*, ed. C. Dendrinos et al. [Aldershot, 2003], 423–56, at 443.49–51), Anonymous Alexandrian (*Panegyricus ad Manuelem et Joannem VIII Palaeologum*, vol. 206, 16–20, trans. Aschenbrenner and John Argyropoulos (*Monody on John*, in Lampros, *Παλαιολόγεια καὶ Πελοποννησιακά* [Athens, 1926], vol. 3, 318.6, trans. Aschenbrenner). For discussion of this tendency in orators working in the last years of the empire see Aschenbrenner, "Reframing Empire," 151–61.
42. On this attempt, to which an Ottoman minister replied, "Oh stupid and foolish Romans!" see Ducas, 34.2–3.
43. Ducas, 34.6–8
44. Ducas, 34.8.
45. 200,000: George Sphrantzes, 35.6 translation in M. Philippides, trans., *The Fall of the Byzantine Empire: A Chronicle by George Sphrantzes, 1401-1477* (Amherst, MA, 1980); 400,000: Ducas: 38.4. Roman defenders: Sphrantzes, 35.6.
46. Ps-Sphrantzes, *Chronicon sive Maius* (expansion by Makarios Melissinos) in *Georgios Sphrantzes. Memorii 1401-1477*, ed. V. Grecu (Bucharest, 1966), 150–448, 456–590, Book 3.8. Translation in Philippides, *Fall of the Byzantine Empire*, 120–21.

47. Ducas, 39.18.
48. Ducas, 39.20.
49. Ducas, 40.17–18.
50. Ducas, 42.14.
51. Ducas, 45.23.

CHAPTER 16

1. A. Kaldellis, *A New Herodotos: Laonikos Chalkokondyles on the Ottoman Empire, the Fall of Byzantium, and the Emergence of the West* (Washington, DC, 2014).
2. Kaldellis, *New Herodotos*, 171–72.
3. Chalkokondyles, 1.5, translations of Chalkokondyles follow those of Kaldellis. Discussion: Kaldellis, *New Herodotus*, 175–76.
4. Chalkokondyles, 1.1.
5. Chalkokondyles, 1.2
6. Chalkokondyles, 1.2.
7. Critobulus, *Ep. to Mehmet*, 1.38–39 (in D. R. Reinsch, ed., *Critobuli Imbriotae historiae* [Berlin: De Gruyter, 1983]). On Critobulus: L. Neville, *Guide to Byzantine Historical Writing* (Cambridge, 2018), 308–12; H. Koski, "Assessing the Historian Michael Kritovoulus as a Historical Figure through Analysis of Michael Kritovoulus' *History of Mehmed the Conqueror,*" *International Journal of Arts and Sciences* 6 (2013), 1–18. The translations of Critobulus follow those of Riggs, with adaptations for clarity.
8. Critobulus, *Hist.* 1.294–98.
9. Critobulus, *Hist.* 1.1, 1.3, 1.8. Nate Aschenbrenner (private conversation) has pointed out that Mehmet begins to exhibit these virtues in Critobulus's text only after the conquest of Constantinople.
10. Critobulus, *Hist.* 1.9
11. Critobulus, *Hist.* 1.12–13.
12. Critobulus, *Hist.* 1.15.
13. Horrors of capture: *Hist.* 1.234–76. Repopulation: 1.280
14. Critobulus, *Hist.* 2.1
15. Critobulus, *Hist.* 1.280.
16. Treatment of prisoners: Critobulus, *Hist.* 1.281–82, 2.3–4.
17. Gennadius: Critobulus, *Hist.* 2.5–8.
18. The first use of the term Holy Roman Empire (*Sacrum Romanum Imperium*) occurs in June 1180, though it becomes more common by the 1250s. Wilson, *Heart of Europe*, 19; H. Weisert, "Der Reichstitel bis 1806," *Archiv für Diplomatik* 40 (1994), 441–513.
19. W. Goez, *Translatio imperii: Ein Beitrag zur Geschichte des Geschichtsdenkens und der politischen Theorien im Mittelalter und in der frühen Neuzeit* (Tübingen, 1958); Aschenbrenner, "Reframing Empire," 184ff.
20. E.g., Enea Sylvio Piccolomini's 1443 work *Pentalogus*, though the ideas in it draw from a long tradition. See J. B. Toews, "The View of Empire in Aenéas Sylvius Piccolomini (Pope Pius II)," *Traditio* 24 (1968), 471–87, at 475–76.

21. Electors: Wilson, *Heart of Europe*, 305–9. Imperial assemblies as checks: Wilson, *Heart of Europe*, 415–19; B. Stollberg-Rilinger, *The Emperor's Old Clothes* (Munich, 2015), 18–67.
22. There were, for example, only twenty-five years with a papally crowned emperor between 1245 and 1415 (Wilson, *Heart of Europe*, 40).
23. Piccolomini, *Or.* 22.1–2. All translations of *Oration* 22 follow M. von Cotta-Schönberg, Oration "Constantinopolitana clades" of Enea Silvio Piccolomini (15 October 1454, Frankfurt), 6th version (Orations of Enea Silvio Piccolomini/Pope Pius II, 22), 2019. hal-01097147.
24. *Or.* 22.8–12.
25. *Or.* 22.3.
26. *Or.* 22.8.
27. His Crusading efforts: N. Bisaha, "Pope Pius II and the Crusade," in *Crusading in the Fifteenth Century*, ed. N. Housley (New York, 2004), 39–52.
28. A. Baca, ed. and trans., *Epistola ad Mahomatem II* (New York, 1990). Discussion: N. Bisaha, "Pope Pius II's Letter to Sultan Mehmed II: A Reexamination," *Crusades* 1 (2002), 183–200; J. Coleman, "Forging Relations between East and West," in *Literary Forgery in Early Modern Europe*, ed. W. Stephens et al. (Baltimore, 2019), 118–34, at 123–24.
29. George's background: Aschenbrenner, "Reframing Empire," 232–34.
30. Angelo Mercati, "Le due lettere di Giorgio da Trebisonda a Maometto II," *OCP* 9 (1943), 65–99, at 85. Discussion and translation: Aschenbrenner, "Reframing Empire," 234–36.
31. Mercati, "Le due lettere," 96. Claim and its larger eschatological scheme: Aschenbrenner, "Reframing Empire," 236–44.
32. Mercati, "Le due lettere," 94; translation: Aschenbrenner, 236.
33. A. Schultz, ed., "Weisskunig: Nach Dictaten und eigenhändigen Aufzeichnungen Kaiser Maximilians I. zusammengestellt von Marx Treitzsauerwein von Ehrentreitz," *JKSAK* 6 (1888): 421–46, at 423; Aschenbrenner, "Reframing Empire," 268–69.
34. Most extensive modern treatment of Maximilian: H. Wiesflecker, *Kaiser Maximilian I: Das Reich, Österreich und Europa an der Wende zur Neuzeit*, 5 vols. (Vienna, 1971–1986).
35. A verse of Matthias Corvinus, king of Hungary, that riffs on Ovid, *Heroides* 12.84. For discussion of this work and the concept of "matrimonial imperialism" see G. Parker, *Emperor: A New Life of Charles V* (New Haven, 2019), 3–4.
36. Discussion: Wiesflecker, *Kaiser Maximilian I*, vol. 4 (Vienna, 1981), 6–15.
37. Marsilii Ficini, *Opera*, vol. 1.961. Discussion: Aschenbrenner, "Reframing Empire," 278.
38. RI XIV 1 n.1273; Vienna, Haus-, Hof-, und Staatsarchiv, Reichskanzlei, Reichsregister II, fol. 154v, trans. Aschenbrenner, "Reframing Empire," 280.
39. RI XIV 2 n.5205; Venice, BNM, MSS Latini, Classe XIV/No 99, coll. 4278, fol. 74r. Latin text in Aschenbrenner, "Reframing Empire," 281; the translation is my own.
40. *Correspondence de l'empereur Maximilien Ier et de Marguerite d'Autriche, sa fille, gouvernante des Pays-Bas*, ed. A. J. G. Le Glay (Paris, 1839), 2.335–38 (a letter to his daughter Margaret from January of 1516).

41. Background: Aschenbrenner, "Reframing Empire," 285. Images of the existing woodcuts: S. Appelbaum, *The Triumph of Maximilian I* (New York, 1964).
42. On Mennel's still unpublished work see Aschenbrenner, "Reframing Empire," 288–92.
43. Arch: Thomas Schauerte, *Die Ehrenpforte für Kaiser Maximilian I.: Dürer und Altdorfer im Dienst des Herrschers* (Munich, 2001); Aschenbrenner, "Reframing Empire," 287. Note as well the reproductions in P. Terjanian, *The Last Knight: The Art, Armor, and Ambition of Maximilian I* (New York, 2019).
44. Tomb in Innsbruck: Aschenbrenner, "Reframing Empire," 286–87.
45. "Aurelian the Revivor" (Aurelians der Widerbringer) is the title given that emperor on Maximilian's Triumphal Arch.
46. Wiesflecker I, 345; Aschenbrenner, "Reframing Empire," 276–77.
47. Aschenbrenner, "Reframing Empire," 283–84.
48. For this process, which cost 1.5 million florins, see Parker, *Emperor,* 87–94. The sum comes from a letter of the English envoy Richard Pace. Charles's own treasurer counted 852,189 florins spent in Germany alone. For these figures see Parker, *Emperor,* 610 n.58.
49. Education: Snouckaert van Schouwenburg, *De republica,* 34. Integrated history of east and west: Aschenbrenner, "Reframing Empire," 292–324.
50. Cuspinianus, *De caes.* 636. Discussion and translation: Aschenbrenner, "Reframing Empire," 323.
51. A. Devereux, *The Other Side of Empire: Just War in the Mediterranean and the Rise of Early Modern Spain* (Ithaca, NY, 2020).
52. Devereux, *Other Side of Empire,* 8–11, 95–154.
53. Context: Parker, *Emperor,* 103–6.
54. *Cortes de los antiguos reinos de León y de Castilla,* vol. 4, 293–98 (trans. following Parker, *Emperor,* 105–6).
55. Parker, *Emperor,* 221–22.
56. Parker, *Emperor,* 115–16.
57. Charles V, *Oratione di Carlo imperatore fatta alli signori Spagnuoli nella sua partenza con promesse di salute a tutti li christiani,* s.l, s.d., Bib. nat. de France, Rés: Oc 159, fol. 4v°, cited by J. C. d'Amico, "De Pavie à Bologne (1525–1530): La prophétie comme arme de la politique impériale pendant les guerres d'Italie," in *La prophétie comme arme de duerre des Pouvoirs,* ed. A. Redondo (Paris, 2000), 97–107, at 106.
58. Cortés, *Cartas* 181, Cortés to Charles, October 30, 1520. Context: Parker, *Emperor,* 345–49.
59. Parker, *Emperor,* 351.
60. *Deutsche Reichstagsakten unter Kaiser Karl V,* 20 vols., ed. A. Kluckhorn et al. (Gotha and Munich, 1893–2009)=*RTA* 1.864–76. Discussion: Parker, *Emperor,* 103.
61. Lanz, *Staatspapiere,* 263–68, quoted in Parker, *Emperor,* 271–72. These words, written in 1538, encapsulate a situation that had already become clear by the early 1520s.
62. References to Luther's *Open Letter* (*An den christlichen Adel deutscher Nation*) follow E. Grosse, ed., *Auswahl aus d. Martin Luthers Schriften* (Königsberg, 1883), 14–44.
63. *An den christlichen Adel,* 40.8–18

64. *An den christlichen Adel,* 14.27–31
65. *An den christlichen Adel,* 15.1–5.
66. Text from H. Schmidt, *D. Martini Lutheri: Opera Latina,* vol. 6 (Frankfurt, 1872), 10–11.
67. Francisco de Salazar, quoted in Parker, *Emperor,* 171.
68. Paolo Giovio, *Vita Pompeii,* 191 in *Vita Leonis Decimi, pontifici maximi: Libri IV* (Florence, 1551).
69. Quoted in Parker, *Emperor,* 172.
70. E.g., *D. Martini Lutheri: Opera Latina,* vol. 6, 19.
71. This was Georg von Frundsberg (Giovio, *Vita Alfonsi* [1550], 49).
72. Andrea Navagero to the Signoria, Valladolid, July 27, 1527, quoted in R. Finlay, "Fabius Maximus in Venice: Doge Andrea Gritti, the War of Cambrai, and the Rise of Habsburg Hegemony, 1509–1530," *Renaissance Quarterly* 53 (2000), 988–1031, at 1018.
73. Charles had inherited control of some Caribbean islands and some possessions on the Isthmus of Panama, totaling perhaps 250,000 square miles.
74. Larger context: Parker, *Emperor,* 345–49.
75. Charles's communication cited in Parker, *Emperor,* 355.
76. Figures: Parker, *Emperor,* 342.
77. G. Poumarède, "Le voyage de Tunis et d'Italie de Charles Quint ou l'exploitation politique du mythe de la Croisade (1535–1536)," *Bibliothèque d'Humanisme et Renaissance* 67 (2005), 247–85, at 267, quoting the papal secretary of state.
78. Details of campaign: Poumarède, "Le voyage," 247ff. Charles's own description of the forces: Charles V to J. Hannart, Cagliari, June 13, 1535, in K. Lanz, *Correspondenz des Kaisers Karl V, vol. 2, 1532–1549* (Leipzig, 1845), 187.
79. Paolo Giovio to Francesco II Sforza, Rome, October 14, 1535, cited in Poumarède, "Le voyage," 267.
80. Poumarède, "Le voyage," 273–74.
81. Parker, *Emperor,* 246–47; Poumarède, "Le voyage," 274–75. Contemporary descriptions: *Die Korrespondenz Ferdinands I,* vol. 5, 452–58, Charles to Ferdinand, April 18, 1536; L. Madelin, "Le journal d'un habitant français de Rome au XVIe siècle (1509–1540)," *Mélanges d'archéologie et d'histoire de l'Ecole française de Rome* 22 (1902), 296–98.
82. Parker, *Emperor,* 256.
83. On this concern see, for example, C. Bornate, "Historia vite et gestorum per dominum magnum cancellarium," in *Miscellanea di storia italianna,* 3rd series 17 (1915, 231–585, at 405–13), where the young Charles is emphatically urged to create a small council of advisors because he controlled "so many and diverse kingdoms and provinces." Discussion: Parker, *Emperor,* 98.
84. On the revolt of Ghent and its aftermath see Parker, *Emperor,* 266; A. Henne, *Histoire du règne de Charles-Quint en Belgique,* vol. 7 (Brussels, 1858–1859), 62–65, 88–95.
85. Franco-Ottoman alliance: D. Jensen, "The Ottoman Turks in Sixteenth Century French Diplomacy," *Sixteenth Century Journal* 16 (1985), 451–70; M. Heath, "Unholy Alliance: Valois and Ottomans," *Renaissance Studies* 3 (1989), 303–15; G. Poumarède,

"Justifier l'injustifiable: L'alliance turque au miroir de le chrétienté," *Revue d'histoire diplomatique* 111 (1997), 218–46.

86. Sack of Nice: J. Dény and J. Laroche, "L'expédition en Provence de l'armée de mer du Sultan Suleyman sous le commandement de l'amiral Hayreddin Pacha dit Barberousse (1543–1544)," *Turçica* 1 (1969), 161–211; L. Durante, *Histoire de Nice depuis sa fondation jusqu'a l'année 1792*, vol. 2 (Turin, 1823), 276–317, an account that reproduces the first-hand account of Jean Badat.
87. Ineffectiveness of these bans in the 1520s and Charles's ineffective response to the Augsburg Confession in 1530: Stollberg-Rilinger, *Emperor's Old Clothes*, 83–113.
88. Appeal for French and British help in 1546: Luis Ávila y Zúñiga, *Commentario del illustre señor don Luis Ávila y Zúñiga, commendador mayor de Alcántara: De le Guerra de Alemaña de Carolo V Máximo* (Antwerp, 1550) and the discussion of Parker, *Emperor*, 319–29. The 1552 appeal: Parker, *Emperor*, 433–45.
89. Peace of Augsburg: A. Gotthard, *Der Augsburger Religionsfrieden* (Münster, 2004); M. Heckel, "Politischer Friede und geistliche Freiheit im Ringen um die Wahrheit: Zur Historiographie des Augsburger Religionsfriedens von 1555," *Historische Zeitschrift* 282 (2006), 391–425.
90. Rumors: *Catalog of State Papers and Manuscripts Relating to English Affairs in Existing in the Archives and Collections of Venice*, Vol. VI/I, 468–71. Charles's comment: *Correspondenz des Kaisers Karls V*, 3.681–83, a letter from Charles to his brother, Ferdinand, dated September 19, 1555, cited in Parker, *Emperor*, 664 n.13.
91. Quoted in Parker, *Emperor*, 464–65.
92. R. Finlay, "Prophecy and Politics in Istanbul: Charles V, Sultan Süleyman, and the Habsburg Embassy of 1533–1535," *Journal of Early Modern History* 2, no. 1 (1998): 1–31, at 2 n3.
93. E.g., Gasparo Contarini, *De magistratibus et republica Venetorum*. See R. Finlay, "The Immortal Republic: The Myth of Venice during the Italian Wars (1494–1530)," *Sixteenth Century Journal* 30 (1999), 931–44; N. Barbarigo, *Vita de Andrea Gritti doge di Venezia* (Venice, 1793), 55; Paolo Giovio, *Opera, Vol. 8: Elogia* (Rome, 1972), 455. *Storia d'Italia*, trans. Alexander, p. 376.
94. Giovio, *Libellus de legatione Basilii magni Principis Moschoviae ad Clementem VII*. Discussion: Price Zimmerman, *Giovio*, 65–66. Larger context: D. Ostrowski, *Muscovy and the Mongols: Cross-Cultural Influences on the Steppe Frontier, 1304–1589* (Cambridge, 2002), 219–43.

CHAPTER 17

1. E.g., John Adams, *A Defense of the Constitutions of Government of the United States of America*, letter 30. For the larger intellectual context see C. Richard, *The Founders and the Classics: Greece, Rome, and the American Enlightenment* (Cambridge, MA, 1994).
2. H. Hearder, "The Making of the Roman Republic, 1848–1849," *History* 60 (1975), 169–84, at 181.
3. Verb of History: G. Mazzini, "Ai giovani d'Italia," in *Scritti scelti di Giuseppe Mazzini*, ed. J. White Mario (Florence, 1901), 264–65. Liberation of Rome: Mazzini, "Italia e

Roma," in *Scritti scelti*, 293–94. Discussion: J. Arthurs, *Excavating Modernity: The Roman Past in Fascist Italy* (Ithaca, 2012), 11.

4. Imperial conquests: A. J. Barker, *The Civilizing Mission: The Italo-Ethiopian War 1935–6* (London, 1968); S. Agbamu, "Mare Nostrum: Italy and the Mediterranean of Ancient Rome in the Twentieth and Twenty-First Centuries," *Fascism* 8 (2019), 250–74.
5. C. Fogu, *The Historic Imaginary: Politics of History in Fascist Italy* (Toronto, 2003), 11; H. Roche, "Mussolini's 'Third Rome,' Hitler's Third Reich and the Allure of Antiquity: Classicizing Chronopolitics as a Remedy for Unstable National Identity," *Fascism* 8 (2019), 127–52.
6. *Il Popolo d'Italia*, May 11, 1936, p. 1, quoted in H. Hyde Minor, "Mapping Mussolini: Ritual and Cartography in Public Art during the Second Roman Empire," *Imago mundi* 51 (1999), 147–62, at 154.
7. Estimates: A. J. Barker, *The Civilizing Mission: The Italo-Ethiopian War 1935–6* (London, 1968), 292–93.
8. A. Bianchi, "Il Centro di Roma: La sistemazione del Foro Italico e le nuove Vie del Mare e dei Monti," *Architettura* 12 (1933), 137–56, at 156.
9. The image is reproduced in Hyde Minor, "Mapping Mussolini," 154.
10. A. Muñoz, *Via dei Monti e Via del Mare* (Rome, 1933), 30, quoted in Arthurs, *Excavating Modernity*, 67–68.
11. B. Mussolini, *Opera Omnia* 22, 47, quoted in Arthurs, *Excavating Modernity*, 50, adapted for clarity.
12. C. Magi-Spinetti, "Colore locale," *Capitolium* 11 (1935), 28, quoted in Arthurs, *Excavating Modernity*, 68.
13. Arthurs, *Excavating Modernity*, 69–72.
14. Arthurs, *Excavating Modernity*, 72–80.
15. Muñoz, *Via dei Monti*, 25, quoted in Arthurs, *Excavating Modernity*, 89.
16. Bianchi, "Il Centro di Roma," 137.
17. Arthurs, *Excavating Modernity*, 78.
18. P. Nalli, *Roma Carcinoma* (Milan, 1945).
19. J. G. A. Pocock, *Barbarism and Religion*, vol. 3, *The Decline and Fall* (Cambridge, 2003), 157.
20. L. Bruni, *Historiae Florentini populi*, 1.10–11, trans. J. Hankins, adapted.
21. Bruni, *Hist.* 1.38.
22. The larger historical project was the *Historiarum ab inclinatio Romano imperio decades III*, with the narrative of Roman decline and fall between 412 and 1410 taking up twenty of the thirty books. Discussion: Pocock, *Barbarism and Religion*, 179–202.
23. N. Machiavelli, *Discorsi sopra la prima deca di Tito Livio*, Pro., in the edition of S. Bertelli, *Il Principe e Discorsi* (Milan, 1977), 125.
24. A. Cohler, *Montesquieu's Comparative Politics and the Spirit of American Constitutionalism* (Lawrence, KS, 1988); P. Rahe, *Montesquieu and the Logic of Liberty* (New Haven, 2009).
25. H. Barckhausen, ed., *Montesquieu, l'Esprit des lois et les Archives de La Brède* (Bordeaux, 1904), 212.

26. *Considérations*, 11. Constitutional concerns in Montesquieu: Straumann, *Crisis and Constitutionalism*, 319–23.
27. E.g., the discussion of opulence in Montesquieu, *Considérations*, 10.
28. *Considérations*, 11. Discussion of these implications: Straumann, *Crisis and Constitutionalism*, 320–21.
29. *Considérations*, 13.
30. E.g., *Considérations*, 14 (on Tiberius's actions against the assemblies), 16 (on Pius and Marcus).
31. *Considérations*, 16.
32. *Considérations*, 17.
33. Christianity and the fall of the West to barbarians: *Considérations*, 19; decline in tolerance: *Considérations*, 20.
34. *Considérations*, 23.
35. Context: J. G. A. Pocock, "An Overview of *The Decline and Fall of the Roman Empire*," in *Cambridge Companion to Edward Gibbon*, ed. K. O'Brien and B. Young (Cambridge, 2018), 20–40, at 20–23; cf. A. Momigliano, "Gibbon's Contribution to Historical Method," in *Contributo alla storia degli studi classici* (Rome, 1955).
36. Edward Gibbon, *The Decline and Fall of the Roman Empire* (London, 1781), vol. 1, chap. 3.
37. Gibbon, *Decline and Fall*, 111, 1068. For these terms and their significance across the first part of the work see the monumental studies of J. G. A. Pocock, *Barbarism and Religion*, 6 vols. (Cambridge, 1999–2015).
38. Gibbon, *Decline and Fall*, vol. 1, chap. 15.
39. "Premature decay": vol. 2, 237. "Passive Connections": vol. 3, 25. Left unsaid is how long one would expect Roman decay to last if a lifespan of 1100 years represented a premature expiration of empire.
40. Gibbon, *Decline and Fall*, vol. 1, 62, 84. For this idea in Gibbon: A. Yadav, *Before the Empire of the English* (New York, 2004), 111–75; Gibbon's "Republic of States": Pocock, "An Overview," 23.
41. Amazon bestseller rank, as of March 20, 2020: #67 in Ancient Roman History, #47 in Italian History.

CONCLUSION: ROMAN DECLINE AND FALL IN CONTEMPORARY AMERICA

1. https://blog.oup.com/2019/03/contemporary-lessons-from-the-fall-of-rome/ (accessed on March 20, 2020).
2. *Playboy* 31, no. 4 (April 1984), 66.
3. The entire speech is reproduced in R. Reagan, *Speaking My Mind: Selected Speeches* (New York, 1989), reprinted 2004, pp. 39–44. Reagan's introduction casts the speech as a call for sanity amid the "student rebellion" of the late 1960s (p. 38).
4. Reagan, *Speaking My Mind*, 38.
5. He confesses that he learned of Gibbon's claims via "a series of articles" written by former Goldwater foreign policy advisor Robert Struasz-Hupé (*Speaking My Mind*, 40).

6. Eerie parallels: *Speaking My Mind,* 40. Diploma factory: *Speaking My Mind,* 43.
7. E. Taft Benton, "Watchman, Warn the Wicked," *Ensign* 3, no. 7 (July 1973).
8. P. Schlafly, *The Power of the Positive Woman* (New Rochelle, NY, 1977), quoted in A. Howard, S. Adams Tarrant, *Reaction to the Modern Women's Movement, 1963 to the Present* (New York, 1997). Schlafly here claims to summarize the views of Amaury de Riencourt. These claims have since reappeared in the twenty-first century (http://pages.vassar.edu/pharos/2018/02/02/feminism-blamed-for-fall-of-rome, accessed on February 23, 2020).
9. "The Greeks and the Romans were homosexuals. Their civilizations did not stand. Did they come in contact with a social disease like AIDS? I don't know the answer. But I wonder . . ." Cremeans's comments, which were first reported in *The Marietta* (OH) *Times,* were discussed in an ad placed by the DCCC in *Roll Call* on September 26, 1994. They were then featured in *The Washington Post* (K. Merida, "Challenger Burned Learning the Ropes," October 5, 1994; K. Merida, "Many Freshmen Are Looking Less Vulnerable," November 4, 1994); and in *The Advocate* (November 1, 1994, 21–22; December 13, 1994, 22).
10. B. Carson, *America the Beautiful* (Grand Rapids, MI, 2012), 182.
11. https://www.rightwingwatch.org/post/phyllis-schlafly-and-alex-jones-have-immigration-meltdown-we-are-on-accelerated-collapse-of-rome-timetable, accessed on February 22, 2020.
12. G. Holland, "Migrants Sank the Roman Empire. Now They're Sinking the US," *Shreveport Times,* June 12, 2018, archived at https://web.archive.org/web/20180618193445/https://www.shreveporttimes.com/story/opinion/2018/06/12/migrants-sank-roman-empire-now-theyre-sinking-u-s/690658002/?from=new-cookie, accessed on February 23, 2020.
13. Spencer's speech itself can be read at https://radixjournal.com/2016/09/2016–9-28-facing-the-future-as-a-minority, accessed on February 23, 2020. For discussion of its claims see http://pages.vassar.edu/pharos/2019/07/26/a-new-roman-empire-for-white-people, accessed on February 23, 2020.
14. Republican commemorations: T. Cornell, *The Beginnings of Rome: Italy and Rome from the Bronze Age to the Punic Wars* (London, 1995), 9–13. For celebrations of imperial figures and divinized emperors see, for example, M. Salzman, *On Roman Time: The Codex Calendar of 354 and the Rhythms of Urban Life in Late Antiquity* (Berkeley, 1990), 130–32.
15. E.g., G. Tsiaples, "Το παλίμψηστο της ιστορικής μνήμης: Η πρόσληψη της αβαροπερσικής πολιορκίας της Κωνσταντινούπολης (626) στις σύγχρονες και μεταγενέστερες ρητορικές και αγιολογικές πηγές," *Byzantiaka* 32 (2015), 79–97.
16. Education as training in virtue: Watts, *City and School,* 1–7.
17. Augustine, *Conf.* 1.17.
18. Although most notable in the speeches Roman historians routinely placed speeches in the mouths of their historical predecessors, this rhetoric was common across literary genres. Notable examples range from Cicero's *Republic* (a first-century BC work featuring Scipio Aemilianus and a cast of Roman luminaries from the second century BC) to Macrobius's *Saturnalia* (a fifth-century AD fictionalization of discussions held

at the home of the fourth-century pagan senator Praetextatus) to elements of smaller texts like Seneca, *Ep*. 71.15 (spoken in the voice of Cato). For the vital role of this activity in socializing Romans: M. Bloomer, "Schooling in Persona: Imagination and Subordination in Roman Education," *Classical Antiquity* 16 (1997), 57–78.

19. On synaxaria see E. Watts, "Theodosius II in Egyptian Anti-Chalcedonian Literature," in *Images of Theodosius II*, ed. R. Flower and C. Kelly (Cambridge, 2013), 269–84, at 279–83.
20. D. Krueger, *Liturgical Subjects: Christian Ritual, Biblical Narrative, and the Formation of the Self in Byzantium* (Philadelphia, 2014), 29–65.
21. This is Romanus, *Hymn* 54.
22. Constantinople: Adamnan, *De Locis Sanctis*, Book 3.3. Baths: Cato, *Ep*. 86.10.
23. The translation follows that of N. Kershaw, *Anglo-Saxon and Norse Poems* (Cambridge, 1922), 51–58.
24. C. Cecchelli, "Itinerario imperial," *Capitolium* 13 (1938), 168, quoted in Arthurs, *Excavating Modernity*, 2.

INDEX

For the benefit of digital users, indexed terms that span two pages (e.g., 52–53) may, on occasion, appear on only one of those pages.